Love in Danger

Love in Danger

Trauma, therapy and conflict explored
through the life and work of Adam Curle

BARBARA MITCHELS

JON CARPENTER

Our books may be ordered from bookshops or (post free) from
Jon Carpenter Publishing, Alder House, Market Street, Charlbury,
England OX7 3PH

Credit card orders should be phoned or faxed to 01689 870437
or 01608 811969

First published in 2006 by
Jon Carpenter Publishing
Alder House, Market Street, Charlbury, Oxfordshire OX7 3PH
☎ 01608 811969

ISBN 978 0 9549727 6 9

Manufactured by LPPS Ltd., Wellingborough, Northants NN8 3PJ

Dedication

The book is dedicated to Adam and Anne Curle, and to my family, with much love.

It is a tribute to all those wonderful people in Croatia who faced fear and danger to bring peace.

It celebrates the courage, positivity and resilience of all those who continue to live daily with internal and external conflict, developing peacefulness within themselves and in their communities.

Contents

Chapter 3   Posttraumatic stress: conceptual evolution, symptoms, psychological and social effects, and approaches to treatment   74

Chapter 4   War and Peace: Osijek, Vukovar , Zupanja, Croatia and the five projects taking part in the case study   120

Acknowledgements

It is a privilege and a pleasure to talk with Adam Curle about his experiences as a peacemaker, reminiscing about his life, people and events, debating current issues, and sharing his excitement last year as he planned his new book. Talking with him, it is easy to understand why he inspires and influences so many people across the world. Anne Curle's smile and her loving kindness also make visits to them both very special.

I am very grateful to Katarina Kruhonja and all the staff and volunteers of the Centar za mir, Bench We Share, Dodir nade, Mir i dobro, and the Coalition for Work with Psychotrauma and Peace for all their hospitality and help in organising and participating in the focus group discussions. There is so much to learn from their courageous and dedicated work for peace. They are valued friends, and there are so many good memories of our early workshops in Croatia 1996 and 1997 with Adam, Tracey Brown and Deborah Curle, and many others afterwards.

I would like to thank all the psychiatrists and psychologists in Croatia who helped with this research, in particular Visnja Matic, Gorana Tocilj-Simunkovic, Dean Adjukovic, and Nikola Mandic and others for finding time to answer questions about their treatment of Post Traumatic Stress Disorder, William West for his encouragement and ideas and Colin Murray Parkes who willingly shared his thoughts about loss and bereavement and provided constructive criticism and comments on the discussion of posttraumatic stress. Thanks to all those who very generously shared their publications.

Thanks to Tom Woodhouse, a wise and patient supervisor, who with consistent kindness and good humour provided encouragement and academic clarity and Betts Fetherston, co-supervisor, for her special combination of academic insight, attention to detail and caring support. Many thanks also to Nick Lewer and Ed Cairns who examined the thesis and encouraged publication of the research. Thanks also to the staff of the University of Bradford, especially John Horton for his helpful criticism of the historical background accounts of Croatia, and the endlessly kind and patient staff of the Peace Studies Department, the Graduate School, and the J.B. Priestley Library.

Brian Thorne of the University of East Anglia has made a significant academic contribution to the theory and practice of Person Centred Counselling. He, along with Dave Mearns, Elke Lambers and Michael da Costa profoundly influenced me during counselling training with them, and Brian's support and encouragement in undertaking this research will always be much appreciated.

Jean Clark has been a great professional counselling supervisor, especially in developing effective treatment for trauma. Her pioneering spirit, openness and creativity continue to be inspirational. I discovered that Brian and Jean both have unexpected links with Adam Curle – Brian and Adam both recently contributed chapters to a multi-authored book, Jean was once Adam's student in Oxford and their professional work is underpinned by strongly held and strikingly similar spiritual beliefs and values.

The period of the research and writing up in Yorkshire is full of pleasant memories of time spent with good friends and colleagues, especially Dave Lane, Jo Brown, Mary Lane, Margaret Nunnerley, Connie Scanlon, Cecile Seetharamdoo, Connie O'Brien, and Karen Abi-Ezzi – often in the Fair Trade Café or the Foyer Coffee Bar at Bradford, or at home, fortified by chocolate!

Special thanks to Phil Mills, who contributed the photograph of Adam Curle for this book, and who we are all delighted to welcome into our family.

Last, I want to thank David, John and Ruthie. They have all been just wonderful. David's encouragement and practical help gave me the confidence to undertake the research. John has patiently kept the computer working, and with Ruthie has also listened endlessly, come up with helpful ideas and coffee and encouraged me to keep going. Ruthie's gentle kindness touches everyone she meets. Throughout the ups and downs of our respective lives over the last few years, they have all stayed consistently loving and supportive to each other and to me, and as a family we are all learning together what it really means to live peacefully.

B.M.

Foreword

by Adam Curle

Recently, I wrote a book which was largely about something I called the Black Cloud. It is a disorder both mental and physical resulting from an emanation of pain, misery and confusion left in the mind of generations of humanity by the despair, desperation and anger of hopelessness and war.

I first identified this horrid condition as initiated during the First World War, but came to realize that it was an almost universal phenomenon, but one which had become apparent with the first of the great mass killings, such as the battle of the Somme.

Initially I believed that the Black Cloud was the massive psychological response to those great killings, a rejection of the stereotypes which sanctioned and accepted the realities, political and military, of the day. And this, I came to see, developed later into an acceptance of new values and a rejection of the older ones of my generation. But many of us were still morally confused. However, the more I explored the bloody world scene, the more clearly I saw that violence could not be checked by just more violence, only by action governed by realistic concern, respect and compassion.

By no means did everyone agree. The twentieth century closed in an atmosphere of angry violence and mega death, much of a despicable but more traditional kind, while the next hundred-year span unveiled new political and military forms and objectives. Perhaps the most notable and virulent of these is what I term 'lethally cunning stupidity' of both British and US leaders – but much less the military.

Fortunately, the mass butcheries of the first great conflict were not repeated, but the various new combatants managed, collectively more or less, in different ways, to make up the shortfall – Pol Pot, the Rwanda Hutus and carnage in the Congo region where the gang of second-class players did a revoltingly thorough job. Through most of the 'civilized' world there was at least a recognised peace Movement – which was a great improvement in Europe from 1918.

However, through the immeasurable period up until today, there has been at least one persistent source of conflict: inequality, often unjust and to every degree of hope and need – political, financial, territorial, personal, intellectual, etc. in every possible field. But of course if we move from the individual to the level of nation or state, the force of desire may reach any level. We know too many examples of rulers who have made some lethal wish come true, plunging their people into war. Or, reminded by the recent two-hundredth anniversary of the victory of Trafalgar, I thought how Nelson's tactical decisions affected the immediate future of English history.

I found it memorable, however, than many of the sailors who played such a vital part in the victory had been press-ganged (hijacked to serve unpaid) and for the duration enslaved. But they felt themselves to be heroes, which made all the difference to them – and perhaps to much wider issues.

Around the same period a very different scene was being enacted: the African slave trade. Here was a situation in which powerful social and economic (and often military) interests vied with the interests of, say, trade with a perhaps impoverished African kingdom. Here the 'commodity' might in the past simply have been slaves, of whom a considerable proportion might die on the Atlantic crossing. Small wonder that the vendors did not ask much for their goods, nor did the customers pay much for their purchases.

And an inequitable ratio has persisted, to some extent, as many of those attending the 2005 G8 demonstrated. There can be small doubt that the like of the World Bank, though run by professionals of personal integrity, continues the established tradition of contrast between the 'local' and the indigenous bodies. At all these levels, from the reputable international down to the pitifully honest, the larger body is to some extent influencing and controlling the smaller.

I would like to make it clear that the majority of the smaller and/or welfare agencies are often heroically well-intentioned; and the same is true of some international agencies, despite occasional prejudice. As a general rule, however, the balance of authority rests with the greater and most potent.

If these tendencies are taken to extremes we should not, perhaps, be surprised if national banks of China, India, Russia and perhaps a few other key world economies come to play the part currently taken by the World Bank and others. It could then hypothetically follow that the larger the institution, the greater is its continuing successful progress. This, however, would not necessarily be the case, for there are obviously other criteria of greatness than size. In the future, I envisage institutional desirability based on a variety of bench-marks. This could lead to a possible 'war' of greater intensity and perhaps on an even larger scale than any recent or existing conflict, one in which the violence was not merely economic and political, but waged with nuclear and other of the most lethal weapons.

How might it be forestalled?

How indeed. Up to now, I have simply stated the obvious point that human beings are aggressive animals. But what drives the violence? Where does its strength and purpose come from? Well, it's really quite obvious. Just consider any excitable or angry dispute. What elevates a disagreement into a quarrel? When and how does an altercation escalate into a fury? The answer is that anger is generated when another person's sense of self feels menaced and his defence mechanism is also mobilized. This means that the most rudimentary type of further development largely escapes control. This may of course be personal – anger, disappointment, resentment – or it can also spill over into material issues of size, quality, improved administration, more appropriate technology, etc. We don't really know how to respond, except though our own further growth.

We *must remember* how we were constantly driven in the past and how we yielded, or sometimes not. The ghastly world wars of the twentieth century in which some reading these words must have fought, stumbled to bloody ends because we couldn't go on fighting – until we had drawn breath to rearm and retrain with improved weapons; and the politicians had found more fine words to 'prove' that we (and they) had made the right decisions; and now this was the time – for action...

By this time, or rather this *rapidly coming* time, we have to find a way out *before* pressing the final button and scuttling off – that is, if the other guys don't do it first. The possible saving grace is that both sides may come to the conclusion that 'the game's not worth the candle' (do they still say, or even think like this?).

In any case, it's desperately important that we attempt to devise a strategy that might, just might, save us all, or at least spare a little wasted effort, such as writing our wills. We really must remember that.

I have tried several ways of trying to broker peace, and no doubt there are many others of which I know nothing. I suspect, however, that in the last resort a single individual's 'work for peace' is just some tactic that we hope will deter the potential enemy, or at least 'defer' the possible offensive. These efforts are of little use; at best they only provide a temporary interregnum which is of little use to anyone, except to increase tension and so perhaps increase the imminent danger of war.

So we must think of something else, something which will not lead to this apparently inexorable cycle of automatic violence. Are we not human beings and are we not supposed to have free will? So why are we periodically driven to desperate measures to avoid being defeated – or equally, of course, winning! The emotional force of death, of whipped-up patriotism, is so damned strong; the most cool-minded pacifist can hardly avoid some reaction.

We, whether we are ordinary citizens or omnipotent rulers, have to ask the most demanding question of ourselves: can we withstand the enormous pressure of dissenting from the powerful universal urge to conform, particularly in times of war or potential war, to what may seem like patriotism? Above all, can we defeat the inward enemy who urges us to fight for our sense of self? But this is a serious wrong. We are not slaves to a piddling 'self', a wisp which will blow away like fog. We have the strength to forge a being that can participate in the work of the Universe; but custom asks us to develop as a slave of the unconscious, a tool of the Black Cloud.

What follows, is, in my view, very important for the whole psychological or physiological approach to the problems with which this superb book is concerned. This is not the final stage. The crucial question is this: what is going on in your mind and mine? The mind, so far as I can understand it, contains many voices of varying strengths and tastes, some confused and some clear, some open and some narrowly closed, some stable and some unpredictable.

Among these, some are more dependable for wiser and humane judgements on vital matters. Their role is crucial if we are to prevent ourselves and humanity from faulty judgements and foolish destruction of ourselves and very many others.

But how do we recognize the other exemplars, the women and men who we may meet on the street, or hear on the radio, or read about. Is there any clear division between the very good, kindly, intelligent, worthy, wise, brave, self-abnegating, generous, etc. etc. and the real, great 'saints'? I believe there is more real sanctity – but what is it, beyond the very complimentary adjectives just listed? I have met a few such saints. They were human beings of high intelligence and great achievements, though modestly worn. There are, of course, others who are rightly praised highly for their particular qualities, abilities or actions. But some human beings have been recognized *by different people for different reasons*, a fact which suggests that they were not honoured, in the one case for intellectual, but for the other, practical, attainments, but as *complete beings*. Some people can be noted for their complete wholeness, their completion, their recollectedness. They are not different from us.

The Black Cloud could stand between us and the Mind of the Universe – by which I mean that gentle, friendly pressure of a loving force which, when we are tired and despondent, insistently pushes its way through the flimsy protection of the 'self' to support and encourage us, and which leaves us profoundly refreshed and somehow wiser. The Mind of the Universe works as quietly and naturally as the circulation of blood in the body. It simply acts to help and succour, remove obstacles to happiness, to strengthen weakness, to reveal reality and to promote growth.

We have to find ways to break through the Black Cloud, firing bolts of positivity and love to penetrate its dense negativity and confusion, letting the healing powers of the Mind of the Universe in amongst humanity to go about their work, integrated into the whole long process of evolution and life cycle: invention, creation, sustainment, destruction and eventually rebirth.

I wonder if the Black Cloud can only be dispelled by the loving work of ordinary human beings, supported by the Mind of the Universe (by which I do not mean 'God'). If I am right in assuming that there is such a thing as a human being (please look at the first part of my recent book *The Fragile Voice of Love*) you will read that the human being contains a number of selves and that their various I's take a probable shifting priority, but that at some stage, a more unified entity evolves as a function of the Mind of the Universe. I have a deep feeling that something of the sort that I am trying to grasp (or that is trying to grasp me?) is a dim and shadowy passage towards a fragmentary understanding of a living reality.

But, factually, if you come to know Barbara, whom I greatly love and respect as a friend and as a wise scholar, through reading this book, or Tom Woodhouse, my dear friend and colleague at Bradford University, and Katarina Kruhonja, the wise and brilliant physician of Osijek and any of the splendid human beings around them, that passage won't seem so shadowy. Soon you will be showing others a way to break through the Black Cloud and tackle the crucial issues of posttraumatic stress and other issues crucial to humanity, which are raised with such compelling force by Barbara Mitchels in these pages.

Adam Curle, January 2006

Introduction

This book is a tribute to Adam Curle, now in his ninetieth year, and to his wife Anne. Both are very much loved by all those who know them in Croatia and across the world. Adam continues to lead a life of spiritual awareness and service, dedicated to living peacefully. He has inspired so many people and continues to receive correspondence from all around the world.

This is also a tribute to the staff and volunteers of five peace projects in Croatia: Centar za mir, Mir i dobro, Dodir nade, Bench We Share and CWWPP. It is a celebration of the work carried out by the projects over more than ten years to create peace and to heal the psychological wounds of the 1991-95 war in Croatia.

The book reflects the results of research to explore the influence of Adam Curle as an academic theorist and peace activist on the community work of these projects in Croatia. It explores the relevance of posttraumatic stress and the role of therapy in the peacemaking process in the context of Adam's work and academic theory of peace. It is a great privilege to work alongside such inspiring and courageous people in Croatia and I will never be able to fully express how it feels for me to be part of their work and their lives. They are all busy people and yet they still manage to find plenty of time for discussions and for friendship. I cannot thank them enough for all that they have contributed to the research.

The research came about because I felt that the impact of posttraumatic stress within the process of peace making following violent conflict has been given little academic attention. The research brings together the disciplines of psychology and the academic study of peace, exploring the psychological effects of war, seeking to understand the experiences of the communities of Osijek, Vukovar and Zupanja following the 1991-95 conflict in Croatia through a rare opportunity to take a longitudinal perspective of the views and perceptions of staff and volunteer helpers from five non-governmental peace-making projects, some of whom have been working in these communities for more than ten years. In some ways the research confirmed what I might have expected, but in other ways, it challenges certain aspects of theory and practice, disclosing areas where further research would be helpful to improve the psychological care of those who are suffering from the trauma of war and in post-war peacemaking.

Adam Curle has shared significant memories of his early life, his work and his long career, and I was fascinated to learn a little more about the life of this man who is a quiet but very influential academic, a contemplative and spiritual person and an effective international peace activist, and to understand how his life experiences played their part in creating his unique way of looking at the world, and how it was that he came to live such an extraordinary life, inspiring so many people.

This book is also about positive examples of hope and courage in adversity, and about commitment to a community and to a belief in peace through love in the dangerous times of the 1991-95 war in Croatia. Here are the stories and some reflections from individuals, psychiatrists, psychotherapists and the staff and members of five non-governmental organisations in Eastern Slavonia, the Centar za mir (Centre for Peace); Mir i dobro (Peace and Good); Dodir nade (Touch of Hope); Coalition for Work with Psychotrauma and Peace and Bench We Share (Zajednicka klupa). Peacemaking is challenging work. But they all persevered in the face of tremendous difficulties. Today they are flourishing and some of these projects have grown, and taken new and exciting directions.

I first met the Curles in 1995, when they invited me to their house in London and I soon became a family friend. Anne is a great cook, and we have shared many suppers along with Adam's special home brewed beer or 'spritzers' both of which look fairly innocuous but are deceptively alcoholic! We worked together in Croatia in 1996, a further workshop followed in 1997, and then that experience led me into greater involvement in peacemaking in Croatia from that time onwards. Adam has encouraged me to explore through research the nature and interactions of conflict and of psychological trauma, and to think about how divided families and communities might heal, and where better to do this than the University of Bradford, where in 1975 he had founded a new Department of Peace Studies, and had been appointed to the first chair of peace studies in England.

This book therefore originated in the research for a PhD thesis, which was completed in 2003. I felt really proud to be part of that Department of Peace Studies, and to be supervised by Prof Tom Woodhouse who, as Adam Curle's research assistant, had helped Adam Curle to found the department in 1975 and who now holds the Curle Professorship. I was co-supervised by Dr Betts

Fetherston who has herself worked in Croatia, and who has a background combining interests in peace, psychology and counselling. Dr Nick Lewer from the University of Bradford has worked with Adam Curle in Croatia, and is an experienced international mediator. All these people have had a profound impact on me and on this research. In 2003, although encouraged to turn the thesis into a book, there was insufficient time to write it immediately. Life constantly moves on and now it is a pleasure to write about some of the new and exciting recent developments created by the Croatian projects which participated in the case study.

I feel very honoured to have become a small part of the work of these projects as a therapist and consultant, making friends and seeing the developments that have happened in Eastern Slavonia over the past ten years. I am very glad that we have been able to talk together about their perceptions and their work, and from the discussions came not only a thesis, but a better understanding of how all these themes interlink, and how these projects have been able to work within their communities holistically to address the wounds of war and to create peace.

Adam Curle would say that his life is no more and no less extraordinary than that of others, but he has a quiet, unobtrusive, influence on many people throughout the world, from world leaders to the residents of remote villages. He has, with governments and leaders, played his part in the prevention and resolution of international conflict, and in local communities, through listening to people, trying to understand them, and being truly himself with them, he helps individuals and groups to understand themselves and others, addressing conflict on inter-personal and intra-personal levels.

This is a not intended to be an academic book – it is a reflection and a celebration of Adam and Anne, the research, subsequent events, wonderful people and thoughts about peace.

Themes of the book – finding a way through the maze of information

This book is built around three interweaving themes. It is difficult to say which should claim first place, or even first mention, because all are of equal importance and each is inseparable from and contributes to the whole. In fact, come to think of it, that is Adam's point about humanity, the Universe and peace.

The first theme is an understanding of conflict and its psychological causes, one of which is undoubtedly the social and economic impact of psychological trauma.

The second theme is the life and work of Adam Curle, an extraordinary man who combines in his life and work so many aspects of academic learning and practical experience – he brings together psychology, anthropology, development, education, mediation and a lifetime of peace activism at so many levels and in so many different settings. To this mix is added a world-view derived from a strong spiritual belief system drawn from both eastern and western religions and cultures.

The third theme is the community based therapeutic approaches to the healing of psychological trauma and peacemaking which have been developed and implemented with the help of Curle and others. This was an unusual chance to take a longitudinal view of peace work over a period of more than ten years in Eastern Slavonia, Croatia, as evidenced in the work of five non-governmental organisations Centar za mir, Osijek; Mir I dobro, Zupanja; Dodir nade, Coalition for Work with Psychotrauma and Peace; and Bench We Share, all of which took part in the research project.

What is new in this book?

This book takes forward Curle's academic work by bringing together the literature on posttraumatic stress and peacemaking for consideration in the context of Adam's theoretical approach, exemplified by insights related to his work in Croatia. This triangulation of perspectives provides a unique opportunity to understand the needs of the post-war community of Eastern Slavonia and to explore the role of posttraumatic stress in the peacemaking process. Of course the task of understanding has only just begun and there is plenty of further research that should be done.

The book charts the movement in academic approaches to peace studies away from an initial emphasis on problem-solving approaches and top down mediation to an understanding of the need for effecting relational change at middle and grassroots levels, and it then deepens the exploration of Curle's work on the psychological aspects of peaceful and unpeaceful relationships, considering his approach alongside that of others, including the use of Carl Rogers' person centred counselling approach in peacemaking.

Modern peace theorists seem not to take sufficient account of the depth of the impact of posttraumatic stress in their study of peacebuilding and reconciliation. Peace theorists also fail to recognise the importance of addressing the effects of posttraumatic stress with appropriate psychological support, and some see little point in opening up the past as a means of healing hurts. Conflict leaves behind it a body of effects, which I have called the 'post-war syndrome', part of which is the psychological impact of war, which I believe needs to be addressed as an integral part of the peacemaking process.

Curle describes the sense of 'alienation' and 'separation' as causal factors of violence. These are concepts that clearly have some resonance with our current understanding of the psychological effects of posttraumatic stress, and so an understanding of the experience of posttraumatic stress may have something to offer to peacemaking following war. To achieve this, I first explored the evolution of the syndrome of posttraumatic stress, its diagnosis, effects and approaches to treatment. This was followed by a case study in which the experiences and views of participants from the five projects in Eastern Slavonia could provide a longitudinal view and illustrations of their work, adding depth to the research.

In the course of this study, insights and leads emerged which led to the conceptualisation of the 'post-war syndrome' along with a greater awareness of the 'compassion fatigue' and 'burn out' which can happen to helpers in post-war situations, contrasted with the positive aspects of posttraumatic stress: 'creative casualties' and 'posttraumatic growth'.

Adam Curle and I share a belief in the interconnections and the constantly changing nature and the co-existence of all things and so, inevitably, before this book is printed, the participants and the events and perspectives reflected in it will have already developed and moved on. Sometimes I have asked Adam to explain something he has written in one of his past publications. He usually looks vaguely puzzled, and in his self-effacing way, he then says something like, 'Well, that was a long time ago... it does not matter much... now I might put it differently...'

But that, too, is the point. The projects, our thoughts and we ourselves are constantly developing and changing. Making peace with ourselves and others means living with impermanence – accepting the passing of time, and changes in life bringing love, loss, triumphs and disasters – and also the challenge of constantly meeting new situations and developing new ways to make peace and live peacefully.

But in all this process of transition, the book is also a chance to take a little time to reflect and to celebrate.

Chapter 1

Adam Curle and the emergence of peace as a subject for academic study

Peace

What's peace? Now first of all it's really
Not a simple issue of no-war.
It's no-injustice, no-intolerance, no-hatred
It's thinking good, not bad of everyone.

It recognises one humanity
In which all lives are precious
And worthy to be loved and given help
Towards fulfilment.

Peace is an inner state
In loving care for anyone in need.
Its qualities are wisdom
And compassion.

Our work for peace is work for harmony among all beings.

Adam Curle (Extract from an unpublished poem)

Adam Curle has a place within the framework of modern conflict resolution theorists, ranking, for example, with Johan Galtung and John Burton. He and they contribute to the academic theory of peace and to understanding the nature, causation and resolution of conflict.

The term 'conflict resolution' is conceptualised in this book as both a process and an activity, the aim of which is 'to transform actually or potentially violent conflict into peaceful (non-violent) processes of social and political change' (Miall, Ramsbotham et al 1999: 22). Whilst the elimination of violent conflict altogether is a desirable goal, in practical terms it is probably impossible, and some would say that it might even be undesirable in some circumstances, for example in asymmetric conflicts, because the more powerful party would remain dominant. Curle refused to mediate in the conflict between East and West Pakistan for this reason. He argues that in order to eliminate conflict there has to be global change eliminating the causes of conflict – the economic, political and social inequalities and injustices and oppression that lead to war (Curle 1999).

The emergence of peace as a subject for academic study

The historical background for this section is taken from the fascinating and readable account of Peter van den Dungen (1996, 1997), which traces the beginning of the study of peace back to 1517, with the publication of *Querela Pacis* by Erasmus. The subsequent Thirty Years' War in Europe (1618-1648) led to considerable philosophical deliberation about the causes and effects of war and the thoughts of many then turned to making and maintaining peace. In 1625, Hugo Grotius published his book *De Jure Belli ac Pacis* (On the Law of War and Peace). During the seventeenth century, George Fox founded the Religious Society of Friends, perhaps better known as the Quakers, who actively promoted a testimony of peace and non-violence throughout Europe, recommending that a European dyet (parliament) should be established to facilitate inter-country co-operation and communication.

The nineteenth century was a time of great expansion of the study of peace. Van den Dungen describes the concern to promote peace growing not only amongst academics but also, perhaps surprisingly, among businessmen, some of whom formed peacemaking organisations and congresses, one of which, 'The United States of Europe', was organised by the writer Victor Hugo and held in Paris in 1849. Peace societies were formed in Austria in 1891 and in Germany during 1892. In the same year, the International Peace Bureau was founded by Berta von Suttner. Alfred Nobel created a legacy for peacemaking, the Nobel Peace Prize, just before his death in 1896.

One prime nineteenth-century peace activist was Jean de Bloch, a Polish railway builder, who took an analytical approach to peace research, setting out a detailed prognosis and warnings of the potential results of the development of sophisticated weapons of war (de Bloch 1898). He and William Thomas Stead (then a famous newspaperman) together funded the Inaugural Universal

Peace Congress in The Hague in 1889 just a year after Tsar Nicholas of Russia had launched the first Peace Manifesto.

Bloch went on to fund the first International Museum of War and Peace in Lucerne, Switzerland. Other peace conferences followed, in Le Hague and elsewhere. The two world wars had led to the development of frightening technological advances in weapons and the machinery of war. Nuclear weapons followed, and the atomic scientist Joseph Rotblat joined with academics and philosophers including Eaton, Russell and Einstein in trying to create a driving force towards peace, because they could foresee the potentially devastating effects of nuclear war. Rotblat was later awarded the Nobel Prize for this work. In a lecture in Geneva in 1932, Dr Maria Montessori proposed the creation of a 'science of peace', and in 1934, Bart de Light published *La Paix Créatrice* calling for a science of peace, drawing from 'psychology, pedagogy, history, science, religion, ethics and philosophy' (van den Dungen 1996:14). In 1945, Gaston Bouthoul's Institut Français de Polémologie opened in Paris.

Following the end of the Second World War in 1945, conflict resolution rapidly developed as a field of academic study perhaps because of the proliferation of nuclear weapons. Its founders in the 1950s and 1960s included Mary Parker Follett, Kenneth Boulding, Johan Galtung and John Burton. The initial drive forward occurred in the United States, where Mary Parker Follett, writing about organisations and labour management, advocated a mutual gains approach in negotiations that may well have led to the development of subsequent problem-solving approaches to conflict resolution (Miall, Ramsbotham et al 1999: 40-56).

Kenneth Boulding, born in Liverpool in 1910, was an economist and also a Quaker, who moved to America in 1937. In 1954, Boulding, with other academics including Anatole Rapoport, formed the Center for Advanced Study in the Behavioural Sciences at Stanford University, enabling academics of different disciplines and junior scholars to meet. One of them was Herbert Kelman, a social psychologist, who with other young psychologists was inspired to start the Bulletin of Research Exchange on the Prevention of War. Social psychology was a major factor in the development of mediation and peacemaking activities. In 1957, Boulding, with other academics, published the Journal of Conflict Resolution, and two years later they founded the Centre for Research on Conflict Resolution (Miall, Ramsbotham et al 1999: 42-43).

The academic study of war has always seemed historically more attractive than the study of peace. In France, Raphael Dubois, Professor of Physiology at the University of Lyon, tried hard to establish the concept of 'peace through science' pleading with the French organisations La Paix par le Droit and the French Association for the Advancement of Science: '...Would it not be wise to endow the science of peace with rich and strong schools, just as one has done for its elder sister, the science of war?' The scope of peace study was widened when Jacques Lambert was appointed to the first French chair in peace research (Chair for the Study of International Institutions for the Organizations of Peace) in the Faculty of Law at the University of Lyon. Lambert outlined a broad range of study, 'embracing moral and psychological dimensions rather than merely legal approaches' (see van den Dungen 1996 in Woodhouse 1998:154).

In Europe, the study of conflict resolution rapidly developed, led by Johan Galtung. Born in 1930, the son of a physician, Galtung's academic background included philosophy, sociology and mathematics. In 1960, Galtung helped to found the International Peace Research Institute in Oslo, followed by the *Journal of Peace Research* in 1964.

Galtung studied the psychological, sociological and economic aspects of conflict, creating tools for analysing and mapping conflict that are now seminal. It was Galtung (1969) who developed the 'conflict triangle' explaining the causation of conflict as an ABC of attitudes, behaviours and structures or contradictions, and the concept of causal factors underpinning social, national and international conflict as 'direct, structural and cultural violence'. Direct violence is the immediate use of force; structural violence may underpin or lie within systemic institutions, for example legal, economic or administrative systems; and cultural violence includes the societal acceptance of unpeaceful behaviours or attitudes, for example prejudice and discrimination. Galtung also made the distinction between negative and positive peace, negative peace being the simple absence of direct violence, and positive peace being a state that has overcome the conditions generating cultural and structural violence. Adam Curle acknowledges the early influence on his thinking of Galtung as the 'father' of peace studies, writing: 'I am intellectually much indebted to him, having assimilated so many of his ideas that I cannot adequately acknowledge them.' (Curle 1981g : 41)

John Burton, another founder of peace studies, was born in Australia in 1915. He gained a doctorate in London, worked for the UN and for the Australian government, and returned to take up a post on the teaching staff of University College London in 1963. Burton first formed the International

Peace Association and later, the Centre for the Analysis of Conflict. He devised strategies for conflict resolution based on ideas derived from a number of sources including psychology, business organisation, and social work. He linked the causal analysis of conflict with methods of conflict resolution, deriving his 'problem solving' approach from Maslow's theory of human needs (Maslow 1954, 1968), systems theory and game theory (Burton 1969) and he developed techniques of 'controlled communication' for use in violent conflicts, international mediation, commercial alternative dispute resolution, and community and family mediation.

Other academics including Herbert Kelman, Roger Fisher, William Ury, William Zartman, Adam Curle and Elise Boulding expanded the study of conflict resolution during the 1970s and 1980s. During this period, through action research, they developed a variety of third party interventions in conflict, including negotiation, mediation and a new social-psychological approach to peacemaking, known as 'interactive problem-solving'. This new approach, which Kelman (1990) implemented in the Arab-Israeli conflict and in Cyprus, combined mediation and facilitated communication.

Elise Boulding refers to Adam Curle as 'one of the great Quaker peacemakers of our time' (Boulding and Forsberg 1998: 34). Adam's first major contributions to the academic theory of conflict resolution were *Making Peace* (1971) and its companion work, *Mystics and Militants* (1972), emphasising the need for psychological change within the process of 'conciliation'. Curle later drew upon his experience in anthropology and psychology to extend his thinking to activities designed to prevent conflict or to create and sustain the conditions for post-war peacemaking. Adam's work in Croatia, combining healing the psychological wounds of war and peacemaking, is an example of the creation of what Elise Boulding termed a 'peace culture' of which she wrote: 'I am not talking about a culture that has no conflict in it... In every relationship there is going to be an element of conflict. If we think of a conflict management as a continuum, at one end those who are different are simply exterminated. Moving along the continuum we find limited war, threat and deterrence. In the middle we find arbitration, mediation, negotiation, exchange, mutual adaptation. At the other end of the continuum we find co-operation, integration, and transformation. Each society can be placed somewhere on this continuum in terms of how it handles the bulk of its conflicts. An individual family can be placed on that continuum, as can individuals. The issue is not a matter of conflict or no conflict, but of *how we respond to conflict'* (Boulding and Forsberg 1998: 34-35). Adam has always held that the peaceful response to any conflict begins within each individual, in their heart, extending to thoughts and then becomes apparent in outer actions. This is the philosophy adopted and implemented by the Centar za mir in their running of the organisation and in their work in the community.

Much later, in 1975, Adam Curle was offered the first academic chair of peace studies to be created in the UK. He was at the time living in Maine, in the USA, and he had reached the time in his life when most people are vaguely thinking about retirement. Even Adam (then a professor at Harvard University) from time to time longingly considered the possibilities of sitting, relaxing, and growing tomatoes in his warm country garden. Instead, he accepted the invitation to found a pioneering new Department of Peace Studies at the University of Bradford, and then set about moving his house and his family to the UK. Only the family know just how much they all went through in making that decision, which involved a major change of lifestyle for all of them, in the service of work for peace. Tom Woodhouse, who was Curle's research assistant, and a member of the department from the beginning, now holds the Curle Professorship of Peace Studies at the University of Bradford, and he too now has an international reputation in the academic study of conflict resolution.

A peace activist in the making

I believe that nature, nurture and life experiences contribute significantly to a person's character and choices in life, and wanted to know a little of Adam Curle's life story in order to understand how it was that he developed such a unique personality and mix of talents and interests, coupled with his commitment to peace. He says that his mother, Cordelia Curle, affectionately known as 'Cork', was the greatest formative influence in his life. His father, Richard Curle, was a talented writer and world traveller, but not a dedicated family man. Cork divorced him when Adam was six years old, and he did not come to know his father with any closeness until his later years.

Adam Curle was born on 4 July 1916, in the shadow of war, on L'Isle Adam, France, within the sound of gunfire from the Battle of the Somme. Although his mother had named him Charles Thomas William Curle after three of her brothers who were fighting in the First World War, he was soon nicknamed Adam by his uncle, and the family immediately adopted that name. He comments that this use of another name then caused him endless trouble with officialdom for over eighty years, but that is the name he uses and by which he is best known. I had difficulty in deciding how to refer to Adam in this book. He, of course says that this is of minor importance. In the end I decided to use 'Adam' when writing of his childhood and personal memories because it feels less distant and otherwise to use 'Adam Curle' or 'Curle'.

Adam was brought up mainly by his mother, but his father put in occasional appearances. He first met his father when was three. He describes Cork as fearless, buoyant and insouciant. She certainly did some unusual things. He remembers being taken at the age of three to the battlefields and war-torn towns in France, and even though he was young, the memory of that visit and seeing for himself the impact of war remains with him.

Until the age of ten, Adam lived happily in Wheatfield, in a comfortable home surrounded by countryside, animals and friendly farming neighbours. In the freedom of this nurturing environment, he developed confidence and awareness, including a psychic sensitivity. He loved nature and as a young child he had spirit companions, a crab, a badger, a centaur and a pegasus. Their function for him at that time was companionship and a source of help in need. He wonders in retrospect if perhaps the crab and pegasus were archetypal symbols (he knew nothing of Greek mythology at that time in his life), the crab perhaps an astrological symbol, and the badger might have been a projection in time, because later he had a real badger, Wadge, as a pet.

Adam loved looking at a windmill in a nearby field and one day, when he was five, he noticed with sadness that the lovely old windmill had gone and another building was being put up in its place. He went home and told his mother about it. She thought little of it until she spoke with neighbours, and was astonished when they told her that there had indeed been a windmill on that field, but that it had been demolished ten years earlier. For the first time, perhaps, Adam internalised the realisation at the age of five that others did not see the things that he could see. He asked his spirit companions why this was. They told him that there is a force in this world that blinds some people to reality. Throughout his life, Adam has continued to combine his spiritual perceptions and religious beliefs with practical and academic learning, resulting in a combination of skills and insights that have formed his unique contributions to the fields of psychology, development, education and peacemaking.

Adam's mother shared her house with a couple, Dorothy, calm and friendly, and Douglas, a musical, creative, but highly volatile man who had suffered from polio and was addicted to morphine to ease the pain in his limbs. Adam later wrote that he loved Douglas, who was more of a dad to him than his own father, and that he learned more from Douglas of what makes a human being than from any other man. But that volatility may have contributed to an event that adversely affected Adam for the rest of his life. Cork was playing music by Brahms on the family piano, and Adam, coming down the hall, heard it. Full of enthusiasm, he danced and sang wildly with the floating piano notes – but someone shouted angrily to him 'Stop!' 'Don't be stupid!' The impact on a sensitive lad was such that he has never been able to dance or to sing spontaneously since that day. Adam nevertheless still has music in his soul, and playing the flute and writing poetry helped him to survive troubled times in later years. He stopped playing a musical instrument at some time later in his life, but he still loves to listen to music. Meditation has long been a vital part of Adam's daily life, and the peace and connection with the universal spirit that he reaches within the silence of meditation is, along with listening to the music of Bach and the love of his family and friends, his source of strength and spiritual nourishment.

Cork was a pacifist and for a long time refused to allow Adam to have a toy gun. He wanted one very badly, and he pestered her until eventually she gave in and bought him the coveted toy gun when he was five years old. He remembers his joy at getting it, and thinking that he would never want anything else, and that this would make him happy forever. Not long after this, a few days later, he remembers that a normal but frustrating household event happened that made him cry. He realised that his happiness had become elusive. He has written many times subsequently of the important insight he gained at this very young age, that happiness cannot be created or sustained by material objects, and that it is an internal thing – that happiness is a state of mind. He has campaigned for many years about globalisation, and the generalised greed and commercialism that creates and perpetuates the causes of conflict and has pointed out how damaging are the illusions so many of us have that happiness that can be gained from materialism.

At Wheatfield, Adam became involved in the local community activities, which included hunting. He remembers being 'blooded' with a fox's tail after the local hunt, but this only served to convince him that hunting is antiquarian, cruel and farcical. He recalls that, when he was annoying to certain local residents who then expressed the feeling that he should have a 'good whipping', he sometimes felt that his mother was his defender against 'an

REPORT FOR

Name...... *A. Curle*

TERM ENDING...... *March 28*......192 *9*

Form...... *5*   No. of Boys...... *8*

Subject.	Place.	Remarks.	No. Boys.	Place.	Master.
Latin	8	*Hardly realise that he is in my form*			*8.7.7.*
English { History		*He could. Is still let 9 careless hardly in saw? v. weak indeed. Considering the number of his absences, this is not surprising.*			*J.D.* *C.W.B.*
{ Geography					
{ Grammar, etc.		*He is equally unsound in grammar etc.*			*J.D.*
{ English Book		*Slow & does not keep his mind concentrated on his work.*			*8.7.7.*
{ Elementary Science					
{ Music					
{ Drawing					
Total English	8				*8.7.7.*
Place in Form by above Marks.	8				*9.7.7.*
Greek or Extra Set	SET = 1	*When he is here, he is her very good.*	7	7	*C.W.F.*
Mathematics ...	4	*Still very weak.*	7	7.	*B.W.F.*
French	iv	*Translation very good. Sentences careless. Grammar very poor. Has no idea of everything in order... has seen very little is ...his ....*	7	4	*R.M.S.*

Next Term begins on...... *Tuesday, April 30*......192 *9*

A school report from 1929, of which Adam is particularly proud. He was 12.

adult gang out to get me', yet his memories of Wheatfield are mainly a sense
of safety and nurture, with the companionship of his faithful dog Julius and
pet badger, Wadge.

At the age of thirteen, everything changed. Adam was sent to Charterhouse
School as a day-boy. He later described to me his time at Charterhouse as an
experience more traumatic for him than his interrogation in a South African
prison. He was horrified at the institutionalised violence and cruelty of the

school at that time, and he witnessed many injustices. He describes the medievalism of the school system, and the fear engendered by the cultivated mystique of the headmaster's floggings with a birch rod. The housemasters and the older boys were also allowed to administer arbitrary beatings, even for minor offences such as having the wrong number of buttons on one's coat undone. Adam was never beaten, but he had a good friend whom he describes as 'normally a gentle and sweet lad', but who was very active, and three-quarters of a century later Adam still recalls only too clearly the trauma of witnessing his friend being beaten many times. As he describes it, his friend gradually became a strangely reckless child, doing daring things, and in reaction to the brutality he became the bad boy of the school. Adam speaks of this period in his life at Charterhouse as one of continual tension, horror and fear. He feels that he survived these years psychologically because he was a day-boy. He was able to come home, play his flute and write poetry. I wonder if and how this prolonged and undoubtedly traumatic experience in adolescence influenced his later interest in psychology, his understanding and empathy for the victims of violence and his lifelong involvement in peacemaking. Adam left Charterhouse at the age of eighteen. His last year there was more enjoyable, and one in which he felt that he was treated as a human being. The school life certainly may have impacted on his friend, who continued to be an inveterate risk-taker. He served as a soldier in the Second World War, was taken prisoner, spectacularly escaped, and eventually returned safely from Dunkirk. In Adam's words, 'Then he went quietly mad. He was unable to work, and although normally a sweet and gentle man, he had awful rages', which Adam remembers persisted right up until his friend's death.

After school, Adam Curle began his academic career with a Diploma in Anthropology at the University of Oxford. He then joined the army, serving from 1940-46 during World War II. He has not told me much about his first army role. He did, however, tell me about a time when he was a young army officer, for some reason travelling on board a ship, and the signal for battle stations was given. He clearly remembers feelings that he describes as '...a pleasant sort of exhilaration' as he scrambled onto the deck, realising that the ship was about to be attacked by a German E-boat. He was not afraid of the battle to come, but rather, excited by the thought of immediate action. Personal danger seems never to have been a concern for him, but even as a young man, the thought of the massive troop movements associated with war filled him with horror, and still does. Precisely how and exactly when he made his lifelong commitment to peace activism remains unclear, perhaps it was a gradual process, but given what we know of his early life experiences, it is very easy to understand how his personal courage and his commitment to conflict resolution led him into the dangerous peacemaking activities that he subsequently undertook.

In the latter part of the war, Adam Curle applied to serve as Chief Research Officer in the Civil Resettlement Units (CRUs) set up by the government to rehabilitate returning prisoners of war. Two men involved in this work, Ben Morris and Roger Hodgkin, were significant influences on him during this time, and he describes them as '...two wise men in my life that showed kindness and right living'. The work of the CRUs also helped him to develop his understanding of the psychological effects of trauma. Ben Morris remained his close friend until his death at the age of eighty.

The work of the CRUs was innovative and pioneering, and that work, coupled with his earlier life experiences, may have been influential on Adam Curle's understanding of the nature and effects of psychological trauma, and of the positive impact of a holistic and community-based approach to the trauma healing. He revisited this work with the CRUs recently as a result of my research, and there is more about it later in Chapter Three.

After Adam Curle left the army, his growing interest in psychology and the effects of war led to the development of connections with the people who were setting up the new Tavistock Institute of Human Relations in London. Some of the Tavistock Institute's founders were still serving in the army and others were, like him, now civilians. He eventually became a staff member there from 1947-50. His writing at this period reflects a continued interest in anthropology and sociology but also an increasing interest in psychology. In 1950, he was appointed to the post of Lecturer in Social Psychology at Oxford. In 1952, he accepted an appointment as Professor and Head of Department of Education and Psychology at Exeter University.

In 1956, Adam Curle was asked to go to Pakistan as adviser on social affairs on a project for Harvard University. From 1956-59 he advised the Pakistan Planning Commission on Social Affairs. During the period 1959-61, he was Professor and Head of Department of Education in the University of Ghana, travelling extensively, helping the government to develop education, social and development plans.

In 1962, the Harvard Centre for Studies in Education and Development was founded. Its purpose, through research, teaching, and fieldwork, was to

develop education policy, essential to create the conditions for peace. It main-
tained a very practical approach, with large field projects in many countries,
including Nigeria, Tunisia, Central America and Barbados. Adam Curle
became actively involved in these research projects and during his time at
Harvard from 1962-73 he and other members of the centre helped to develop
and implement other research in a number of countries. At Harvard
University, Curle was initially a Visiting Professor of Education, and then the
first Director of the Centre for Studies in Education and Development, and
subsequently Professor of Education and Development. During this time, he
was consultant to the government of Pakistan on education under the
auspices of the World Bank, and was directly involved with Pakistan's first
five year development plans.

In 1973, Adam Curle was appointed by the University of Bradford in
England to the chair of the first university department of peace studies, a
pioneering project instituting peace studies as a new academic discipline in the
United Kingdom. He retired from this post in 1978, and he now lives in
London with his wife, Anne, continuing to actively support peace work in
many countries.

In November 2000, in recognition of his academic contribution to the study
of conflict resolution and of his many international peacemaking activities,
Adam Curle was awarded the Gandhi Peace Prize. A certificate of that award
now hangs in his study. Pinned to it is a tattered and much treasured photograph of Mahatma Gandhi.

Love in danger

Adam Curle has many times in his life been in danger during his work as
a mediator. He has had to make some very tough decisions. He had family
responsibilities, his first wife Pam and two daughters, and then his second wife
Anne and his youngest daughter Deborah, who in 1996 and 1997 was part of
our team for the workshops in Croatia. His family needs must have often
competed with his work. In the course of an international mediation in Africa,
he was told that in order to preserve the secrecy of the mission his plane could
not be given any special exemptions. 'It is with regret that we tell you we must
try to shoot you down...' he was told by the general. Undeterred, he still made
the journey, and once airborne, he recalls looking out of the window (again
with a frisson of exhilaration in the presence of personal danger) and
watching the tracer bullets curving up towards their ramshackle and defence-

less little plane. He survived, but only he knows what that decision cost him to make.

There were other threats at times directly and indirectly to Adam Curle and worse, to Anne and to their family. He was arrested in South Africa and questioned by the police. He says that he survived this without compromising the safety of any other person by giving a good deal of useless information and by confusing his interrogators. He says, looking back on this time that he was terribly afraid of course, but that he was far more concerned about possible threats to his family than to himself. After his release he travelled to England. Soon after his arrival, he noticed that a South African agent was following him, presumably hoping to kidnap and return him for more interrogation. Fortunately, Adam recognised him and was able to persuade the UK government to take protective action for his family.

Anne has never said much about these events, but they must have been very hard for her to bear. Anne is extremely brave and resourceful, having had many adventures herself. Before she married Adam, she drove overland from Jordan to Pakistan with a female friend. She was an able horsewoman (Adam is not a confident rider) and he remembers fondly and with admiration a time when she jauntily rode along a crumbling mountain pass with her right foot casually slung over the horse's saddle, overhanging a sheer drop of 1,000 feet, happily unaware of her husband's concern, and nonchalantly eating an apple! Anne is a wonderful cook. She is a natural and imaginative homemaker and in Maine, Yorkshire and then in London, she created with Adam and Deborah a happy family environment to which he could return from his demanding work and in which he could relax, think and write in peace. Anne also accompanied Adam sometimes on his journeys. She went with him to Croatia during the height of the 1991-95 war, and during his peace work they risked their lives to be with the people that they wanted so much to support.

You can tell a lot about a person by their home. Adam's study is crammed full of books, letters waiting to be read, writing in progress, and memorabilia collected during a life full of activity. There are much loved carvings, paintings and photographs jostling with scraps of paper bearing addresses, telephone numbers and notes – all competing with journals and papers for space on his desk. Amongst these, there is probably the hearing aid that has been missing for the past week. He is frequently looking for things that some gremlin has mischievously moved from where he last remembered putting them – his stick, reading glasses and several spoons.

Adam has a letter from the Dalai Lama pinned up over his desk, above a signed photograph in which the Dalai Lama's face absolutely fills the room with joy, humour and hope – it is one of his most valued possessions. He also treasures an old and fragile statue of Buddha carved in gilded wood, given to him by family friends. An oil painting depicting Jesus hangs on another wall. Opposite is a framed etching made for him by Diana Francis of a cockerel, a snake and a pig chasing each other's tails in an eternal circle, representing the 'three poisons' of ignorance, greed and hatred, which according to Tibetan Buddhist theory, are the main causes of unpeacefulness.

Adam Curle dislikes bland food and prefers savoury tastes to sweets. His favourite breakfast is very dark toast, moistened with olive oil with chillies, topped with peanut butter, tomatoes, cucumber and possibly a little marmite. He and Anne until recently brewed their own beer – much approved by their friends. The kitchen has many little touches of Anne's craftwork and like his study, has many reminders of their travels. Very few things are thrown away. Adam and Anne disapprove of any waste of the world's resources – they recycle whatever they can and their letters arrive in ingeniously re-used envelopes.

Adam is a prolific writer and poet, and has produced to date around 264 books, papers, articles, monographs and poems. I tried to collect a comprehensive list, but regularly more early titles come to light, and of course, he keeps on writing! His most recent book has just been published (Curle 2006). He feels that in poetry he can express his feelings most clearly. The major part of his earlier work published after 1970 relates to the theory and practice of peacemaking, but following the publication of his book of poetry *Recognition of Reality* (Curle 1987), he has increasingly expressed his philosophical views. Adam is a Quaker, but also profoundly influenced by non-western philosophies, including Tibetan Buddhism. His approach to peacemaking adopts the spiritual values and perceptions of both Quakerism and Buddhism, set in the context of the teachings of modern quantum mechanics and atomic science, sociology and psychology. He describes this holistic world-view clearly in *To Tame the Hydra* (Curle 1999), particularly in the powerful poem 'Indra's Net', describing his perception of the nature and interconnectedness of all living matter on physical and spiritual levels – the foundation of his philosophy. In *The Fragile Voice of Love* (Curle 2006) he explores the basis of his philosophical and spiritual approach in greater detail, and he goes on to write more of his thoughts about the impact of the 'Black Cloud' by which he means the psychological consequences of non-peaceful experiences and the impact of conflict and non-peaceful ways of life.

Adam Curle is a natural communicator, and he speaks at least seven languages. He also has the ability to empathise at a very deep level. We have explored the concept that psychic ability is simply a particular level of communication and empathy. He is certainly able to 'tune in' to the thoughts and feelings of others. He does not understand Tibetan, but on one occasion when he was listening to the Dalai Lama giving a lecture in that language, he soon realised that the translator had made a mistake. Adam Curle and the Dalai Lama later became friends, and although now they can only meet infrequently, they stay in communication, and they do not always need words.

Adam occasionally startles me by answering aloud a question that I have in mind, when I have not yet spoken. I remember one time when he did this whilst we were all sitting at supper. I have forgotten now what I was thinking about, and his answer, but I remember looking at him in amazement and thinking something like, 'Good heavens, you can read my mind.' Adam grinned and then said, quietly, 'Yes, I can.' I have never found this intrusive, and trust that he would never use that ability insensitively. Anne, too, is psychically gifted and she has experienced psychic phenomena. Both have used their gifts only to understand and to help others. We talked once about whether it is a good thing to work at the development of psychic powers, and Adam was very clear in his view. He said that these powers may develop and come from long spiritual practice, and if they do come this way, then they will be used wisely and only for good, because they have an underpinning of spiritual understanding and discipline behind them. If they are deliberately developed for other reasons, then they are potentially liable to misuse.

I remember a time, a few years ago, when I was visiting the Centar za mir in Osijek. I had gone there alone that year because Anne had been unwell and Adam had stayed at home. They were both sad that they were unable to be with their much-loved friends in Osijek. It was a hot day and the Centre staff were frantically busy and stressed. It seemed that there was too little time and too much work to do. They had no time to stop and take a rest. I asked how I could help. I was thinking of phone calls, typing or photocopying. Katarina Kruhonja, who was a founder and at that time the Director of the Centre, smiled, then she asked if I would do for them what Adam would have done for them if he were there. I replied 'Of course, what would Adam do?' Katarina said, 'Well... Adam would go and sit down by the river and meditate for us for a while.' Until that moment, I had not realised how empathic Adam is to others needs, and how simply and quietly he combines his spiritual practice with his interactions with others, wherever they are in the world. An understanding about doing, being and loving developed that day, as I sat by the river thinking of Adam and Anne, of Katarina, and the staff of the Centar za mir.

Adam's unusually varied background in psychology, education, anthropology and peace studies gives him a unique theoretical approach to the academic study of peace. This is particularly apparent when he makes links between psychological trauma and the cycle of conflict. The community approaches which have emerged in Croatia though the work of the Centar za mir in Osijek and other local organisations have, I think, been very much influenced over the years by Adam Curle on personal and professional levels, which, for him, are really indivisible.

Chapter 2 explores Adam Curle's theoretical approach to peacemaking in the context of his life and work, and the ways in which he put his innovative approach to peacemaking into practice in Croatia. It is really important to say here that this work in Croatia is only a very small part of Adam's life and work as a whole. He has done so much in so many countries over the years that it is not possible to write about it all here. His involvement with peace work in Croatia came later in his life, but he says that his contact with the Centar za mir and the other projects has greatly influenced his thinking about the process of peacemaking. He and Anne have made many friends in Croatia and they are very proud to be associated with these projects, and of all their achievements.

Chapter 2

Psychological aspects of war and peace

Violence breeds new violence. Suffering breeds suffering. War breeds
new war when the generation of the traumatised grows up. Untreated
trauma remains written in the body, as well as in the individual and
collective memory.

Stanislav Matacic (1998: 350)

The psychological aspects of the process and dynamics of conflict and relational change in peacemaking gradually emerged as a focal issue in
conflict resolution theory. Adam Curle, with Burton, Mitchell, Kelman, and
others addressed the question of whether conflict is an inevitable aspect of
human relations. The contribution of psychology to conflict resolution theory
led to the movement towards effecting relational change at community level
as part of the peacemaking process. At the same time, there was a movement
in conflict resolution away from an emphasis on the technical skills and
methods of conflict interventions (for example conciliation, mediation,
containment, controlled communication and problem solving), to build on the
concept of creating and sustaining psychological change in peacemaking.
Curle, who was an active mediator in many international conflicts, gradually
moved from his 'top down' mediations with national leaders to a much more
holistic approach including relational change at community, interpersonal and
intrapersonal levels.

The impact of Social Psychology and its influence within conflict resolution theory was particularly focused on understanding the causes and nature
of conflictual relations and developing ways to effect relational change for
peace. Curle developed his psychological approach to peacemaking through
a progression beginning with his work with the British Army Civil
Resettlement Units (CRUs) in 1946 healing the psychological trauma of

returning former British prisoners of war; his connections between counselling and peacemaking in 1971; and then his association with the Centar za mir. I was then able to help to take his work forward with Mir i dobro in Zupanja, Croatia in 1996 and 1997, and from that time I have continued to work with the Centar za mir and to keep in touch with the staff and volunteers of the other projects.

It was Adam Curle's work that inspired me to explore the relationship of psychological trauma, the cycle of conflict, and the community approaches to heal the wounds of war in Eastern Slavonia.

Is conflict an inevitable part of human relations?

Some theorists see violence as an intrinsic part of human relations, to be contained and controlled, whilst Adam Curle, and others like Ury, might answer the assertion that war is only a natural part of human nature with the response, 'Yes, and so is peace' (Ury 2000: 55). Following the First World War, many influential thinkers and conflict resolution theorists considered practical ways to stem violence and prevent further conflict. William James, who was referred to by Deutsch (1995) as the 'first peace psychologist', questioned the assumption that war is inevitable (James, 1995: 23).

Einstein, questioning whether there might be a psychological element underpinning conflict that could be addressed within education, wrote in a letter to Sigmund Freud:

> There are certain psychological obstacles whose existence a layman in the mental sciences ... is incompetent to fathom: You, I am convinced, will be able to suggest educative methods, lying more or less outside the scope of politics, which will eliminate these obstacles.

> The ill-success, despite their obvious sincerity, of all the efforts made during the last decade to reach this goal leaves us no room to doubt that strong psychological factors are at work, which paralyse [sic] these efforts' (Einstein and Freud (1933: 3-1) in Langholtz (1998a: 5-6)).

Despite his profession, Freud's response indicated no confidence in finding a psychological way forward. His view was that the animal part of human nature is prone to violence. So, even Freud envisaged conflict resolution more in terms of containment than relational change and the way forward as an international collective exercise of control over this natural human violent tendency. Freud's reply was: 'Thus, under primitive conditions, it is superior

force – brute violence, or violence backed by arms – that lords it everywhere.'
He added: 'There is but one sure way of ending war and that is the establishment, by common consent, of a certain control which shall have the last word
in every conflict...The League of Nations...has no force at its disposal and can
only get it if the members of the new body, its constituent nations, furnish it'
Einstein and Freud (1933: 10-14) in Langholtz (1998a: 5-6). The League of
Nations no longer exists. The United Nations has a limited containment role,
but Freud's point concerning the limitations of delegated power to control acts
of aggression remains valid. In 2003, the United States of America and the
United Kingdom invaded Iraq to find and remove alleged weapons of mass
destruction by armed force, despite the refusal by the Council of the United
Nations to authorise that drastic action.

The concept of harnessing the principles of social psychology for conflict
resolution developed slowly. Betts Fetherston (2001: 1) reminds us that
'Conflict resolution, like peace research, evolved as a critique of realism in
international relations'. In realism, states are in conflict over resources and
power, depicting a scenario where human nature is viewed as inclined to strife
and anarchy unless violent conflict is contained and controlled. Conflicts are
seen as objective, caused by 'knowable, measurable, reducible objects, outside
of and separate from the subject' (Fetherston 2001: 2), and often based on
competing interests. Appropriate methods of controlling this type of conflict
therefore logically involve settlement strategies including mediation, negotiation, and arbitration, dividing up those things that are capable of division and
re-organisation of distribution.

Transforming conflictual relations

This section explores this transition within conflict theory from high-level
interventions with national leaders, including international mediations and
conciliations, to include efforts to transform conflictual attitudes, perceptions
and behaviours at community (grassroots) level, with particular reference to
the work of Burton, Galtung, and Adam Curle.

John Burton's early work differed from Curle's conciliation and mediation
activities with international leaders. Burton advocated 'controlled communication' techniques (Burton 1968; 1969), bringing together social scientists and
representatives of nations in conflict in seminars designed to study the
conflict objectively, hoping that perceptions would change, leading to more
effective communication. Curle commented, 'This is better than someone

going back and forth between two countries attempting to change the perceptions of people separately. The disadvantage is that leaders cannot very well participate in Burton's seminars, and so, if their subordinates come to see things differently, they face the tough and unpopular task of persuading leaders at home that they were wrong' (Curle 1971c: 242). Curle's approach relied heavily on the knowledge, tact and diplomacy of the mediators working with the leaders in the conflict, requiring the mediators to undertake background research, considering that 'information about the situation in particular and about conflict in general is indispensable', preferring this to the 'ignorance of the details of a conflict' involved in Burton's method of controlled communication (Curle 1971c: 190). Gradually, however, the strategies and interventions of both Burton and Curle changed as their theories were influenced by insights derived from experience.

Burton attempted to build a unified theory of conflict resolution, relying on social and psychological theory in contributing to a new paradigm of the nature, causation and resolution of conflict with constant efforts to criticise, challenge and change accepted ideas in existing conflict resolution theory and practice. John Burton saw conflict resolution as a manageable process, believing that strategies could be developed to contain or ameliorate existing conflict, combined with conflict prevention. He was actively involved with conflict intervention in Malaysia, Indonesia and Cyprus, and his pragmatic approach was reflected in his development of a conflict resolution skills manual (Burton 1990a).

Eventually, Burton became convinced that conflicts were not generated primarily, or even at all, by shortages of material goods or claims to territory, but suggested that they arise from subtler tensions. He distinguished between needs (defined as non-material and therefore not easily divisible) and interests (which are material and therefore subject to the potential limitations of supply and demand). Interests might be negotiated to achieve compromise solutions (Burton 1990: 242 and Miall, Ramsbotham et al. 1999: 47). Burton's work then became focused on whether responses to clashes of needs should be coercive and containing or responsive and goal directed (Dunn 1995: 203).

Fetherston (2000: 4-5) points out that Burton's theory supplies a new 'objective' basis for violent conflict. Since needs are not divisible, malleable or controllable, containment will not help and conflict occurs when needs remain unmet. Burton developed the analytical process of 'problem-solving', highlighting the decision-making dilemma of achieving needs satisfaction as opposed to needs suppression by power. His use of the word 'Provention' indicates leaving behind the containment in conflict prevention and moving towards the far more challenging task of creating conditions of peace promoting new, non-conflictual relationships (Burton and Dukes 1990a: 274).

Curle perceives conflict as a dynamic force, potentially leading to change within the individuals, systems and the structures in which conflictual relationships are embedded. His research and publications over several years, in *particular Making Peace* (Curle 1971c), published together with *Mystics and Militants* (Curle 1972a), and his later work *Tools for Transformation* (Curle 1990b), had a decisive influence on the academic field of peace studies because it provided a more holistic understanding of conflict transformation operating at several levels, extending beyond suggestions of elimination or control of conflict or manipulation of communications or perceptions. Whilst it is accepted that mediations vary, it is not appropriate to assume that all disputes can be settled with mediation. Curle did not accept this normative approach, and he identified, for example, 'asymmetric conflicts' where the power imbalance is such that mediation for an equitable outcome is impossible, and it was with great regret that he refused to mediate between East and West Pakistan for this reason. There could have been a settlement, but in his view, it would have been one of negative peace, sustaining a continuation of the oppressive power imbalance (Curle 1990b: 92-93).

In his early work, Curle identified sequential elements of conflict resolution: research, education confrontation, conciliation, bargaining and development (Curle, 1971c; Curle, Dugan 1971). It was later that he began to address the psychological issues of peacemaking. These included actively changing perceptions, breaking down stereotypes and prejudice and enabling the parties to understand each other. As seen from the brief biographical account of his work in Chapter 1, he was much involved in education and development work in the UK and overseas, and it is understandable that his early publications emphasised the political power of education in effecting psychological change for development and for peace, (Curle 1961; Curle 1962a, 1963a, 1963b, 1963c, 1964a; 1965; Curle, Yudelman,. 1965; Curle 1966, 1968a, 1968b, 1970b; 1974a; 1974b; 1974c). He recommended that education and development could be used to transform the position of the 'underdogs', hopefully without becoming 'dead dogs' (Curle 1974a), suggesting that education could raise awareness, so empowering the oppressed to confront and challenge their oppressors. From such challenges, conciliation, bargaining, and eventual change might follow, (Curle, 1971c; Curle, Dugan, 1971; Curle 1974a).

In *Preparation for Peace*, Curle (1981d: 19) recognised that 'top down' mediations are only 'treating a sore on a body riddled with disease' and cannot provide the whole solution to conflict. He continued to see mediation as a necessary activity to address and contain conflict as it happens, but alongside this he emphasised the necessity of transforming those economic and social conditions and psychological attitudes which he identified as leading to conflictual behaviours, seeing these changes as necessary on individual, collective, national and international levels (Curle 1999). His approach to peacemaking therefore moved from the 'top down' model of mediation with national leaders (limited because it often has the effect of maintaining underlying problematic social structures), to a focus on peacemaking activities with community leaders and influential professionals referred to as the 'middle way' (Curle 1992b). He recognised that community support is necessary for lasting peace. 'Although the first step towards a settlement may be a political or legal agreement, this will mean little without willing and enthusiastic assent by most of the people' (Curle 1997b: 4). He describes the extension of his work to empower communities at 'grassroots' level in *Tools for Transformation* (Curle 1990b), and *Another Way* (Curle 1995) and further elucidates the rationale for this approach in *To Tame the Hydra* (Curle 1999) and in his latest book, *Fragile Voice of Love* (Curle 2006). My research explores relational change at community level, in particular, healing the adverse psychological effects of war, a significant part of the 'post-war syndrome,' my term for the collective economic, psychological and social effects of war.

Adam Curle and I discussed the concept of the post-war syndrome during the research, with particular reference to the long-term effects of war and the relationship between therapy and peacemaking. He has long suggested that there is a cycle of violence in which the adverse psychological effects of war lead to alienation and separation, creating a climate in which 'fear, suspicion and dislike dominate' and that '...these emotions arise because of some present or past – at times very remotely past – circumstances' (1997d: 2). He has developed this theme in his most recent book, referring to the 'Black Cloud,' which is his term for the 'compound of fear and misery...distilled and expelled by suffering humanity in the form of sad and muddled feelings', which are the cumulative negative emotional effect of human cruelty and misuse of resources (Curle 2006: 1). He makes the point that the Black Cloud becomes '...lodged in and expressed through the memories and emotions and inherited traits of the men, women and, most sadly, the children of much of the world. In particular many of the vulnerable and receptive adolescents are sucked into the ambience of fear, anger, muddle and chaotic violence', adding '...as time passes the different tragedies and miseries of the past blend confusingly with the afflictions of the present to challenge the skills of the most insightful therapist' (Curle 2006: 8).

Having asserted that peace agreements can only work if supported by professionals, community leaders and by the general population, Curle (1975b: 10) wrote approvingly of the work of Gene Sharp and George Lakey on the non-violent empowerment of the oppressed. Taking an increasingly holistic approach, he encouraged multi-level approaches to effect psychological and behavioural change at all levels of society, an example of which is his association with the Centar za mir and Bench We Share in Osijek, and with Mir i dobro in Zupanja, Croatia, aspects of his work which are explored in this book.

The influence of social and organisational psychology on conflict resolution theory is particularly apparent in the area of conflict analysis, and in the study of the dynamics and processes of conflict, explored in the remainder of this chapter.

The influence of psychology in conflict resolution theory: effecting relational change

In considering multi-level psychological change, both Burton and Curle were influenced by systems theory in which '...attention is given to the role of social learning and culture in the way in which social systems change' (Miall, Ramsbotham et al. 1999: 47). Curle's view of the importance of the role of education in effecting psychological change for peace has already been considered. Anatole Rapoport postulates that socio-cultural systems have underlying assumptions (default values), which are more resistant to change than those of their individual members. Individuals may be subject to this first order learning, forgetting that they can make choices in order to attain goals. Second order learning is the ability to challenge and change commonly held social assumptions, and he suggests that the most effective way to produce such learning is through a participative design process Rapoport (1966: 442) in (Miall, Ramsbotham et al. 1999). Burton asserted the need to change society's default values to include problem solving methods and philosophy (Burton and Dukes 1990b: 2). Galtung and Curle went further, asserting the need to challenge and change cultural and structural violence within society (Galtung 1996, Curle 1981g: 53). Burton concurred with this approach, but pointed out its political risks (Burton 1990: 256).

For Curle, peacemaking links in with the humanistic psychological approaches that aim to encourage internal reflection, questioning personal and external belief systems, empowering individuals to take action to effect personal and social change. He strongly advocates intrapersonal change: '…a final dimension of reconciliation, that we should be reconciled with ourselves' (Curle 1975a: 12).

As will be argued later in this book, the approaches of Burton and Curle to peacemaking are underpinned by principles of social psychology stemming ultimately from the work of the psychoanalyst Sigmund Freud (1856-1939). The prevailing positivist approach to social science, with its separation of facts and values and the criticisms made by Karl Popper caused Freud's theories to be regarded by some as 'unscientific'. The logical positivists of the Vienna Circle sought to eradicate metaphysics from scientific knowledge (Smith 1998: 97). A book review of *Mystics and Militants* (Curle 1972a) published in *The Times Education Supplement* on 25 August 1972 reflects a similarly critical attitude to Curle's approach. Today, some people might criticise certain counselling modalities for similar reasons, stating, perhaps, that they are 'too touchy-feely' with insufficient evidence-based theoretical underpinning.

In mediations and conciliations, the mediator is facilitating psychological change, and effective communication is an important part of that process. Organisational psychology has contributed an understanding of communication in the context of negotiation to conflict resolution theory, for example, in Fisher and Keashley's 'consultation' approach, research suggests that in deep-seated conflicts, there are moments when interests are salient and others when miscommunications and misunderstandings are more relevant. As the conflict escalates and de-escalates, different interventions may be appropriate (Fetherston 2000: 7).

A wide range of academic disciplines and a number of religions, particularly Quakerism and Tibetan Buddhism, underpin Curle's peacemaking theory (Curle 1981b, 1999). There have been criticisms, particularly by Pat Bracken, Derek Summerfield and others that western psychiatric and psychological approaches in general are underpinned by Cartesian dualism and potentially lacking relevance and meaning in non-western cultures. Curle's approach, however, incorporates both western and non-western philosophy, positing interconnectedness, and implicitly rejecting Cartesian dualism. The limitations of Cartesian thinking in psychiatry may contribute to some of the difficulties encountered by practitioners in accurately defining and diagnosing specific mental illnesses, for example Post Traumatic Stress Disorder (PTSD), in epidemiological surveys and in evaluations of the impact of psychological and social interventions following war. These issues are explored further in Chapter 3.

Curle's concept of personal and collective psychological change in the process of peacemaking emphasises personal responsibility and the potential for self-development through education and other activities, but contrasting with western individualism and Cartesian dualism, because his approach is based on an assumption of the interconnectedness of all matter. He advocates individual development in the context of society as a whole, emphasising individual and collective responsibility. There are potential conceptual tensions between the notions of individual development, self-actualisation and autonomy accepted by western psychiatry and psychology as a necessary and healthy part of human development and the Buddhist concept of the interconnectedness of all matter contrasted with the pervading sense of separation and alienation which is identified as one of the causal factors of conflict and war.

Evolving links between psychotherapy and peacemaking

In earlier writing, Curle had suggested 'reversing the cycle of violence' by '...changing the energy expressed in explosive violence to energy manifested in wise and compassionate action' (Curle 1997d: 1). By that time, he had become actively involved in supporting community peacemaking in Croatia, and in that 1997 paper, he mentions the Centar za mir in Eastern Slavonia. It was in 1995 that Adam and I met together to plan our future work in Zupanja, Croatia. This area, because of its geographical position, had suffered constant shelling almost daily over a prolonged period of five years. Tracey Brown and I were by then experienced in trauma counselling, working individually and together as part of a team. Deborah Curle had a master's degree in psychology and at that time was training as a counsellor. Together, we volunteered to work under Adam's supervision with the teachers and psychologists in Mir i dobro in Zupanja to develop ways to help the children in their community heal from the traumatic experiences of the recent war.

The 1996 trauma workshops in Zupanja went very well. The participants had the idea that following on from the healing of the psychological trauma, they could develop their work with the children in the community to defuse conflictual attitudes and to work to create and sustain peaceful attitudes. They asked if we could design another workshop with them to explore these aspects of peacemaking, and Deborah and I went out again to co-facilitate that work in 1997. In those early workshops in Zupanja, we established direct links between therapy and generating relational change for peace. Adam Curle refers to those workshops in two papers *Counselling in Croatia: a peaceful future?* (Curle 1998) and *Counselling for Peace* (Curle 1997a). He later wrote that he considered that the necessary shift in perception to counter alienation and violence could be effected through the work of '…wise therapists, by experienced community workers and indeed by individuals who realise that feelings are beginning to overcome judgment' (Curle 1997d: 2). It is this role of community-based therapeutic work within the peacemaking process as a means of effecting psychological change for peace, which came to be the foundation of my research and is explored further in this book.

In *Making Peace*, Curle (1971) described the longitudinal progression of conflict along a continuum from unpeaceful to peaceful relationships, which can be charted in a matrix comparing levels of power with levels of awareness of conflicting interests and needs, providing a foundation on which to develop activities to assist in the peacemaking process (Lederach 1996: 64-71). The concept of 'awareness', developed in *Mystics and Militants* (Curle 1972a), became a constant theme within Curle's approach to psychological change in the process of peacemaking. During his tenure of the Chair of the Department of Peace Studies at the University of Bradford, his approach to peacemaking, whilst still including strategic approaches, increasingly encouraged wide social and psychological transformation, through research, education and other means, as evidenced by the principles outlined in his inaugural lecture:

> There must be concern for changing perceptions, for enlarging awareness of social reality: and there must be concern for changing the balance of power where strength is being employed to enhance or maintain the strong at the expense of the weak. These will have very different implications for both analysis and action in different settings, but in all cases they involve a purposeful alteration of the existing situation. (Curle 1975b: 11)

In working with the CRUs in 1945, the psychologists and psychiatrists explored the effects of posttraumatic stress in the context of conflict, and there were elements of therapy alongside psychosocial work for the rehabilitation of the former prisoners of war.

During the 1970s, whilst considering conflict resolution strategies and relational change, Curle also made his first link between conciliation and psychological therapy:

> Conciliation is a function that may operate within any peacemaking context. It is a psychological technique, or rather, the rudiments of one, which I believe may be refined and developed as a therapeutic technique. (Curle 1971c: 177)

This link between therapy and conciliation represents the beginning of the development of Curle's thinking about the process of relational change in peacemaking, refined in the course of his long peacemaking experience. His life and work is characterised by his attention to the personal relationships of everyone involved, at all levels. Effecting appropriate psychological change for peace presents many difficulties, particularly after war. Where people suffer the trauma of violent conflict, their experiencing becomes embodied in a post-war revision of their social norms and meanings, and the physical and psychological stress suffered by a community in war may lead to feelings of separation, alienation, bitterness and hatred. This was certainly true at that time in Croatia (Agger 1996; Allwood, Bell-Dolan et al. 2002; Arcel, Folnegovic-Smalc et al. 1998; Curle 1971c; 1972a, 1975a, 1992d). Curle became involved in many subsequent projects that incorporated both healing for the trauma of the war, and the encouragement of peaceful attitudes (Curle 1992a, 1992c, 1992e).

The influence of psychology in conflict resolution theory: peaceful and unpeaceful relations

Curle describes peaceful interpersonal relationships from the pragmatic viewpoint of their mutual effect:

> Between a man and a woman, for example, a peaceful relationship, despite occasional tiffs, would in general provide for mutual support, comfort, and a pleasurable life; in an unpeaceful relationship, one or both of the couple would make the other feel anxious, guilty, inadequate, frustrated, angry etc: and their life would be more unhappy than happy. (Curle 1995: 10-11)

He accepts that any human relationships are variable and may not always be positive, but construes peacefulness as a balance in which 'the various parties did each other more good than harm'. He points out that this terminology has the advantage of 'covering any exigency of human relationships, interpersonal, (even intrapersonal) familial, communal, international and so on' (Curle 1995: 10). He gives an example of the practical impact of such relationships:

> A peaceful relationship would, on a personal scale, mean friendship and an understanding sufficiently strong to overcome any differences that might occur... On a larger scale, peaceful relationships would imply active association, planned co-operation, an intelligent effort to forestall or resolve potential conflicts. (Curle 1971c: 15)

He then extends this pragmatic definition of peaceful relations to interstate relations:

> A peaceful relationship between larger groups, such as states, would be characterised by close and relaxed political and economic ties, ensuring that if any differences arose they would be quickly and amicably resolved. An unpeaceful relationship would be the opposite; serious differences might lead to a breach of diplomatic relations, dangerous confrontations, and even in the last resort to war. (Curle 1995: 10-11)

Curle perceives violence as encompassing illegality, force and the destruction of harmony. In *Another Way*, he extends the definition of violence beyond that of physical force, emphasising that physical violence represents 'only some of the ways in which force is used unlawfully':

> Violence is something that does harm to people; in the sense of words, deeds or situations that damage the ability to develop fully the human potential for feeling, creation and happy maturity. (Curle 1995: 4)

His notion of 'harm' implies deprivation of the basic human satisfactions perceived necessary to achieve our full human potential, as defined in Abraham Maslow's theory of human needs and motivation (Maslow 1943, 1954, 1968). He wrote 'Maslow is one of the very few psychologists of repute whose work was directed towards demonstrating that human potential, and hence the reality of human nature, was far higher than the average achievement' (Curle 1981b).

Maslow posited a hierarchy of human needs based on two groupings, 'deficiency' and 'growth' (Maslow 1943). He added to the original list, over time, in other publications. The deficiency needs are, starting from the basic (lowest) level: Physiological – hunger, thirst, bodily comforts; Safety and security – out of danger; Belongingness and love – affiliation with others; Esteem – achievement, competence, approval and recognition. Within the deficiency needs, he suggested that unless the need at each lower level were met, the higher levels would be difficult to achieve. The higher levels of growth needs are: Cognitive – to know and understand and explore (Maslow and Lowery 1998); Aesthetic – symmetry, beauty, order (Maslow and Lowery 1998); Self-actualisation – to find self-fulfilment and realise one's potential; Transcendence – to help others find self-fulfilment and realise their potential, and spiritual fulfilment (Huitt 2002; Maslow 1971). Despite a lack of evidence to support this hierarchy, it seems to continue to enjoy a wide acceptance.

Curle combines these disciplines to define the primary satisfactions for humanity, which the more abstract principles of justice and equality would serve, as:

> *Safety* (protection from violence from whatever quarter), *sufficiency* (enough food and basic material requirements so that potentialities are not inhibited by material factors), *satisfaction* (where material progress is not gained at great psychic or cultural cost) and *stimulus* (where the sense of potentiality – intellectual, emotional and social – is kept in view). (Curle 1995: 96)

Later, in *To Tame the Hydra*, he adds to this list, service (the chance to take some role in the ordering of local, national or international affairs) (Curle 1999: 32).

Curle also indirectly adopts Galtung's analyses of the physical and social manifestations and causes of conflict in this definition of peaceful relations:

> What characterises unpeaceful, as opposed to peaceful, relations, is, of course, their violence towards human beings. It may be the direct violence of person to person: or the violence of a system that legislates unjustly towards various categories of people – for example, gypsies in parts of Europe, or an economic structure which, without actual malevolence, but certainly uncaring, ensures the prosperity of the rich at the expense of the poor. (Curle 1995: 10-11)

The next section explores some of the conceptual analyses of the process and dynamics of conflict which influenced Curle's thinking, or are relevant to this study.

The dynamics and process of conflict

Curle acknowledges his indebtedness to the work of Johan Galtung, (Curle 1971c: 27); and his writing evidences Galtung's profound influence in *Making Peace* and in *Reconciliation, Violence and Anger* (Curle 1975a: 7), reflecting Galtung's (1969) conceptualisation of violence in varying forms: direct violence (the use of force upon others); structural violence (the systems of inequality or injustice in society that create or perpetuate violence, for example poverty or racial discrimination) and cultural violence (the attitudes and behaviours in society that support, encourage or tacitly permit violence to continue, for example prejudice and greed). In the same work, Galtung also created a different, but related, causal model which Miall, Ramsbotham et al. (1999: 14) illustrate as a 'conflict triangle' or the 'ABC' triangle, representing the attitudes, behaviours and contradictions leading to violent conflict.

Miall et al (1999: 52), referring to their interpretation of Galtung's conflict triangle in the discussion of conflict resolution strategies, describe Galtung's structural approach as addressing the 'contradictions', Burton and Kelman's controlled communication techniques as addressing the 'attitudes' and the bargaining/negotiation, mediation/conciliation, and arbitration/adjudication of Zartman and others as addressing the 'behaviours'. In this analysis, they have not included the transformative approaches creating radical interpersonal and intrapersonal psychological change which Curle regards as essential in creating and sustaining peaceful relations (Curle 1990c).

Curle also describes a different, but related concept, 'the cycle of violence'. This is a cycle in which factors such as alienation and separation deplete human compassion and sensitivity, allowing or causing violence to occur. The violence causes psychological damage, leading to further alienation and separation, and then further violence is perpetuated. He suggests that this cycle of violence can be addressed with interventions to effect psychological change using experienced community workers, individuals, therapy and the work of community groups such as the Centar za mir (Curle 1997a: 2).

The dynamics of conflict and its resolution may also be conceptualised as a cycle in which surrounding circumstances (the attitudes, behaviours and contradictions of Galtung's triangle) lead to conflict formation; appropriate interventions are applied to stop conflict when it occurs, which may include UN style peacekeeping forces (peacekeeping); mediation, problem solving and communication skills are offered to contain and transform conflictual behaviours (peacemaking); and finally, effecting social change through various means, including humanitarian aid, to help to heal the physical and psychological effects of war, educate and create a peaceful society to prevent the recurrence of violent conflict (peacebuilding).

The causes of unpeaceful relations, and the psychological processes that contribute to the development or perpetuation of conflict

Many modern psychological and therapeutic approaches (including many for healing psychological stress following violent conflict) are linked or adapted from Freudian principles, including psychoanalysis, psychodynamics, psychodrama, cognitive therapy and behavioural therapy. Person-centred therapy, gestalt therapy, transactional analysis and other approaches widely used in the healing of the psychological trauma of war are also developments stemming from psychoanalytical principles.

The concepts of Freudian psychoanalytical theory also underpin some expositions of the psychological dimensions of conflict. For example, Mitchell (1981) uses terminology (rationalisation, projection, transfer, displacement, repression) indicating the psychoanalytical foundations of his approach. These concepts might not only underpin some psychological aspects of peace theory, but also influence the way in which many Western mental health practitioners understand the psychological effects of war, and the way in which returning former prisoners were treated after the second world war. The psychoanalytical approach also underpins much of the modern diagnosis and treatment of psychiatric disorders including posttraumatic stress disorder, which is discussed further in Chapter 3.

Perceptions and attitudes

I am making the assumption that attitudes and perceptions originate in a person's genetic inheritance and are then influenced by the impact of culture, conditioning and circumstances. Attitudes and behaviours stem from many origins including character or personality, socialisation and ethnic, cultural or gender differences. Normalisation and generalisation is inevitably inappropriate where there is so much possibility for variation, and therefore any observations I make here may be justifiably distinguished or challenged on the grounds of diversity.

Character

Character and personality may be defined to include the 'mental and moral qualities' of an individual (Pearsall 1999: 237, 1065). There are huge debates from the large body of literature within psychology on personality theory and character formation about the nature and extent of the respective roles of innate or genetically inherited qualities and the influence of culture and conditioning on character or personality formation. I am adopting Adam Curle's view that character formation is derived from genetic inheritance, combined with the influence of upbringing and life experiences, (Curle 1995: 17). Character is assumed here to be inextricably linked with culture and conditioning, involving subjective processes of attitude formation and socialisation, which may include political identity (Roshchin 1986: 7). An issue for peacemaking is whether conflictual attitudes become embedded in personality and if so how and why they are so embedded. These topics are not addressed in this book, but would benefit from further research.

Carl Rogers, a psychologist, was influential in developing the Person Centred Approach to counselling and psychotherapy and in his later years, in peacemaking activities (Thorne 2003). He was born in Illinois, Chicago in 1902 and died in 1987. He began training in scientific agriculture at the University of Wisconsin, but as he became drawn to Christian ministry, he changed his study to history. He married, and then trained in clinical psychology, taking a post in the field of child protection. His therapeutic background included both psychoanalysis and behaviourism. Later, as a professor in the State University of Ohio, he first presented the principles of 'client-centred' therapy (Rogers 1942) and subsequently further developed his theory, renaming it the 'Person-Centred Approach' (Rogers 1961, 1980; 1995; Rogers and Stevens 1967).

Rogers' Person-Centred Approach to psychotherapy has had a profound impact upon social and educational thinking and is widely used in counselling, group-work and in peacemaking activities (Rogers and Malcolm 1987; Rogers and Ryback 1984; Rogers and Sanford 1987; Rogers and Whiteley 2003a; 2003b). Rogers' approach values empowerment, self-awareness and self-development (Rogers 1942, 1961, 1980, Mearns and Dryden 1990; Mearns and Thorne 1988). Curle and Rogers never met, and although Curle never directly refers to the work of Rogers, there are several striking similarities in their thinking. Rogers' view is that character and personality are not static, but in a constant state of change and development as part of the process of self-actualisation (Rogers 1989; 1992; 1995). Rogers' theoretical approach, including that of the development of personality, reflects Freudian principles. He suggests that humans develop a self-concept which '…is an organised configuration of perceptions of the self which are admissible to awareness'. Such configurations are subject to constant change. These perceptions form an 'organised picture, existing in awareness either as figure or ground, of the self and the self in relationship, together with the positive or negative values which are associated with those qualities and relationships, as they are perceived as existing in the past, present or future' (Rogers 1995: 501). Curle refers to the ever-changing nature of the elements of self which we call 'I' (Curle 2006: 15-16; 2003). Denial of awareness, Rogers warns, may lead to psychological tension (Rogers 1995: 510). This view reflects Freud's concept of repression. Rogers suggests that we generally adopt ways of behaving that are consistent with our concept of self, and that where behaviour is inconsistent with our self-concept, it may not be 'owned' by the individual (Rogers 1995: 507-509). This has clear implications in societal situations where, for any reason, violence is prevalent or is positively valued.

Rogers' concept of the self-actualising tendency is integral to his concept of personality formation, and to counteracting conflictual attitudes. Rogers and Curle utilised both the self-actualising tendency and deliberate social conditioning through education and therapeutic approaches in their peacemaking work. Rogers' peacework in Northern Ireland and South Africa encouraged an atmosphere of acceptance in which people could let go of their bitterness and begin to try to understand each other, (Rogers 1982b: 88; 1987b; Rogers and Sanford 1987). During his lifetime, Rogers became increasingly involved in peacemaking activities, seeking to enhance mutual understanding and to change conflictual attitudes, (Rogers 1982a, 1982b; 1986; 1987a; 1987b; 1987c; Rogers and Malcolm 1987; Rogers and Ryback 1984; Rogers and Sanford 1987; Rogers and Whiteley 2003a, 2003b).

Kohlberg (1969) argues that a child's social development follows progressive definable stages. At first, the child absorbs norms from fear of punishment, then to be encouraged, to win approval, to conform to social pressures and then from compliance with an unnamed abstract social contract and finally is guided by 'some abstract principles of conscience that appeared from who knows where', cited in (Roshchin 1986: 15). Kohlberg's view partly accords both with Freud's concept of the development of the super-ego and with Rogers' concept of internalisation of the conditions of worth, save that

Kohlberg's description of the initial stages appear to come from a mechanistic behaviourist standpoint. Personality theory has shifted in recent years from its focus on Freud's theory of unconscious drives to the concept of generalised 'schemas', or embedded patterns of thought, which form the scripts upon which we subconsciously formulate our decisions and actions.

Earlier in this book, the question arose of whether violence is innate in the human character. William Ury (2000: 33-37) finds little evidence for an innate human tendency to violence, but Curle accepts that the urge to show anger, to destroy, is just one part of our animal nature:

> We probably share with most of the animal kingdom a utilitarian impulse of potentially violent aggression when our vital interests, or those of our group (family or nation) are imperilled. (Curle 1995: 13)

Curle adds that humans are undoubtedly 'very prone to violence', killing and doing damage in a pointless way, in contrast to animals, who '… will fight others to guard their mates or offspring, to secure a mate or to protect their territory (Curle 1995: 13). However, he distinguishes humans from animals for a different reason. He believes that humans, having the gift of imagination, are able to use it creatively, but imagination also fosters the development of self-concepts and societal illusions that may lead to violence. His 'Leopard Parable' is an example of the development of collective societal illusions (Curle 1995: 14-15), but he adds an optimistic rider…

> …there is much more to human nature than violence. We love one another; we build complex social structures for living together and caring for each other; we are amazingly intelligent; we create beautiful things; we have great and largely untapped potentials... (Curle 1995: 134)

Ever pragmatic, Curle concludes that 'Whether or not we have an innate aggressive or violent streak is a less important issue than whether or not we can guide this force (whatever its source) into constructive effort' (Curle, 1995: 13). Curle and Rogers both emphasise the need for the development of awareness and through the establishment of self-discipline over action and intent.

Rogers attributes the cause of violence mainly to culture, conditioning and reaction to life circumstances. He said that in his experience of people, he found 'no such innate tendency toward destructiveness, toward evil'. However, he adds a qualification:

> How do I account for the evil behaviour that is so obviously present in our world? In my experience every person has the capacity for evil

behaviour. I and others, have had murderous and cruel impulses, desires to hurt, feelings of anger and rage, desires to impose our will on others… Whether I, or anyone will translate these impulses into behaviour depends, it seems to me, on two elements: social conditioning and voluntary choice. (Rogers 1982b: 87)

Culture

I have taken a brief overview of enculturation from the perspective of conflict resolution, adopting Cohen's view of culture as "A system of meanings and values shared by members of a community, thus informing its way of life and enabling it to make sense of the world" (Cohen 1996: 109). Race, ethnicity, religion, race, tradition, class, age and gender are therefore seen here as components of culture (Kimmel 1998).

Korn (2002) posited that enculturation stems from the registration of sensory information in the brain as percepts. These percepts are given meaning when they are subjected to cognitive interpretive processes and organised in the higher areas of the brain, forming concepts (including memories) which help us to make sense of the world. These concepts are then encoded into thought patterns and words, facilitating communication, and allowing us to develop belief, value and operating systems. Culture defines the categories, standards and guidelines for society at different levels. Roshchin suggested that western psychology had perceived socialisation as a process of influences directed towards a person in which that person is a passive object, culminating in conformity with societal norms. He added that this perception is developing into 'a broader representation of the characteristics of political consciousness and of the person's behaviour' (Roshchin 1986: 11). Referring to political socialisation, he suggested a new term, 'the political development of personality', defining this as 'the process of active assimilation by the individual of the ideological and political values and norms in their society and their formation into a conscious system of socio-political principles determining the positions and behaviour of the individual within the political system of the society '. This new concept implies a conscious and active response on the part of the individual as subject, not object. Freudian theory would, perhaps, differ, positing that social and political activity may be the rationalised product of unconscious egotistic urges – an emergence of inner drives rather than the result of external controls or influences.

Curle suggests that we do not appreciate the impact of culture and encul- turation on the psyche – 'We fail to see ourselves as being the sum product of every influence that has played on us since, and even before our birth...' (Curle 1995: 17). He extends the influence on human development of personality and culture into the metaphysical – the subtle impact of our total interconnectedness:

> We are not simply the product of our parents' genes, but of our whole human environment, its culture, teachers, our experiences, the artistic and philosophical influences that have played on us. All of these are incorporated into our being, just as our being is incorporated into that of countless others. Every change in our circumstances also changes us. (Curle 1999: 45)

He challenges the prevailing Cartesian dualism of western culture that embodies the separation of mind and body and the further false perception of events as having discrete chains of causation, enhancing the illusion of sepa- rateness. He perceives reality as a 'co-arising' of events, 'a vast system of interlocking systems' extending into the universe, of which our personal sub- systems form a part. Those who reject a dualist stance must accept a collective responsibility and cannot wholly allocate the culpability for perceived wrong- doing to others. The illusion of separateness is now firmly embedded (Curle would say, detrimentally) in many modern western psychological approaches, which seek to empower individuals to reach their full human potential through introspection and autonomy, rather than interaction with others and co-operative enterprise. Rogers strongly refuted such challenges in relation to person centred therapy, stating that in his groups, people became more real- istic and socially aware (Rogers 1982b: 85).

Curle, in considering the epidemiology of violence, gives examples of the circumstances in which violent cultures emerge (Curle 1995: 61-62). He suggests that greed causes violence in the modern materialistic global pursuit of power and profit, and he identifies further cultural influences for violence in macho and competitive societal attitudes, war-like traditions, or extreme views or subservience to violent leadership (Curle 1995: 62). Both Curle and Rogers emphasise that the development of human awareness could enhance peaceful attitudes through a glimpse of our interconnected place in a greater cosmic scheme.

Rogers wrote:

There is a formative directional tendency in the universe, which can
be traced and observed in stellar space, in crystals, in micro-organisms,
in more complex organic life and in human beings. This is an evolutionary tendency toward greater order, greater complexity, and greater
interrelatedness. In humankind, this tendency exhibits itself as the individual moves from a single cell origin to complex organic functioning,
to knowing and sensing below the level of consciousness, to a conscious
awareness of the organism and the external world, to a transcendent
awareness of the harmony and unity of a cosmic system, including
humankind. (Rogers 1979: 133)

Stress

Stress may be a causal factor of conflict, and contradictions causing stress
may be intrapersonal or interpersonal. Traumatic experiences may cause
internal conflict, for example between a generalised perception of the world
as a safe place and the impact of adverse external events. Social psychology
proposes a human tendency to reduce psychological strain as far as possible,
'avoiding tension and anxiety, reducing levels of uncertainty and ambiguity,
lessening any sense of insecurity, and avoiding, as far as possible, irreconcil-
able pieces of information, and uncomfortable complexities' (Mitchell 1981:
72). People therefore struggle to resolve contradictions in their lives or
thinking, and are happier when they learn to accept paradox.

Certain levels of stress may act as incentives to action, increasing efficiency
in performing physical, computational and intellectual tasks, so they may be
perceived as beneficial, and even sought out by some individuals (Mitchell
1981: 73). For this reason, some people might experience conflict positively.

In his mediation work, Adam Curle noticed the 'mirror image' in which
adversaries in conflict tend to perceive each other in similar ways (Curle
1990c: 34-36). He refers to the task of the mediator as enabling the parties in
conflict to recognise that mirror image they have of each other. He gives an
example of similar words spoken by opposing sides:

We are only fighting to defend ourselves from the ruthless aggression
of our enemies...They are brutal and violent and only want to destroy
us, whereas we are a peace-loving people, as all the world should
know... remember the atrocities they have committed and tell the world
the truth when you return home. (Curle 1990c: 35)

High levels of anxiety, coercive or physically damaging behaviour or uncertainty and the knowledge that others feel hostility to oneself or one's group are also likely to produce uneasiness along with perceived levels of threat as the levels of uncertainty and coercion increase. There is then a tendency to misperceive the adversary's position or proposals, even though they may hold the belief that there is a very precise understanding (Mitchell 1981: 75).

Tolerance of stress varies from person to person. Some individuals may attempt to restore equilibrium by 'closing' specific stimuli to conscious awareness. It is in these circumstances that selective perception, selective recall and group identification may lead to stereotyping of the other party in a conflict situation, lessening the ability to empathise with the other, increasing the tendency to universalise one's own frame of reference, the likelihood of tunnel vision, and an increased probability of perceived polarisation of the environment in which the conflict occurs (Mitchell 1981: 82). Mitchell warns that in a conflict, in the effort to maintain cognitive consistency and reduce stress, the parties may avoid dissonant information, enabling misinformation and stereotyping to flourish unchallenged. Language may be used to obscure information, for example by using euphemisms – 'collateral damage' rather than killing civilians, or 'taking out' rather than murder.

The deliberate internal censoring of information may encourage a sense of separation from the other party, de-humanising and objectifying the other. It may reduce empathy, removing the psychological barriers and moral restraints that might otherwise cause stress at the thought of inhumanity to others, so enabling acts of cruelty to occur (Kelman, H. C. 1973). Curle recognises these processes within a conflict situation, including them in his concept of alienation and separation.

Alienation and separation

Curle identifies the main causal factor of violence and an unpeaceful state of mind as 'a sense of alienation from our common humanity' by which he means a lack of awareness of our true nature (Curle 1995: 55, 61-62). Curle adopts the eastern view that all matter is interconnected and that one of the illusions from which humankind suffers is the illusion of separation. A difficulty for critical analysis is that the concepts of alienation and separation are understood differently by eastern and western philosophies.

Curle's approach draws from both modern psychology and from Buddhist ideology. In *Another Way*, Curle summarises the tenets of Tibetan psycho-philosophy, explaining the sense of alienation which arises from the 'three poisons' of ignorance of our true nature; acquisitive greed or yearning; and hatred or jealousy (Curle 1995: 16-20). He defines the first poison, 'ignorance', as an erroneous perception of self and others. 'We have this illusion of an unchanging and independent self, which distinguishes us and isolates us from all the other unchanging and independent selves by whom we are surrounded' (Curle 1995: 17). Curle conceptualises all matter as interconnected and fluctuating in response to the impact of people, environment and events. He suggests that our true nature is 'empty' in that there is no permanent 'you', or 'I', but only inconstant, momentary, configurations of self, 'focal points in an unending system of life' (Curle 2003). It is, he argues, the failure to understand this true nature that causes a sense of alienation and separation, leading to unpeacefulness. The second 'poison' is greed, lust or acquisitive yearning. This stems from the illusion that happiness can be conferred by external people, objects or events, and is evidenced in much of the present global pursuit of power and profit. The third 'poison' is jealousy and hatred, generating negative feelings 'ranging from slight distaste to angry loathing' (Curle 1995: 20), caused largely as a result of despair caused by the failures generated by acquisitive greed or yearning.

Curle may have encountered John Bowlby's developing theory of attachment and separation during his work as a psychologist at the Tavistock Clinic. Adult feelings of alienation may arise as a result of experiences in childhood of various forms of domination, submission and rejection during which the child may have repressed their inner experiencing. The theory of attachment and separation adds another perspective, suggesting that the disruption of close loving attachments early in life can affect a person's ability to make and keep relationships in later years (Bowlby 1969). The potential effect of separation on children who are parted from parents, carers and loved ones during war is discussed in Chapter 6.

Psychological reactions to traumatic experiences in adults or children may result in severe feelings of alienation (Herman 1992). The sense of alienation generated by traumatic experiences may be exhibited behaviourally in varying degrees of severity as a lack of interest in others, a lack of empathy, an inability to form or keep relationships, or in rejecting and violent conduct (Herman 1992b). Dissociation to the extent of clinical illness in the form of Dissociative Identity Disorder (formerly known as Multiple Personality Disorder) may be associated with prolonged or severe child abuse (Putnam 1989; Putnam,

Guroff et al. 1986). There is a recognised risk of personality disorganisation following prolonged trauma (Kolb 1989: 811-812 in Herman 1992b).

Curle also adopts Thomas Yeomans' (1994) concept of the 'soul wound' as a potential cause of psychological alienation, describing it as a hurt inflicted on a child who comes into the world, not welcomed for himself/herself as a 'soul' (in the sense of the central organising element in the mind rather than in a religious sense) but who is treated as a 'bundle of potential capacities'. Such a soul wound may cause difficulty in making and maintaining relationships (Curle 1995: 59-60). This is similar to the 'conditions of worth' described by Rogers, preventing a child from developing an appropriate sense of self-esteem. These different approaches all have some relevance to conflict. The inability to empathise or to form attachments may lead to conflictual attitudes and behaviours. There are examples in prisons and politics of people who have committed acts of great cruelty following the effects of life experiences which have caused them to feel alienated from their fellow human beings.

Education as an agent for psychological change in peacemaking – challenging and changing group norms

As Curle increasingly became aware of the inadequacies of current educational provision, he sought ways to combine social psychology and education to develop new teaching methods and approaches. During his time as professor and Head of the Department of Education and Psychology at Exeter, he developed and implemented his belief that education could be improved to give people a more solid foundation with which to cope with life, perhaps reducing subsequent psychological dysfunction. He realised the importance of education in providing people with the psychological stability necessary to live constructively, building positive co-operative human relationships (Woodhouse 1991: 33). He advised the Government of Pakistan on education, development and social affairs and helped to create their five-year education and development plans. In 1962, the Harvard Centre for Studies in Education and Development was founded with Curle as Director. Its purpose, through research, teaching and fieldwork, was to develop education policy. He holds that education and development is a vital to counteract alienation and separation, creating the conditions for peace (Curle 1971: 174-176). During his active involvement with teachers and psychologists in psychosocial projects in the former Yugoslavia after the 1991-1995 war, he was disappointed that educationalists in Bosnia and Croatia were unwilling to implement peacemaking programmes as part of their national school curriculum (Curle 1997a; 1998). However, following our workshops, the teachers in Mir I dobro managed to informally include peacemaking activities into the art, literature and language lessons in their local schools.

Individuals tend to try to conform to group norms, expectations or attitudes, and 'create an environment in which only the most determined individuals can resist pressures towards consensus' (Mitchell 1981: 73). If adults find it hard to resist group norms, then this argument supports educational efforts in peacemaking to establish non-conflictual attitudes within groups and this is particularly important in their formative years.

Mitchell refers to the actions that some people take in order to retain their 'group identity' or group membership. The intense human desire to belong may lead to group identity as a means of establishing or maintaining self-esteem and the identification with the group may result in a desire to perceive the group as possessing desirable qualities and 'outsiders' are seen as lacking those qualities. Information contradicting this belief may be ignored. This attitude may create divisions in communities and society, and extreme forms of alienation and oppression may occur such as xenophobia or nationalism (Mitchell 1981: 88).

The natural human instinct to conform to authority figures may lead (in the context of group membership) to actions which individual morality would normally have prevented. In the Milgram experiment at Yale University, participating group members obeyed instructions to administer electric shocks (which they believed to be both painful and potentially lethal) to others on the instructions of a researcher who they believed to be a scientist wearing a white coat and appearing as an authority figure (Milgram 1974).

Mitchell (1981: 93) identifies behaviours in which a person or group, unable to act with hostility towards the direct cause (perhaps in a latent conflict), instead directs its hostility towards another weaker substitute person or group in a similar way to the Biblical description of the 'scapegoat' driven out by the desert tribes into the wilderness, carrying both sins and collective punishment. The plight of the Roma in Croatia, a minority who are victims of widespread hostility from all other ethnic groups exemplifies stereotyping leading to alienation and negative group identity.

Circumstances which may lead to unpeacefulness

Ury suggests that the growth in violence within global culture is a relatively recent development, supported by archaeological evidence that humans possibly lived in relatively peaceful co-existence until they began warfare in the last ten thousand years. He posits that conflict arose from the circumstances of competition over resources (Ury 2000: 35). Adam Curle regards the prevalent 'global pursuit of power and profit' and materialism as a major cause of violence, but for different reasons, proposing that these attitudes arise from two other societal illusions: that happiness is conferred by something outside ourselves and that happiness is permanent (Curle 1995: 15-16). In Chapter 1 is the story of Adam's toy gun, and his very early realisation at the age of five that happiness is not conferred by material objects, but that it is an inner state. His peacework endeavours to address materialism, uncovering the privilege associated with possessions, wealth, birth, position, religion or race, and the violence inflicted on people by injustice, oppression, manipulation, exploitation, terror, by degrading or inhuman practices and all the other countless ways in which we demean and harm each other, physically or psychically. He lists the societal circumstances likely to engender these conditions, creating or encouraging violence:

1.   Communities suffering the instability of war or rapid change, especially for long periods.

2.   Groups subjected to particular forms of stress, for example: war, homelessness, famine, poverty, and long-term unemployment

3.   Oppressed minority groups

4.   Communities separated from wider society by unbridgeable gaps of poverty or deprivation

5.   Elements of society where the culture of acquisition (competitive materialism) erodes emotional security

6.   Communities where traditional culture has been replaced by non-specific universalised forms or practices having little social value (Curle 1978b: 1-6)

Curle suggests that although these circumstances will not always produce violence, the likelihood of violence is increased if those experiencing these circumstances have also suffered psychological damage, producing a sense of alienation and separation. He gives as examples of damaging situations 'the soul wound', traumatic experiences, exposure to extreme racial religious or political views, addictions, unquestioning dependency on leaders, exposure to violence on television or in the media or upbringing in a macho culture or war-like tradition (Curle 1995: 62).

Psychological effects of war: loss, bereavement and trauma

War leaves in its wake many consequences including destruction and damage of private and public property, social disruption, bereavement, physical or psychological injuries, economic loss and unemployment. All of these may lead to psychological reactions to changes in physical and social circumstances caused by the conflict. The psychological consequences of war may be generally categorised as varying experiences of loss, bereavement and trauma.

Loss

Following our work with Mir I dobro in Zupanja in 1996, Tracey Brown and I wrote a resource pack 'Loss, Bereavement and Trauma' with practical information and activities to help the project members and other professionals or volunteer helpers offering psychological support following traumatic events (Brown and Mitchels 1997). A sense of loss can occur in relation to any of the social, physical and economic changes concomitant with war, any of which may be traumatic. Loss may be an event in which a person is deprived of material objects or a sense of loss may be the emotional response to the damage and destruction of physical objects; economic changes causing financial hardship; the removal from home, friends and familiar surroundings; reduction in self esteem through violence; unemployment; or the deprivation of some attribute or quality for any reason, for example, the loss of mobility after being wounded (Kocijan-Hercigonja, Skrinjaric et al. 1998b: 343; Stalekar, Gregurek et al. 1998: 110-111); loss of physical functions, sexual drive, self esteem or trust after torture (Arcel, Folnegovic-Smalc et al. 1998: 45-4; Loncar 1998: 212-217; Popovic 1998b: 218-221; Tocilj-Simunkovic 1998: 222-228).

Bereavement

The term 'bereavement' is used here to mean the loss, through death, of the companionship and support of family, friends, colleagues and others, or separation from a person or people. Vukovar, Osijek and other towns experienced mass bereavement caused by terrorism, bombing, or other military action and

Aspects of loss following war

After war, aspects of loss might include:

- Security – emotional and physical
- Safety
- Service
- Personal integrity and dignity, through imprisonment, torture, rape, or coercion
- Work
- Financial security, income
- Home, or a place to live
- Routine, and familiar surroundings
- Local amenities
- Opportunities for development
- Positive intellectual, emotional or physical stimulus
- Trust in self or others
- Friendship
- Emotional support of friends, family, and colleagues
- Administrative systems
- Transport and travel
- Social support
- Education
- Recreation
- Spiritual support

in some towns and villages, very few families survived the war without some bereavement of relatives or close friends. In some areas, people disappeared through military or terrorist kidnappings and a number of these people remain missing (Moro, Franciskovic et al. 1998b: 87). In the area of the case study, comprising Eastern Slavonia and the Vukovar region of Western Sirmium, 15,000 Croats were killed and some 3,000 Croats were missing (Kruhonja 2000: 14). Several thousands of Serbs in this area were killed. Some families in 2002 were still waiting to hear the fate of their missing relatives. The absence of reliable information causes uncertainty about how to react emotionally. Families understandably do not want to give up hope of recov-

ering the missing person, but they may also need at some time to allow themselves to grieve and to adjust to their altered situation. The natural grief and
frustration of relatives of missing people has been expressed intermittently in
public rallies and protests, and some participants commented during the case
study that this grief had on occasions been cruelly stirred up or prolonged by
political activists.

Bereavement may alter many aspects of family life (Popovic 1998a: 169;
1998b). In a country where there is no state financial support for widows, children, the elderly or the unemployed, the loss of working adults can lead to
poverty. Children may be forced by necessity to change roles to take the place
of missing adults, taking new emotional and physical responsibilities (Danieli
1992; Brown and Mitchels 1997: 50). Children often respond bravely to the
challenges of new responsibility, but they also may lose the freedom and fun
of their childhood. In Osijek, one of the slogans painted during the war by children on a wall in Sjenjac, Osijek, reads 'Vratite nam nase djetinstvo' – 'Bring
us back our childhood'. Compounding the grief of bereavement for many thousands of people in this area was internal displacement from familiar
surroundings or refugee status, both involving massive loss (Kebo, Sehovic et
al. 1998; Moro, Franciskovic et al. 1998b; Popovic and Dizdarevic 1998).

The psychological experience of grief and bereavement is well documented
(Dyregrov 1995; Kubler-Ross 1991; Parkes 1986a, 1986b, 1988, 1991, 1993,
1995, 1998a, 1998b, 1998c, 2001; Worden 1995). Although described as
'stages of grieving' (Kubler-Ross 1991; Worden 1995), grief should not be
regarded as a predictable psychological process following a specified course,
but certain identifiable emotions may occur, or recur, at different times for
each person. The manner and the duration of grief depends upon a number
of variable factors, including the culture, age and personality of the bereaved,
the circumstances of the loss, and the degree of support available, (Moro,
Franciskovic et al. 1998a): 86.

Bereavement is one of the most painful losses for children Dyregrov (1995)
and Harris Hendricks, Black et al. (1993: 12), report that, in a post-war study
of children conducted in Lebanon, when asked to select the most painful
memories, 60% of the children listed the death of someone close to them.
Children, because they are in the process of development on so many levels,
may be particularly vulnerable to the psychological effects of trauma, loss and
the disruption of their family support and loving attachments. During the
1991-1995 war, separation from parents and carers by death or displacement

was reported as a major cause of psychological suffering for children (Kocijan-Hercigonja, Skrinjaric et al. 1998a: 335-36, 1998b: 343; Matacic 1998: 348-350; Pantic 1998: 352).

Trauma

The term 'trauma' is used here to mean a traumatic event, or its psychological consequences. The syndrome of posttraumatic stress is discussed in detail in Chapter 3. Trauma may result from direct experience of violent conflict, or it may arise from witnessing the events of war (Kocijan-Hercigonja, Skrinjaric et al. 1998a, 1998b). Frequently, those who witness the suffering of others, even if they are themselves physically unharmed, experience deep emotional pain in response to the events, perhaps to a greater degree than if they had suffered the experience personally (Harris Hendricks, Black et al. 1993: 12). Even hearing reports of frightening events may cause vicarious trauma, and this may affect professionals and volunteer helpers, particularly medical and mental health workers (Adjukovic and Adjukovic 1998; Franciskovic, Pernar et al. 1998; Halilovic 1998: 284).

Traumatic situations that occur during war may cause changes in the economic status and lifestyle of the family. Attention may be given primarily to survival and provision of material necessities, to the detriment of nurturing relationships. Children may be affected by the loss of loving attention from parents who, in their attempts to meet their own needs or the needs of the family as a whole, may deny their children's psychological suffering (Kocijan-Hercigonja, Skrinjaric et al. 1998b: 342; Pantic 1998: 352; Matacic 1998: 347).

Children may be more likely to suffer complex emotional reactions to trauma. Practitioners who worked with children and families during the 1991-95 war in Croatia add that 'PTSD in adults frequently remains PTSD even if it becomes chronic. Original PTSD reactions in children can later develop into many different pathological directions and can be expressed in a wide spectrum of psychological disorders when the child reached adulthood' (Matacic 1998: 345). A report, *Community Trauma in Eastern Croatia* (OSCE 2002), gives details of the continuing effects of the war on the community in this area.

A considerable body of research was carried out in Croatia after the war and documented by local psychiatrists, psychotherapists and helpers, with recommendations for future psychological and social care of survivors and refugees (Arcel and Tocilj-Simunkovic 1998). The degree of trauma suffered may increase in proportion to the number and severity of the events experienced (Harris Hendricks, Black et al. 1993: 12). The impact of trauma and the duration of its effects may be influenced (as seen earlier in considering loss, by the personality and resilience of the person affected, the circumstances of the events, and the degree of emotional and physical support available. In Chapter 3, consideration is given to whether adult resilience to trauma is possibly linked with earlier childhood experience. It is known that previous traumatic experiences earlier in life can increase the impact of new events upon children. Vidovic (1991) reports that, in Croatia during the recent war, children who had suffered earlier separations were seen to be the most vulnerable to traumatic stress, depression and associated problems of behaviour.

Stiefel describes the most profound effect of war as the destruction of relationships. The erosion of trust is particularly poignant in a country where there has been internal civil war. In addition to the physical disruption of normal daily life by war, colleagues, families and friends may find themselves divided in loyalties. Former friends and neighbours become enemies, and faith in government, or in those in positions of power or authority, is eroded. Erosion of trust is one factor which could lead to Yeomans' 'soul wound' (Yeomans 1994), causing difficulty in making and maintaining relationships (Curle 1995: 59-60). Violent episodes causing trauma could lead to the 'Stress Aggravated Soul Wound', which could precipitate a degree of unpeacefulness in relationships that leads to gross cruelty (Curle 1998). This conviction led Curle to work with communities which suffer the effects of violent conflict.

Recovery from the trauma of captivity: Adam Curle's work with the rehabilitation of former prisoners of war

This section explores Adam Curle's innovative work with the treatment of traumatic stress in the Civil Resettlement Units (CRUs) during 1945-1946 with returning prisoners of the war. The project was run by A.T.M. (Tommy) Wilson, psychiatrist, and Eric Trist, psychologist, both Lieutenant Colonels in the Royal Army Medical Corps. Curle, then a British Army Major, was appointed Chief Research Officer for the project. They wrote several accounts of their experiences (Curle and Trist 1948; Curle, Wilson et al. 1952; Wilson, Trist et al. 1990; Curle 1999: 67-69). Adam Curle also wrote two contemporary papers on this work published by the War Office (Curle 1946a, 1946b), copies of which are now sadly unavailable.

I read all the available accounts of the CRUs' work, and talked about them with Adam, as a result of which he revisited that work, considering its contemporary relevance (Curle, 2001; 2001b). He describes the formation of the project as an urgent governmental response to a perceived need:

> As it became clear in 1945 that war was coming to an end, a group of very senior British army officers approached the government with an urgent plea for provision to be made for some 120,000 British prisoners of war who had been captured in 1940. These officers had been themselves been captured during World War 1 and argued that their lives had been ruined because no-one had realised the damaging effect of their long captivity. Some provision, they said, must be made for the young men who would soon be returning from German prison camps. (Curle 2001b: 3)

Former prisoners who returned from south-east Asia had special provisions elsewhere because of their extreme physical and psychological needs.

The CRUs were in twenty army camps, each in a different county, set up to help the former prisoners of war (POWs) bridge the 'very difficult social and emotional gap between captivity and freedom' (Curle 2001b: 4). The geographical locations were chosen for the convenience of the POWs and staff, with local facilities and opportunities for the men to gain practice in job interviews and work experience. Each unit serviced the needs of 240 men, who usually stayed for a month at a time. Where necessary, some would stay for a longer period. The permanent staff wore military uniform, and they were subject to normal (but relaxed and non-doctrinaire) discipline. The POWs all attended voluntarily, and there was no compulsion to participate in any activity. They could come and go as they wished (Curle 2001b: 4).

Curle explains that the units offered ample medical and dental facilities, and psychiatric treatment was available in an inconspicuous location to preserve privacy, but the emphasis of the effort was social. The aim was to help the POWs to 'feel at ease' and to be 'eased back into their social and familial roles' (Curle 2001b: 4). Help was provided to 'master the complexities of post-war society', to deal with rationing of food, clothing and furniture, and to handle the problems of finance, taxation and accommodation. The units were concerned to help the men gain satisfying employment. They recruited local businesses to enable them to find out about a wide variety of jobs, with 'job rehearsals' to experience different work, facilitating realistic choices. Information was provided about training and interview skills. The units held regular seminars and workshops with a 'participating' officer (rather than a chairing or facilitating officer) and their emphasis was on empowerment of participants. He remarks that 'the exchanges that took place gave volunteers the chance to break down the feelings of shyness, to deal with experiences in a way that could help them to become closer to their families and others in the civilian community' (Curle 2001b: 4). The most important stepping stone was reintegration into family life. The volunteers could have weekend visits home at any time, but Curle noted that many could not face domestic life until they neared the end of their stay in the unit.

The POWs had experienced an alienation from civilian life, through the process of 'militarisation'. Civilians were transformed into soldiers whose identification with their army unit was cemented by battle situations in which small group solidarity and mutual trust was essential to survival. Following capture, reliance on the group intensifies. The captives, deprived of weapons and their leaders (who were sent to other camps) evolved a democratic system of 'reciprocal respect and care'. From this description, it would seem that their difficulty in returning to civilian life stemmed from a combination of earlier militarisation and then institutionalisation during their imprisonment. Curle describes the symptoms that the POWs experienced as 'desocialisation'. He reports that the men spoke of feelings of alienation from their families and the society to which they were returning, including their wives and children.

> Most of them had enjoyed a blissful first few weeks, but then their mood had changed. They were depressed, felt that were losing touch with their families, and wanted to return to such minimal security as was offered by the CRU. They suffered from insomnia, and from loss of appetite and sexual drive. Some had aimlessly left home; a certain number had committed petty crimes. Many felt vaguely guilty for having allowed themselves to be captured, seeing this as a failing both the army and their families.(Curle 2001b: 3-4)

As research officer, Curle undertook a survey of one hundred and fifty men, one hundred of whom had been in the CRUs, and fifty of whom had not. The participants were chosen by other colleagues, and each sample group was selected according to a rough estimate of balance of age, marital status and level of education. A control group of forty men in reserved occupations (who had not been in the services) also took part in the study. Curle used participant action research using questionnaires and socialising with the men at home, work and in pubs. They identified patterns of role behaviour in fifteen illustrative types of relations with partners, children and other close family members, neighbours, employers, workmates and wider society which they termed the 'criteria of social participation'. The researchers allocated scores according to norms for behaviour, which they defined as the 'statistical norm' (characterised by terms like 'all right', 'just ordinary', and 'decent enough fellow'); the ideal 'supranorm' (enthusiastic approval); and two narrow and limited infranorms ('not so bad, I suppose'). Behaviour furthest below the statistical norm was characterised by extreme disapproval. Hugh Murray, a statistician, undertook detailed analysis of the data gathered. The result of the analysis indicated that '…a significantly larger proportion of those who had been to the CRUs were better settled than those who had not', Curle reported, adding: '…this vindicated the CRU experiment; statistically there is a very low probability that some other factor could have been responsible for the result' (Curle 2001b: 5). He was convinced that the approach of the CRUs worked in re-socialising the men, but their research did not explore which of the therapeutic elements in the programme had been most effective.

Curle describes the CRUs as 'transitional communities'. He sees their value in providing an atmosphere of freedom and individual empowerment, in the context of a familiar military environment. He notes that 'perhaps encouraged by the lack of restrictions, the great majority took full advantage of available facilities and opportunities' (Curle 2001b: 4). His belief was that these freedoms created a contrast with the prisoners' former conditions of captivity and army life, enhancing their sense of self-esteem and empowering them through freedom of choice to reach greater self control and to take greater emotional and social risks. His ideas link here with the core conditions of empathy, acceptance or unconditional positive regard, and congruence embodied in Rogers' client centred approach to counselling and psychotherapy. Rogers later added a further condition, 'presence' (Rogers 1995), which, like the CRUs, provides an atmosphere of equality and mutual respect in which individuals feel free to explore their feelings and experiencing without criticism or rejection, thus encouraging internal reflection, questioning personal and external belief systems and empowering individuals to effect personal and social change, reaching towards their full human potential (Curle 1971c: 117-125).

Curle comments on the beneficial psychological effects of the conditions in the CRUs to counteract alienation and separation:

As a man became reconnected with his society he was eventually able to drop his protective mask, and to view the world around him objectively, not as a mirage reflecting the shimmering distortions of his own fears and pains. Because the inner hold of the culture upon him had weakened, he was also able to adopt new and more realistic modes of behaviour, but this was not possible until the more painful effects of his captivity had been reduced. (Curle 1971c: 125)

Referring to the 'shell shock' described during the First World War, and the subsequent development of the concept of posttraumatic stress, Curle points out that Wilson and Trist firmly rejected any idea that the former prisoners were 'ill' or 'abnormal' (Curle 2001b: 4). 'They were, in the rather horrible but excessive parlance that evolved, de-socialised, or unsettled' (Curle 2001b: 4). He does not entirely refute the validity of the modern (DSM IV) diagnosis of posttraumatic stress disorder (PTSD) discussed in Chapter 3, but he comments that 'many psychiatrists claim that there is no clinical entity that justifies recognition as such' and adds: 'This is not to suggest that the great number, and great variety of people diagnosed as suffering from PTSD are not suffering. They are. But they are suffering from the misery of lost happiness, peace of mind, beloved persons and haunting memories' (sic) (Curle 2001b: 1). He suggests that a sceptic would comment that this is jumping on a coun-selling bandwagon, and that PTSD is no more than the common lot of humanity, but he posits an alternative interpretation 'which may constitute an approach which would enable us to identify a significant cluster of related symptoms among the much wider concept of PTSD' (Curle 2001b: 1). The importance of the work of the units is that it provides insights into the nature of the suffering, and ways in which help may be provided, without labelling the sufferers as ill or abnormal. For the returning prisoners of war, the transi-tional community of the CRUs provided appropriate conditions for them to recover from their state of militarisation and desocialisation and ease back into their family and community lives.

Eric Trist also noted the significance of the 'creative casualties'. 'These were people who had coped with pain, confusion and separation from their loved ones without losing hope or the ability to help and encourage their companions in captivity. These were the men who scored supranormally in the survey'. 'These creative casualties had, by surviving threat and hurt, gained an exceptional new awareness and power' (Curle 2001b: 5). No explanation is proffered for these men's psychological strength. Chapter 3 contains discussion of 'posttraumatic growth' and other positive aspects of suffering, exploring the views of contemporary practitioners about the factors which seem to enable some people to survive painful or traumatic experiences with reported positive outcomes varying from little or no residual psychological damage, to significant psychological, social or spiritual growth.

A general inference might be drawn from the work of the CRUs that individuals may experience uncomfortable psychological states following traumatic experiences, which do not constitute formal illness, but which may improve with psychological and social support. Chapter 3 deepens the exploration of the psychological states associated with trauma, focusing on the syndrome of posttraumatic stress. This is followed by the case study, introduced and reported in Chapters 4 and 5, which includes the perceptions of the participating projects of the therapeutic approaches used to alleviate the suffering following the war in Croatia. Finally, the analysis of the research data in Chapter 6 carries the work of the CRUs further through discussion of its relevance to potential recovery from the psychological effects of the war in Eastern Slavonia, considered in the context of the needs of peacemaking and the current debates about the diagnosis and treatment of posttraumatic stress.

The quotation cited at the beginning of this Chapter is from Stanislav Matacic, a psychiatrist working with children in post-war Croatia. It demonstrates the extent of his concern, and also indicates a way forward towards future peace – that society needs to address psychological trauma and to take steps to initiate systematic social change. This is the concept of peacemaking which Curle began in the CRUs and implemented in Eastern Slavonia.

Chapter 3

Posttraumatic stress

…The study of trauma has become the soul of psychiatry. The development of posttraumatic stress disorder (PTSD) as a diagnosis has created an organised framework for understanding how people's biology, conceptions of the world and personalities are inextricably shaped by experience. (Van der Kolk and McFarlane 1996: 4)

Before beginning this chapter, I want to clarify that when I use the term 'posttraumatic stress' I am describing what I believe to be a normal human reaction to traumatic events. There is no implication from me, anywhere in this chapter, that posttraumatic stress is or will necessarily lead on to any form of mental illness or to PTSD. I believe that whilst many people who have been through traumatic experiences are suffering, and they may be suffering a great deal, they are not all 'ill' and these people have every right to be angry at those who try to impose widely generalised diagnostic mental health labels on them. This research shows that community-based approaches to healing the psychological posttraumatic stress following war have benefited local communities without creating or using mental health labels. However the research also shows that we have to understand that some of the people who experience prolonged or severe suffering following a traumatic experience may be in need of psychological or medical help, and these people have a right not to be ignored or marginalized. The problem that we face in a post-war situation therefore is how to understand these different situations, and to offer the right kind of help, at the appropriate time, to the people who need it.

In the last chapter, I explored the contribution of social psychology to the development of conflict resolution theory, the emergence of the importance of relational change and the psychological causes and impact of war on communities in their experiences of loss, bereavement and trauma. This chapter now explores the nature and effects of posttraumatic stress, with a brief overview of its historical development and theoretical underpinnings and the evolution of the DSM IV TR diagnostic criteria of PTSD. This chapter then takes a look at some of the psychophysiological effects of posttraumatic stress and its effects on children and their families. In the context of the traumas of war, there are other phenomena to be considered: Herman's concept of 'complex posttraumatic stress', the comorbid diagnoses of anxiety and depression and the effects of posttraumatic stress on professional helpers in the syndromes of 'burn out' and 'compassion fatigue'. With the needs of those working with trauma in mind, their vulnerability to posttraumatic stress, stress prevention and preparation for coping with the effects of posttraumatic stress are considered. Trauma also has a potentially positive effect and there is discussion of 'posttraumatic growth' linking in with the 'creative casualties' identified during Adam Curle's work with the CRUs. Finally, I have attempted to consider critically the attempts to create normative measurements of posttraumatic stress, bearing in mind that DSM IV-TR may have overlooked significant differential factors in people, society and stressor events, taking into account the criticisms of Bracken, Summerfield and others.

Later in the book, these themes of trauma, treatment and the potentiality of development and growth from trauma are extended through the perceptions of the staff and volunteers from five non-governmental organisations in Eastern Slavonia, who have been working in this field for over ten years. This research carries on from Curle's earlier work in the CRUs, contrasting his approach to trauma healing and peacemaking with some of the main approaches currently used by these organisations in Croatia, leading to suggestions for further research to design culturally appropriate combinations of psychotherapeutic and peacemaking approaches for communities following war.

Over the past two decades, the concepts of posttraumatic stress and PTSD have become widely accepted in western psychiatry (van der Kolk and McFarlane 1996). The concepts of posttraumatic stress vary, as do approaches to treatment, and we should not assume that posttraumatic stress necessarily follows the same pattern in all people and societies (Yehuda, R. and McFarlane 1995: 1). Cultural differences in the experience of posttraumatic stress are explored later in this chapter. Epidemiological research relating to PTSD reveals no common methodology for assessment; for example, there are many different measurement scales used, and cultural perceptions or other factors may affect the validity of diagnosis. In some post-war situations, humanitarian aid providers may not routinely ask about symptoms, test for

PTSD or even provide any education about it (Weine, Kuc et al. 2001). The posttraumatic stress syndrome may exist, but Weisaeth argues that it may remain unacknowledged and in some cases this could be serious because the failure to diagnose or to provide (or accept) appropriate early treatment for posttraumatic stress could potentially lead to the later onset of PTSD (Weisaeth 2001).

In order to understand the evolution of the syndrome of PTSD as a psychiatric illness, the chapter first sets out a brief background overview of the study of hysteria in western psychiatry. Herman and others have identified three types of reactions to traumatic experiences that emerged into the public consciousness: 'hysteria', 'shell shock' and 'combat neurosis'. Herman also suggests that there is a commonality in the symptoms, which has evolved into the normative syndrome of posttraumatic stress.

Not all theorists agree with Herman's proposition, because some of the specific features of PTSD as currently defined in DSM IV-TR differ from the symptoms of hysteria from which Herman (1992b) suggests the syndrome of posttraumatic stress originally developed. Moreover, PTSD represents just one aspect of psychological suffering after trauma; for example, anxiety disorders are common following bereavement (Parkes 1998a). Other concepts of the nature of suffering may be equally valid in different contexts and cultures (Bracken 2002: 67). Herman also suggested that working with psychological trauma means 'bearing witness to horrible events', something we would perhaps wish to avoid. 'War and victims are something that the community wants to forget' but perhaps, on the other side, the 'victims wish to forget but cannot' (Herman 1992b: 7-8). The tensions between remembering and forgetting unpleasant events were much in evidence in the case study in Eastern Slavonia, and are relevant to both the recovery from trauma and to the process of peacemaking.

Hysteria: beginnings in the study of traumatic stress

Hysteria had been regarded for centuries as a medical condition of women, named after its deemed origination in the uterus (Herman 1992b: 10-11). The neurologist, Jean-Martin Charcot challenged these beliefs, and in the latter part of the nineteenth century, began a systematic study of 'the Great Neurosis' in female patients from the Salpetriere, a hospital asylum in Paris. By 1880, the cause of hysteria was proved to be psychological in that it could be artificially induced and relieved through the use of hypnosis, which

Charcot used with patients in public demonstrations. Sigmund Freud, Pierre Janet and William James were among the influential physicians to hear him lecture and witness his methods of treatment. Charcot's empirical and positivist approach to research involved accurate observation and recording of symptoms and the 'vocalisations' of the hysteric patients, but he gave no attention to their inner lives (Herman 1992b: 11). Freud, with his colleague and mentor Joseph Breuer and Janet carried Charcot's research further by talking with hysterical patients, listening to their stories and paying attention to their emotional experiencing. Through hearing these personal histories, they concluded that the symptoms were disguised representations of psychologically traumatic events that were apparently unavailable to conscious memory. The women's affective response to these emotionally unbearable events in their lives had produced an altered state of consciousness, which Janet termed 'dissociation' and Freud termed 'double consciousness'.

Following Charcot's work, unresolved questions arose as to the relative significance of potential causal factors of hysteria: the event, individual reaction, or the timing of the event in a person's life. Jones recorded that, in *Preliminary Communication* (Freud and Breuer 1893), the authors attempted 'to describe simply the mechanism of hysterical symptoms, but not the inner causes of the affection itself' (Jones 1964: 240). It was in *Preliminary Communication* that the famous expression 'hysterics suffer mainly from reminiscences' came (Herman 1992b: 12). Breuer and Freud accepted Charcot's theory that trauma causes hysteria, but they extended his thinking, envisaging the causal factor not as the traumatic event itself, but the individual's reaction to it. Between 1893 and 1896, Freud published his new theory of hysterical symptoms in a footnote to a translation of one of Charcot's books. The footnote includes these comments: 'I may mention here: the kernel of the hysterical attack, in whatever form this takes, is a memory, the hallucinatory living through of a scene that was significant for the outbreak of the illness' (Freud, in Jones 1964: 241).

By the mid 1890s, Breuer, Janet and Freud had discovered that relief from hysterical symptoms could be obtained by bringing the traumatic memories, along with their accompanying feelings, into the patient's conscious memory and enabling the patient to verbalise them – the 'talking cure' had evolved (Breuer and Freud 1955: 30 in Jones 1964: 239).

Freud's concept of the psychological defence mechanisms, particularly repression of emotion and the principles which led to Freud's 'talking cure' underpin many current approaches to the treatment of trauma, including the cognitive behavioural techniques approved by the British National Institute for Health and Clinical Excellence (NICE) for trauma treatment. Many modern practitioners believe that it is helpful to re-visit the traumatic experiences, talk about the traumatic events and allow the painful feelings and memories to emerge in an atmosphere of physical and psychological safety. They believe that reframing the experiences with the aim of integrating them into day-to-day living is also likely to relieve the suffering of posttraumatic stress. I accept this belief as a value, but with the clear recognition of the limitations to this approach and the belief that it is not normative or exclusive. People, cultures and circumstances vary, creating different therapeutic needs. A holistic approach involving social and psychological support is necessary in many situations, particularly in the treatment of posttraumatic stress following war.

At the time Freud first published *Aetiology of Hysteria* in 1896, he attributed the origins of hysteria to memories of real experiences of childhood sexual abuse of the women concerned (Freud 1962: 203 in Jones 1964: 246). Herman comments that: 'A century later, this paper still rivals contemporary clinical descriptions of the effects of childhood sexual abuse. It is a brilliant, compassionate, eloquently agued, closely reasoned document' (Herman 1992b: 13). In a manuscript, *Repression in Hysteria*, Freud suggested that 'phantasies arise from an unconscious combination, in accordance with certain trends, of things experienced and heard. These trends are toward making inaccessible the memory from which the symptoms have emerged or might emerge' (Freud 1897b). However, less than a year later, Freud began to doubt his original thinking about the reality of childhood sexual abuse (Jones 1964: 247), and he then focused on the process of psychoanalysis, exploring his clients' inner world of fantasy and desires. Herman suggests that Freud's patriarchal attitudes and the anti-feminist political and social situation of the time led to his revised thinking. The implication that these 'perverted acts against children' were endemic in society depicted a social situation which many of Freud's professional peers rejected and which Freud himself found hard to believe (Herman 1992b: 14-15). In the United Kingdom, in the early days of child protection legislation, professionals and the courts were sometimes reluctant to acknowledge the awful reality of extreme forms of child abuse. In one of my workshops, the participants (who were mainly teachers and psychologists) initially strongly denied that any child abuse existed in Croatia. As we talked about what they had actually seen and heard in their work, they gradually acknowledged the prevalence of domestic violence, which was at times witnessed or experienced by children. Child sexual abuse was, however, perceived by the group as unthinkable at that time. A psychologist in the group found it too emotionally painful to look at textbook pictures depicting typical physical injuries caused by child abuse. Several years later, new child protection legislation had been enacted in Croatia, and that same psychologist is now working with children and families, not only in treatment of anxiety and depression, but implementing aspects of child protection including prevention of child abuse and treating the effects of childhood trauma.

The concepts of 'shell shock' and 'traumatic neurosis'

Soldiers experienced emotional reactions, symptoms of lethargy and withdrawal after the American Civil War, which at the time were attributed to 'nostalgia' due to being far from home. They also experienced physiological symptoms in the chest area with unknown aetiology, which were known as 'soldier's heart' and 'irritable heart' (Bracken 2002: 66). During the First World War, a British psychologist Charles Myers (1940) noted that some soldiers showed symptoms of screaming, weeping, inability to move, unresponsiveness and mutism, and he attributed these symptoms to organic damage to the central nervous system from the percussive effects of exploding shells, naming the syndrome 'shell shock' (Herman 1992b: 20). Research into army history uncovered further recorded symptoms of shell shock as 'daze, fear, trembling, nightmares and an inability to function' and also symptoms of neurological dysfunction: blindness, deafness, semi-paralysis, amnesia, and 'extraordinary, unnatural ways of walking' (Shepherd 2000, in Bracken 2002: 66). 'Conversion hysteria' is another condition described in soldiers during the First World War, with symptoms including 'paralyses, contractures, muscle rigidity, gait disorders, seizures, tremors, spasms, blindness, muteness, fugue states, and other symptoms of nervous system dysfunction'. Military doctors also noted syndromes of 'neurasthenia' and 'disordered action of the heart' (Bracken 2002: 66).

The discrepancy in neurological symptoms would suggest that neither shell shock nor conversion hysteria are identical with the modern diagnosis of PTSD as described in the DSM IV-TR criteria, but they do have features in common with hysteria, and it is not surprising that following the First World war, mental health professionals considered that prolonged exposure to violent death had produced a neurotic state in men similar to hysteria. The concept of individual vulnerability or moral weakness in response to trauma as a causal factor of the neurological and emotional symptoms led some British psychiatrists, notably Lewis Yealland, to take a condemnatory moral view of this syndrome, using inhumane and punitive treatments. In his *Hysterical Disorders of Warfare*, published in 1918, Yealland advocates treatment using shaming, threats and punishment and applying electric shocks to remove the hysterical symptoms of mutism, sensory loss or motor paralysis. He reported his treatment of a mute soldier with electric shocks to the throat for hours until the soldier eventually spoke, exhorting him during treatment to 'remember, you must behave as the hero I expect you to be... A man who has gone through so many battles must have better control of himself' (Showalter 1985: 177 cited in Herman 1992b: 20).

During the First World War, other practitioners in Britain, including the physician W.H.R. Rivers, took a different view, arguing that brave soldiers of high moral calibre could suffer from this condition. He treated shell-shocked soldiers, one of them the war poet Siegfried Sassoon, with compassion, dignity and respect, encouraging them to speak and write of their experiences. The aim of treatment was to return the men to combat. Despite his anti-war philosophy, Sassoon returned to the battle lines expressing guilt at having survived when many fellow soldiers had perished, and also explaining that his loyalty to his comrades was the main reason for his return (Herman 1992b: 22).

One might think that the high incidence of Dissociative Syndrome in the trenches during the First World War resulted from the tension in the combination of danger and pressure to be brave, with repression and denial of feelings of fear or distress. Abraham Kardiner, a psychiatrist working in America with war veterans, published a clinical and theoretical study, *The Traumatic Neuroses of War* (1941), in which he recognised the similarity between hysteria and combat neurosis. The use of the term hysteria was however, seen as pejorative, and the term 'traumatic neurosis' emerged. Kardiner's treatment of soldiers during the Second World War included psychoanalysis and also the induction of altered states of consciousness using hypnosis or 'narcosynthesis' using the drug sodium amytal, to assist cathartic re-experiencing of traumatic memories (Herman 1992b: 24-25). Kardiner and a psychiatrist Herbert Spiegel recognised the importance of the relationship between the soldiers, their unit, and their leaders as a factor in protection from overwhelming terror and in assisting recovery, and this was certainly Siegfried Sassoon's reason for his return to the front. By contrast, two other psychiatrists, Roy Grinker and John Spiegel, suggested that the constant danger of war created an emotional dependency on peers and leaders which they perceived as a negative trait (Herman 1992b: 25).

During the rehabilitation process in the CRUs, Adam Curle noted the importance of relationships with comrades and officers to the soldiers whilst in active service and as prisoners and the contribution of mutual comradeship to their recovery process (Curle 2001b).

Herman mentioned a similar psychosocial approach that developed in America. During the Vietnam War in the 1970s, some anti-war veterans, with help from sympathetic psychiatrists, shunned the psychological help offered by the government through the Veterans' Association, forming self-governed 'rap groups' to relieve their psychological trauma and to raise awareness of the effects of war. The rap groups' political pressure resulted in a legal mandate for a new model of psychological treatment through self-help and peer counselling named 'Operation Outreach' within the Veterans' Administration. A five volume report of research carried out for the Veterans Administration (Egendorf 1981) confirmed the relationship of trauma with combat exposure, and contributed to development of the formal diagnostic criteria for posttraumatic stress disorder (Herman 1992b: 27).

Posttraumatic stress and the development of the diagnostic criteria for Posttraumatic Stress Disorder (PTSD)

The *Diagnostic and Statistical Manual of Mental Disorders* is a manual used by psychiatrists and psychologists as a normative reference for the diagnosis and treatment of psychiatric disorders. The first edition, DSM I (American Psychiatric Association 1952), contained criteria for 'gross stress reaction' which was conceived as 'a disorder which resolved rapidly unless there was pre-existing personality pathology' (Bracken, P. 2002: 45).

The next edition, DSM II (American Psychiatric Association 1968), included the disorder 'transient situational disturbance' which was present if the response to the event was short lived. If the disturbance persisted, then it became a form of the more general condition 'anxiety neurosis'. DSM II still attributed long-term symptoms to the personality or other pathology of the patient, stating that 'if the patient has good adaptive capacity, his symptoms will usually recede as the stress diminishes. If, however, the symptoms persist after the stress is removed, the diagnosis of another mental disorder is indicated' in (Bracken 2002: 45).

After the Vietnam War, there were many suicides and severe psychiatric problems among the veterans returned from Vietnam. The work of Egendorf, Wilbur Scott, and others for the war veterans provided a factual foundation for subsequent political pressure on the government for recognition of the suffering caused by the trauma of war, and facilities with which to help the veterans. This led to the publication of the diagnostic criteria for Post Traumatic Stress Disorder (PTSD) in DSM III (American Psychiatric Association 1980). The group of arousal symptoms included feelings of guilt for surviving. This edition specified three categories of PTSD (acute, chronic and delayed) defined by the onset and duration of symptoms. Bracken (2002: 47), however, criticises the diagnostic criteria for PTSD published in DSM III for failing to take into account the political background from which it had arisen.

The definition of posttraumatic stress disorder in DSM III was amended again in the subsequent DSM III-R revised edition (American Psychiatric Association 1987). In the revised edition DSM III-R, (1987) survivor guilt was dropped from the criteria. The list of avoidance symptoms was expanded and the third group of symptoms re-named 'increased arousal'. This edition contained new criteria for the syndrome in children, and altered the criteria for the onset and duration of the disorder.

A major change followed in the next edition, DSM IV (American Psychiatric Association 1994) with new wording in category A: 'The response of the person includes intense fear, helplessness or horror'. This both extended the diagnostic field and shifted the emphasis from the stressor as a causal factor to the subjective psychological reaction of the person to it.

DSM IV-TR, published by the American Psychiatric Association in 2000, followed the 1994 version with a text revision taking into account recent research. The diagnostic features and criteria for Posttraumatic Stress Disorder (PTSD) as presently defined are set out in DSM IV-TR on pages 463-468.

The current criteria for PTSD

The criteria are set out in four distinct groups. The first, A, describes both exposure to a traumatic event that involved actual or threatened death or serious injury, or a threat to the physical integrity of self or others and also the individual's response to it, involving fear, helplessness or horror. It notes that, in children, this reaction may be expressed by disorganised or agitated behaviour.

The second group, B, describes the persistent re-experiencing of the event in one or more of several specified ways. These symptoms include recurrent and intrusive distressing recollections of the event, including images, thoughts or perceptions, which might be expressed by children in repetitive play involving themes or aspects of the trauma.

There may be recurring and distressing dreams of the event, or children may have frightening dreams in which the content is not necessarily recognisable. The person may act or feel as if the traumatic event were happening again and they may have a sense of reliving the experience, illusions, hallucinations or episodes of dissociative flashbacks. They may occur any time, including on awakening or when intoxicated. Young children might re-enact the traumatic events in their own way. The criteria include intense psychological distress and physiological reactivity to internal or external cues that symbolise the traumatic event.

The third group, C, describes the persistent avoidance of stimuli associated with the trauma and a numbing of general responsiveness, which was not present before the trauma occurred. The ways in which individuals may experience this avoidance include efforts to avoid thoughts, feelings or conversations associated with the trauma, or to avoid activities, places or people that arouse memories of the trauma and they may be unable to remember important aspects of the trauma. They may feel detached or estranged from others and experience a marked loss of interest or wish to take part in activities that are significant to them.

Another typical symptom may be described as 'emotional numbing', a restriction of the range and depth of feelings, and the person may also see little or no future for themselves or others. For example, DSM IV-TR explains that they may not expect to have a career, marriage, children, or a normal life span.

The final group of symptoms, D, are those of a persistent increased psychological arousal which was not present before the trauma. There follows a list of symptoms, of which at least two must be present for the diagnosis. These include difficulty falling or staying asleep, irritability or outbursts of anger, difficulty concentrating, hypervigilance and an exaggerated startle response.

If these symptoms cause clinically significant distress or impairment in social, occupational or other important areas of functioning and they persist for more than one month, then PTSD may be diagnosed. If symptoms persist for up to three months, the condition is defined as 'acute', and if longer than three months, it is 'chronic'. PTSD is specified as 'delayed onset' if it starts more than six months after the originating traumatic event.

Samuel Pepys – a case of posttraumatic stress?

Pat Bracken (2002: 65, citing Daly 1983) mentions that an interesting historical account of symptoms very much resembling those of posttraumatic stress disorder is provided by Samuel Pepys, who witnessed the great fire of London which began on 2 September 1666 and raged over a period of four days, destroying four-fifths of the City. Intrigued, I followed up this lead. Pepys, who seems from his writing to have been naturally curious and also a very sensitive man, meticulously kept a diary in which he recorded his thoughts, feelings and accounts of events in his daily life. Its entries speak for themselves.

On the first day of the great fire, Pepys, who was then thirty-three years old, gives the reader the first indication of the unusual nature of such an event in his own life, recording that he was 'unused to such fires' (Latham 1978: 120). Despite being horrified by what he saw and heard, Pepys was clearly fascinated by the events and it seems from the diary that he must have spent many hours watching what was happening. His diary entries, made whilst the fire still ferociously raged through shops, offices and houses, record his increasing sense of shock and dismay at the destruction of the city, and his empathy with the plight of people and their animals abandoning their homes and fleeing in desperation for their lives. In a further diary entry on 2 September 1666, Pepys poignantly describes his perceptions and feelings on seeing the progression of the fire through London. 'Poor people staying in their houses as long as till the very fire touched them and then running into boats or clambering from one pair of stair by the waterside to another.'

Later that day he went out again, writing: '…it made me weep to see it. The churches, houses and all on fire and flaming at once and a horrid noise the flames made and the cracking of the houses at their ruine. So home, with a sad heart' (sic) (Latham 1978:123). Also see Bryant (1949: 306-310).

Then the entries for 3 and 4 September 1666 (Latham 1978: 123) show that the fire came close to Pepys' own office and home, and he had to make his own hasty arrangements at 4 a.m. to safeguard his work papers, his personal belongings and to protect his wife '…thinking of the certain burning of this office…'. Pepys' home was not burned down, although the fire came very close to it, and the fire passed it by. On 7 September, he recorded in his diary that he '…did sleep pretty well, but still, both sleeping and waking, had a fear of fire in my heart, that I took little rest'.

Several days later, on 15 September, he was puzzled by his continued alertness at night time, having worked hard all day, and he noted '…it is strange to see how clear my head was…whereas one would think that I should have been dozed' and although he expressed his infinite joy and relief at being safely back in his own chamber with his wife, he added, 'But much terrified in the nights nowadays, with dreams of fire and falling down of houses'.

Five months later, the intrusive memories and the hypervigilance still remained, or perhaps had returned, triggered by sights, smells and sounds that were reminders of the trauma of the great fire. On 28 February 1667, Pepys wrote: ' I did within these six days see smoke still remaining of the late fire in the City; and it is strange to think to how to this very day I cannot sleep a-night without great terrors of fire; and this very night could not sleep till almost two in the morning through thoughts of fire' (Latham 1978: 138).

The symptoms of hysteria, shell shock and combat neurosis each differ from PTSD in some respects, and the modern definition of PTSD evolved from earlier, different criteria. The reality is that, after traumatic events, people do suffer. Whatever we choose to call it, whether it is anxiety, depression, PTSD, or something else, as Curle points out in *The Wounds of War* (Curle 2001), it is still suffering – however we might conceptualise and label it. Our concern as practitioners must be to find ways to help people through that suffering using treatment approaches that work in the context of different situations and cultures.

Cultural aspects of the syndrome of PTSD

The notes on 'specific culture and age features' relating to PTSD in DSM IV-TR contain just one paragraph mentioning culture. It simply suggests that those who have emigrated from areas of social unrest and civil conflict may have elevated rates of PTSD and may be reluctant to divulge experiences of torture and trauma due to their vulnerable political immigrant status, therefore needing specific assessment. No comment is made in the notes concerning cultural differences, implying an assumption that PTSD is cross-culturally normative.

Some cultures see the self as contextual: 'Linked to each other in an interdependent system, members of organic cultures take an active interest in one another's affairs, and feel at ease in regulating and being regulated' (Schweder and Bourne 1989: 132). The extent of the fluidity of the self-other-world boundary varies culturally. In some African and Maori cultures, for example, this extends from the self to family, society, out to the physical universe and into metaphysical and spiritual realms. In Hindu and Buddhist cultures, individual boundaries may be seen as illusory, Inuit culture curtails the importance of the individual, whilst Confucianism emphasises the role of the individual as part of the community (Schweder and Bourne 1989 in Holdstock 1994: 243). Holdstock also points out that there are many cultural variables such as modernisation, hierarchical group membership (caste and social class), and the dominance of masculine or feminine aspects within a culture (Holdstock 1994: 243). It is hardly surprising therefore that researchers have questioned the validity of the western individual trauma model in cross-cultural situations.

Western therapeutic approaches use a model of individualised catharsis and healing of 'memories' and 'emotions' and this may be criticised as inadequate, as it risks missing the key themes that converge in the collective experience of trauma. Some practitioners suggest that emotion and memory can only be meaningfully experienced in social interaction and a cultural framework. These cultural variables present challenges for therapists who work in cross-cultural situations. If the culture is organic, then western therapy may at best be unhelpful or at worst, exacerbate the trauma. Bracken's position is very clear:

> I believe that therapy can have the effect of increasing the isolation of suffering individuals by encouraging a narrow focus on their own memories, thoughts and beliefs. Such people need, more than anything else, to feel part of a community again, to feel close to other people, to feel at home in the world. Western psychotherapy can have the opposite effect. (Bracken 2002: 291)

However, Bracken's criticism may be based on too great a generalisation. Many therapeutic approaches seek to establish a climate of non-judgmental empathic relationship in which the client strengthens their ability to maintain psychological connection with others and, where necessary, practise social skills. Group therapy provides an opportunity for participants to listen to others, empathise, and establish social connections. If Bracken means that a focus on the content of memories in therapy is egocentric, this would be a valid criticism if the client focused on the intrusive memories to the exclusion of awareness of their external circumstances and the feelings and needs of others. Active and fulfilling participation in society should be a goal of therapy. This need for 're-socialisation' was one of the problems identified by Curle and others in the work of the CRUs.

There are also difficulties with measurement instruments of PTSD across cultures, because perception of emotions and interpretation of phenomena, for example dreams, varies culturally (Marsella, Friedman et al. 1996). Gender differences have been noted to affect the arousal reaction to fear of death and specific cultures attenuate or amplify differences in posttraumatic stress in males and females (Norris, Perilla et al. 2001). Measurement instruments and their psychometric properties may also present problems in both translation and in cultural adaptation (Klejin, Hovens et al. 2001).

Some cultures do not find it helpful to talk about the past:

> Some evidence suggests that detailed inquiries may intensify symptoms. This is particularly true for some refugees from Africa and South East Asia, who tend to experience trauma and recovery in ways distinct from the narrative experience of many Western societies, which are often linked to Judeo-Christian notions of catharsis, confession, reparation and redemption. (Desjarlais, Eisenberg et al. 1995: 130)

Given current understandings of the physiology and psychobiology of posttraumatic stress, it is possible that raising repressed experiences to consciousness may indeed trigger emotional and physiological reactions, which may initially intensify symptoms, but it can be argued that this may promote healing in the longer term. Further, talking about traumatic experiences is not the only approach to trauma healing and where appropriate it may be combined with other approaches or not used at all. It may help some people but not others. In Croatia, talking was seen as an important part of psychological recovery.

Therapeutic approaches derived from Freudian principles maintain that repression of emotion underlies the syndrome of PTSD and that varying degrees of exposure to the traumatic event are necessary to achieve symptomatic relief (MacKay and Cross 2001). In cognitive and behavioural therapeutic approaches that seek to alter perceptions and interpretations of the traumatic events and reactions to them, re-exposure is inevitable in talking about the events. Therapies that seek to change the social meaning of the events or to change the limbic system's 'pattern matching' of sensory input to affect (e.g. visual kinaesthetic dissociation) also involve a degree of re-exposure to the traumatic stimulus. My research revealed that in Eastern Slavonia the therapeutic approaches to trauma treatment which are based on the perceived benefits of exposure currently prevail, despite the focus groups' reporting a cultural tendency to repress emotions. The significance of this finding for the design of therapy programmes for the relief of trauma and for future research is discussed in the final chapter of this book.

Culture, along with other factors, also affects coping mechanisms and social systems may affect expectations of recovery. Cultures may create systems of meaning defining trauma, for example, some may take a fatalistic approach, believing that trauma has external causes (ancestors, spirits, or gods) that must be continually encountered during life, requiring rituals for appeasement or for protection. De Vries points out that the benefits of a supportive culture have concomitant costs. Culture can function as a protective and supportive system of values, lifestyle and knowledge, affording social protection, buffering socially integrated individuals from the impact of traumatic events. However, as de Vries rightly notes: 'Strong attachments to persons and lifestyles lead to a deeper sense of loss when the life of the culture is disrupted' (de Vries 1996: 400).

In Croatia, psychiatrists treating PTSD in Eastern Slavonia noted that, in relation to helping patients with chronic PTSD return to work, cultural, social and political factors seem of more importance than medicine and psychiatry (Mandic and Javornik 1998), but they leave the evaluation of these factors to further research.

Writing of traditional healing, Wilson and Walker also make an unequivocal claim for the importance of culture in the healing process: 'Culture-specific and transcultural ritualistic practice can effectively decondition altered psychological states and restore vitality and well being' (Wilson and Walker 1989: 22). Traditional healing is often based on the belief that the body cannot be separated from the mind, and the mind and the sufferer exist in a social context as part of an organic whole in which the meaning of health and disease are communicated from birth to death (de Vries 1996: 403). In situations where traditional healing in non-western medicine does not appear to distinguish mind and body, somatic illness and psychological illness may be inseparable.

Psychophysiological and somatic effects of posttraumatic stress

Biomedicine adopts a naturalist epistemology. The PTSD criteria are seen as normative and social and cultural factors are rarely taken into account in explaining or treating PTSD in the west (Bracken 2002: 28, 49). The approach of psychiatry research also reflects an assumption that people physically react to traumatic stimuli in similar ways: 'These responses to extreme experiences are so consistent across the different forms of traumatic stimuli that this bimodal reaction appears to be the normative response to any overwhelming and uncontrollable experience' (van der Kolk 1994b: 254).

I can only attempt here to provide a very brief descriptive overview of the physical response to traumatic stress. At the moment there is insufficient understanding of all the physical mechanisms of posttraumatic stress, and among the leading researchers van der Kolk, suggests that further research is required, because 'The precise interrelation between hypothalamic-pituitary-adrenal (HPA) axis hormones and the catecholamines in the stress response is not entirely clear' (van der Kolk 1994b: 254).

1. Human reaction to stress and the normal recovery pattern

Anxiety is a normal, adaptive response to environmental threat, necessary to survival and reproductive success. 'It is a form of vigilance which enables an organism to be alert to environmental changes so that it can be prepared to meet whatever emergencies may arise' (Stevens and Price 2000: 100). It is generally accepted in evolutionary psychiatry that these 'fight or flight' mechanisms evolved to enable animals and humans not only to sense and identify danger, but to respond appropriately in order to escape it by 'fighting, fleeing, freezing or submitting' (Stevens and Price 2000: 101). It is also suggested that anxiety has a biphasic function in which moderate amounts of anxiety promote adaptive efficiency, whilst excessive amounts militate against efficiency (Yerkes and Dodson 1908).

The human response to a perception of danger is characterised by specific biological reactions. 'In a well functioning organism, stress produces rapid and pronounced hormonal responses' (van der Kolk 1994b: 255).

> Arousal prepares the body for violent action. The heart rate increases, the blood pressure goes up, adrenaline is secreted, energy stores are mobilized in the liver and released into the bloodstream, and blood is redistributed from the internal organs so as to carry oxygen and energy to the muscles and brain. At the same time, the thyroid gland is stimulated to increase the efficiency of body metabolism. (Stevens and Price 2000: 101)

In response to a traumatic stimulus, both left and right brain are stimulated. In the left brain, there is an almost simultaneous activation of adrenergic neurons and release of catecholamines from nerve terminals and the adrenal medulla. The catecholamines: norephinephrine (noradrenalin) and epineph-rine (adrenalin) are secreted by the locus ceruleus and distributed throughout much of the central nervous system, helping to initiate the fight or flight behaviours. (van der Kolk 1997: 255). The effect of the catecholamines is to raise heart rate and blood pressure, muscle reactions speed up and fats are broken down more slowly. At the same time, the right brain responds to the stressor. The Hypothalamo-Pituitary-Adrenal (HPA) axis hormones activate a cascade of reactions eventuating in a release of glucocorticoids (cortisol) from the adrenal glands. The effect of high levels of cortisol could produce a sense of anxiety and distress or conversely, happiness, peace, elation and comfort. The endogenous opioids may induce analgesia.

There is a negative feedback loop in which the production of cortisol inhibits the production of catecholamines. 'In acute stress, cortisol helps to regulate the release of stress hormones via a negative feedback loop to the hippocampus, hypothalamus and pituitary, and there is evidence that corticosteroids normalize catecholamine-induced arousal in limbic midbrain structures in response to stress' (van der Kolk 1994b: 255). In normal situations, therefore, the hormones will gradually return to their usual lower levels and achieve a balance in which the body returns to its normal daily functioning.

It might be suggested that PTSD is simply an exacerbation or extension of the normal stress response. However, the biological changes in PTSD are

> ...abnormalities...found to be different from those in other psychiatric disorders that have been associated with stress, such as mood and other anxiety disorders. Together, these points suggest that the biology of PTSD is not simply a reflection of the normative biology of stress, as has been consistently hypothesized. (Yehuda and McFarlane 1995: 1709)

2. Psychophysiological effects of trauma

PTSD is characterised by a chronic psychobiological dysregulation of the hormonal system (van der Kolk 1997: 16). The normal recovery from stress described above appears not to occur. In exploring the psychophysiology of PTSD, certain assumptions, adapted from the work of John Wilson and Alice Walker (Wilson and Walker 1989), are made:

- Traumatically stressful experiences disrupt the physiological and psychological equilibrium of the person, impacting on organismic functioning, and affecting both physical levels of homeostasis and optimal levels of psychological arousal.

- The disequilibrium that occurs in response to trauma affects all four levels of organismic functioning: physiological, psychological, social-interpersonal and cultural.
- Organismic functioning on one level affects other levels.

Wilson and Walker (1989: 22) suggest that 'Traumatically stressful experiences produce state-dependent learning that has both physiological and psychological correlates'. They add that:

> In some persons, especially those who have endured extremely prolonged and physically arduous experiences, there may be relatively permanent changes in nervous system functioning that result in chronic hyperarousal and a cognitive information-processing style that functions in trauma-associated ways in nearly all situations. (Wilson and Walker 1989: 22)

This would seem to reflect the 'complex PTSD' described by Herman and discussed earlier. Nevertheless Wilson and Walker also suggest that the altered psychobiological state produced by traumatic experience can be reversed to restore normal organismic functioning and healthy growth and development. This can be done through a process of deconditioning the altered psychobiological state using medication, exercise and transformative cultural rituals (Wilson and Walker 1989: 22).

Whilst a temporarily altered state may be reversed, it is unclear what the outcome might be of damage to the hippocampus resulting in lesions. Lesions by definition are permanent. Van der Kolk cites the research of Le Doux and colleagues, whose experiments implied that cortical lesions may prevent the extinction of emotional responses to traumatic stress and that 'emotional memory may be forever.' (Le Doux, Romanski et al. 1991) in (van der Kolk 1994b: 261). However, the human brain sometimes makes remarkable recovery after physical trauma or stroke and perhaps further research is needed to show the potential of recovery after cortical lesions have formed.

The diagnostic criteria for posttraumatic stress disorder in DSM IV-TR groups symptoms in terms of their perceived effect: increased levels of arousal and hypervigilance; intrusive re-experiencing of the traumatic event; and avoidance of reminders, dissociation and psychic numbing. Recent research has endeavoured to understand the physiological basis for the emergence of these symptoms following trauma, which are briefly summarised here. The main underlying symptom of PTSD is hypervigilance, which is thought to be the result of the chronic psychobiological dysregulation (van der Kolk 1997: 16). Sounds, images and thoughts associated with the trauma can cause increased heart rate, skin conductance, and blood pressure. Heightened autonomic arousal (through stress or medication) can precipitate visual images and emotional states associated with the prior traumatic experience. In those who have posttraumatic stress disorder, a dysfunction occurs in the control of hormone production and there is an imbalance in the levels of hormones including the catecholamines and cortisol. Whilst a balance could stimulate active coping behaviours, increased arousal in the presence of low cortisol levels may promote undifferentiated flight or flight reactions (Yehuda, R., Southwick, S.M., Mason, J.W. et al 1990 in van der Kolk 1997: 18). It is likely that serotonin has a role in maintaining the hormonal balance, helping to achieve an appropriate response to the stressor through stimulus discrimination, because decreased serotonin levels also correlate with impulsivity and aggression.

> Serotonin probably plays a role in the capacity to monitor the environment flexibly and to respond to behaviours that are situation-appropriate, rather than reacting to internal stimuli that are irrelevant to current demands. (van der Kolk 1994b: 257)

Appropriate responses to stimuli may also be affected by the amygdala. Michael Davis and his colleagues, in researching the role of the amygdala in stress arousal, refer to the work of Le Doux (1987, 1992), which found evidence that the amygdala is critically involved in explicit cue conditioning and stimulus discrimination (Davis, Walker et al. 1997). The natural patterns of behaviours produced by conditioned fear can be blocked by lesions of the amygdala, and produced by its electrical stimulation.

Earlier research with animals indicated that stress is capable of inducing some degree of analgesia (van der Kolk, Greenberg et al. 1985: 318). These researchers subsequently found that if PTSD subjects were faced with a stimulus resembling the original stressor, even twenty years after the original identified traumatic event, their bodies produced endogenous opioids equivalent to 8 mg morphine (van der Kolk 1994b: 257). The researchers then proposed that some of the increased arousal symptoms of PTSD – hyper-alertness, startle responses, difficulty falling asleep, anxiety and unpredictable explosions of aggressive behaviour – were similar to the symptoms of opiate withdrawal and they suggested that this might be the result of the cessation of production of endogenous opioids (van der Kolk, Greenberg et al. 1985).

Another distinctive feature of PTSD is the persistent re-experiencing of the traumatic event. Research in the last two decades has led to some further understanding of the biological systems of the laying down and triggering of memories. Van der Kolk describes the cycle of hyperarousal and re-experiencing of trauma:

> ...traumatised patients seemed to react to reminders of the trauma with emergency responses that had been relevant to the original threat but had no bearing on current experience. They were unable to put the trauma behind them, victims had trouble learning from experience; their energy was funnelled toward keeping their emotions under control, at the expense of paying attention to current exigencies. They became fixated on the past, in some cases being obsessed with the trauma, but more often by behaving and feeling as if they were traumatised over and over again without being able to locate the origins of these feelings. (van der Kolk 1994b: 253)

Van der Kolk suggests there could be a physiological explanation for this constant, almost addictive, re-experiencing of the past, and posttraumatic stress may be seen as a cyclical process, inextricably linked with the process of laying down and retrieval of memory on cognitive and physiological levels. The process by which events are perceived and stored in memory usually occurs below the level of conscious awareness (van der Kolk 1994b: 260). The amygdala, an organ in the brain's limbic system, is thought to have a 'gateway' function in the formation and storage of memory traces. Some theorists argue that:

> When a deeply traumatic event occurs... the emotional reaction is so strong that communication between the amygdala and the hippocampus is barred, preventing the sensory memories from passing from one to the other and keeping them trapped in wordless form in the amygdala. (Griffin and Tyrrell 2001: 10)

The amygdala is thought to function in the attribution of emotional meaning of incoming stimuli and assignation of free-floating feelings of significance to sensory input, which the neocortex then further elaborates and imbues with personal meaning. It integrates internal representations of the external world in the form of memory images with emotional experiences associated with those memories (van der Kolk 1994b: 260). This process may be speeded up or inhibited by stress (Joseph 1998: 175). Whilst low and intermediate levels of arousal can improve learning, high stress levels may cause injury to the hippocampus which 'assists in storing words, places, conversations, written material, contextual details and spatial relationships in long-term memory' (Joseph 1998: 169-170). He therefore suggests that hippocampal injury disrupts the ability to convert short-term memory into long-term memory. This means that traumas which are prolonged or repeatedly suffered are often more difficult to remember than a single episode of severe turmoil. There is some corroborative evidence that high levels of stress may induce hippocampal atrophy, because in Cushing's syndrome the overproduction of corticosteroids leads to hippocampal atrophy and memory loss.

Pitman, Shin and Rauch explored the decrease in hippocampal volume in people with PTSD, using neuroimaging techniques. They note the decreased hippocampal activity and increased brain sensitivity to norepinephrine, with hyper responsivity to threat stimuli because the under responsive medial prefrontal cortex fails to inhibit it. They suggest five possible explanations for their observations, which are worth considering since the choice of explanation impacts on treatment approaches.

1. That there is a pre-existing brain abnormality which increases the risk of exposure to PTSD causing events – less ability to avoid risks, or to learn from past events
2. A pre-existing abnormality increases vulnerability to PTSD after exposure to traumatic events
3. The traumatic exposure causes the brain abnormality, and the abnormality produces PTSD
4. The traumatic exposure produces PTSD, and that leads to the abnormality
5. Traumatic exposure produces PTSD, and sequelae, which then lead to complications (e.g. alcoholism), which then leads to the abnormality. (Pitman, Shin et al. 2001: 54)

Modern research on the psychobiology of trauma still leaves definitive attributions of causality open, suggesting that further research is required.

3. Somatic symptoms of the posttraumatic stress syndrome, including anxiety, acute stress, panic attacks and depression

PTSD is categorised in DSM IV-TR as an anxiety disorder, sharing the hyperarousal symptoms of anxiety and panic attacks. However, physiologically, PTSD also mimics other psychological disorders, combining the hyperarousal of anxiety with the vegetative nature of depression and the endorphin-related symptoms of dissociation. The somatic symptoms of anxiety and hyperarousal arise as a result of the endocrinal activity described earlier. In panic attacks, phobias, Acute Stress Disorder and Posttraumatic Stress Disorder, symptoms may include insomnia, palpitations, tremors, sweating, feeling cold, diarrhoea, confusion, blushing, tension headaches, choking sensations or giddiness, decreased libido and gastrointestinal disturbances. Muscular aches in the head or back, restlessness, heaviness, or fatigue in the legs, and pains in the abdomen, head, shoulders, back or pelvic area are also common (Ljubotina and Arcel 1998: 235; Herman 1992a: 390; and Kraljevic, Bamburac et al. 1998: 172).

In generalised anxiety disorder people may experience cold, clammy hands, dry mouth, nausea, urinary frequency, trouble swallowing (described as 'a lump in the throat') and an exaggerated startle response (American Psychiatric Association 1994: 433). 'Inner restlessness', 'often short of breath', 'lack of energy' and 'inner tension' were frequently reported in a Croatian post-war refugee study (Ljubotina and Arcel 1998). If trauma is prolonged, the longer-term effect of arousal can lead to circulatory problems, hypertension, ulcers and gastrointestinal problems, and dysfunction of the thyroid glands (Popovic and Dizdararevic 1998). Following trauma, the body's immune system may be depleted, and the body becomes more susceptible to infections and to other immunological ailments. There is an interesting parallel drawn between anxiety and the immune system, which both have defensive functions. The immune system can overreact (anaphylaxis), underreact (immune deficiency), respond to the wrong cue (allergy) or wrong pathogen (autoimmune disease), so that anxiety can be excessive (panic), deficient (hypophobia), or a response to a situation that is not dangerous (phobia) (Stevens and Price 2000: 102).

In one Croatian study, the authors discuss their work with a patient with rheumatoid arthritis, which they describe as an autoimmune disease commonly associated with or exacerbated by stress. They note that research indicates an increase in the numbers of patients with rheumatoid arthritis during and after the 1991-1995 war, and stress and anxiety are identified as significant causal factors of the disease. They recommend an integrative psychological and medical approach (Kraljevic, Bamburac et al. 1998: 173). Depressive states may be indicated by 'lack of energy', 'insomnia' and 'loss of appetite' (Ljubotina and Arcel 1998: 235) and suicidality may be increased (Pavlovic and Marusic 2001).

Research in sexual assault was reported as rare in the socialist former Yugoslavia, and when rape and sexual assault of both men and women occurred during the war, there was a social taboo about discussion of its effects (Arcel 1998; Loncar 1998: 216) and Croat and Bosnian mental health experts were reported to be culturally unprepared to treat sexual assaults at the beginning of the wars (Arcel 1998: 205). The somatic symptoms of posttraumatic stress in victims of torture or sexual assault may be complicated by additional physical injuries, requiring medical attention. Women's menstrual cycles may be disturbed following posttraumatic stress or sexual assault, or they may suffer pregnancy as a result of rape. There was a need for social support and psychological assistance for women who had babies as a result of war-related rape. Following sexual assault, sexually transmitted disease may be present. Both men and women may experience feelings of guilt and shame, low self-esteem, and distortion of self-image, resulting in attempts at self-harm or suicidality (Loncar 1998; Pavlovic and Marusic 2001; Popovic 1998).

Effects of posttraumatic stress on children and their families

The term 'child' here is defined as a person under the age of sixteen years, and 'young person' includes persons between sixteen and eighteen years of age.

Atle Dyregrov, a specialist in trauma work with children, writes that we do not know enough about the trauma processing and the different development tasks of childhood (Dyregrov 1995: 46).

There is a considerable worldwide body of research on the effects of war, grief and posttraumatic stress on children (including child soldiers) and their families (Dyregrov 1995). There were also some studies carried out following the war in Croatia (Kocijan-Hercigonja, Skrinjaric et al. 1998a, 1998b; Matacic 1998; Pantic 1998), which are considered later in the book in the context of the case study.

In peacebuilding, to generate long-term social change it is vital to encourage non-conflictual attitudes in children, since they will build and influence the next generation (Curle 1973, 1973g, 1974a, 1974b, 1984a; Masheder 1986). After the 1991-95 war, teachers and others working with children in Eastern Slavonia noted increased aggression and anti-social behaviour in schools and this disturbed behaviour was also reported as occurring at home. They attributed these behaviours to the trauma of war. The effect of posttraumatic stress on children and their development is relevant to both the treatment of trauma and to peacebuilding, but little is known about its effects.

Atle Dyregrov, a specialist in trauma work with children, writing from a western cultural perspective, says, 'Unfortunately, we do not know enough about the interplay between trauma processing and the different development tasks of childhood' (Dyregrov 1995: 46). In the field of psychobiology, little appears to have been done to explore posttraumatic stress in children from a psychobiological perspective in the context of either western or non-western cultures, and this is an area for further research.

Anxiety disorders, chronic hyperarousal, and behavioural disturbances have been described in traumatised children, (Bowlby 1969, in van der Kolk 1994: 258-259). In addition to single incidents, long term sexual abuse is increasingly recognised to produce complex posttraumatic syndromes (Cole 1991; Herman 1992a, 1992b: 96-114) that involve chronic affect dysregulation, destructive behaviour against self and others, learning disabilities, dissociative problems, somatization, and distortions in concepts about self and others (van der Kolk 1988; Herman 1992a, 1992b). The field trials for DSM IV-TR showed that this group of symptoms tend to occur together, and that the severity of the syndrome was proportional to the duration of the trauma and the age of the child when it began (van der Kolk, Roth and Pelcovitz 1992). The proposal that 'emotional memory is forever' (Le Doux, Romanski et al. 1991 in van der Kolk 1994: 261), implies that the consequences of war trauma on children may be very serious, potentially affecting their subsequent ability to function fully as adults and parents.

The effect of separation from attachment figures in childhood has long been recognised in western psychiatry (Bowlby 1969; Winnicott 1957). Separations may arise from bereavement, illness and marital or family break-up, internal displacement in wartime, refugee status, for child protection or other societal reasons. Children in a Croatian study who had suffered earlier separations were found to be most vulnerable to traumatic stress, depression and associated problems of behaviour (Vidovic 1991). Separation may exacerbate the effects of traumatic stress, perhaps leading to complex posttraumatic stress. In studies of Croatian and Bosnian refugee and displaced children, practitioners noted higher levels of PTSD symptoms compared with local children who had also experienced the 1991-95 war, and that 'the intensity of the problem increases with prolonged exposure to a traumatic experience' requiring psychological monitoring and appropriate preventive or therapeutic measures (Kocijan-Hercigonja, Skrinjaric et al. 1998a: 261). Matacic questions whether the adult experience reflected in the DSM IV TR criteria for PTSD might differ from the experience of children, suggesting that the syndrome of post-traumatic stress may manifest in a wide variety of ways as child survivors grow and develop (Matacic 1998: 346). He makes the point that in post-war situations, looking only for the diagnostic criteria of PTSD in children and adolescents could result in overlooking many other developmental phenomena.

Traumatic events may cause impairment of memory. It is suggested that children with PTSD are more at risk for traumatic memory loss than older individuals (Joseph, S. 1998: 171). In infants, the memory system that encodes affective quality of experience matures before the central nervous system. The central nervous system links the representations of events with symbolic and linguistic organisation of mental experience. With maturation, there is an increasing ability to link experience with existing mental schema, but this process is also vulnerable to disruption. In normal child development, the hippocampus matures slowly until the 3rd or 4th year, and the myelination cycle is not complete until well after the first decade. There may be prolonged immaturity of the corpus callosum, which is limited in its ability to transfer information between right and left hemispheres until well after the age of five. As the right hemisphere and right temporal lobe are dominant for storage of personal and emotionally laden experiences, callosal immaturity prevents the language-dominant left hemisphere from gaining access to this data. Joseph explains that this may be why most individuals have difficulty recalling events that occurred prior to age three and a half, because these memories are stored, but cannot be easily retrieved and expressed (Joseph, S. 1998: 171).

In children with PTSD, various stimuli, including stress induced corticosterone production, may decrease hippocampal activity, including hippocampal mediated memory storage and categorisation but some mental representation may be laid down by means of the system that stores affective memory without symbolic, spatial or temporal processing. These psychobiological effects of the posttraumatic stress syndrome may affect the child's reactions to stimuli, and also their general behaviour and attitudes. The hyperarousal, intrusive symptoms and depression of PTSD may impact on their ability to concentrate on daily tasks and schoolwork and to assimilate and remember new information.

The age of the child will influence the effect of traumatic stress on their development and the way in which they respond to the trauma. One Croatian study of the psychological problems of children in war notes that:

The changes and problems influencing the child's development in wartime depend on the kind and intensity of trauma experienced as well as on the age of the child. To children under seven, problems of separation and the parent-child relationship are the most important factors, while to school children (pre-adolescents and adolescents) the most significant factors are the community and society, the attitudes and values of the society in which they live. (Kocijan-Hercigonja, Skrinjaric et al. 1998a: 336)

1. Children under seven

'The similarity between grief reactions in children and adults is striking. This is so for grief and crisis responses' (Dyregrov 1995: 46). However, he notes that the expression of symptoms varies according to age and developmental stage.

Preschool children are learning to trust others, developing basic security and attachments, and developing control over their body and impulses. They are developing identity and autonomy, and seeking to understand their outer world, they are facing death or crisis at their most passive and vulnerable age, and may have a limited capacity for understanding what is happening, or the long- term implications of the events. They may have heightened anxiety about separations and rejections, and are more vulnerable to the death of a caregiver. Their lack of understanding may be to some extent a protective factor, as is their openness and ability to be concrete and direct. Their reactions to death may include anxiety about strangers, crying, clinging, and the need for much reassurance. They may show regressive behaviour such as bedwetting, soiling and sleep disturbances. The depressive symptoms may be apparent in loss of interest in play and temper tantrums (Dyregrov 1995: 43-44).

In children under seven, predominant problems relate to separation, sleeping, feeding, changed behaviour and various forms of physical disturbances for which paediatricians cannot find an organic cause. (Kocijan-Hercigonja, Skrinjaric et al. 1998a: 336-337)

2. Children over seven

School age children are 'decreasing their dependence on their parents, and increasing contact with the world outside the family'. They have a 'greater repertoire of coping strategies to meet and handle death and crisis situations' and in fantasies, 'through changing, undoing, reversing, or taking revenge, they can counteract feelings of helplessness' (Dyregrov 1995: 44). Schoolwork may suffer from the child's inability to concentrate or apathy. Depressive symptoms are common after bereavement, and anxiety or guilty feelings may emerge, but the child may be unable or unwilling to share their feelings with adults or their peer group. Dyregrov suggests that denial or suppression of feelings seems to increase with age, (1995: 45).

If feelings are suppressed for any reason, or there subsists a family or societal culture where negative or painful feelings are not freely expressed, reactions to posttraumatic stress may emerge in psychosomatic symptoms, subconsciously giving a tangible reason for complaint. It has already been noted that in research with adults in Croatia, the majority of refugees sought help for somatic complaints rather than psychological reasons. Children and young people may tend to react the same way as they move towards adulthood.

> The problems most frequently found in schoolchildren are related to a changed attitude towards everyday duties, school, and authorities, but also to other problems, such as psychosomatic reactions and diseases, depression and even suicide attempts. (Kocijan-Hercigonja, Skrinjaric et al. 1998a: 336-337)

3. Adolescents, and young people of 16–18

In adolescents, Dyregrov (1995: 44-45) describes the developmental tasks as directed towards mastery of biological, psychological and social changes, developing adult sexuality and the adult sexual role. Concerns centre on dependence and independence, fear of rejection and ambivalence towards parents. The 'magical thinking' of childhood may be reactivated and inappropriate feelings of responsibility for events, guilt and self-reproach may arise. Adolescents may, however, envisage the longer-term consequences of death and loss.

Dyregrov then makes a point that is highly relevant to the psychological aspects of peacemaking. He suggests that the intensity of adolescents' feelings or the avoidance of confrontation may cause their reactions to be expressed more through behaviour and conflicts with the environment. 'Violent human-caused deaths may activate adolescents' own destructive fantasies and aggression' (Dyregrov 1995: 45). They may endeavour to gain a control over death and engage in risk-taking activities. In a peaceful situation this may be sublimated to sport, but this has obvious implications in a post-war situation where the trauma is severe and recent, where weapons may be available and where the political, cultural or social climate may encourage such behaviour.

Children and young people of any age who have suffered loss and bereavement might also have to cope with changing roles within the family, carrying out additional or new household tasks or wage earning work to replace the role of lost adults. Competition may arise between attendance at school and other tasks. Children and young people may find themselves with competing social and family pressures or needs. Through physical or psychological causes, adults may become dependent on their children. Refugee children may have this additional stress and responsibility of role reversal (Harris Hendricks, Black et al. 1993: 12).

Another finding of Kocijan-Hercigonja, Skrinjaric, et al. was that there was a significant difference between parents' and children's evaluation of the children's problems, the children reporting more problems than the parents had noticed. This led the researchers to conclude that the parents had a tendency to deny their children's problems, indicating a disturbed parent-child relationship, and possibly also an emotional condition of the parent. The researchers noted that the intensity of mental disturbances in refugees differed not only in relation to the duration of exile, but in relation to the attitudes and beliefs of the family concerned (Kocijan-Hercigonja, Skrinjaric et al. 1998a: 338). The conclusion of the study was that families should be treated as a whole. Systemic family therapy is the treatment of choice for family dysfunction by psychologists in Croatia.

Awareness of the impact of trauma on children and young people is essential because the effects of trauma may persist in the long term and some practitioners suggest that if untreated, posttraumatic stress may lead to subsequent PTSD or other mental illness (Herman 1992a: 89). If exacerbated by additional factors, it may lead to complex posttraumatic stress.

Complex posttraumatic stress

Complex posttraumatic stress is a term used by Judith Herman to indicate a condition in which posttraumatic stress is exacerbated by additional factors (Herman, 1992a; 1992b: 121; 1993). Her research, spanning fifty years' literature on survivors of prolonged domestic, sexual or political victimisation, led her to assert that a new category of posttraumatic stress is required to reflect the severity of the effects of such suffering. Herman, in complex PTSD, adds to somatization the dissociation and affective sequelae of prolonged trauma, suggesting that 'chronically traumatised people are hypervigilant, anxious and agitated, without any recognisable baseline of calm or comfort' and over time, they begin to complain of 'insomnia, startle reactions and agitation'. They may also experience a variety of headaches, gastrointestinal disturbances, abdominal, back or pelvic pain, and tremors, choking sensations or nausea (Herman 1993: 90). Other practitioners have noted the need for an expanded concept, suggesting for example 'complicated PTSD' (Brown and Fromm 1986 in Herman 1992a: 88). Herman confines her definition of this syndrome to the category of people who have suffered prolonged, repeated trauma, in a state of captivity. The victim is unable to flee and under the control of the perpetrator. Captivity creates a relationship of coercive control, which may be exercised 'by physical force (as in the case of prisoners and hostages), or by a combination of physical, economic, social and psychological means (as in the case of religious cult members, battered women, and abused children)' (Herman 1992a: 87).

Herman characterises three broad areas of disturbance that transcend simple PTSD: symptomatic, characterological, and vulnerability to repeated harm at their own hand or that of others (1992b: 119). Herman cites a number of authorities for her claim that: 'A history of abuse, particularly in childhood, appears to be one of the major factors predisposing a person to become a psychiatric patient. Though only a minority of survivors of chronic child abuse become psychiatric patients, a large proportion (40-70%) of adult psychiatric patients are survivors of abuse' (sic) (Herman 1992a: 89). One has to be very careful about reliance on such sweeping generalisations extrapolated from research data, but if there is any possible implication of a potential risk of later mental illness or impairment of health or development for any of the numerous child survivors of war who have suffered some sort of abuse, then this must constitute some ground for the provision of appropriate help for those children.

Dissociation may be exaggerated in complex PTSD. Herman suggests that those affected may have 'become adept practitioners of the art of altered consciousness. Through the practice of dissociation, voluntary thought suppression, minimisation, and sometimes outright denial, they learn to alter an unbearable reality' (Herman 1992a: 90). Disturbances in the sense of time, memory and concentration are reported. The future is foreshort-ened, but eventually the past may also be obliterated, leading to 'traumatic amnesia'. Dissociation to the extent of a clinical diagnosis of Dissociative Identity Disorder (formerly called multiple personality disorder) may be associated with prolonged or severe child abuse (Putnam 1989; Putnam, Guroff et al. 1986; Kolb 1989; American Psychiatric Association 2000: 526-529) and there is a risk of personality disorganisation following prolonged trauma.

Herman describes in detail the phenomenon of 'learned helplessness' that may also arise in captivity. During imprisonment in which external control over bodily functions (possibly deprivation of food, sleep, shelter, privacy or personal hygiene) is coupled with fear of death or serious harm and perhaps also the capricious granting of small indulgences, the captive may develop 'traumatic bonding', a psychological dependence on the captor resulting from enforced infantilism, in which identification can occur and which may result in the captive perceiving the captor as both oppressor and saviour. Isolation of the victim enhances the dependency and captors may then seek to exacerbate alienation by requiring the victim to witness or commit criminal acts against others (Herman 1992a: 92-93). For former political prisoners, or prisoners of war, the relationship with the former captor may continue in the freed captive's inner life, resulting in a preoccupation with tracking the oppressor's career, continued fear, and a feeling of continuing danger. Future relationships may be affected; as Herman puts it, 'all relationships are now viewed through the lens of extremity' (Herman 1992a: 94).

Adam Curle and others worked with these and many other problems reported by the former prisoners in the Civil Resettlement Units. The case study in Croatia raises the issue of whether some of these effects of prolonged trauma may subsist in communities subjected to continual shelling as happened in Zupanja, or which were placed under siege, for example Vukovar, or for those people who were held in the generalised long-term 'captivity' of war. In group psychotherapy with refugees from Bosnia and Herzegovina, the pattern of learned helplessness and continuing fear of persecution was apparent amongst those who had been in detention camps, particularly those who had been ill treated (Simunkovic and Arcel 1998: 146).

Herman notes that survivors of trauma may carry within them a burden of unexpressed anger. In war, this is likely to be primarily against perceived perpetrators, but (as Herman indicates in cases of captivity), it may also be against all those who are perceived as remaining indifferent and failing to help, and it may be turned into self-hatred and suicidality. Efforts to control this rage may further exacerbate the survivor's social withdrawal and paralysis of initiative. Occasional outbursts of rage against others may further alienate the survivor and prevent the restoration of relationships. An internalisation of rage may result in a malignant self-hatred and chronic suicidality, but this should not be confused with self harming which Herman suggests is usually to regain a sense of reality through a jolt to the body (Herman 1992b: 109). She describes the additional risk in complex PTSD of repeated harm, self-inflicted or at the hands of others. She suggests that this is an internalisation of victim-isation that goes beyond the re-living of the traumatic events in PTSD, to render the survivor vulnerable to future abuses of power, or to feelings of guilt and shame that may lead to self-harm. On a community level following war, the potential effects of such unexpressed anger in high numbers of people may have profound social and political consequences, both in relationships within the local community and in work with providers of humanitarian aid after the war, who may encounter in transference and counter-transference the effects of unexpressed rage.

As seen from the earlier discussion of the physiology of posttraumatic stress, the symptoms of PTSD and complex PTSD share much in common with the arousal symptoms of anxiety and the apathy of depression, making accurate differential diagnosis difficult. They all have in common (to varying degrees), a sense of isolation and alienation from the external world, which may deter people from seeking early intervention and if unresolved, may lead to long-term difficulties in personal and social life, potentially leading to a subsequent need for psychological and social interventions.

Anxiety and depression: conditions associated with posttraumatic stress

The symptoms of PTSD overlap with those of other disorders. Reported studies of traumatised groups with PTSD contain high numbers of individuals who also met the diagnostic criteria for another psychiatric disorder, including substance abuse, anxiety, panic attacks and depression, to the extent that 'it is the exception rather than the rule for individuals to meet the diagnostic criteria for PTSD in the absence of meeting criteria for another psychiatric disorder' (Yehuda and McFarlane 1995: 1708).

Following war, local and refugee populations and those professionals and volunteers who seek to help them may be affected not only by PTSD defined according to the DSM IV TR criteria, but they may experience the symptoms of generalised posttraumatic stress manifesting in many different ways, including associated psychosomatic illnesses (Saraceno, Saxena et al. 2002). In Bosnia and Croatia, mental health practitioners noted that anxiety and depression are psychological conditions that frequently arise following experiences of trauma, and which may co-exist with posttraumatic stress, or are formally diagnosed as common comorbid conditions with PTSD (Arcel, Folnegovic-Smalc et al. 1998; Bleich and Moskowitz 2000; Henigsberg, Folnegovic-Smalc et al. 2001; Ljubotina and Arcel 1998).

1. Anxiety

There are a number of anxiety disorders. Acute Stress Disorder, together with PTSD, Generalised Anxiety Disorder, Panic Attacks and Phobias are all classified as anxiety related. Acute Stress Disorder has similar symptoms to those of PTSD, but they are of shorter duration, and acute stress disorder is a differential diagnosis for PTSD. I do not want in this book to give detailed accounts or to make comparisons or evaluations of these disorders or their prevalence in Eastern Slavonia, but perhaps a general awareness of their features here may prove helpful in providing a contextual background to the consideration of the focus group discussions from Eastern Slavonia.

All the anxiety disorders involve a degree of emotional and physical arousal. Panic attacks may occur within the stimulus-arousal pattern of PTSD and in Acute Stress Disorder. Phobias may also include arousal symptoms when faced with feared objects or situations. Phobias may be conceptualised differently in varying cultures, for example, fear of spirits and magic would only be considered phobic if the fear were excessive within the person's specific culture. Reminders or memories of either specific or generalised incidents of war could give rise to panic attacks or phobias related to the traumatic events, e.g. fear of planes, loud noises, or open spaces.

Generalised Anxiety Disorder is an excessive worry about a number of events or activities occurring more days than not over a period of six months or more. The worry may be accompanied for adults by at least three (or for a child, at least one) of the symptoms which include restlessness, being easily fatigued, difficulty in concentrating, irritability, muscle tension and disturbed sleep. The intensity of the worry is out of proportion to the events of the person's daily life.

2. Depression

Depression is described according to levels of its severity and duration. It may include Major Depressive Episodes, Major Depressive Disorder and Dysthymic Disorder. Additional complicating factors such as manic or psychotic episodes may accompany depression. The criteria for Major Depressive Disorder include a depressed mood present for most of the day, nearly every day, for a period of at least two weeks, markedly diminished interest or pleasure in all or almost all activities, fatigue or loss of energy, feelings of worthlessness or excessive or inappropriate guilt, diminished ability to think or concentrate or indecisiveness, recurrent thoughts of death (not just fear of dying) and suicidal ideation without a specific plan, or a suicide attempt, or a specific plan for committing suicide. Major Depressive Disorder is associated with increased pain and physical illness, deceased physical social and role functioning and a high risk of mortality by suicide, with increased risk of death rates in individuals aged over 55 (American Psychiatric Association 2000: 371).

Dysthymic Disorder is a less severe form of depression, characterised by a chronically depressed mood present for most of the day, for more days than not, for a period of at least two years. In children, the mood may be irritable rather than depressed, and the minimum period for the criteria is one year. During the period of depression, at least two of these additional symptoms are present: poor appetite or overeating, insomnia or hypersomnia, low energy or fatigue, low self esteem, poor concentration or difficulty making decisions, and feelings of hopelessness. Individuals also may experience low interest and self-criticism, seeing themselves as uninteresting or incapable (American Psychiatric Association 2000: 377-380).

Depression may occur as a reaction to life events (reactive depression to psychosocial stressors), or as a result of general medical conditions, substance abuse or other causes. In post-war situations, drugs or alcohol may be used by survivors to relieve their symptoms of posttraumatic stress, and substance dependence (particularly cocaine or alcohol) may contribute to the onset or exacerbation of major depressive disorder.

Herman (1992a: 391) suggests that prolonged depression is almost always found in clinical studies of chronically traumatised people. Following the war in the former Yugoslavia, many of those who sought and received help from humanitarian aid programmes had suffered catastrophic life events (Moro, Franciskovic et al. 1998) that generated posttraumatic stress or reactive depression (Arcel, Folnegovic-Smalc et al. 1998; Weisaeth 1998). Some practitioners also noted psychotic symptoms associated with these traumatic experiences (Bleich and Moskowitz 2000). The co-existence of a number of similar or overlapping symptoms makes differential diagnosis difficult. The people who took part in the focus groups in Eastern Slavonia resented the imposition of 'labelling' and diagnosis, and chapter 5 includes their comments on the implications and value of diagnosis (or not) for medication and for psychological and social recovery from the experiences of war.

'Burn out' and 'compassion fatigue'

Posttraumatic stress reaction is not confined to those who directly experience trauma. The syndromes of 'burn out' and 'vicarious trauma' are encountered by professionals and helpers who may themselves experience the symptoms of PTSD. In professional and volunteer helpers, the phenomenon of 'compassion fatigue' may arise from a combination of the nature of the work and from posttraumatic stress. Professionals and helpers working with refugees after the war in Croatia found themselves working long hours, in difficult conditions and often with inadequate training and experience of the problems they were facing (Franciskovic, Pernar et al. 1998; Ljubotina and Arcel 1998: 321). A study identified exacerbating factors of stress in helpers as personality, environment including working relationships, and the nature of the work (Adjukovic and Adjukovic 1998: 314). Professionals and helpers can feel unsupported in their work by their own administrative bodies. Croatian health officials were perceived by some health workers to be operating from a biological medical orientation, and causing frustration by failing to understand community needs for psycho-social help, assuming that good will and compassion is sufficient (Hecimovic 1998: 128). There is a need for training and redeployment, risk assessment and contingency planning for personnel who work in these situations.

Compassion fatigue is characterised by a defensive withdrawal from the close supportive relationships with clients or others required in the course of daily professional duties. The helper may be unwilling or unable to engage or cope with the stress of empathic communication and rapport. From a psychoanalytic perspective, transference and counter-transference may operate to affect the therapist's perceptions and reactions to their clients (Ladame 1999), and this may affect work with psychotraumatised people, causing difficulties in sustaining the therapeutic relationship and in offering appropriate empathy

(Klain and Pavic 1999; Milivojevic 1999). Klain and Pavic point out that

> The therapist may be cast in potentially positive roles within the trauma membrane, such as protector, rescuer, comforter, or fellow victim, or in negative roles outside the trauma membrane such as perpetrator or fellow victim turned enemy...' Patients' experiences may be so horrific that in telling their story they unconsciously try to shock the therapist or to elicit feelings of horror or guilt – 'in such a way that the patient has assumed the perpetrator role and the therapist is now the victim. (Klain and Pavic 1999: 467)

This syndrome can affect work with individuals (Milivojevic 1999) and also the dynamics of group work (Urlic 1999). Therapists may find that they are bodily and emotionally exhausted, depressed, lacking in energy, anxious, lacking in self confidence and feeling helpless, perhaps combined with fatigue, loss of appetite or sleep disturbances – all symptoms of 'burn out' (Klain and Pavic 1999: 470; Milivojevic 1999; Urlic 1999). The need for implementation of preventive measures and to provide appropriate supervision for helpers was recognised in Croatia and The Society for Psychological Assistance in Zagreb set up a training project in 1994 to address the mental health needs of helpers, (Adjukovic and Adjukovic 1998: 314-315; Klain and Pavic 1999).

In Chapter 6, the implications of vicarious trauma for staff and volunteer helpers in post-war projects are considered in the context of programme design, training, and preparation for fieldwork, preventive measures and appropriate supervision.

Vulnerability and risk factors for PTSD

The concept of PTSD embodies a characterisation of the effects of environmental factors in psychiatric illness. There appears to be no linear relationship between the severity of stress exposure and psychiatric consequences – after a traumatic experience, cultural, individual and social risk factors may impact on psychological response to trauma (de Jong, Komproe et al. 2001). Research shows that certain factors may generate an apparent risk of vulnerability to PTSD, although this must be viewed with some caution since in some cases, although the evidence is indicative of a possible link, no clear causal links are established. Consideration of potential vulnerability may assist in the prevention of the onset of PTSD by appropriate preparation and preventive techniques.

Biological risk factors include a family history of mental disorders (McFarlane and Yehuda 1996: 157), gender, and possibly also heightened 'conditionability' (the susceptibility to conditioned responses) or neuroendocrine vulnerability factors such as a low cortisol response to stress (Shalev 1996: 85-86). Shalev suggests that personality traits, including neuroticism, introversion, and prior mental disorders also influence the risk for developing PTSD (Shalev 1996: 86), as do Lauterbach and Vrana (2001). O'Shea's research confirms the relevance of personality, a background of psychiatric problems and personal meaning of the traumatic event, but identifies additional etiological factors: genetics, issues of proximity or the intensity of the initial emotional response to stress (O'Shea 2001). It is suggested that life events causing early traumatisation may create vulnerability to later trauma (O'Shea 2001; Herman 1992b: 119). Other predisposing factors include environmental and social conditions before the trauma, individual characteristics, nature and dimension of the traumatic events, features of the posttraumatic environment and cognitive appraisal of the events (de Jong, Komproe et al. 2001; Ljubotina and Arcel 1998: 232). Vulnerability may be increased by posttraumatic factors such as lack of social support and exposure to subsequent re-activating stressors (Yehuda and McFarlane 1995: 1707).

Some authors suggest that there was a philosophical shift involved in the inclusion of PTSD in DSM III which resolved a previous quandary of how to classify a chronic condition in normal people who developed symptoms after an extremely traumatic event (Yehuda and McFarlane 1995: 1705), but as Pitman, Shin et al point out, that premise of pre-existing normality is one of a number of assumptions which are not yet fully clarified. Bracken (2002: 78-79) refers to the work of McFarlane, an Australian psychiatrist, who during the 1980s worked with firefighters following a bush fire in Australia. McFarlane followed up the men's psychiatric records, and reported that only a small number of the men, described as 'anxiety prone', developed the intrusion/avoidance symptoms of PTSD, and that 'pre-morbid vulnerability accounted for a greater percentage of the variance of the disorder than the impact of the disaster' (McFarlane 1989: 227). Bracken notes McFarlane's suggestion that, 'Once anxiety symptoms and/or depression have become established, a feedback effect begins to occur where the intensity and frequency of the memories of the disaster are increased' (cited in Young 1995: 138). Bracken sees a further issue here:

Young makes the point that if we accept that depressive or anxiety states can bring about the intrusive-avoidance symptoms of PTSD at all [sic], then we have to accept the possibility that at least some of the cases of late onset PTSD are induced by anxiety or depressive states which occur independently of the actual event, which then becomes the focus of these intrusive-avoidance phenomena. (Bracken, P. 2002: 79)

I agree with Bracken's suggestion that this has serious implications for the study of PTSD, because its present definition implies that the symptoms flow from the traumatic stressor.

Preparation and 'stress inoculation'

It has been shown that preparation for exposure to trauma reduces the likelihood of adverse psychological effects occurring (Chemtob, Bauer et al. 1990). The process of preparation for forthcoming stress is sometimes referred to as 'stress inoculation' Preparation '...reduces uncertainty, increases one's sense of control, and teaches automatic responses that are less readily eroded under stress' (Shalev 1996: 87). Shalev cites the work of Hytten (1989), which found that helicopter pilots who were trained in survival manoeuvres coped well in a real crash. Their survival tactics were not the same as those learned in training, yet the training was perceived by survivors as helpful. Hytten concluded that the training had instilled the expectancy of a positive outcome.

Van der Kolk suggests that coping with stress entails mobilising the skills of self-care, gaining social support, and being able to rely on external protection when internal resources are insufficient. Parenting and childhood experience is important – 'Secure attachment bonds serve as a primary defence against trauma induced psychopathology in both children and adults' (van der Kolk, B. A. 1996: 185).

The ability to recruit a social network in the aftermath of the experience provides resilience to traumatic stressors, giving a more rapid modulation of the stress reaction (McFarlane and Yehuda 1996: 158). It is really interesting to note that Adam Curle's work in the CRUs also confirmed the powerful healing effect of a social network and the views expressed in the focus groups in Eastern Slavonia reiterate the beneficial impact of a community approach in healing the wounds of war.

Positive aspects of trauma: creative casualties and posttraumatic growth

There are people who triumph over adversity and who seem to develop despite, or because of, their suffering. Linley notes that some researchers have 'made the case for the adaptive nature of PTSD, while others have described it as a continuum of normal adaptive behaviour rather than a distinctly abnormal reaction' (Brewin, Dalgliesh et al. 1996; Williams, R. and Joseph 1999 in Linley 2000: 353).

Eric Trist noticed the positive effect that the experience of being a prisoner of war had on some of the soldiers in the Civil Resettlement Units, and he referred to these men as 'creative casualties'. Somehow he felt that they had gained in awareness and in personal power. Adam Curle was impressed at the time by the positive outcomes that the former prisoners had created out of their suffering and he wrote about it when he revisited the work of the CRUs in recent years (Curle, A 2001b: 5). The phenomenon of positive psychological growth following suffering was noted and considered by psychologists in different circumstances some fifty years later and the term 'posttraumatic growth' was first used by Tedeschi and Calhoun in 1995 to describe their perceptions of a new phenomenon. They identified this in clients who had experienced trauma, in which they identified three broad areas of change: self perception, relationships with others, and philosophy of life (Tedeschi 1999; Tedeschi and Calhoun 1995; 1996; Tedeschi, Park et al. 1998 in Linley 2000: 353). Tedeschi and Calhoun (1996) subsequently devised the 'Posttraumatic Growth Inventory', a measurement scale addressing these three areas of growth.

1. Self-perception

Trauma can challenge our world-view and the schemas within which we operate. Whilst this may threaten to demolish existing belief systems and values, it may also present an opportunity for productive revision, facilitating the development of a more resilient personality. 'This acknowledgment of vulnerability, concurrently with an appreciation of strength, allows an appreciation of self (Collins, Taylor et al. 1990) which in turn develops more positive emotions, leading to enhanced self-esteem, greater self-reliance, and increased self-confidence' (Aldwin and Sutton 1998 in Linley 2000: 354).

Perceptions of increased strength and resourcefulness can result from surviving trauma (Joseph, Williams et al. 1993), and this confidence may generalise to other situations:

>...living through life traumas provides a great deal of information about self-reliance, affecting not only self-evaluations of competence in difficult situations, but the likelihood that one will choose to address difficulties in an assertive fashion. (Tedeschi and Calhoun 1996: 456)

Some survivors of childhood sexual abuse report increased self-knowledge and resourcefulness (Linley 2000: 353). One person of whom this was undoubtedly true was Bertha Pappenheim. Judith Herman's account of her life (1992b: 19) describes her experience of considerable suffering as a child and young adult, yet she made a remarkable recovery and achieved much in her adult years in her subsequent career. As a young woman, she was a patient of Joseph Breuer, and she was diagnosed with 'hysteria'. He refers to her as 'Anna O' in his case notes. It was she who first described Freud's psychoanalysis as 'the talking cure'. Bertha Pappenheim suffered from intrusive memories of prolonged sexual abuse during her childhood. She entered into almost daily psychoanalysis with Breuer, over a period of two years, after which Breuer suddenly terminated his work with her. The reason for this is unclear, but Breuer may have been aware that she had become emotionally attached to him. Following the cessation of his treatment, she suffered a crisis and was admitted to hospital, but she eventually recovered her mental health after an illness lasting several years.

Under the pseudonym of Paul Berthold, Bertha Pappenheim translated into German a paper by Mary Wollstonecraft on women's rights and then wrote a play entitled 'Women's Rights'. Under her own name, she then achieved many things which were pioneering for her time – she directed an orphanage for girls, founded a feminist organisation for Jewish women and travelled throughout Europe and the Middle East to campaign against the sexual exploitation of women and children. Her spirit and passion earned the admiration of Martin Buber, who commemorated her after her death.

2. Changed relationships with others

Linley (2000) explains that changes in perspective may lead to a 'greater appreciation of the role of others in our lives, as well as allowing the dismissal of minor aberrations when our focus is set on the broader tapestry of life. Compassion for others is emphasised, and greater altruism develops with the experiential knowledge of the suffering of others. Evidence from a

Netherlands study indicates that those who have faced death (but not had a 'near-death experience') undergo over time 'positive change and were more self-assured, socially aware, and religious than ever before' (van Lommel, van Wees et al. 2001: 2042).

Where the trauma is a shared experience, for example a family bereavement, the common grief and loss may bring other family relationships closer in united grief and the family may need to reorganise the roles of its members to carry out tasks formerly fulfilled by the deceased. Coping with disability or with mental illness in a family member may also require radical changes in role or adaptation to new ways of life.

3. Spiritual growth

The loss of a loved one, or a close encounter with death or risk of dying may create a sense of the value of life (Tedeschi and Calhoun 1996), and may provide the motivation to address formerly unsatisfactory relationships. Religious belief may be a source of solace.

Some people who become terminally ill refer to a new inner strength and greater spiritual awareness, which arises after the shock of the realisation of their prognosis. Some have even welcomed their illness as an opportunity for growth. One area in which people report change is the revision of priorities. More than half of the cancer patients responding to a survey described this type of change (Taylor 1983 in Linley 2000: 353). Near-death experiences (NDE), or deathbed visions, may be defined as 'the reported memory of all impressions during a special state of consciousness, including specific out-of-body experience, pleasant feelings and seeing a tunnel, a light, deceased relatives, or a life review' (van Lommel, van Wees et al. 2001: 2040). These near-death experiences have been reported by psychologically healthy people who were for a period of time, clinically dead, but resuscitated. A Netherlands cardiac care unit carried out a study of 344 patients who had undergone 509 successful resuscitations. Findings included reports of life-changing experiences. 'People who had NDE had a significant increase in belief in an afterlife and decrease in fear of death compared with people who have not had this experience' (van Lommel, van Wees et al. 2001: 2041). The authors add that 'Depth of NDE was linked to high scores in spiritual items such as interest in the meaning of one's own life, and social items such as sharing love and accepting others' (van Lommel, van Wees et al. 2001: 2042), and (Ring 1984). The scientific explanation for NDE remains unclear; explanations put forward

vary from one or a combination of spiritual, psychological, neurophysiological or physiological processes.

4. Liminality

Liminality is a term stemming from the Latin word 'limen' or threshold.
Jean Clark extensively explores the term in her autobiographical pamphlet
Change is Boundaries Dissolved, subsequently summarised in a book chapter
(Clark 1988, 2002). Clark uses the term to describe a transitional state in the
process of psychological change and development. She describes the process
of separation from the familiar, passing into a state of liminality and finally
into psychological reintegration. Liminality might also be an appropriate term
for the whirlpool of chaotic thoughts and feelings of posttraumatic stress
through which many people pass before reaching the quieter stretches of the
river of life in which healing lies.

Here is another of those strange connections that happen in life and which
I find it hard to believe are just pure coincidence. Jean Clark is a Person
Centred Counsellor who has now retired and also a Fellow of the British
Association of Counselling and Psychotherapy. She was for some time my
professional counselling supervisor and has now become a good friend. Jean,
like Adam Curle is a poet and a pioneer in many ways. She has worked with
Carl Rogers, Colin Lago and others in exploring various aspects of counselling
including race, ethnicity and culture, boundaries, founding and cessation of
counselling services, aspects of private practice, and trauma treatment. Jean
was always very supportive and encouraging of my work in Croatia, and she
was very enthusiastic about this research. Jean told me recently that she had
studied with Adam Curle in Oxford in the 1950s. She wrote to Adam. He was
delighted to hear from Jean and he remembered their work in Oxford. Their
creativity flourished in correspondence and telephone calls and this year they
have met together once again. I feel very privileged that I have been able to
bring together in this book the thoughts of two people for whom I have great
respect and it is such a joy to all of us that it has brought them together again
after so many years.

Adam Curle suggests that peace is not only a state of 'not war' but is an
internal psychological state. He asserts that the sense of alienation and separation engendered by violence and conflict might be healed by the
development of awareness, which he envisaged as a vital part of the peacemaking process. In the process of developing awareness, and transforming an

internal psychological state of unpeacefulness to peacefulness, it may be necessary to let go of former assumptions (some of which, after an experience of
conflict may have been already shattered by trauma) and to allow the psyche
to enter into a state of confusion and uncertainty in order to reconfigure the
sense of self in relation to others and to the external world. Carl Rogers'
Person Centred Approach to counselling is based on the belief that the core
conditions of empathy, acceptance (or unconditional positive regard) and
congruence create the optimum conditions in which this deep psychological
change can occur. The work of community groups such as the Centar za mir,
Dodir nade, Mir i dobro, Bench We Share and CWWPP endeavour to create
physically and psychologically safe environments in which the confusion of
liminality might be experienced safely.

Comments on the foundations of western psychiatry and mental health care, focusing on the diagnosis and treatment of trauma

Another link lies between the work of Adam Curle and that of Dr Patrick
Bracken, a consultant psychiatrist practising in Bradford, who, with his
partner Joan Giller, has many years' experience working with trauma
following violent conflict. They worked with the Medical Foundation for the
Victims of Torture in Uganda in the late 1980s. In Bradford, Dr Bracken has
established an innovative system of home treatment for people with severe
mental illness based on an approach of social care rather than more formal
traditional psychiatry, empowering people to work in a user-provider part-
nership in the organisation and provision of services. Dr Bracken brings
together insights from doctorates in philosophy and psychiatry and was instru-
mental in the development of the Philosophy Group of the Royal College of
Psychiatrists. He has written widely on the theoretical underpinnings of posttraumatic stress, (see Bracken 2001, 2002; Bracken, Giller and Summerfield
1993; Bracken 1998), and he is critical of some current western approaches to
the diagnosis and treatment of PTSD.

Bracken suggests that mental illness was seen as a social stigma, and that
when the doctors working within residential institutions for those who were
mentally ill began to systematically classify and study their charges, and
when psychiatry eventually emerged as a profession, western society then
imported into the diagnosis of mental illness the existing stigma of social
rejection. It is true that in some cultures, social stigma exists in relation to

mental illness. Adam Curle notes that in his work with the CRUs in 1945-46, the men did not wish to be seen as 'ill or abnormal' (Curle 2001), and refugees taking part in a study in Bosnia certainly did not see themselves as 'mentally ill' (Weine, Kuc et al. 2001). The focus groups in this research confirm that social stigma still exists in Eastern Slavonia in relation to mental illness and hospitalisation. An alternative view which Colin Murray Parkes puts forward, however, is that mental hospitals were developed to provide asylum and care for people who were seen as a danger to society, and that, by defining them as sick rather than sinful, psychiatrists were able to rescue them from the punitive labels of sinfulness and diabolical possession which preceded the movement (Parkes 2003).

Bracken posited that Descartes' ontological dualism underpins modern psychiatry, along with the information-processing models of mind and thought, separating the inner world of the mind from the outer world with which it is in contact. Thoughts, perceptions, beliefs, and desires are seen as things, which adhere within the mind (Bracken 2002: 22-23). Curle, from a Buddhist standpoint, described this separation as an illusion, seeing mind and matter as inseparable. Midway between these two approaches lies Husserl's transcendental phenomenology, bracketing the body, history, ego and lived life of a person to form their 'empirical ego' in contrast to the 'transcendental ego' of their pure consciousness (Bracken 2002: 24). Bracken suggests that, since Karl Jaspers published his influential work, *General Psychopathology*, (Jaspers 1963) which was overtly based on Husserl's ideas, twentieth century psychiatry has 'continually sought to separate mental phenomena from background contexts' (Bracken 2002: 25).

The implication of this approach in modern psychiatric practice is that psychosis and mental distress are seen as disordered individual experience. Not all psychiatrists would agree with Bracken. Some modern psychiatrists are likely to understand the assumptive world of the individual as a reflection of their perceptions of the world around them, and of the interpretations of that world by parents and others, as exemplified in the process of enculturation (Korn 2002), and that therefore mental phenomena cannot be regarded as separate from their background contexts. Mental activity may be seen as a function of the physical brain, in which it arises, and the mind as a social phenomenon, an organ of communication, influenced by social and other external stimuli.

Psychiatrists are trained in medicine, and moral and spiritual issues are not perceived as relevant to biomedicine, which adopts a naturalist epistemology, which Bracken explains as

> ...The belief that all phenomena can be explained in terms of natural causes and laws without attributing supernatural, spiritual or moral significance to them ... Science provides its criteria of truth. A combination of naturalism, empiricism and positivism came to dominate the methodological framework for medicine and the behavioural sciences such as psychology, and has continued to do so up to the present time. (Bracken 2002: 28)

Whilst a naturalist epistemology may rule out the supernatural significance of phenomena, it does not rule out their spiritual and moral significance. A point relevant to psychiatric treatment is that Bracken, citing Samson (1995), also comments that social and cultural factors are secondary and may or may not be taken into account; and they are usually understood to affect the content and not the form of psychiatry phenomena. This, if it represents general psychiatry practice values, has implications for international mental health provision for posttraumatic stress.

Following the medical model, psychiatric diagnosis and prognosis relies on standardised instruments (usually questionnaires), which are used to identify and quantify psychiatric disorders, leading to operational definitions of symptoms and syndromes and normative diagnostic criteria. Standard collections of diagnostic criteria, for example the DSM IV-TR criteria for PTSD, appear to operate with an implicit normative assumption that all psychological problems cross-culturally have the same form. The cognitivist 'computer' model of mind, with the brain conceptualised as the hardware and mentation as the programmes running, involves an operational belief system in which 'thought and emotion is understood to involve similar basic elements and structures cross-culturally' (see Bracken 2002: 31, 35).

Personality theory has shifted from its previous (Freudian) focus on unconscious drives to the concept that our perceptions and memories of the world are organised into generalised 'schemas' forming the unconscious scripts upon which we formulate decisions and actions, and upon which enculturation is based (Korn 2002). Schemas, our basic assumptions, reflect our fears and hopes, and are assumed by cognitivists to be the way in which the mind assimilates, compartmentalises and discards complex information.

... Schemas embody the rules and categories that order raw experience into coherent meaning. All knowledge and experience is packaged
in schemas. Schemas are the ghosts in the machine, the intelligence that
guides information as it flows through the mind. (Goleman 1985: 75)

The schematic approach now dominates psychiatry, influencing definitions
and treatment of trauma. Bracken (2002: 37) cites Aaron Beck's theory of
depression as an example of the relevance of schemas in general psychiatry.

Beck (1972: 129-130) proposes that erroneous or dysfunctional assumptions
may be internalised within schemas early in life, (e.g. a toddler is chastised for
being naughty and told that he is a bad boy) then subsequent events may
trigger the schema that has been laid down and automatically regenerate its
pattern of negative thoughts (parents tell him off for small disciplinary
matters, a teacher criticises his schoolwork, his boss criticises his work...
therefore each event may be interpreted in his mind as confirming the earlier
schematic belief that he is a bad person). As more experiences occur which are
interpreted by the individual as reinforcing the schema, the schema becomes
embedded in the psyche. Beck believes that such negative thoughts underlie
the clinical state of depression. The treatment is to recognise that there are
alternative interpretations of events and to actively encourage the patient to
recognise their dysfunctional thought patterns and through exercises and
'homework' to challenge and change or 'reframe' them when they occur,
generating a more positive thinking pattern (e.g. We all sometimes make
mistakes. The criticism was about an error at work. Work practice could be
improved, but getting something wrong does not necessarily make one an
entirely bad person). This approach can be helpful in changing negative
patterns of guilt and self-blame and the phenomenon of 'survivor guilt' of
those who survive a traumatic event when others did not.

The significance is that depression is seen as a disorder of cognition. Affects
(feelings) reflect and accompany cognition. They reveal the depression,
although they do not cause it, and are the essential criterion in diagnosis. As
we have seen already, frequently those who have suffered trauma blame themselves inappropriately in some way for the event or for their reactions to it
(Herman 1992b: 68). Some treatment approaches seek to alter cognitions in
the treatment of posttraumatic stress. There are a wide variety of therapeutic
approaches that may be used to alleviate the psychological or somatic symptoms of posttraumatic stress.

This chapter deepened the exploration of posttraumatic stress, and this theme continues next with a case study in Eastern Slavonia, exploring the psychological effects of traumatic experience in the community following the 1991-95 war, the therapeutic approaches commonly used, and the recommendations of the projects on ways in which to address the psychological suffering of the post-war syndrome. The case study uses action research with focus group discussions to explore the views and perceptions of five local nongovernmental organisations – Centar za mir, Mir i dobro, Bench we Share, Dodir nade and the Coalition for Work with Psychotrauma and Peacemaking – providing a longitudinal perspective of the experience of the community and of social and peace building activities in Osijek, Vukovar and Zupanja since 1992.

Chapter 4

War and peace: Osijek, Vukovar, Zupanja, Croatia and the five projects taking part in the case study

The case study, which formed part of my research in Eastern Slavonia, took place in the context of the experience of extreme violence in this area during the 1991-95 war. It was apparent from discussions with project members that some of the local population also retain memories or thoughts of earlier conflicts, particularly the events of the Second World War. In order to understand the context of Adam Curle's work in Croatia and the role of the projects which took part in the case study, this chapter provides some background information about specific events during the 1991-95 war in the former Yugoslavia directly relating to the areas in Eastern Slavonia within which the case study took place: Osijek, Vukovar and Zupanja.

I will briefly describe my perceptions of Eastern Slavonia in the period of post-war recovery and introduce each of the five projects taking part in the case study, with a short overview of the development and work of each project. It must be emphasised that much of the information available about the history of the area and the projects is anecdotal or based on participants' accounts of events from memory; so the details that are set out here may not always be accurate. Inevitably there are variations in individual perceptions and interpretations of the meaning of events. Following the theme of post-war recovery and to provide a context to the current mental health provision for the area in which the projects work, I have also written a little about the therapeutic interventions currently in use for the treatment of psychological trauma in Eastern Slavonia following the 1991-95 war.

Experiences of the 1991-95 war in Eastern Slavonia

I looked, but could find very little written information specifically about the events of the 1991-95 war in Eastern Slavonia. Books that proved helpful for general background information and statistics are *The Balkans* (Glenny 2000), which gives an overview of the Balkan wars from the author's first hand knowledge of the area as a journalist; *The Death of Yugoslavia* (Silber and Little 1996) and *I Choose Life* (Kruhonja 2000), written by the staff of the Centar za mir from their personal local experience and research. There is also *Sign of Hope* (Jegen 1996), a book written by a nun who visited the Centar za mir in Osijek during the war. This is an account of her personal observations at the time of her visit and includes anecdotal accounts of events from her conversations with people at that time. Additional information has been taken from other cited local and international sources.

Eastern Slavonia lies on the southern edge of the former Austro-Hungarian Empire, now bordering Serbia, Bosnia and Hungary. For hundreds of years the area enjoyed a peaceful co-existence of Croats, Serbs, Czechs, Slovaks, Ruthenes, Italians, Hungarians and – until 1945, Germans (Silber and Little 1996: 139). German is a second language spoken by many adults in this area, but I noticed that children and young people now frequently speak English, which is a standard second language in the national school curriculum.

There are several religious groups in the region, which in some writers' perceptions also correlate with ethnic differences, for example Agger comments that an important cultural indicator of ethnicity in the Balkan context is religion. 'Serbs are Orthodox, Croats are Catholic and Bosnians are Muslim' (Agger 2001: 243). In Eastern Slavonia, there are also other religions present in small numbers, including Jews, and some attempts are being made to respect their cultural needs – for example, there is currently a project for reconstruction of the synagogue in Vukovar.

At the time of the declaration of Croatia's independence from Yugoslavia on 5 June 1991, from some accounts, extreme nationalist attitudes were developing on all sides, although I was told by several local residents in Eastern Slavonia that the outbreak of war was an unexpected shock. Anecdotally, the first signs of violence were said to have occurred in late April and early May 1991, in the village of Borovo-Selo near Vukovar. Following these incidents, President Tudjman warned the public of the likelihood of civil war for Croatia's independence and the division of Yugoslavia. In Eastern Slavonia, random attacks continued by both Croats and Serbs. Political and ethnic attitudes polarised, represented by the pro-Serb JNA (Yugoslav National Army) and the Croatian National Guard.

Vukovar

Vukovar was a thriving town on the Danube, very close to the border with Serbia. Between January and August 1991, there had been elections and reports of harassment, including the incidents in Borovo-Selo. The account that follows is taken from Glenny (2000) and from anecdotal local information. There may be a bias because of a lack of detailed information about events from a Serbian perspective, the deaths and injuries amongst the Serbian population of the town and the absence of information about any Serbian graves.

The population of Vukovar at the 1991 Council of Europe Census was 44,000. The ethnic mix of Vukovar and Beli Manastir at that Census was given as 42.49% Croat, 35.11% Serb, 6.7% Hungarian, 22% others (including Slovak, Czech, Albanian, Montenegrin and Ruthenian). In August 1991, Vukovar came under artillery and mortar attack. The population reduced to 15,000 as the inhabitants fled. The remaining townspeople hid in underground shelters.

The JNA began a bombardment of the town and on September 14 the Croatian National Guard laid siege to the JNA barracks. Serb paramilitaries, supported by the JNA, killed eighty civilians outside the town and buried the bodies in a mass grave. For the next fifteen days, attacks led to hundreds of casualties and two bombs fell on the hospital. Vukovar held out, but in November 1991, a new offensive began with attacks by the federal air force. Ground troops neared the town centre and for two weeks hand-to-hand fighting followed. Finally Vukovar was cut off and 700 residents hid in the hospital complex. On 17 November 1991 the JNA destroyed almost the entire town save for a few pockets, notably the hospital. Next day, Vukovar surrendered.

During the three months of bombardment and siege, the Vukovar police registered 520 dead, of which 156 were Croatian national guardsmen. The rest were civilians and eight children. 1,850 people were seriously injured. It is noted that these figures possibly do not include hundreds of bodies that remained uncollected in the streets on the last days of the siege.

The troubles of the residents were not yet over. On 19 November 1991, The JNA entered the hospital ahead of the international monitors who brought vital medicines and were to supervise the evacuation. Women and children were allowed to leave, escorted out, or were handed over to the Croatian authorities. It is reported that some 400 men remaining at the hospital, including hospital staff, patients, civilians, political activists and Croatian fighters, were removed and are missing, presumed dead. Ian Traynor reports that Cyrus Vance, the U.N. mediator was not permitted to enter the hospital at that time. Those Croatians who were spared death were taken to a detention centre and subsequently released in 1992.

It is thought that many of those taken from the hospital were beaten, killed and then buried in a mass grave near Ovcara, just outside Vukovar. The number of people buried at Ovcara has been estimated as 261, but local accounts cannot be specific. A report in the *Guardian* of 14 June 2003 gives an account of these events and the arrest of Colonel Veselin Sljivancanin for this war crime. Two other former army officers connected with this event, General Mile Mrksic and Captain Miroslav Radic, have surrendered to the Hague Tribunal. Three army officers have now been indicted for war crimes relating to the events in Vukovar and their trials began in 2005.

I could find no local account of the numbers of Serbian losses, nor of any mass graves of Serbs. For the Serbian population in Vukovar at the present time, this lack of acknowledgment of their loss reflects an inequality in the formal recognition of the events of the war, perhaps influenced by political or social pressures. Most of the once beautiful town of Vukovar was destroyed. The famous 'ice cream cone' shaped water tower of the town still stands, although reduced by shelling to a skeletal structure. It has now become a national symbol of survival against overwhelming odds. It is in the context of these traumatic events that the Coalition for Work with Psychotrauma and Peace came to work in Vukovar in 1995 and remains there, working with all the resident ethnic groups.

Osijek

Osijek, on the River Drava, lies in Eastern Slavonia close to the Serbian and Hungarian border. It is the fourth largest city in Croatia, has an airport and a population in excess of 100.000. It is the 'industrial, cultural, educational and administrative centre of the Slavonian and Baranian regions, with their rich agricultural land and oil resources' (Jegen 1996: 13). It has a rich cultural heritage of art and music, a large university and a teaching hospital. Its well-known gymnasium school has amongst its former pupils a Nobel Prize winner.

Osijek dates from a prehistoric settlement. The Romans built a camp, Mursa, later destroyed by Atilla's Huns in 441. In the seventh century a Slavic settlement was established and the Croatian and Slavonic settlers named it Osijek, perhaps from the word 'odsjecen' meaning 'cut off'. Osijek thrived as a port and market town, gaining an entry in the records of the Croatian-Hungarian King Emrik as 'Ezek', eventually attracting Turkish occupation and rule and subsequently Austrian administration, with many successful immigrant traders. The city retained separate administrative regions until 1809, when a unified Osijek was proclaimed a 'free and royal city', growing rapidly into second place to Zagreb in Croatian industrial development. There were buildings from each era, reflecting a rich ethnic and cultural mixture of traditions.

The proximity of Osijek to the borders rendered it vulnerable to attack during 1991-95 war. For most Osijek residents, the most memorable period of that war is the period during which the city was shelled from August 1991 until June 1992. Within this period, from November 1991 until January 1992, the shelling was the most severe. The JNA had pulled out of its barracks in the city and from a new position, bombarded Osijek. Most of the population fled, leaving some ten thousand people in the city. After the ceasefire in January 1992, 'the terrible bombardment was greatly reduced and the UN reported that some 40 shots were exchanged daily' (Curle 1995: 113). Around eight hundred people were killed and many more people were wounded (Jegen 1996: 14). The city, surrounded on three sides by Serb forces, continued to experience sporadic shooting and other war-related incidents until 1995, but was never overrun. Adam Curle commented that it was 'brilliantly defended' by Branimir Glavas, who later became the Zupan (governor) of the province (Curle 1995: 113).

Today, considerable mortar damage to buildings is still apparent, but repairs are gradually progressing as the economic climate improves. The population is now of mixed ethnicity, mainly Croats, some Serbs and a few other ethnic groups. Many of the population of all ethnicities who fled from this region as refugees have returned after the war, but employment is scarce and housing issues are very complex. Many of the houses left empty by fleeing families were taken over by local remaining residents, title deeds were lost or destroyed and proof of title and boundaries is now very difficult. In 1992, the Centar za mir (Centre for Peace, Non-Violence and Human Rights) came into being, addressing both the psychological and the social and human rights issues of the war. It has generated many new projects to meet local needs, one of which is a legal advice and advocacy centre to help local residents. Ten years later, it is thriving and increasingly active in the community.

Zupanja

Zupanja is a town with a population of around fifteen thousand people in Eastern Slavonia, on the River Sava, situated opposite Orasje in Bosnia. Since the two towns of Orasje and Zupanja are not for from the 'Posavina corridor' – a strip of land that connected the two main concentrations of Serb population during the 1991-95 war and the route for transport of supplies and reinforcements – they became a site of constant fighting. The two towns were subjected to initial bombing from the air and then sporadic artillery fire over the duration of the war and suffered heavy casualties. There had been a bridge over the river, but it was blown up in 1991. A ferry was the only way across the river until the US army established a floating raft-bridge to take essential supplies and passengers.

The town evacuated many of its population to safer areas, including professionals and even some spiritual advisors, leaving parishioners bereft of their spiritual leadership and professional support. The hospital continued to work, but with no ambulance service and with a staff shortfall of eight physicians (Curle 1995). The main school roof was damaged by artillery fire, but luckily the children were not there. Because of the irregular but constant shelling, it was too dangerous for the children in the town to go out to play, or to walk out in the open through the streets to school. Schools were forced to close, but brave teachers remained in the town and they went regularly to the local family houses to teach the children at home. The teaching style had been formal up until this time, but the new more informal style of teaching which developed during the war may subsequently have become a significant factor in the Mir i dobro approach to peacebuilding.

The war experience of Zupanja was one of sustained sporadic bombardment over years and the psychological impact of this on the community was intense, because people had to risk their lives each time they went out in the streets. Shelling was unpredictable. There was no 'safe' time to go out. Many families had pet or working dogs, which were by tradition kept outside, and in 1996 I was told that many of the family pets had 'gone mad' because of the noise of the constant shelling. Despite all this, Adam Curle commented, following one of his regular visits to Zupanja during the war, that the mayor and everyone he spoke to in the town was 'passionate for peace'. 'There is no angry talk of fighting back or revenge, no "ethnic" hostility. Instead there is much encouragement for the peace group' (Curle 1995). The 'peace group' Adam mentions is Mir i dobro, started in 1992 in the early stages of the war and one of the projects participating in the research.

In January 1992, a cease-fire was signed and a United Nations Protection Force (UNPROFOR) formed to protect a newly formed Republic of Srpska Krajina, the territory of which covered over 30% of the total area of Croatia, extending up to Osijek and on to the Hungarian border. In 1995, the Croatian military and police forces undertook joint operations, regaining most of its former territory, with the exception of Eastern Slavonia, Baranja and Western Sirmium. Many Croatian Serbs left the reclaimed regions in a mass exodus, flooding into Eastern Slavonia (Kruhonja 2000: 15). On 21 November 1995, the presidents of Bosnia-Hercegovina, Serbia and Croatia signed the Dayton Agreement, bringing the fighting to an end. From 1996-1998, the United Nations Transitional Administration for Eastern Slavonia (UNTAES) remained in control of Eastern Slavonia, Baranja and Western Sirmium, to oversee a peaceful reintegration of the community.

The United Nations' High Commissioner for Refugees (UNHCR) established that Eastern Croatia had the highest concentration of mass graves and missing persons in the country (UNHCR 1995). After the war, the population comprised a high percentage of Serbian refugees and the Croatian government commenced the task of guaranteeing human civil and minority rights to all residents. Katarina Kruhonja (2000: 16) writes that, by co-operation between UNTAES, local Serbian authorities, local and international non-governmental organisations and the Croatian Government, 'In two years, the territory was demilitarised without major incidents, public services and schools were reintegrated into the system and personal documents were issued to the majority of the residents who accepted Croatian citizenship'. Local elections were held at the end of the two-year period. A report by the Organisation for Security and Co-operation in Europe (OSCE), *Community Trauma in Eastern Croatia*, dated August 2002, gives details of the continuing effects of the war on the community in this area. By the year 2000, referring to the return of refugees and internally displaced persons, Katarina Kruhonja records that the 'political, legal and economic framework for return had not been created' leaving continuing problems of homelessness, unemployment, land disputes and contested property ownership. The work of the projects took place all through the 1991-1995 War and then the Centar za mir and CWWPP, continued for the following ten years; Mir i dobro and the Bench We Share slowly reduced their work and new projects like Dodir nade developed. The focus group discussions took place between 2000 and 2003. It is now 2006. I have now had the opportunity to look back on the research, to reflect on events that have happened since then, and, with the project staff, to consider the work of the projects from the beginning until the present time, which includes exciting new developments – recently the Centar za mir has created a new Community Mediation Project under the leadership of Sonja Stanic and it is proving highly successful, providing mediation services in Osijek and Baranja and with a planned service for Vukovar.

Eastern Slavonia: post-conflict recovery

In my research, I wanted to consider the perceptions of the focus groups in the context of Curle's work and his theoretical approach to peacemaking, so I have included here information which may help to explain the social and economic situation in which the projects are now working. It may also help to clarify the nature and extent of Curle's relationship with the staff and his influence on the work of the projects which participated in the case study.

Centar za mir (The Centre for Peace, Non-Violence and Human Rights)

The development and work of the Centar za mir in Osijek is described in *Another Way* (Curle 1995: 111-130). It is also described in *Sign of Hope* (Jegen 1996), a book which was written about the Centar za mir following a two-week visit by a Catholic nun, Sr Jegen, to Osijek in 1995, towards the end of the war. A subsequent report funded by the European Union provides more formal documentation of the work of the centre (Kruhonja 2000). The account here is derived from these sources, also from informal conversations I had over the years with Curle and some of the many people involved with the centre.

Osijek now has a population of around a hundred thousand people, with some thirty thousand additional refugees. The present population may have changed from the former mix of mainly Catholic Croats with some twenty per cent Orthodox Serbs, some Hungarians and some Muslims. On Easter Day, 2002, the Catholic cathedral in the main square was packed with thousands of standing worshippers. Politically, there has been progress in the city. The new Zupan (mayor) is described by Katarina Kruhonja as 'a peace-worker' and he is a member of the Centar za mir. The Centar za mir staff spoke with pride of his conciliatory approach to community conflict and protests, his willingness to listen and the beneficial influence this has had on the local community.

Economic problems persist. In the fields around the city, there were still patches where mines remained for years after the war, preventing the redevelopment of agriculture. Some local people told me that there were 'hundreds and thousands of mines' during the war. Nobody knew how many actually remain and perhaps they are all gone now, because there is evidence of farmers resuming their agriculture in most areas. The roads surrounding Osijek are now safe to drive and Osijek is gradually gaining trade and redeveloping its industry. The historic old buildings and churches are being repaired. The gymnasium (secondary school), the university and the hospital are all fully functioning. Galleries, cinemas and Internet cafes are open and thriving. Beside the beautiful bridge over the River Drava is a new park, with a playground, zoo and an open-air swimming pool. The Osijek airport is operating again and the tourists are coming back. There is still, however, a continuing problem of unemployment because the local factories making furniture, soap and shoes were destroyed in the war and there is insufficient money at the moment to replace and update the damaged machinery. Many of the groceries and luxury goods now sold in the local shops are imported.

Katarina Kruhonja, a founder and subsequently Director of the Centar za mir, is a doctor, formerly a specialist in nuclear medicine at the University Hospital of Osijek. She is also a mother and a member of the Catholic Church. She describes her religious belief as central in her life. At the start of the war, she endeavoured to create an influence for peace in public prayer meetings outside the army headquarters in Osijek and broadcasting prayers on the local radio network.

Krunoslav Sukic ('Kruno') the co-founder of the Centar za mir, is a gentle man, a teacher, philosopher, father and an atheist committed to non-violence, human dignity and rigorous intellectual exploration. Katarina Kruhonja says:

> It was during the shelling of Osijek; ... I met him and a few other intellectuals and we were talking about what could be done in this situation and what we could do. From this meeting only the two of us stayed together in discussion and from those discussions the Centre started. (Jegen 1996: 20)

Their families had been evacuated and they had time to talk and to plan. Katarina Kruhonja explained:

> We accepted that we could not stop the war – that we could not influence what was going on, but we were responsible for the future, for

our children and for the generations that were coming and for a new State that was just beginning. (Jegen 1996: 21)

Other like-minded people soon joined Katarina Kruhonja and Kruno Sukic. A local teacher, Dusanka Ilic and Branka Kaselj, administrator, registered the Centar za mir with the anti-war organisation, Anti-Ratna Kampanja (ARK) in Zagreb. Others joined them. An ARK peace activist, Vesna Terselic, mentioned their peacemaking activities to Adam Curle, inviting him to visit Osijek. In April/May 1992, Curle visited Osijek for a few days with Nick Lewer, Judith Large, Erich Bachman and others (Jegen 1996: 22). The visitors contributed to community activities in the university, centred on topics relevant to peacemaking and this was effectively the launch of the Centar za mir. Adam Curle thought that further planning and discussions might be helpful. He therefore returned a few weeks later, in June 1992, to facilitate a workshop for twenty people, sharing their experiences, developing a sense of interconnectedness and exploring together ideas for the future. This workshop was held in less formal circumstances.

It will be difficult, if not impossible, to assess the extent of the influence of Curle's approach on the project members who have come to know him well during his long contact with the Centar za mir. The first workshop in June 1992 must have been very influential, providing a context for the theoretical foundations of peacemaking laid down between Curle and the Centar za mir at that time.

Curle later wrote about this workshop in *Another Way* (Curle 1995: 119-120). This description is summarised from his account. A workshop participant described her reactions to the war as feeling '…like a fist around my heart' (Curle 1992g). He explains that he realised that the participants hoped for some kind of help in their difficult situation to function fully as individuals and as a team. Curle believes that we need

> …to escape from the mindless automatism that governs so much of our lives, from senseless worries and fears, from prejudice, from ego cherishing and irritability, from vanity, from illusions of guilt and badness, from belief in separate existence. These and all other negative emotions are like a fist around the heart. (Curle 1995: 119)

Curle felt that he could not teach these ideas as a skill. It is here that his long-held philosophy of living peacefully by direct action, rather than talking about peace, came into play. One has 'to be rather than to do' (Curle 1995:

119). They used the workshop for 'sharing and mutual help; the learning would come to all of us from this, rather than any formal instruction. In fact, the first lesson would be that we all have something to give and something to learn' (Curle 1995: 119).

The workshop was not entirely unstructured. Together the participants and Curle devised role-plays and exercises. Using the metaphor of the fist around the heart, the participants considered what things made the fist tighter or looser, using awareness and listening exercises. Curle emphasised to the group his personal belief in the essential goodness of people and that '...if we approach people with respect and expecting them to behave decently, it would evoke their better nature. But if one expected the worst, one would find it' (Curle 1995: 120). Curle and the participants explored their 'blind spots, prejudices, irrational reactions including anxieties, dislikes and guilt; things that could impair our judgment and our relations with colleagues and others' (Curle 1995: 120). He adds, 'We considered our interconnectedness with all human beings, with all life and with the planet. In doing so, we tried to rid ourselves of conventional views of the dichotomised self and other, friend and enemy' (Curle 1995: 120).

Curle adds that, in the workshop, in the context of Osijek and generally,

> We traced the connections between what we had been discovering and different facets of violent situations; we explored these from human, economic and political points of view, considering refugees, homelessness, psychological and physical traumas of war, separation of families, social dislocation, deprivation and poverty. (Curle 1995: 120)

Finally the participants 'learned something of the principles of non-violent protest and conflict resolution and thought about their application in particular situations (Curle 1995: 120). This sharing of ideas, he felt, generated psychological change, noting that references to 'I' and 'me' changed to reference to 'we' in discussion of future plans (Curle 1995: 120).

By the summer of 1992, the Centar za mir had premises in rooms of the cloister of a former monastery. It began a programme of education and human rights advocacy. Some team members confronted and reasoned with the military when they attempted to unlawfully evict people from their homes, risking their own safety. Katarina and Kruno were personally threatened for such activities. Katarina later commented that this was a moment of great importance for her, because, having decided to ignore the threats despite having the responsibilities of motherhood, she felt somehow liberated on a spiritual level and empowered to continue work which she felt was vitally important to the cause of peace.

The Centar za mir places considerable importance on meeting the needs of the local community. Its early emphasis was on a 'listening project' in which the centre members held meetings with many groups in the local community. This led to the planning of workshops and activities specifically designed to meet local needs. The Centar za mir avoided the mistake made by so many non-governmental organisations offering post-war humanitarian aid, which is to offer interventions and facilities without sufficient local consultation. The Centar za mir is now a structured organisation with around 100 members and 150 associates. It is non-partisan and describes its work as

> Non-governmental, non-partisan and non-profit citizens' associationfocused on working for peace, protection of human rights and freedoms, promotion and implementation of creative methods of problem solving and conflict resolution on individual, group and political level. (Centar za mir 2000)

The work of the centre now reaches into many areas of the country and includes civil rights education, legal and practical assistance, community mediations for housing problems necessary to assist refugees returning home, facilitation of self-help groups for those who have suffered loss and bereavement, groups for parents, peace education programmes and psycho-social programmes for women who have suffered domestic violence. It has designed and implemented a number of innovative psycho-social programmes, including 'peace teams' of local volunteers of different ethnicities and international helpers to assist in re-integrating the multi-ethnic community, bringing 1,100 people from opposing ethnic groups together.

Between 1992 and 2000, five hundred teachers working with the project have given peace education workshops to over 5.000 pupils and students. Current programmes include community mediation training and many educational and self-help workshops for support with social situations: anxiety and stress; divorce, refugees, parents of children with schizophrenia or other mental illness and a wide variety of other topics.

Hundreds of people have participated in the workshops and groups over the years, and displaced families have been enabled to visit their former homes. In 1998, Katarina Kruhonja, director of the Centar za mir and Vesna Terselic shared an award from the Right Livelihood Foundation (generally known as the 'Alternative Nobel Peace Prize'). The Centar za mir has now grown into an organisation well known throughout Europe, attracting visitors from across the world.

The work of the centre has developed further in response to the needs of the local community. Requests for legal advice and advocacy on housing, human rights and property issues led to the formation of a legal centre, which is now housed in a separate office and staffed by a group of lawyers, with responsibility for advice, legal education of the public and with an active caseload. They have handled more than 3,999 human rights cases and over 20,000 people have received legal aid (Centar za mir 2000).

The centre has reached out to the local community through the media and publications, including 'Burek', a newsletter for youth. It has communicated with over 200,000 residents in Osijek and the surrounding areas through publications and distribution of materials concerning tolerance and human rights and the development of a democratic society. The centre now has two offices. The main office, provided by the government, is in the main street in Osijek. It is used for administration, meetings and training. The second office, a short distance away, is used for the legal and human rights work. The legal staff explained that separate funding specifically for the legal work continues and is sufficient to continue to employ the lawyers and sustain the work of that office. The Centar za mir relies on donations for its main funding and in 2002 it lost its European grant, so money is now shorter and staffing levels had to be reduced.

In May 2002, just after the case study, the Centar za mir celebrated its tenth anniversary with their bi-annual Week of Peace and Culture. The first 'week of Peace and Culture' in the monastery garden in 1992 was described by Curle as 'a wonderful occasion', with music, dancing and workshops on peace, mediation and the creative solving of conflicts, intermingling serious talks with performances by the children, parties, feasts and poetry. In 2002, for the first time since the war, after great efforts of persuasion and diplomacy by the Centar za mir staff in overcoming the doubts and anxieties of local government, the police and the local theatre administration, Djordje Balasevic, a singer and peace activist from Vojvodina was invited to perform in Osijek. It was a movingly peaceful and popular event, with some three hundred people attending and a public demonstration of the work of the Centar za mir towards peaceful reintegration of the population.

In 2004, the Centar za mir developed a new mediation project, (Medijacija Centar za mir), under the very able and committed leadership of Sonja Stanic and funded by donations through the British Embassy, to train community mediators in three towns in Eastern Slavonia: Beli Manastir, Osijek and Vukovar. They have now in one year trained groups of mediators in two regions and the third, Vukovar, is under way. The Medijacija Centar za mir is negotiating for premises to be provided by local government for mediations and the volunteers, having received training free of charge, will in return offer a free mediation service to the community. The Medijacija Centar za mir has already carried out mediations in these local communities and it is hoped that the provision of permanent premises with an administrator will create not only a service, but a new ethos within these areas. Those mediators who have received training include lawyers, judges, teachers, other professionals and volunteers. This pioneering project coincides with new legislation now in force in Croatia to empower parties to engage in mediation within the court process in specified circumstances and the ministry of justice is now in the process of planning implementation of new mediation systems within the courts, in co-operation with the judiciary. I feel very proud to be associated with this project as its first consultant supervisor and we plan that at the end of the first three years of the project Medijacija Centar za mir, the supervision role will be taken over entirely by local staff.

From the first visit in early 1992, Curle visited the Centar za mir regularly, three or four times each year, accompanied by his wife Anne when she was able to do so. They continued their visits until prevented by unavoidable circumstances. Adam is now almost ninety years old and he is no longer able to travel there and both he and Anne are much missed. Both are held in great respect and love by the centre staff and members, not only as mentors but also as good friends. The staff from the Centar za mir, Bench We Share and Mir i dobro have many times mentioned their appreciation of the work and friend-ship of Adam, Anne and all the people who visited them regularly during and after the war, encouraging them in their efforts and helping with funding. This commitment made by Adam Curle and others to personal long-term support and encouragement is reflected by a similar attitude from many staff and volunteers of these projects towards those in the community with whom they work.

The Bench We Share Project (Zajednicka klupa)

The Bench We Share has many achievements. Dusanka Ilic was involved with the Centar za mir in Osijek from 1992. In 1994, they could not enter the occupied territories of Baranja, Eastern Slavonia and Western Sermium. Dusanka and others from the Centar za mir began working with the Meeting House Project, organising meetings in the neutral territory of Hungary for people divided by the war. The Bench We Share project was formed to undertake reconciliation work at grassroots level in the local communities, and in 1996, when freedom of movement was allowed into Baranja, an area of Croatia controlled by UNTAES, the project began to respond to the need for re-establishing trust and the reconstruction of the multi-cultural community in that region. The political and physical opening up of the area after the war encouraged the centre to work towards reintegration of returning refugees with the remaining population and to counter the sense of alienation and separation experienced by some members of the community. The Bench We Share project provides community mediations, psychosocial support in villages where there is tension, peace education and empowerment of local peace groups in villages in Eastern Croatia.

The name of the Bench We Share (Zajednicka klupa) is perhaps derived from the old, possibly Turkish custom of 'divan', still practised in some areas of Croatia, where people sit together outside their homes on wooden benches in the summer sunshine and winter good weather, to talk and share news. The return to a communal sharing of space and discussion symbolised by the wooden bench was perceived as an important step in inter-ethnic reconciliation. Dusanka Ilic invented a greeting, 'Palisood'. I heard it being used, and asked her what this word meant, since it did not sound Croatian? Dusanka explained that it is an acronym, meaning 'Peace and love in spite of our differences'. It is still used – an email came with it recently! All those associated with the project are presented with a beautifully hand-carved wooden bench. Adam Curle has one proudly displayed in his study.

The Bench We Share, with Dusanka Ilic, welcomed Gordana Kovac as administrator in 1999 and the project widened its role, undertaking community tasks and encouraging people of all ethnicities to work together in shared tasks in which they could take the initiative and responsibility. An example of these local projects is the restoration of a park and a castle in Darda. From this work and regional discussions, other independent peace groups arose.

Inspired by the story of the recovery of Coventry after the second world war, the Centar za mir and the Bench We Share project worked in co-operation with the Department of Reconciliation of the University of Coventry and the staff of Coventry Cathedral Community for Reconciliation. Together, they ran a series of workshops bringing together ethnic groups who had been alienated by the war, with some residential visits for selected participants in the UK. These pioneering workshops for post-war reconciliation in Croatia earned recognition with the Coventry Cathedral Cross of Nails award.

The Rev Clive Fowle has been associated with the Bench We Share for several years and the project constituted a case study in his research (Fowle 1999).

In recognising the importance of the work of the project, he cites the Rev. Dr Stephen Plant:

> It is clear that small-scale relationship building projects, such as the Bench We Share, are of the highest importance as the larger aid agencies move on elsewhere. Reconciliation will take a generation and more. And, like all relationships, this requires dedicated work by a committed few who refuse to let the effects of war destroy their essential humanity. (Plant 1998 in Fowle 1999: 106)

The Bench We Share association is now independent, run by Dusanka Ilic and Gordana Kovac. They have many ideas for further reconciliation through community projects, but at the moment funds are needed to continue their work. They are working in liaison with CWWPP to develop new projects in Vukovar and they may become involved with the Jewish community there in the rebuilding of the synagogue. They are also developing a new project, Deset Zrna (Ten Grains) – the theme of which is to encourage inter-ethnic co-operation at grassroots level to donate food for people suffering from hunger across the world.

Dodir nade, created in 2001 by the Centar za mir, is now carrying forward the work of the Coventry Project.

Dodir nade (Touch of Hope)

In October 2001, the Centar za mir held an international consultation in Coventry to design and develop a new project. Its Croatian name, Dodir nade, literally translated, means 'Touch of Hope'. It was designed to continue the Coventry project begun by Bench We Share, developing it in new directions, providing an inter-faith and multi-ethnic forum for the healing of the psycho-logical and spiritual hurts of war and to promote reconciliation. With its first director, the Rev. Marijan Persinovic, a number of professional staff and volunteers from the Centar za mir and the Rev Clive Fowle, it facilitated a series of workshops in Croatia. For its first two years, it also ran annual resi-dential courses in the UK. designed to promote awareness and inter-ethnic tolerance and understanding.

Dodir nade continues to run a rolling programme of training in Eastern Slavonia and it is supported by the Community for Reconciliation's 'Footprint', an organisation formed and funded by a number of churches in the UK. They raise support for the work through charitable donations and fundraising events.

Dodir nade will have completed the fifth year of its programme by 2006. The project workshops are proving popular in the three local communities of Vukovar, Osijek and Baranja where they are currently offered and it is hoped that the project will extend its work if funding permits. The project publishes a newsletter in the UK, *Footprint* (Fowle 2002).

Mir i dobro (Peace and Good)

Zupanja shows considerable evidence of post-war recovery. Many build-ings have been repaired and the number of shops is increasing, but local residents told me that there is insufficient employment for all and since the end of the war in 1995, many people have not yet found full time work because local industry and agriculture have not yet been re-established. The local bank, along with others, suffered a post-war financial crisis, causing further loss of money invested by some Zupanja townspeople (Croatia National Bank Council 1999). The population of Zupanja comprises mainly Croats with only a small minority of other nationalities, but I have not been able to find any helpful statistics. During the case study, local residents from Zupanja mentioned the predominance of Croats in conversation, adding that they have experienced few problems with social inter-ethnic integration of the commu-nity. This, perhaps, reflects the peaceful attitudes noted earlier by Adam Curle (1995). By the banks of the River Sava, there is now a memorial cross for the dead, standing close to the site where a splendid new bridge is in the process of planning and development.

In 1992, during the war, Mara and Stirpan Cʻovic, Djurdja and Zvonko Zivkovic, Tomislav Lanka, Evica Lincic and other local residents founded the project Mir i dobro. They were later joined by a psychologist, Visnja Matic and a number of local volunteers – mainly housewives, teachers and social workers. All wanted to help the local community to adjust to the trauma of the war, to re-build trust and confidence and, acknowledging the prevalence of anger and emotional pain, they were particularly concerned to encourage non-violent attitudes in the children of the community. During the 1991-95 War, they organised pioneering meetings and workshops for groups of local people interested in helping their community. In 1996 and 1997, Mir i dobro ran workshops for people working with children in the community, combining counselling and peacemaking activities which could then be used for the benefit of local children.

Many members of the workshops were teachers. They were concerned to find ways to help the children in their schools, finding difficulty within the prevailing formality of the education system in creating an environment in which children could express their feelings. Very subtly they introduced into the local school curriculum time for discussion within the classes in art and literature. In 1997, Deborah Curle and I were invited to see a bright and optimistic display of creative art and poetry made by pupils of a village school just outside Zupanja, dedicated to their hope for future peace. This was just one example of the impact of Mir i dobro within the local community.

During the war, Mir i dobro volunteers met in each other's homes for mutual encouragement and support. Its members no longer meet together regularly, but individually some continue to undertake voluntary work in the community, including support groups for people injured by mines, workshops for parents and children, and direct work with children in need in their locality. I do not have details of all the projects and voluntary work carried out by members since 1996, but some are known. Tomislav Lanka, a teacher, author and local historian, facilitates peace-education activities and exhibitions in local schools; and Djurdja Zivkovic, a teacher, is currently involved in a day care centre offering creative work and group therapy for children with special needs. In Easter 2002, an exhibition of artwork by the children at the local day care centre was held in the Museum in Zupanja. Visnja Matic, a clinical psychologist, continues to work with children and is currently completing postgraduate training in Gestalt therapy. She now works in a residential children's village. Mara and Stirpan Covic would like to start a small local factory for refugees making clothes, providing work, an income and training.

Some of the children of the Mir I dobro members became involved in work for peace. Sonja and Jessica Zivkovic helped brilliantly as translators in the workshops. Sadly, Jessica was later killed in a tragic accident, and she is remembered by us all with much love and appreciation of her work with us.

The Coalition for Work with Psychotrauma and Peace (CWWPP)

In Vukovar, rebuilding continues, but slowly. Lack of funding for building and unemployment continues to cause considerable hardship for local people. The hospital is partly repaired. Two Catholic churches are being restored and there are plans to restore the Jewish synagogue, which was destroyed in the second world war. The railway station remains in ruins and the nearest station is at Vincovci, a few kilometres away. Mines have been cleared from the road-sides and travel on the main road between Vukovar and Osijek is no longer hazardous in bad weather, when it was once dangerous to leave the tarmac surface. Most fields are also now cleared of mines and agriculture is resuming.

Local trade and industry is slowly growing and small businesses, shops and cafés are opening up. Close to the newly restored Hotel Dunav on the banks of the Danube is a large and beautiful memorial cross for all those lost in the war, with outdoor candle lamps kept constantly alight in memory of those dead and for those who are still missing. I was told by local residents that the mass grave nearby at Ovcara contains, they think, the remains of two hundred or more Croats. There is today very little public mention in Vukovar of the Serbs who were killed during the 1991-95 war and, although there may be other graves, no further information could be elicited about losses amongst the Serbs or other ethnicities.

Social integration continues to present difficulties for some areas, particu- larly Vukovar, because many Serbian refugees from other towns came to live in Vukovar at the end of the war and the Croats who continue to live in the region, are possibly now outnumbered; they find it difficult to integrate socially with those whom they perceive as former enemies. The schools are open, but ethnic segregation continues. Lessons take place in two separate sessions – one in the morning and one in the afternoon for Serbs and Croats respectively. One focus group remarked that in Vukovar, some local cafés are known to favour either Serb or Croat customers and that children of different ethnicities do not play together. There are a few Roma remaining in the area. From conversation with local residents, I understand that the Roma continue to be politically marginalized and socially ostracised by all the other ethnic groups.

The Coalition for Work with Psychotrauma and Peace (CWWPP) was conceptualised at a meeting of the Balkan Group of International Physicians for the Prevention of Nuclear War in 1994 and founded in 1995 with the help of Dr Charles Tauber, who became its Director. Since that year, the project has continued to operate under his direction, in cooperation with international organizations and local agencies. CWWPP has been active in Eastern Croatia since 1996, in Brcko since 1997 and has had a small presence in Vojvodina and in the Posavina region of Bosnia Herzegovina. The information that follows about the background of the CWWPP is taken from its Mandate (Coalition for Work with Psychotrauma and Peace 2000).

The CWWPP works with individuals, families, groups, the community and society, combining the treatment of psychological trauma, social reconstruction and peacebuilding.

The Mandate describes the issues with which the CWWPP is involved as including:

1. Health, in particular widespread psychological and physical health issues resulting from long-term conflict-related stress.
2. Techniques of non-violent conflict resolution and conflict prevention.
3. Reconciliation within and between groups in the community.
4. Community building and social reconstruction, including 'democratization'.
5. Return and reintegration of displaced persons and refugees.
6. Human rights 'in conjunction with other aspects of our work' (Coalition for Work With Psychotrauma and Peace 2000).

The techniques used by the CWWPP include education and capacity building, the formation and support of local groups, networks and coalitions, supervision and research. The CWWPP mandate provides information about the region, which is cited here because it indicates the organisation's perceptions of local issues and its approach to the work of the project.

We estimate that somewhere between 5% and 15% of the population, depending on the area concerned, has been in prisons, concentration camps or prisoner of war camps and thus has been physically mistreated in some way. This ratio is even higher among the refugee population. In our experience, there have been few people in the region in which we are working who have not been traumatized. While this varies to some degree, errors in assessment in the past have, in our view underestimated rather than overestimated the epidemiological studies of the physical or mental health of the regions in which we are working. Furthermore, there is little sociological data to indicate how societies have been affected by the War. In addition, there is no data with regard to the aspirations or the interests of the indigenous population.

A number of seriously affected groups have been ignored. Three groups which come to mind most readily are: Men, including ex-soldiers and policemen who have frequently seen and have sometimes carried out things that no human beings should see or do. Youth, who are likely to be ignored and who have the potential for the future for either great good or great problems. Such persons are also likely to transmit their traumas to future generations if not treated. The elderly, who frequently cannot care for themselves. We feel that these three groups require special attention. This is not to say, however, that other groups (including women) are presently getting adequate care. (Coalition for Work with Psychotrauma and Peace 2000)

The CWWPP continues to address the needs of the local community by the provision of therapy and counselling training groups for War veterans, self help groups and individual therapy and the project is involved in the plans for the future rebuilding of the synagogue, but the work of the CWWPP in the community is currently restricted by a lack of funding. Dr Charles Tauber has served with the project in Vukovar with great courage and commitment since 1996. The pressures of work and the continued uncertainty of funding under-standably create physical and emotional demands on the project staff and volunteers. Their work in the early days was carried out in very difficult conditions because much of Vukovar was destroyed in the war, and although the physical conditions have now improved, the work is still demanding and the project needs additional resources to enable staff to carry out the management and fieldwork tasks that they would like to offer the local community.

Psychological interventions for the treatment of posttraumatic stress in Croatia following the 1991-1995 war

Before writing about the case study, I am setting out a little of the background to the treatment of posttraumatic stress in Eastern Slavonia following the war and at the present time. The case study took place in the context of a variety of therapeutic approaches to the treatment of PTSD commonly used within the medical and psychiatric services and humanitarian aid projects in

Croatia. I wanted to find out from the focus groups (among other things) whether the present therapeutic approaches in their view meet local needs and whether additional approaches, not currently used, might be helpful in the context of healing the psychological effects of trauma following war.

This overview of the therapeutic approaches most commonly used in Croatia generally and Eastern Slavonia in particular, is not the result of a formal survey, but simply based upon informal enquiries through discussion with the project members and correspondence with psychiatrists, medical practitioners, psychologists and non-governmental organisations in Zagreb and in Eastern Slavonia.

1. Trauma treatment: practice regulation, ethics and training

In Croatia, psychiatric practice is regulated by the Croatian Medical Bar. The Croatian Psychological Society regulates the practice of clinical psychology. Currently, the practice of psychotherapy and counselling are not regulated, but training is available from non-governmental and private organisations. Psychiatrists are trained at the medical school of the University of Zagreb. Psychologists are trained at the Department of Psychology at various Universities, including the Universities of Zagreb, Rijeka and Zadar. Some psychiatrists and psychologists now practising in Croatia have received training abroad.

2. Commonly used therapeutic approaches for psychological trauma in Croatia

In order to find out about the types of therapies used to treat trauma related psychiatric illness and psychological trauma generally in Croatia and in particular in Eastern Slavonia, I made informal enquiries by email of two psychiatrists in Zagreb, both practitioners, one of whom teaches in the University; a psychiatrist in Osijek and three clinical psychologists from Osijek and Zupanja. In Vukovar I spoke with Dr Charles Tauber and with one clinical psychologist and I researched the Croatian Medical Journal.

The consensus amongst these practitioners is that the main therapeutic approaches currently used by mental health professionals generally in Croatia are psychoanalysis, cognitive and behavioural therapy, Gestalt therapy and transactional analysis. Other treatment approaches were mentioned as in less frequent use, notably systemic family therapy, neuro-linguistic programming, reality therapy and rational emotive therapy. After the research finished, I heard in 2006 that the Rogerian person-centred approach to psychotherapy is currently developing both in use and popularity.

Other therapeutic approaches mentioned as used in Eastern Slavonia included bibliotherapy; biodynamic bodywork, eye movement rapid desensitisation and reprogramming (EMDR), neuro-linguistic programming (NLP), rational emotive therapy (RET), reality therapy, reiki, spiritual healing, Rogerian person-centred approach, socio-educational approach, specialist trauma treatments (not specified) and systemic family therapy. The Rogerian person-centred approach was mentioned as underpinning the general counselling ethos of one non-governmental organisation's treatment programme, but none of the practitioners in that organisation specifically implemented person-centred therapy as a discrete therapeutic approach at that time. Critical incident de-briefing (CID) and de-fusing are sometimes used following traumatic events. Some practitioners reported that they had heard of the use of specialist trauma treatments, but they were not aware which specific treatments were available. Some practitioners mentioned that clinical psychologists use EMDR for the relief of intrusive symptoms, but none of the practitioners in the case study used EMDR themselves.

I was grateful to Prof. Dr Nikola Mandic, psychiatrist and head of the psychiatric unit at the Clinical Hospital, Osijek, for finding time to talk with me about the treatment of psychological trauma in Osijek during and after the War. He kindly gave me a copy of a paper on PTSD that he had co-authored (Mandic and Javornik 1998). At that time of our discussion, many of the psychiatric in-patients in Osijek hospital were, in Dr Mandic's view, experiencing conditions related to trauma or transitions, by which I understood him to mean the effects of loss, bereavement and trauma resulting from internal displacement, refugee status, or other disruptions of family, work and social life. The common symptoms that he noted were PTSD, adjustment problems and anxiety for the future.

3. Resources for trauma treatment in Eastern Slavonia

The hospital at Osijek serves the whole population of the area and has departments for biological psychiatry, social psychiatry and pharmacotherapy. In 2002, there were a number of specialist treatment clinics, including one for PTSD. Other facilities for the area then included three 'day hospitals', one of which treats PTSD using therapeutic communities, psychodynamic therapy and reality therapy. There are also two smaller units: one offering residential care and therapy for neurosis and borderline personality states and the other providing psychiatric care and therapy for children and adolescents. There is also a day centre for psychotrauma, with a telephone help line, and there are clubs for war veterans. In addition, just outside Osijek, there is now a 'village' facility offering residential and psychological care for children.

Psychotic symptoms are usually treated with pharmacotherapy, with a short stay in hospital and then discharge home. Many of the hospital psychiatric patients had co-diagnoses of somatic illness including asthma, bronchitis, myocardial infarcts, ulcers, cancer of the breast, rectum and colon, diabetes, allergies, migraines and psychomotor disorders. This ties in with the observations of the focus group participants and the literature review, where it is noted that the hormonal imbalances of traumatic stress may be experienced as somatic symptoms, or lead to physical illness, although further research is needed to explore any direct causal link. The co-existence of physical and psychological symptomology and the fluidity of the symptoms of posttraumatic stress may lead to misdiagnoses or to difficulty in providing appropriate treatment. Prof Dr Mandic's paper on PTSD refers to problems with the diagnostic criteria, insufficient therapeutic procedures and the need to balance social cultural and political factors with medical and psychiatric elements in assessment procedures (Mandic and Javornik 1998: 7).

Prof Dr Mandic supports community based approaches for the treatment of PTSD, including work in schools and raising public awareness of issues related to family organisation, parenting and drug use. A particular post-war problem that he identifies is the disruption of attachments following transitions and bereavement and he mentioned the particular difficulties of fatherless families. The approaches of music therapy, group therapy and play therapy are used with children who have lost one or both of their parents.

Chapter 5

Case study in trauma, therapy and conflict: the views of five focus groups from Croatia

Chapter Four provided a contextual background for a case study to explore the experience of the community in Eastern Slavonia during the 1991-1995 war and in the post-war recovery period from 1995 to the present time, focusing on Osijek, Vukovar and Zupanja, the areas in which the five projects participating in the focus group discussions function. The projects were then introduced, following on from the earlier exploration of psychological trauma and posttraumatic stress in Chapter 3. Chapter 4 also included a brief overview of the current therapeutic interventions available in Eastern Slavonia for the treatment of posttraumatic stress.

This chapter describes the views and perceptions of the five projects on the topics of the present peacefulness or unpeacefulness in the communities of Vukovar, Osijek and Zupanja; the therapeutic approaches used in these communities to alleviate posttraumatic stress; and, from the perspective of healing the psychological trauma of war, the ways in which the focus group participants would like to take the tasks of peacemaking forward.

In Chapter 6, I will bring together all the data gathered in the research and literature reviews, exploring the potential impact of the research on Adam Curle's approach to psychological change in peacemaking, in the light of the current debates on peacemaking and the criticisms made by the focus group participants of current approaches to the treatment of trauma in Eastern Slavonia.

The context of the focus group discussions

In action-based participatory research, the researcher is both subject and object of the research. To some extent therefore, because of my long-term involvement with the work of the projects, inevitably there must be some influence on the focus group discussions, however hard I might have tried to remain as unobtrusive and neutral as possible. In order to understand and evaluate any possible influence that I might have had, I will say something here about my background and association with the five participating projects over the years.

My professional background is a combination of disciplines. I qualified as a lawyer in 1975, in a general practice including human rights and crime. Since 1980 my practice focus has been mainly in child and family law. A gradual progression from law to therapy then seemed to me to be entirely logical. As a lawyer I could see that the courts provide external control, but I wanted to help people at a deeper level to effect permanent change to improve family life and relationships. Psychotherapy provided the means to help people to effect enduring internal change, and from 1989, I have worked with individuals, children and families in both therapy and forensic assessments. Mediation was a very natural next step to facilitate changes in family and community relationships. I love to work with groups and so have been involved for a long time in lecturing and course facilitation.

At the request of Mir i dobro, I had travelled with Adam Curle to Zupanja in 1996 to co-facilitate a workshop focusing on work with children towards recovery from posttraumatic stress, with two other psychotherapists, Tracey Brown and Adam's daughter Deborah. The workshop was very successful and I made friendships with some of the participants that continue to this day. In 1997, at the request of Mir i dobro, Deborah Curle and I visited Zupanja again to co-facilitate a second workshop in peacemaking. Tracey was not with us for that second workshop, but she had made a lasting impression on the participants with her openness and her willingness to express her feelings, particularly in a poem she had written which she shared and which touched them deeply. They remembered her with affection and some had kept a copy of her poem and had felt inspired to write poetry themselves. The second visit with Deborah was wonderful and full of hope. It was summertime and in that period, one of the young girls who had translated for us in the first workshop was getting married. The young bride and bridegroom walked through their village in a marriage procession followed by their family and friends, followed by an informal, moving service in the local church in which a relative from Zagreb sang 'Ave Maria' – the sights and sounds of that wedding created a lasting memory for me, full of a feeling of joy and hope for the future.

During 1996, I visited the Centar za mir with Adam and met with the directors and some of the staff and volunteer helpers for the first time. In subsequent years I have been back to Croatia many times, visiting the projects taking part in the case study, and I became a Consultant to the Coalition for Work With Psychotrauma and Peacemaking (CWWPP) and to the other projects in mediation and psychotherapy.

In autumn 2001, I facilitated an exciting international consultation held in Coventry, UK, to which the members of the Centar za mir and Bench We Share projects came, together with people from the UK interested in helping to found a new project which the consultation group named Dodir nade (Touch of Hope). Those present included the Rev Clive Fowle, representatives from the Community For Reconciliation, Footprints, Coventry cathedral and other churches. The first three years' workshops and rolling programme for Dodir nade was designed and developed. Some of the people participating in the case study in 2003 were involved in that original consultation and it is so good to see how in the present day, Dodir nade is still a thriving project and its rolling programme of workshops and community based trauma healing continues.

I had also kept in touch by email with the projects and had developed friendships with some of the project members. My role for them is therefore a mixture of professional and personal roles: friend, professional consultant, mediator, psychotherapist and from time to time, a workshop facilitator. It was really good to be able to go back to Croatia and stay in Osijek for three months with Tom and Erna Kruhonja. I cannot thank Tom and Erna enough for their hospitality and for welcoming me into their home. The Centar za mir was so helpful in organising the focus group discussions and in finding time to carry them out. I wanted in return to give something back to the Centar za mir and the other projects, so during that time I facilitated around ten workshops and team building sessions with the Centar za mir and provided consultancy and mediations on a voluntary basis for other non-governmental organisations in the area.

Reflections on gathering, presentation and analysis of the research data from the case study

Reflections on gathering data from the focus group discussions

The data from the case study was derived using the method and methodology of a combination of content analysis, grounded theory and heuristics. Data was gathered through participatory action research with individuals and focus groups, categorised and then considered in the context of the literature reviews relating to peacemaking and to posttraumatic stress through a process of internal reflection incorporating images, understandings and interpretations using my observation, intuition and tacit knowing.

Separate focus group discussions were held with each of the five participating projects. All the discussions were tape recorded with the consent of the participants, to assist subsequent transcription. The discussions were mainly in English, with immediate translations by experienced professional interpreters into Croatian as necessary. The Mir i dobro focus group discussion was conducted mainly in Croatian (with immediate interpretation into English for me) and the transcript was very kindly transcribed and translated into English by Visnja Matic, a psychologist and a good friend, to whom I owe many thanks for all her help. I feel very sorry sometimes that I don't have Adam Curle's fluency in languages, but although I have tried to learn Croatian, English has had to remain our medium for communication. We have been lucky that there have been so many excellent and highly experienced translators for workshops, focus groups and other events over the years – too many to mention each translator individually – but all of whom have provided their skills for the cause of peace.

Of course, a transcription of an audio recording cannot record body language, or the non-verbal aspects of group interaction. I therefore had to rely on notes, journal entries and memory of events to supplement the transcriptions with recollections of the body language and contextual information to aid analysis.

The data for the case study is drawn from transcriptions of the tape recordings of the focus group meetings, personal notes and journal entries made during the case study, my memory of events considered in conjunction with notes and transcriptions, correspondence and relevant conversations.

I first developed the research questions at the University of Bradford under the supervision of Tom Woodhouse and Betts Fetherston. They were first written out in English. The focus group participants were each provided with three documents: an information sheet explaining a little about the research; a form ascertaining the participant's view on anonymity and asking whether they consent to participate in the research; and the research questions. Translations in Croatian were provided together with an opportunity for discussion of the documents, questions and clarification at the beginning of each focus group. Some of the participants did not wish to be identified and therefore anonymity was provided for everyone by using coded references for each response.

Analysis of the data

I have done my best to reflect in order to understand and evaluate the impact of my values and belief system in the gathering and analysis of the research data. In analysis and presentation of the views and perceptions of the participants in the case study, I have tried to use empathy to understand their experience. Denton advocates the use of an open mind in understanding the life world of the research subject (in his work it was counsellors) and refers to achieving an understanding, which is 'always open to new perspectives and interpretations' (Denton 1981: 598). During the case study, it was obvious that, because of my association and friendships with some of the project staff and volunteers, a stance of neutrality was not possible in the focus groups and that to attempt it would 'defeat the epistemological purpose of immersing yourself in a setting' (Mason 2000: 64). However, I tried in the focus groups to take a stance of empathic neutrality during their discussions. By this, I mean the use of empathy towards the people participating in the case study and neutrality towards the information as it was gathered and later on in the subsequent analysis. I tried to listen with my eyes, ears and heart, giving undivided attention. At first I tried to remain relatively silent, save for asking the research questions, relying on body language to demonstrate empathic attention. This effort to stay comparatively silent throughout the focus group meetings felt unnatural to me and I sensed that it had the effect of flattening the dynamic flow of the debate. Then, accepting that inevitably my presence would affect the process and the responses, I used active listening skills, including verbal and non-verbal responses, indicating that I had understood what was said, adding occasional supplementary questions for clarification and to encourage the flow of responses and using reflexivity throughout to remain aware of the possible influence of my interventions. The group process then felt much more natural and flowing.

I used an adaptation of William West's model of data categorisation and analysis, derived from a combination of heuristic and grounded theory approaches (West 2001). The transcriptions were first printed out and then divided up, using intuition and tacit knowledge, into separate units of meaning (data units). Each data unit varies in size from a few words to several sentences, but each one is capable of standing alone. Where one collection of words expresses more than one unit of meaning, the second or subsequent interpretation was considered as a separate data unit, and therefore in this chapter some participants' responses are included more than once. Each data unit was then copied and pasted onto a card. The data units were colour- coded, using a different coloured card for each of the five participating groups. Each data unit card was then labelled with a coded identifier for the focus group and the individual participant, to preserve individual anonymity. They were also referenced to identify the research question to which the participant was responding.

The data units were then sorted into categories according to their meaning. Some carried more than one meaning. These were then replicated and separately categorised, for example: 'They smoke too much and they are using drugs. Thirteen years old. I think that this is very, very serious'. I interpreted this as containing several units of meaning, the first based on smoking, the next on the use of drugs and another relating to the concern of the speaker about the age of the young people referred to in respect of both smoking and drinking. Other inferences are possible, for example, there could be an implied acceptance of some degree of smoking, in that using the expression 'too much' may suggest that the speaker was not concerned at young people smoking in general, but only at them doing so to excess. However, in this analysis, I made no additional inferences without further direct or contextual corroborative evidence.

In analysis, I was interested in the literal content and the words and language used, but also took an interpretive reading of the data in 'constructing or documenting a version of what you think the data mean or represent, or what you think you can infer from them' (Mason 2000: 109). I read the data reflexively, endeavouring to assess and evaluate my part in it, relying on the research questions, context, intuition, research data and tacit knowledge to derive the units of meaning from the transcriptions.

The data units were first considered in direct relation to the research question addressed by the speaker in the focus group discussion. I then followed a procedure succinctly described by West – 'The first unit is put into a category with a provisional name to it. The second unit is compared with the first and, if sufficiently similar, is put into the same category, otherwise a new category is named' (West 2001: 127). West defines each category as containing six or more units, but here all the data units were taken into account and each category was defined, irrespective of the number of units it contained. This research was not quantitative and I simply wanted to reflect the variety of perceptions but not to attribute any statistical weight or inference from the number of data units in the different categories. Next, the categories were considered in relationship with each other and higher order models constructed, consisting of a core category, main categories and sub categories. This created generalised additional themes for analysis, for example, the psychological effects of war, creating and sustaining peace and effecting psychological change.

West comments that 'It is assumed that, in principle, another researcher given the same data would arrive at much the same model' (West 2001: 127). However, the categorisation of the case study data (and indeed, the selection of literature for review) in this research was intuitive and based on tacit knowledge derived from my own particular combination of academic disciplines and experience. It therefore seems unlikely that another researcher's perceptions would be precisely the same, but the use of a unique combination of experience in the course of analysis is a potentially positive aspect of this type of research. The use of reflexivity and openness in data analysis enables readers to understand and evaluate the basis upon which these choices were made.

The data were further considered in the context of broad themes derived from Adam Curle's approach, for example, his concepts of 'peaceful' and 'unpeaceful' and also within themes intuitively derived from my own background and experience, for example 'domestic violence', 'blocked mourning' and 'listening'.

To preserve the integrity and impact of the statements, direct quotations from the focus group participants are reproduced in this book as they were spoken or translated, without changing the original vocabulary or grammar. For ease of reading, the identifier codes have been omitted, and I have added my own words in square brackets where necessary for clarification.

Views of the focus groups considered in the context of earlier research on peacemaking and posttraumatic stress

The research questions are set out before the relevant responses. I want to celebrate and acknowledge the wide variety of perceptions and views of the focus group participants, so have included both representative responses from the focus groups to the questions and also relevant minority responses given in the discussions.

Each focus group discussion was placed in the contextual framework of the local community and the work of the projects.

The Questions

1   Have there been any psychological consequences of the war for people in your local community and if so, what are they?

The 'local community' was translated in the groups to mean the local geographical community in which the projects work and the groups defined these as Osijek, Vukovar and Zupanja. All the focus groups mentioned that they had clearly seen psychological consequences of the war. Some of the participants spoke to me outside the focus groups about their own personal experience of the war. In the focus groups, the main discussion was about the experiences of others – family, friends and people in the local community.

Some of the quotations below were given in response to other research questions (for example, about the peacefulness or unpeacefulness of the community) but these responses are included here because I have interpreted them as a reference to the psychological consequences of the war.

Extent of psychological effects amongst the community

> *Also we have a lot of traumatic experiences. So-called posttraumatic diseases... we have a lot of such experiences.*

> *Comparing my work before and after the war, I can see increase of psychological problems. I am sure that there is some psychological consequences.*

> *The consequences of the war have been incredible... that is pretty much every person in this community... I don't think that there is any person who has been spared.*

> *I thought that in a sense that somehow after the war we are all ill. We are all affected somehow.*

When I think back about the psychological experiences of the war for some people, umm, it is pretty widespread. It is a range of all kind of effects that you could notice in people's faces. Very often, what I saw and heard was a kind of deep pain. Now mostly it was pain and it was pretty general as a feeling among people, that people were feeling hurt due to all the things that had happened to them, either because various members of the family were killed, or their best friends were killed and the pain was pretty devastating for most of them.

Psychological problems are worse in those who are vulnerable

I have in my family such problems and also I saw the people before. I know they were just a little bit ill. So they were treated by medicine, by drugs and everything, but now they had to be moved to institution or somewhere else because they couldn't stand with the depression of the war.

Psychological problems seen as more complex now than before the war

People ask for help for problems which are more complex than before.

Anger, aggression and domestic violence

There were stories of arguments that flared up suddenly and ended in the use of lethal weapons, causing fatalities:

A year ago, in May in Vincovci, a man went into a post office and something happened, I don't know, a post office person treated him a little roughly and he came back ten minutes later and threw a grenade. That kind of incident occurs on a fairly regular basis, much of it not reported, in pubs and in other places.

Somebody suddenly comes into a restaurant and starts shooting around or has a quarrel with a friend and then takes out a gun and bang – straight into his head.

They are aggressive at their children ... the war is at this moment in their house because they quarrel.

Officials in Osijek/Baranja County and in Vukovar/Sirmium County have said to us that the number one and number two problems in their counties are suicide and family violence.

Also there is more abusing in families.

Several teachers noted an increase in aggressive and anti-social behaviour at school, with the use of abusive ethnic or political language such as 'Chetnik' or 'Ustase'. They felt that the incidence of domestic violence had increased, perhaps exacerbated by economic and other family pressures. They also linked the experience of domestic violence at home and the aggression they noted in children at school.

In my school there is an increase in aggressiveness

In schools, what I noticed is that in some children from their families [have] got that intolerance for other nationalities 'Ah you are Serb and I am going to kill you, you are Chetnik'.

I observe more and more children with unusual behaviour patterns, aggressiveness and violence.

Children, which were maybe three or four years old back in 1991, now they are teenagers and they are very aggressive.

I am teacher... all of my colleagues said that children became much more aggressive than they were before. And of course it is all in connection with different psychology illness. PTSP, [PTSD in Croatian] different traumas ...and people try to put their hurts under the carpet, but it make very big press on them and the war at this moment is in the house because they quarrel. They are aggressive at their children.

Children take in a lot of aggressiveness, which probably they have experienced at home.

Apathy and depression

Apathy was sometimes associated with a sense of danger and a foreshortened future. Some thought this was also linked with the present high levels of unemployment.

There is a lot of depressed people... total apathy in the villages. Some people in the town, they have some vision, but really the whole community in danger. They still feel endangered.

And people are more and more confused and more and more apathetic...

I think people don't see a vision of the future.

Unemployed people, youths, cannot see a future.

Suicide

Participants thought that there had been an increase in the levels of suicide following the war and that this constitutes one of the most serious concerns for psychological health. They mentioned potential contributory factors including family problems, difficulties over former refugees returning to their homes, the courts and government taking too long to resolve property disputes and a general lack of effective psychological help in the community and in schools.

Officials in Osijek/Baranja County and in Vukovar/Sirmium County have said to us that the number one and number two problems in their counties are suicide and family violence.

There is a problem – what do you call it when someone kills himself – suicide. There arise a lot of suicides. Elderly and youths.

I heard that every week, one person who were in the army, every week one of them commit suicide. This is direct consequence of the war.

Suicide may be seen as an extreme response to depression, apathy, hopelessness, alienation, hardship or powerlessness in the post-war situation. Here is an extract from a conversation between two participants which reflects a general perception and examples of powerlessness caused by domestic, financial or property problems, exacerbated by the lack of effective psychological help:

I don't know for sure, but the population they are rising among those who participated in homeland war and now they don't have enough money to live and they have problems with their families, so they choose …

Another person finished the sentence for the previous speaker –

… Death. A lot of actions about property, private property unsolved still. A lot of people lives in a house that isn't their house and the owner want to get back into that house. I don't know how the courts have maybe not enough time. I think that now the government isn't enough … how I can say … maybe capable to do this, that this process will pass quickly. And about institution who can help to the people who has psychological problems so let's say in schools majority we have psychologe [psychologists], but …I cannot say they have a lot of effects. And the other in hospital, if you will come to the doctor, he say 'Hello. How are you?' 'Do you better today?' 'Yes, you are better '. 'Ok. Do you need some medicaments?' … 'Yes please.' After that he written a receipt and then he say 'Goodbye.'

Suicide was also considered to be a consequence of a perceived lack of societal trust and empathic awareness leading to a cultural reluctance to talk about problems, combined with the prevailing lack of therapeutic help.

People actually hide their problems. No-one in their surroundings is aware of what their problem. Surprise when you read in a newspaper for instance that someone is killed – make the suicide – or something like that and you just surprised, but why – he didn't look like – and everything. And it is certainly communication, trust and all these values. Also which actually

cause that more people are more ready to hide their problems, suppress
them, have no, probably, one to whom they can talk, openly, honestly and so
we have increased the number of suicides.

Addictions to alcohol, drugs and smoking

Participants were concerned about a perceived increase in the use of drugs,
alcohol and smoking – in particular they felt this was a serious concern in
respect of young people

Alcoholism is widespread.

There is a large amount of addiction to drugs, particularly prescription
drugs...particularly benzodiazapines. There is a wide range of overuse of
prescription drugs such as anti-depressants and neuroleptics. There is an
increasing amount of illegal drug use ... and there is a combination of drug
use.

Drink and smoke enormously ...

They are unemployed, but I don't know how they have in this case the
money for alcohol, because it is very expensive, but usually people start to
drink.

They smoke too much and they are using drugs. Thirteen years old. I
think that this is very serious.

Other psychological effects

The participants commented on other fears and psychological symptoms
following the war:

They still feel endangered.

They mentioned specifically symptoms of anxiety, flashbacks and psychosis.
In private conversations people told me:

I'm afraid of open spaces.

I am afraid of darkness.

I suffer from sleeplessness.

I was sleepless at nights. There were so many questions in my head and
sort of haunting me ...

There were comments on general tension:

...You see it on the faces ... people here don't smile. They don't show their

teeth when they smile. I think it is much on everybody's mind. It is bound to have such huge consequences for every aspect of their life because of the lack of provision of how to deal with it. There is no real psychological safety net.

As far as I can tell personally, you can feel in the air that there is emotions and problems around. You can feel it in Vukovar. You can feel it in Osijek. Maybe you don't notice it so much but when you go away, like I went away to Zagreb and then you feel there that the air is clearer in a way. It sounds a bit vague, maybe …

Emotional numbing was mentioned by two participants in discussing an exhibition of photographs of the exhumation of a mass grave:

The point is that people around here, when they see such an exhibition, they grow more or less numb to both their and other people's pain. They will review the exhibition with more or less interest for the detail, which they haven't, like, seen yet, because they have seen a lot already… ' Oh, this is a good picture of a skull'. 'Oh look it is missing a nose.' That is how they will react, because they have already suppressed whatever they could suppress, they are practically emotionally numb.

Participants felt that mourning following bereavement may also be blocked by the general culture of silence mentioned earlier, exemplified by a lack of ability or willingness to openly express deeply held feelings and that work to improve communication is an essential part of recovery. Their views about communication are discussed later in the chapter.

Physical illnesses and psychosomatic effects of the war

Participants, including a medical doctor, described physical illnesses in their community which they attributed to the effects of the war. Some felt that therapy could reduce psychosomatic symptoms.

Heart problems. Heart attacks. Young people who were too young, forty, thirty-four, twenty-nine, die from heart attacks.

Circulatory system problems including strokes, heart attacks and high blood pressure in young people

Asthma.

Gastro- intestinal problems, which is ulcers and Crohn's disease and all the rest of it.

Everything up to endocrine problems, thyroid problems and diabetes mellitus.

Disinhibition or inhibition of the immune system leading to conse-
quences such as cancer.

And just from the experience of the therapy, I know that once the person
is healed from the inside, it all affects even for the physical health as well.
Psychological health and physical as well.

'Burn out', compassion fatigue and vicarious trauma

'Burn-out', compassion fatigue and vicarious trauma are constant problems
for local non-governmental organisations' staff and volunteers. Some staff and
volunteers have been working in difficult post-war conditions for over ten
years. One participant mentioned secondary traumatisation as an unrecognised 'important priority' in health care, relevant to post-war helpers.

In the beginning there was more enthusiasm and voluntary work. Now,
we are all exhausted, tired and embarrassed. We have found that our private
life and our families also were suffering and they also need help, support and
time for themselves. So our enthusiasm becomes weaker.

The focus groups emphasised the need for support for the helpers,
suggesting that preventive therapy would be helpful in this situation, with
breaks in their work to recover lost energy.

I am working for project for three years and I notice that it could be very
important to call it [ask for] help for helpers. To have some kind of workshop
for us who are working on this problem, you know.

We also have psychological problems of helpers. A lot of people who were
involved in helping others were almost burnout. A lot of people on our last
workshop ... we all talk about that we feel that we are tired and that we need
healing ...

One participant acknowledged that she had not recognised her own need for
help:

I have believed myself stable, balanced, strong and rational person, but
sometimes I found it was fake.

The lack of internal resources to help others may extend to health professionals. This account was given by a clinical psychologist:

The psychologists and psychiatrists themselves need help. They are trau-
matised. An example of this is a veteran who came to see his psychiatrist and
the psychiatrist said 'How are you?' and the veteran started to tell him about

> *his problems and the psychiatrist said to him 'Don't talk to me, I have my own problems. I don't want to listen to you now. Just take your prescription and go.' That was his exact words. Even the professionals are burned out because they have their own traumas and their own worries and problems ...*

The clergy have similar problems:

> *The clergy have the exact same problems. We have heard this from the clergy of all religions ... that their parishioners come to them and they don't know how to handle the situation themselves because they are not trained in it...and they get secondarily traumatised by it and so they can't really handle the situation either. So where do the people go? They have nowhere.*

Some group members made a clear distinction between physical and emotional or spiritual energy, in themselves and others.

> *... also another aspect which you can try to define is that one member, a war veteran said that he feel himself zero in a spiritual way, so very damaged, because he have no internal resources to help others. When he was injured physically, or whatever, but having internal capacity to help others he felt 'I am ok, but now, when I can't give nothing, when I have nothing to give to others, then I feel I am zero.*

2   Are there any therapeutic interventions currently offered to heal the psychological effects of war? If so, what are they and where and by whom are they offered? Are there any therapeutic interventions not currently available that, in your opinion, would benefit your community?

I had already informally asked psychiatrists, psychologists and medical practitioners in Eastern Slavonia and Zagreb about the therapeutic interventions for psychological trauma currently available in Eastern Slavonia. Their responses are summarised in Chapter Four. The responses of the focus groups to this question, together with their views on additional therapies that they feel would benefit the community, are set out below.

Medication

> *Most of people who need therapeutic interventions receive medical and psychiatrist. Then most of the psychiatrists prescribe only medicine or tablets, but for most of the people this is not good. This is most of them*

become addicted and then when they are addicted, most of them cannot work and cannot be in good communication. And I know that some of psychiatrists and doctors find some kind of group work, for more talking, but most of the interventions are medical interventions.

The majority of the interventions given in this area are drug interventions and that's very unfortunate. People go and they get drugs for everything. They get the most wild and weird and unbelievable sometimes combinations of drugs which are prescribed for them and that is the basic method of treatmen

Therapeutic approaches used in Eastern Slavonia

Therapeutic approaches mentioned by professionals in the focus groups were described not as treatment modalities but more often as techniques, for example establishing trust, then encouraging the re-experiencing of traumatic events in the context of a sense of safety and then reintegrating the experience. Psychologists said:

When people are very traumatised, you have to spend a lot of time building trust and building therapeutic relationship. I think it is so important to give people some space, to be themselves and to have a lot of confirmation that what they are saying it is ok to feel and that is how you start building the relationship I always find – and the trust as well – for them to talk about safe things first, before you enter those minefields.

When I was working with women who had been raped, in concentration camps, you know, not only had they lost their identity, they had been humiliated. One woman was asked to stand in front of ten soldiers naked, so they could choose – she did not feel human any more, she said she felt nothing and you have to do so. You are both re-living the trauma and you are both having to look at things back. All these things happened to you. You are still in there somewhere, even though all these things happened to you. I believe very much in the psychodynamic approach, but also on behavioural tasks for people who are very depressed. Give them one little thing to do per day, in order to make them feel that they have mastered something, that they feel more empowered and more in control of their life again ...

I think combine the treatment for each individual, treat each individual as a whole and do not just treat that one specific trauma, look at the other things that have happened in their lives and what kind of personality they have.

In the end of the day I keep stressing that it is not the therapeutic methods you use but the therapeutic relationship you have with the person that heals really, so whatever you choose, you tailor it for the individual and the relationship you have with that person is the most important aspect.

Since specific therapy modalities were not discussed in detail in the focus groups, I made enquiries of psychiatrists, psychologists and psychotherapists in Osijek, Vukovar and Zagreb and referred to the Croatian Medical Journal and other relevant research publications for general information about the main therapies used in Eastern Slavonia.

The groups briefly mentioned the use of bodywork with mine victims and others, eye movement desensitisation and reorganisation (EMDR), the work of Victor Frankel and the Rogerian approach.

One participant mentioned the use of bibliotherapy, psychodrama and psychological skills in one NGO's group-work with victims of rape. These women are offered a two-week holiday by the sea with support from staff and volunteers:

A great emphasis of our work is going to the beach every day, like in the afternoon or so, in order to have the opportunity for women to relax, actually and to openly and informally talk about their wounds and hurts, in their own way, or just based on individual conversations or so and what we do, we listen carefully and see how we can actually help them by some advices or just by listening.

The speaker said that she would like to see follow up support for the mothers after their return to their own community.

Therapies available are insufficient for the needs of the local community

The groups' perception was of a general lack of facilities currently available to alleviate trauma. They expressed the need for more trained professionals and volunteer helpers and for the government to allocate better resources for mental health.

I am living in a small village and there is nobody who could give therapeutic intervention or help person in need. In our community, during and after the war, we had a lot of traumatic events, killing, wounding, suicide, but there were [not] any therapeutic intervention.

It was established before the war some kind that we call SOS telephone.

You can ring and talk with somebody who should be supporter. And we have a citizens' organisation who try to help for drunkards, but I think that at the moment it is just a little bit. Not enough for our situation.

In schools we have psychology, but these work … I cannot say that have a lot of effects.

There is … and Mir i dobro in Zupanja … there is the Centre for Professional   Rehabilitation at Osijek and there is … in Osijek, another psychologist, but that is basically about it.

In Osijek there is one who is trying to give that kind of help but groups are too big and he is doing it only in his working hours … in Croatia I don't know if there is a programme for this psychological support. Maybe only for those who were fighting. Maybe for them. For civilians like us I don't think so …

She is very much traumatised and she just think that she can't walk … and people like her they need some kind of support. They are not covered by any specific groups. I don't know how it should be organised. How it should be offered … Osijek is for instance not too big City, but it is also not too small, so there are many people who are not covered by anything. They should have something. There should be organised something for people.

And the constant complaint that you get from people is that there is no psychotherapy, that they don't have any place to express their emotions. There are for example, no SOS lines. The shelter facilities in Osijek are for three or four beds. I mean, that's it. In an area which really needs it. There is nothing in Vincovci, there is nothing in Vukovar and there is nothing in Zupanja. There is nothing anywhere.

The groups did not blame mental health professionals entirely for the inadequacy of mental health provision at that time – it was seen mainly as a resource problem, resulting in overwork for staff:

To be fair to the professionals, they are all overburdened. They have something like fifty patients a day, they report. It's insane.

I think that there is no currently offered psychological help. Because there is a lot of psychologically damaged people and all doctors, all potential which we have from our medicine people, they are also loaded with the work they do. And so, these minor, as they think, as it is public opinion, these minor problems, are not treated and not taken as serious.

However, whilst they understood the resource problems, the groups also felt that a more empathic and approachable attitude from mental health professionals would encourage people to seek therapeutic help. The perceived emphasis in hospitals is on treatment by medication and not on listening to patients:

> *Institutions have a constant lack of capacity and they are motivated to see as many patients as possible, hence the effect of that is a lack of individual care.*

> *And … in hospital, if you will come to the doctor, he say 'Hello. How are you? Do you better today? Yes, you are better. OK. Do you need some medicaments?' 'Yes please.' After that he written a receipt [prescription] and then he say goodbye.*

> *Roughly an interview lasts less than five minutes, average two or three and he sees him and he says 'Oh, a manic depression with paranoia, here is something to pick you up. Oh, in case this picks you up too high, here is something to put you down and here is something to keep you normal and, oh well, if you get nervous during the day, you can take one of these.' You end up after the interview with the psychiatrist with, like four or five prescriptions and of course people are laymen and they tend to mix them or to abuse them, or whatever.*

There is a perceived social stigma attached to seeking mental health care:

> *There is a public opinion in our nation, in our country, that seeing psychiatrist, or asking for psychological help, is a sign of illness … so people think that if they go to a psychologist or if they go to a group to talk about psychological problems, that they are crazy. So other people name them or stigma to them … public opinion should be changed. It is not like America, maybe, where everybody is going to psychological, psychologist or consultations or somewhere else.*

> *Also, we have a problem with fear or anxiety of stigmatisation. In our small community, people aren't enough free to ask for psychological help.*

Recommendations for improvement in psychological therapeutic services

> *More professionals, more training, more funds, isn't it obvious? … and more Croatian speaking professionals. It would be downright silly to have a therapist which needs a translator, right?*

What Croatia really needs is same as any post conflict area in the world is a couple of thousand professional psychiatrists, which would actually cover the area.

But, recognising this as impossible given present resources, a way forward, suggested by all the groups, is for trained local people to do the work:

Within the NGO organisations that are here in this region, not only to talk about the specialised help that psychologies or any kind of therapies can offer, but even us, who are not psychologists but who have a goodwill and who have some kind of sly notions about what trauma is and how to deal with trauma, that is an enormous help to people very often. And then they realise. That they might become aware that they are having a problem and then it comes to their conscious level and they say 'Aha, yes, I haven't been aware of that, so now I know. It is something I have to deal with and I have to cope with.'

The only answer is to train large numbers of non-professional, peer counsellors and to supervise them and that's our approach ... actually, peer to peer counselling appears to be the only real way to meet the need.

There is, however, a perceived problem about the provision of training and resources in the country areas:

There is a reasonably good, not quite a Western standard, but a fairly high standard of psychology and psychiatry in Croatia ... The knowledge does exist in Croatia somewhere. The problem is that it is not getting out to the field, and to the outlying areas.

The creation of an emotionally safe environment in which to talk is seen as helpful by all the groups:

I think that one of the therapies that was important was simply the chance of talking. People who had suffered all kind of pain and trauma during the war, when they had a chance to talk about it I think even that was a kind of therapy and help to them. The therapy that we did ... was simply through kind of talking and creating a safe space to speak openly about their angers, about their fears, about their pains. So, creating such a safe space for people to talk about it and giving them a chance to say 'Hey, I am here. I am ready to listen' means a lot.

When they start to verbalise, whatever problems they have, it is a kind of therapy.

In Osijek I met with several local psychologists. Their view was that the provision for psychotherapy is currently inadequate to meet local needs and some of them are using their own initiative and funds to improve their skills and service provision. Some are funding themselves to undertake a three-year post-graduate course of training in Gestalt psychotherapy.

Self-help and support groups were seen as important in post-war recovery. During the case study, I was told that a local resident was planning to set up an Alcoholics Anonymous meeting in Osijek, with support and advice from Dr Tauber. That meeting is still thriving and there has been an Alcoholics Anonymous conference held recently in Osijek. One group agreed together that public psychological education was important, with self-help and self-stabilisation measures taught through the media.

3   Based on your experience, in what ways would you say that your local community is peaceful or unpeaceful?

Physical danger

The groups all felt that Croatian society is not yet peaceful. They agreed that there is no longer overt war, but there was still physical danger:

> My experience is that fact is that mortar shells are not falling on our heads any more. If that is peace, then our local community is peaceful, but I want to say that I don't feel safe now because violence is still existing and maybe very strong forms and there are also many weapons left from the war and it is very dangerous. And there are also many minefields still remain. And people cannot go and cultivate their lands because they don't feel safe. Last year, about 1,010 people were injured or killed by mines. Then it's be a lot unpeaceful. We need a lot of money to de-mine the fields and professional help, to feel safe. And changes in community of course, to feel safe.

I asked for clarification of the violence in 'strong form' and this is the reply:

> For example violence between those who stayed on occupied territories and those who returned and remainees ... it is not a national problem between Serbs and Croat, but between these two groups, regardless of their nationality. For example, in one village and I think there are more villages like that, one neighbour put strong poison on his neighbour's land just before the harvest. She ruined everything. It is not possible to plant anything on this field for at least five years. That is very strong violence.

Lack of ethnic integration

Participants noted this generally in Osijek, but it was particularly apparent in Vukovar:

Because of the traumatisation there is a lot of inter-ethnic tension.

In Vukovar, where this gap is still very strong among people where you have the coffee houses, only for the Serbs or only for the Croats and the children simply don't play together on the streets and so on… I mean there is a hope definitely, there always is, but we have to be aware of how slow the process is.

Because of the high traumatisation levels, these tensions are increased even further.

There were very varied perceptions of present evidence of ethnic tension:

It is much better than it was ten years ago, but in the same time very far away from a peaceful society.

It seems to me that it is even a kind of silent war going on … They live together. It is not love and peace, but it is a step forward and tolerated.

In schools what I noticed was that some children from their families got that intolerance for other nationalities. 'Ah you are Serb and I am going to kill you.' 'You are Chetnik' so they are not making up these. They heard something like that in their families and that is very dangerous, too because they are just children.

Serbs don't like Croats. Croats don't like Serbs. Moslems don't like both of them and both of them don't like Moslems.

Serbian and Croatian nationality have a lot of similarities. They have more or less within themselves- those nations have similar systems of value and neither of them is xenophobic, or fascistic, or whatever. It is actually downright stupid to say that the entire nation is like this or like that – people are people, people are messy, what can I tell you?

The groups were interested in the issue of difference and similarity, pointing out that difference may lead to marginalization. They mentioned the Roma (referred to below as the gypsies) as a minority ethnic group of people who are widely ostracised. A participant told this story:

We had one workshop in one village in B*****, after that one woman said 'I am very sorry that Hitler isn't live, that he will kill all of the gypsies.'

She then added her own view that

The Roma are for me good people for me in spite their different behaviour.

Ethnic tension was not noted as a particular problem in Zupanja. In that region, other evidence of unpeacefulness was felt to be more pressing:

We live in ethnically clear community and we haven't a lot of these problems.

I think that there is not ethnical issue here any more, than here we have lack of morals, knavery, educational problems.

Religious divisions

The predominance of one religion was noted in some communities and schools. The participants perceived social difficulty for children who are attending schools that hold religious education classes focusing on one faith, if their parents did not wish their child to attend these classes.

But they just put, let's say, church in the school. They are learning pray, but just in this one way. Let's say the Roman Catholic Church occupy the schools. I don't like it. And if you don't want as a parent your child will go, because it isn't obligation, it is just choice, it is very difficult, because in this case this child is separate of the majority. Which is very difficult for children.

Inter-faith co-operation was seen by one participant as limited:

The co-operation between the other churches, particularly the Roman Catholic and Orthodox Church are very bad, for example ... Before the war, they was going to each other, celebrating together share celebration, now they are too working in school teaching religion and speaking, but after that, finish. Not saying hello.

A Catholic priest, a Methodist minister and a Seventh Day Adventist minister, each working for non-violence in Croatia, gathered with a multi-faith congregation during a visit to the U.K. to celebrate a service together and all three laughingly said that this shared celebration was 'highly illegal' within their respective churches. Nevertheless, they had the courage and the will to share their faith and it was a very moving service. Members of the congregation afterwards commented on this as a powerful contribution to tolerance and understanding in a multi-faith society.

The break up of friendships, families and divorce

The groups reported that before the war there had been many inter ethnic friendships, relationships and marriages and that the ethnic divisions of the war had resulted in the break up of friends and families and an increase in the divorce rate:

> So you could see many divorces around among the Croats and the Serbs, because the politics became so important in their lives that they realised that they could not longer live any more together.

> The pain is not only connected to the loss of members of the family or to loss of the property and material losses, but it is also loss of friendships that it happened among people and this mistrust that happened actually was affecting the families deep inside as well.

The ethnic separation was noted to have been developing before the war came. In the generalised atmosphere of mistrust, good actions may be overlooked. One whole focus group present agreed with this statement:

> This big gap that was growing and growing within the families, within the neighbours, within the communities and it also happened later on at the level of the nation ... it happened due to the politics of the media, that you had a very powerful picture in the media of your enemy and of course then you generalise ... You don't see that not all people were bad during the war... but there were many who tried to help. There were many who were offering their hand, but then in the pain that you are going through, in the trauma that you are suffering, you cannot see further, you cannot step out of your feet, out of your shoes and then you think that everybody is to be blamed and of course then you generalise things and everybody is guilty and then it takes time, a lot of time, to regain the trust, to create a new picture again, to help people start seeing things differently and understanding things differently.

Political manipulation, inequalities and power struggles

Some participants were angry at the manipulative use of the war for economic or political ends by those in power or those seeking power, citing as an example the former war veterans who try to obtain better conditions than others because of their war service.

> All of us have contributed to our country, not only soldiers. So, I don't like it when some categories are privileged.

Of course there are those who are politicians and who manipulate with history and with this war, but many of them you can see on television that they use their position as war veterans to fulfil their very basic needs.

Local residents mentioned to me the deliberate stirring up of the feelings of parents and relatives of missing persons for political ends. The comment was that people are not encouraged to accept their loss and to grieve and move on. The relatives' hope that their missing loved ones are still alive is constantly stirred up, causing them more anguish.

Earlier in this chapter I mentioned an exhibition in Osijek of photographs of mass grave exhumations, showing mutilated corpses constituting graphic witness to cruelty, suffering and violent death. This was an exhibition created by a group of women and as we were looking at the photographs, I was aware of their very powerful emotions. As we walked round the stands, one woman indicated a photograph to me and with tears in her eyes, said, 'That is my son.' Others there had lost their husbands and some indicated photographs of their friends, neighbours and relatives. These women want to continue to show the exhibition regularly despite suffering intense emotional pain. They told me that they wanted children, even those born after the war ended, to see these photographs, so that they should know and remember what happened.

Tangible reminders of past violence are felt to be depressing

Every day you walk through the ruins, every day you are facing these destructions, every day it is like a little salt is being put on your wound and it is painful and it hurts. So if they could have a normal town rebuilt again and if people could have some jobs, some kind of material security in their hands, there would be some kind of orientation, some kind of vision for the future.

One participant spoke of her work with women who had babies as a result of rape during the war. These babies constitute tangible reminders of traumatic experience. She said that many of these children are now being looked after in residential care because they were physically and emotionally rejected by their mothers and by the local community. I was told about one residential home in which several rape victim mothers were encouraged to stay in the same house as their babies, but despite encouragement to develop attachments with their babies, they preferred to live on one floor and have their babies looked after on another floor by staff.

4.   Are there any conditions necessary to generate and / or sustain peace?

Management of the reintegration of returning refugees

There were comments that reintegration should be a careful and well thought out procedure:

> *Return process should have been done more carefully, in a more integrated manner. Here is a new house, my foot … there is a guy who killed your brother living next door to you, that's not the way to do it.*

Speaking of Vukovar:

> *You have to work with each group. You cannot deal with the groups together at the moment. That is just not possible. You have to deal with the traumatisation. You are talking about long-term solutions.*

The establishment of economic equality and alleviation of financial and physical hardship

> *After the war, there is injustice … What you experience in society is the gap between the poor and the rich, which hasn't been present in this society before the war. Now this is becoming very evident and obvious. And I think it has contributed to the whole situation of neither war nor peace in the community and in society.*

A condition of peace suggested was that people should be empowered in various ways to act for themselves:

> *At first I start to talk with my friend and after that I started to talk with some other and we made some agreement about some workshop, about what they would like to talk, or what is the problem. It mean make an interview, then an animation and after that, third step from conflict to reconciliation and after that some evaluation and agreement what we would like to do together.*

> *In Darda, people organised themselves to put in order a park and a castle, which is a monument, on the list of United Nations. And they find enough power to engage municipal local authority and different organisation who had big mechanisation for do this and I am very proud because it. I am very satisfied.*

Another local organisation was mentioned in which the people of Beli Manastir had gathered together to create workshops for peace, leading to an independent peace group.

Creating a space in a community to share opinions freely, generating mutual respect and understanding

> *I would like to say that it is very important to enable people to hear each other and to know that they are not the only ones who have problems. Maybe, very, very similar problems. It is very important too and that is one step for opening communications between them. If they can talk, then they can also reason and when they reason they will know more and they will not be maybe afraid of something.*

> *One workshop for retired people from Vukovar, it was on the topic 'What is home to me and where is it?' There were Serbs, Croats, returnees and those who stayed... One woman she turned to her neighbour and she said to her 'You know, when I saw you on the street I turned off my head, because I didn't want to see you. You were just air to m.' Because that lady was a Serb and she stayed in the village. This lady she is a Croat and she came back. And she said, 'Also, now I see I was plainly wrong. People, those who hurted me left long time ago and from now on I will drink coffee with you and I am very sorry because of my behaviour.' That was a big step for her. Really very big step because her voice was very high. She was under great pressure if she said anything and she felt a great relief. After that she said that she now feel herself free to walk through the village.*

Bringing justice and responsibility for actions into public awareness

> *Because that is very important that people who did really bad things through the war should be brought to court. It is not like the question of the Hague, where Milosevic ends up, but it is also the question of people who were not on a very high political position, but who were still deeply involved ... That responsibility for the actions. If it is necessary that punishment, if it is proved that people are guilty of the things they did, that this should be clearly said and clearly be done in the public at the court level.*

A problem was identified of retention of the victim role, a lack of personal responsibility for actions – attributed by some to a general culture of power-lessness, created politically by earlier governments taking responsibility for decision-making and financial support.

> *People should be involved actually in creating things and then they might perhaps, when they are actually involved in creation, then they will be a little*

bit more antagonistic and suspicious about destroying things that they created with their own hands.

In the former system, everything seemed to be so easily accessible and everything comes like from the sky, so you simply get things and people were not aware how these things appear in their life and how they were acquired. Certain financial benefits and so on.

To counter this effect, people should be encouraged to take individual responsibility:

... like being an entrepreneur and starting your own business, small family farm, or whatever this might be.

You cannot expect always somebody else to solve the problems for you, but you are the one who can also start doing that.

5.   In your opinion, what blocks do you see to making or sustaining peace?

The necessity of personal change

We should work on changing our attitudes about our relations with others, (war starts at first in our head). We should learn to accept other human being as much as different he could be.

I think that at first we need peace with ourselves.

I can say that the most important thing is to gain peace from within or from inside ourselves. So working actually from the inside toward the outside. Which means that I prefer working with people who are open and ready to work on themselves first in order to create the peaceful atmosphere working on the soul level and the spiritual level.

Is very important. Is very, very important because ... you can be more healthy. And if I don't solve my problems then I can't help other people. That's the way I see it.

Economic hardship

One project group suggested that economic hardship, together with family problems, contributes to higher rates of suicide. In other groups, the struggling national economy, unemployment and also the lack of international funding were identified as major blocks to peace.

... Given that Croatia did not receive all the economical assistance and aid that it needs, given that we cannot gain access to funds that this and similar organisations would need and given that there is not real international will to sustain peace here, what is to talk about? Croatia needs money to recover its economy. It needs foreign assistance to change its attitudes. Croatia needs foreign assistance to mediate with. Croatia needs foreign assistance to treat from psychotrauma. Croatia needs foreign assistance in whichever aspect of life you can look at.

Like this lady was telling me yesterday. She was really old when she lost her job and she said 'The only thing I could think about was how would I have money to buy food for my children? I didn't have time to deal with everything else that happened to me during the war. I have enough just thinking about how to get money and to survive.'

I'm coming back to economy and its high unemployment and people are extremely unhappy and are struggling to survive ... I think that there would not be so much tension if the economy was OK.

I am willing to bet that a good percentage of all those war veterans would be willing to change all of this and all of their war pride and everything what they have experienced and what they are, like proud of, for a decent living in Hungary, somewhere in Poland, somewhere in Portugal.

The whole economic situation in the country is such that in the post- war period it is very difficult for the people to live real peace.

For instance with economical situation, it seems to me that more and more we are reaching the moment when violence could happened, when people cannot just go on the street ... and I don't see that we have means to deal with these problems. On an institutional way we don't have ... how to solve that, we don't have means of dialogue, of solving problem, or of dealing with such situation.

The effect of past politics

The perceived effects of the past communist government have already been mentioned in relation to the effects of war. The participant quoted below clearly saw the research as a useful means of making his point. He commented on the prevailing psychological and social attitudes of peacemaking:

I am deliberately using this opportunity to address some foreign intel-lectuals about this. Communist society was oppressive spiritually. Hence, even before the war, these very same people, which now actually in addition suffering consequences of the war, have inherited negative attitudes. They are not self-confident, they are not dependable, they are not self-reliable. They were raised to act and feel quite the opposite. 'Shut up, don't rock the boat. You'll be taken care of.'

Some mentioned that citizens of Croatia have lost their freedom of expression over the last ten years. 'We need broader space for critique, for criticism towards our political subjects.'

To live normally means to have freedom of expressions and I am not sure that in the situation which we had last ten years, most of Croatians or citizens of Croatia had real freedom of expression.

Now we have a peace, if peace is the opposite of war. But we have not good life as was. We lost security. Our trade union is totally destroyed. Workers' rights are very less. Very bad. They can make a strike but in the end it looks as if some joke.

Negative influence of modernisation, loss of old values and new 'western' values

We have had transition from traditional lifestyle to more 'western' kind of life ... which we connect with its negative aspects.

That main obstacle or block, blockades towards mental health of individuals and of our society as a whole is lack or confusion in values and all this confused values is used by politic, not for building a vision or norms, but just to divide power.

I am glad that ... and ...named problems of modernisation,, of too quick modernisation of Croatian society ... and the result of that modernisation is that we were overwhelmed by many devices such as motorcars, as computers, as informations, which we couldn't control or use in a proper way.

I think that both family and we have failed in education. After the war we have more delinquency, addiction and violence. We need help to rebuild value system.

Poor example set for the public by leaders, politicians and the media

Participants noted a lack of effective communication and some politicians are perceived as in pursuit of their own interests and seeking power.

Many people who appear on television in all kinds of debates have no idea about what real non-violent communication is.

They are the top of society, intellectual society, spiritual society, spiritual talk, they are the leaders. They are the people who lead this society and what do you have? The level of conversation among them is one you would find at the marketplace and it's a very poor example to other people!

... not for peace politic, but from politic how to save my chair in parliament, my position in parliament.

There was praise at the Centar za mir for the present Zupan of Osijek who was described as 'a person very dedicated to non-violence and a member of the Peace Centre'. He was described as setting a positive example of listening to young people and dealing with protest by organising discussions.

The destabilising effect of media manipulation

This was seen as generating fear and mistrust during the war, until

Everybody was afraid of everybody.

Mass media promote differences; there are only crime, scandals and bad news.

I would add perhaps a lack of trust in general. Toward the system, toward people. They don't trust even to their family members any more because they lost their trust in general I would say. That is sad to see.

So somebody who was living next to you for about twenty, thirty years and you consider the person as a close member of your family, overnight turns out to be your awful enemy and people could not just believe that such kind of manipulation could happen and that people could turn overnight and become enemies for just no obvious reason.

Speaking of Vukovar:

I just feel it so much here. People are so suspicious. I am sure that is from the war, because I have never experienced that anywhere else in Croatia for the thirty years I have been coming here. People are extremely suspicious of other people here.

All the groups mentioned the social effects of dividing friends, neighbours and families, one described 'a deep feeling of mistrust.' In some cases the division caused divorce, particularly in inter-ethnic marriages.

Crises of identity

In the former Yugoslavia, ethnically mixed marriages had been common and Croatia contained a variety of ethnicities in its population. During the war, there had been considerable internal displacement of refugees, who had been forced to change their place of residence. After the war ended, some refugees returned home and others settled elsewhere. Three groups mentioned the issue of psychological problems of identity following the war.

> *The identity issue is, in my experience in the field, probably the crucial one. People during the war have lost their identities and they, even before the war, probably had problems with their identities.*

> *This identity thing just keeps running through pretty much every group we run ... It is a constant theme of pretty much every group I have run in the past seven years.*

> *Actually war re-asserted their identity. During the war, they were either Croats or Serbs.*

> *So you could see many divorces around among the Croats and the Serbs, because the politics became so important in their lives that they realised that they could not live together any more.*

The confusion of identity extends to property:

> *This bad situation, the conflict between returner and people who stayed means that you cannot know who is owner of something. It is totally confused.*

Culture of silence, repression of feelings

The participants described a culture of silence, in which feelings of pain and loss are repressed. The grief and loss of friends and relatives was described as 'a kind of deep pain' experienced as 'devastating' for many. There follows an extract from an exchange in one focus group between two participants, one of whom lives in Eastern Slavonia and stayed throughout the war. The other came there with an NGO to provide humanitarian aid in 1995. They are speaking of a woman of mixed marriage who had lost her husband:

> *She was very sad about it obviously. She had problems with it and she began to cry at one point, she broke out spontaneously crying and her friends really repressed her. They said, 'You are crazy to cry.' And when she was in a group last year she said to me 'You mean it is actually OK. if I cry because*

I lost my husband?' Now I mean that in the west we would not even question that. We would encourage it, so this kind of blocked mourning, this is really the sort of pushing down on her, to repress her emotions … let's say societal repression of emotions. I have heard about that kind of thing from other people as well and with other patients and with other clients. I kind of think that this was to keep the collective sanity during the war, to keep everybody on the sort of level that you need to keep functioning…

Don't open the Pandora's box because you will go crazy … because you will go crazy and influence everybody else also.

And after the war there is another … reason for that suppressed mourning. You are not supposed. Nobody else does it, you know. People are pushing, pushing ahead, struggling to survive. If you start crying with mourning, you are going downhill all the way. You are not coming back, trust me, so no mourning. Just keep functioning.

The evening before the focus group meeting, I had gone with members of this group to see the exhibition of photographs of exhumations of mass graves mentioned earlier in this chapter. In the group, I mentioned the exhibition and referring to the context of what we had been saying about suppressed mourning, I asked, 'How does that fit in for people who go there with the expectation that they should suppress their mourning and then seeing that. I wonder what your thoughts are?' Looking back, I am not sure whether I should have asked this question. It had come to mind first as a question to put to an NGO professional group containing psychologists. On another level I was aware that emotional pain was surfacing in this group because we were talking of the psychological consequences of the war and also painful feelings and memories had been triggered by the exhibition. The therapist in me wanted to acknowledge that pain, aware that the talk of repression was perhaps indicative of how at least one of the group members might be feeling now. The response was open and honest:

I felt terrible. The point is that people around here, when they see such an exhibition, they grow more or less numb to both their and other people's pain. So I dunno, I am not emotionally numb, that's why I reacted yesterday. In that case I might was well ask the four of you, [indicating the group members not present during the war] why you didn't react like I did? People here react in an understandable way. They were supposed to grow numb, otherwise they would not be able to sustain the pressure.

At this point I realised the intense impact of the earlier event on the speaker and also the distinction he was making between the reactions to it of those who had experienced the war and those who had not. I responded, 'There is maybe a great difficulty for people who were supposed to grow numb, but who were also faced with reminders?' and he, with another person, agreed.

6   In your opinion, does therapy to alleviate the psychological effects of war have a role in making or sustaining peace?

Healing is important for peace

The response to this question from all the groups indicated that addressing the psychological effects of war was seen as an important part of making peace and a prelude to reconciliation. There follows an extract from a lively debate.

One participant, who had experienced the 1991-95 war in Eastern Slavonia, said:

The answer is obvious. Yes of course. People hurt all over for ten years. You have seen that lady yesterday. She showed you a picture from the funeral of her own son. I don't know how she can take it ... well, you be the judge of how much she hurts. Right, and imagine all those people hurting for a decade now ... therapy is needed, mediation is needed, peers are needed, whichever method of releasing pain from the people you apply, yes it is needed ... and here it is hundreds of thousands of people. At least 10% of them are war veterans. America has struggles dealing with their own war veterans for two decades now, three and they are still dealing with that conflict and they didn't do it. We are barely trying to scratch the surface – you need everything you can get sent over here.

First of all I agree with everything just said. The simple answer to the question is, yes it [therapy] does help, it does lower tensions, it does get people – to come back to Adam's work, he speaks always about creating the conditions for peace. Well that is exactly what therapy is doing. It is creating – first of all it is creating trust. It is lowering the state of internal agitation and internal disorder. Putting people into a much more rational state. It is allowing them to control their emotions. It is allowing them to think more rationally. It is allowing them to get in touch with both themselves and with other people.

The speaker then gave a practical example of the process of peacemaking in several groups in Eastern Slavonia, in which addressing psychological trauma had been part of the group work process, enabling subsequent reconciliation to take place, adding:

…in my judgment some of those people would not have been able to do it had they not had that preparatory work.

I said:

So, in a way, you are describing therapy as a prelude to being able to bring people together?

Yes, exactly. (One speaking, the other joining in)

I asked:

As a necessary part of preparing people for the conditions of peacemaking, have I understood you right?

Yes, absolutely .

The point being, defuse them first, right, and then merge them, let's say so.

A psychologist in the group concurred:

I agree with what's being said here, you need to – the psychotrauma – you need help, psychological help, before people can start to talk to each other. You need to deal with their own issues before they can even start to live with other people. Absolutely such a necessity.

Individual healing

I would like to say psychology support. People said it to us and they was asking us they need something who is ready to lead them to talk together, to recognise that everybody is hurted from something and that they have something in common. And I see that the most important is to understand and hear our differences and after that time, to find what is common and useful for all of us…

I asked 'Do you think that help with those psychological problems is important in making peace? Or is it not important?

This is very important if you have opportunity to share a problem with the other people, because in this case I see it as a mirror, which said to me, 'Yes, I can see you are a good person.' You can see people listen you and appreciate you and that they gave you empathy.

In Zupanja, the need for healing trauma before reconciliation was taken for granted:

People who have experienced loss or other traumas in the war, they are
not interested in making peace and conciliation and I think that is normal.

In Osijek, healing the hurts of war is a main aim of the Dodir Nade project:

We have to work for reconciliation, but the main step from conflict to
reconciliation is this which we do in Touch of Hope, healing hurts. If person
will ... avoid ... this step, in this case I cannot believe that   this person or
persons will be ready ... for reconciliation and non-violence in modern
community.

First we have to make reconciliation with us, with ourselves, then we can
do something ....

If I can just agree with [the person] just speaking from the experience of
war veterans. It is obvious that they need some kind of spiritual change,
whether we call it spiritual or just psychological improvement or whatever.
The fact is that when we ask them what would that be, they couldn't really
define. They know they feel empty. They feel they need inner satisfaction or
whatever, but the fact is that people don't actually know what they lack
because they have never experienced, they have never had that kind of
psychological support. It is, yes, the thing most needed in this area.

The Centar za mir group emphasised peacemaking praxis in their discussion, but they see the healing of psychological trauma as part of that process.
Trauma is seen as a psychological block to overcome:

When you help people, when you are there for them in the society, when
they know there is somebody who cares, and that is very important to help
them overcome the feeling of pain, the feeling of trauma, and you open and
create a space for feeling and seeing things differently.

In Centar za mir and Dodir nade, the participants included spiritual dimensions in psychological health and also in peacemaking:

I certainly believe that the spiritual level will have the impact on the local
community being the peaceful one. And I believe that the ill person cannot
create a peaceful community or just be a part of it as a truly peaceful one.

I asked: 'Do you think that therapy to help people with psychological
trauma is part of that way of getting well, or is it other ways of getting well that
you see as important?'

I believe that all factors are important for a person to be healthy. So the
psychological level, the spiritual level and the physical one. The physical is

*more the consequence of the spiritual one. And … from experience I have
noticed that people who have opened themselves in order to receive some
kind of spiritual change and spiritual improvement or growth, they are now
actually ready to cope with all the problems and all the factors which come
into our lives. Because, in one way, when I said about this ill person, I
thought that in a sense that somehow after the war we are all ill. We are all
affected somehow and that to me, just receiving this spiritual, I would say,
growth … make us strong in order to cope with the rest of our life, with all
the reconstruction.*

7.   What kind of therapeutic interventions, if any, would you see as helpful in building peace in this community and why?

*Therapy, it is for us medical doctors doing on tablets, prescriptions, so …
something from our tradition or understanding is too short, too narrow. So
I would say something like recovery, or healing in a more broad sense.*

*And what … interventions? So it could be really different. Very different
range from doing psychotherapy for those who went through traumatic experience and they need that … really putting in the place values and norms in
society which would be very healingful for people.   A lot of love and respect
again as a part of our life … But love, for me is … the most important … it
is necessary that people will be talking about their hurts and have the
courage to cry in front of the group. Crying is so important as laughing.
These two things for me is a good therapy.*

The consensus from everyone in the groups is that talking about the
psychological consequences of traumatic events is helpful in the context of
peacebuilding:

*I think if I can talk about my anger, my hate, my fears, my love. I would
feel better.*

*People cannot see the future, they need sometime to tell several time,
same story, how they were hurted. Several times. Not just one. Same story
and when they passed this they will feel better, less intention, and it is my
expectation that they will be able to see a future, sky and sunshine … but we
should do it very, very sensitive.*

*Nobody has time to listen to people. I think that talking several time
about own hurts, it can help, and the tension which you feel when you hurt
will maybe go down, will be less. It is very helpful. … I hear that psychology*

*is very good and people said it to us, but it is very difficult to make them open.
Because it is unusual to say that 'I am hurt' among the group of people who
are the majority who don't know each other.*

One participant described post-war workshops as:

*Talking and creating a safe space for people to speak openly about their
angers, their fears, about their pains.*

Does therapy require psychiatrists or psychotherapists?

The therapeutic space can be created by ordinary people for each other.
Community and psychosocial activities were mentioned by several people as
helpful in recovery from trauma and in peacebuilding. These are explored
further in relation to the next research question.

*If there were things that people could work together to find a common
aim, lets say, you know, building a centre together, employing people, getting
people to work physically, actively together and communication, … I think
that's an important thing as well as all the psychotrauma.*

*The type of gathering where people would listen each other, could talk,
open discussion, dialogues on key questions of society, could also have therapeutic effects.*

*The political aspects of such interventions are crucial, especially what
[another contributor] mentioned as verbalisation of fears, negative emotions,
expressions of horrifying events which many suffered and so on.*

But:

They are not to be mistaken as a replacement for therapy.

One person emphasised the social impact of therapy. Therapeutic change
should have a positive impact on relationships and day to day functioning:

*There is the social aspect, then you are dealing with the psychological
aspect and then you have to use what you learn in therapy out with people
and socialise and use those skills and how you learned through therapy you
are using outdoors, right. You can't only function in a therapy room. You
need to function outdoors.*

*Many people are still not ready to share all of their deepest feelings with
somebody in the group. Maybe one combination of group and individual
therapy would be good, because someone just feel need to talk to one person
and to share his feelings, or hers. Then, after that, other time it's not impor-*

tant, maybe he or she would be willing to share this kinds of feelings with the group. You know, like a process.

Referring to individual or group work, some participants said that if a person was not ready for groupwork, or felt that they needed to talk individually, this could be with a psychologist or other professional and explained: 'just as a first step, as some kind of triage', 'a bit like opening the door, you know.'

Of course it could happen that on the workshop, someone will come to you and say, 'Listen, I have a problem and I want to talk to you in private' so professional help very good.

Many people mentioned the reluctance of people to come forward to seek or to accept help.

We have a problem here with fear or anxiety or stigmatisation. In our small community, people aren't free enough to ask for psychological help.

In Croatian culture there is a huge taboo on going to see a psychiatrist or somebody and talking about your emotions, so maybe to work in this area, you might need to ease them in slowly before they are even ready to go through such huge psychological, you know, process.

Some participants described the empowering effect of active listening in workshops which enables people to speak about their feelings. One person quoted words said by a man who had first felt free to talk about his feelings in the context of a workshop:

I don't want to talk to other people about my problems. My friends who I meet on the street, they are not interested in my problems. They asked how I was but they are not really interested in hearing the response.'

Reluctance to seek help may also be seen differently:

I have observed something interesting in a negative way. People who need psychological help don't respect enough our efforts and contribution, sometimes they refuse or ignore it, because they are so engaged with existential problems and have no time or energy for anything else.

Offering therapy before reconciliation

I have seen a certain number of programmes go in those directions ... trying to make a certain thing, a park, here in Vukovar, working on certain issues. I think the traumas here (and I speak for here, not for anywhere else and I speak only from my own experience) ... are too deep for that. In my opinion, the kind of therapeutic intervention you need to do is straight psychology and you need to do straight sort of therapy and advice. And I think you have to do it with each group individually, at first. I don't think you can mix the ethnic groups because, to use examples, if somebody thinks that the other group has killed their brother or their father, they cannot talk about too much together and if they are working together those problems will be right under the surface and they will be almost directly ready to come out and they will be explosive and we have seen that a couple of times.

One participant summarised the debate:

Theories of reconciliation, one is that you start with projects together and the other is that you start to prepare people, with individuals and it is not quite clear yet which one works. In social psychology there is research on getting groups back together and working to an overall aim does get people to work back together. It does not mean that they will automatically heal and that their psychotrauma will heal, or anything like that, but it will help them see each other as humans again, maybe and then create another one of the pillars for a society.

Well, as I have always said, this issue has arisen before. My first idea is, first you guys defuse them. They have issues, they are likely to explode. Do you really want to meet someone who is on the other side of the front? At the same day? At the same place? Eye to an eye? What will happen? What is likely to happen?

One person mentioned a non-governmental organisational activity in Split, called Peace Initiative, the aim of which was to build a sustainable society after the war. Peace Initiative was run by 'therapists from the States' and organised two seminars each year, of fifty to fifty-five people, using large and small group work, in which role-play was used to encourage participants to discuss their fears and problems. The participant had attended three of these seminars, felt it very helpful and would like to see more of this kind of activity.

Work with children and families

Working through school programmes is necessary to generate and sustain peace, to understand and accept differences.

It doesn't matter ... which ethnicity or religion or who stayed or who was displaced person. It ... will be very well to try to do something together with children and parents, then they will listen. A facilitator will lead the discussion on the good way.

We have done great workshops for children who have been bereaved of parent. That was great work, children were collaborative and they liked our meetings. After a few years we stopped this project because they grew up. Now, we work in counselling centre where people could come or phone. But we found that interest is lower and lower.

Work with children in schools could be used.

Speaking of two child relatives who are orphaned, one person expressed a view with which the whole group agreed:

No-one has ever asked 'How do you feel?' The question in our society would be 'How are you?' and the answer would be 'Good' and that is that. So nobody ask about your feeling inside family. In school you don't have a psychologist … it is not a part of the culture, but it is also not part of the structure. We have not that and we need that.

Another group member expressed a view with which the group concurred, that preventive measures should be taken to help the present and future generations of children from being affected by the unexpressed suffering of others in their family affected by the war, parents and older siblings:

I don't see anybody who is working on prevention, especially in schools with children… OK, this generation is damaged and we can't help them a lot. But what we can do … We can help them to endure. To live with their damages, but we have to prevent those children who are still healthy not to be affected with the damages of the older ones.

In schools there is no any psychological help, which could be said that it is offered to children or to their parents. There is no communication with parents. Teachers, they don't communicate with parents. I think that it is a pity from both sides, that teacher or parents, parents especially, they don't like to say about their own hurts. They have effect on their children.

Participants' suggestions for educational programmes are set out under the sub heading 'Education for peace' under the responses to the next question.

8.   In your opinion, are there any other activities that may be helpful in building peace in this community?

There may be reasons for making a distinction between psychosocial activities and therapy, but sometimes the boundaries are unclear:

I remember one that we start work with the children in school and someone put in programme proposal for therapy, but we aren't psychologists or psychiatry [psychiatrists] so they said that we mustn't do this ... and after-wards we change this word and said 'psychological support' not 'therapy'.

I work mostly with children and it was helpful. I have tried to do work-shops with parents, adults, but I don't dare to do it any more, because there were so much emotions and I didn't know what to do. I am not a person who could do therapeutic interventions.

They have taken these other activities as instead of the therapy, or they have taken them as the therapy. That has been a fundamental mistake. They have seen sewing groups and they have seen work groups and they have seen building parks and all those kinds of activities as psychosocial therapy, the be all and end all and not included the therapy.

Public psychological education

It seems to me crucial to get round the taboos, to lower the taboos first of all, to say that these are the ways that you can help yourself. TV campaigns, radio campaigns, brochures, these sorts of measures.

Education for peace

Four groups felt that education is vitally important in the peacebuilding process, as a means of generating attitude change in this and future generations.

Building peace should be affirmed like human value.

I think that pupils and parents should take the initiative and that the most useful is working on prevention.

The purpose of the education would be

Learning non-violence, increasing self-esteem and self-confidence

and it was suggested that

Suitable ways of working with children are workshops in small groups (about ten children), either with children with behavioural disturbances or non-violent education. Also there is education between pupils-mediators. These pupils work with peers.

Other teachers include peace education in their lessons:

There are these little steps that each of us can make, either in an organ-ised way, or simply by doing. I do that every time by teaching, when I do. When I have my lectures with my students, we talk about things like 'What do you see as tolerance in your society?' We decide that you are tolerant or that your colleague is tolerant and how you understand this as a notion. Do we need it in our society? And things like that.

In Zupanja the group mentioned that one school had formed a committee with pupils and parents and had designed and implemented a programme of non-violent education. Another participant commented:

I think that projects like this one are only on paper. People just transcribe programme from somebody else. In my school we haven't a lot of problems and our programme (transcribed) hasn't been realised.

Group work for psychological change

Working with ... groups teaching them communications, changing their attitudes to an attitude of self-reliance, giving them the independence to deal with their own issues. It empowers them. It gives them a new self confidence. Getting rid of a lot of that block on mourning. In that way encouraging people to do sort of co-therapy on each other. Those kinds of interventions are necessary.

The group discussed different approaches to post-war ethnic reintegration:

Things like community work. People could work together to find a common aim ... building a centre together, employing people, getting people to work physically, actively together and communication ... you   know I think that's an important thing as well as psychotrauma.

Social reconstruction ... maybe you first need to work with individuals before you get people together ... and I know that in reconciliation work there are at least two different trends and one would say start with football games with two activities together and then dealing with the trauma; and the other one deals with individuals first and then you can put the group together and have joint activities. So we don't know which is working.

There has been an interesting psychological examination on the issue ... two groups of children who were made each other's enemies and then had to be reconciled. You had to have the overall aim you have to reach together and that actually did work in bringing them back together...

Rebuild this community for each other, not to be so divided, to realise they actually all need each other.

One participant felt that a reintegration programme requires therapeutic support to ensure success:

At the end of the day providing psychotherapy or some support so that to have a group doing therapy and reconciliation or joint activity together to make sure this works.

Ever practical, another person commented:

Groups are more economic.

It was suggested by CWWPP that a group programme should ideally last three years, because it takes this length of time to prepare and train people. However the lack of funding places constraints on this ideal. They were critical of the three-month programmes that they had to run at that time for economic reasons.

Positive aspects of the war

It is much better today than it was ... it is easier to go from our country to the neighbouring countries and once the communication among people [is established] there is a possibility of prevention of course.

It is better than it was before...five or six years ago, Serbians living in this area round Osijek would not even imagine they would be part of Croatia, or Croatian returnee or displaced person would not imagine that they could live together with their neighbours and now it is going on. They live together. It is not love and peace, but it is a step forward and tolerated. So in a way we are going a little forward from the situation ten years ago, but in the same time, I don't see that we have capacities, approaches, methodologies, resources inside society really to solve these current conflicts on a way to overcome that and to heal society.

Political, economic and social change

One participant suggested that mental health would be improved through a reduction of insecurity by establishing trust in politicians and implementation of human rights laws and practice.

For instance people probably would be thinking about be more [better] mental health if they would have higher level of trust on our politicians for instance. This feeling of insecurity and ... [if] our politicians will be honest or doing by norms in society would very much influence the mental health of [the] whole population. If human rights practice and laws would be implemented it would help the mental care of those victims whose rights are endangered.

I think that solution is in economic development and then we could solve other problems.

You need political national and international work. You need economic, I would say equal economic treatment and that is definitely a question of human rights...It must come at all levels, institutional, international and national, regional and local level and you have to have an integrated approach to see and to try to tackle the political leaders, then meet political parties and then grassroots levels of the community and with each group do different action in all fields also. That is my ideal.

Peace study centres

My personal desire, is to see one day in Osijek, a peace study centre, in order really to develop different strategies, different promotions, actually what peacemaking and peace sustainability is all about. Because that is what we lack the most.

One participant noted the lack of professionalism in peacemaking and said that she hoped for a formal training and evaluation system, similar to the rigorous training of a teacher. She hoped that there would be set up academic and training institutes for peacemaking in Croatia. There have been discussions about an institute for peace studies, or a centre for social transformation and hopes have also been expressed for a specialist academic peace study centre in Osijek associated with the university, similar to the Department of Peace Studies at the University of Bradford.

This chapter has set out the perceptions and views of the focus group participants on the broad themes of the peacefulness and unpeacefulness of the communities of Osijek, Vukovar and Zupanja.

The exploration of this theme is deepened in the next chapter, bringing together all the data from the research and reflecting on it in the context of Curle's approach to psychological change in peacemaking, exploring the ways in which the data carries Curle's work forward and identifying some areas which might benefit from further research.

Chapter 6

The relationship of trauma, conflict, therapy and peacemaking: taking Adam Curle's approach forward

I think that at first we need peace with ourselves.

A lot of love and respect again as a part of our life...But love, for me is...the most important...it is necessary that people will be talking about their hurts and have the courage to cry in front of the group. Crying is so important as laughing. These two things for me is a good therapy.

...the point being, defuse them first, right and then merge them, let's say so.

(Quotations from the focus groups, 2002)

This chapter brings the perceptions and views of the focus groups together with the academic theory of peace and the research relating to posttraumatic stress and Posttraumatic Stress Disorder (PTSD), all of which are considered from the perspective of Adam Curle's approach to peacemaking.

First, the psychological suffering described in the case study data is considered in conjunction with western definitions, diagnoses and measurements of mental illness, focusing on the concept of posttraumatic stress, PTSD and the problems in diagnosis of PTSD and other psychiatric illnesses. Next, I explore the potential difficulty of understanding the complex psychological reactions to the war in Eastern Slavonia and the difficulties of diagnosis and assessment in the light of the diagnostic criteria of psychiatric illnesses related to anxiety, depression and posttraumatic stress. The focus group discussions indicate a perception of widespread continuing suffering on many levels. In many cases the reported symptoms do not represent any formal psychiatric illness, but it is possible that in other cases, undiagnosed psychiatric illness may exist.

Whatever the diagnosis or terminology used may be, whether we call it depression, PTSD, or something else, it is still suffering – however we conceptualise and label it. The concern of those involved in humanitarian aid following war must be to find a way to help people through that suffering in ways that work in the context of different situations and cultures.

The resources available to the community to alleviate the psychological effects of war are considered in the context of the problems described by the projects concerning the availability and effectiveness of therapy, the types of psychological help available and the social and cultural reasons for the perceived stigma associated with receiving psychiatric treatment or psychological therapy. Particular attention is given to coping with memories of the past and to consideration of the needs of children within the community (which often remain unrecognised) and the ways in which children and their families might benefit from psychological and social assistance.

One of the outcomes of this research was the realisation that the psychological and social effects of war might be considered collectively as the 'post-war syndrome'. This should be clearly distinguished from a mental illness, but has components that would benefit from psychological, social and other forms of support. The post-war syndrome is not a finite concept. Its psychological aspects are constantly changing as new conditions arise, encompassing individual and community experience and will vary according to many factors including geography, resources, culture, the traumas experienced and the nature, experience and response of individuals.

I was also very interested in the concept of collective suffering and community healing and this chapter reflects upon what one focus group participant describes as the 'silent war' in the context of Adam Curle's perceptions of peacefulness and unpeacefulness and how the activities of the projects carry his theoretical approach to peacemaking on into the future, particularly the recommendations of the focus groups for the creation of structural and cultural change for peace in the community, in particular the reintegration of returning refugees, human rights, justice, economy and education.

The final part of this chapter addresses the social and psychological healing of the wounds of war. The earlier sections identified and explored the problems and confusions of understanding the nature of the psychological suffering of the post-war syndrome and the problems of diagnosis of complex symptomology, leading to difficulty in identifying appropriate treatment approaches. Added to this is a perception of a lack of resources for treatment, the extensive societal needs of the post-war syndrome and a vital need for peace building. The task of the community is therefore complex and difficult, and we explore the needs of a community involved in healing the psychological effects of war and at the same time working for peace. Curle's innovative approach to the treatment of posttraumatic stress with returning former prisoners of war in the Civil Resettlement Units (CRUs) during 1945 is a starting point for a community based approach to address the post-war syndrome. His approach in the CRUs is extended from the original focus on individual recovery and re-socialisation, to the work of the projects in the multi-level recovery of a community in the context of the process of peacemaking and the psychological and social support which might be helpful to individuals and the community in alleviating the suffering in the aftermath of war and to facilitate the transition of the community into peace.

Psychological suffering: how useful are definitions and measurements of psychiatric illness in the context of the psychological effects of war?

Does the concept of posttraumatic stress and the criteria for posttraumatic stress disorder described in DSM IV have any relevance for the communities of Eastern Slavonia? If it does, what that might be? In the discussion that follows, reference to 'PTSD' means the psychiatric illness of Posttraumatic Stress Disorder defined by the criteria set out on pages 463-468 in DSM IV-TR published by the American Psychiatric Association in 2000. The participants in the focus groups were not necessarily describing PTSD or any other formally diagnosed psychiatric illness and unless they specifically mention PTSD, we have to assume that they were describing, in their own way, the general psychological effects of war.

For clarity, in the text here, formal DSM IV TR diagnoses are denoted by the use of initial capitals (e.g. Major Depressive Disorder) and informal descriptions are all in lower case, for example 'posttraumatic stress' (meaning the stress associated with traumatic events but where a formal diagnosis of PTSD has not been made, or where some, but not all the criteria for PTSD may be present); 'depression' (meaning a depressed mood, or a psychological state not formally diagnosed as Major Depressive Disorder, Dysthymic

Disorder, or any other mood disorder); and 'anxiety' (meaning an anxious mood, or a psychological state not formally diagnosed as any anxiety disorder).

Medical documentation records that, between 1991 and 1993 in Croatia, over 300,000 people from Croatia's total population of 4.7 million are reported to have been expelled from their homes and that the majority of the population was directly exposed to missile attacks on their towns and villages and some witnessed combat (Kostovic, Judas et al. 1993). Around 6,000 people were captured and imprisoned. Some were held for several months before release, experiencing or witnessing rape or other torture. Refugees arriving in Croatia after the war had experiences including loss, bereavement, imprisonment, rape, torture and deprivation. (Kozaric-Kovacic, Folnegovic-Smalc et al. 1995). This led to an unusually high proportion of civilian victims who had suffered traumatic events (Henigsberg, Folnegovic-Smalc et al. 2001: 544). Psychiatrist researchers reported that this situation made PTSD 'one of the most frequent psychiatric disorders in Croatia' (Henigsberg, Folnegovic-Smalc et al. 2001: 544), but the precise nature and extent of the psychological and psychosomatic consequences of the 1991-95 war remain unclear in Croatia generally and in Eastern Slavonia in particular (Henigsberg, Folnegovic-Smalc et al. 2001: 544). 'Research is needed to better define the medical concept of trauma and the range of phenomena of traumatic stress in the context of the Croatian post-war situation' (OSCE 2002: 3).

One of the problems of defining the concept of trauma is that the term 'traumatic stress' confounds two distinct constructs, 'stress' and 'mental traumatisation' and Shalev (1996: 77) points out that the term 'posttraumatic' '...fosters a retrospective definition of events as traumatic, based on their pathogenic effects'. The failure to distinguish between different traumatic stressors, for example road traffic accidents and war or holocaust, creates 'an unbalanced foundation for an etiological theory of stress-related disorders' (Shalev 1996: 78). The traumatic stressors to which the focus group participants referred, or to which they had been exposed, varied according to personal circumstances and their local community's experience of the war. Not all people exposed to traumatic stressors develop PTSD. Psychological reactions are influenced by societal and individual factors.

As seen in Chapter 3, stress is an adaptive response to arousal, setting up psychobiological reactions, which eventually subside to restore homeostasis. PTSD appears to be a disturbance in (or a departure from) the normal pattern

of arousal in which homeostasis does not occur and the psychological disturbance persists. Pitman, Shin et al. (2001) proposed five possibilities about the
human psychobiological reaction to PTSD, which, summarised, are that:

- a pre-existing brain abnormality increases the risk of exposure to PTSD
  causing events
- a pre-existing brain abnormality increases vulnerability to PTSD after
  exposure to traumatic events
- the traumatic exposure causes a brain abnormality and that abnormality
  produces PTSD
- the traumatic exposure produces PTSD and that leads to the abnormality
- or traumatic exposure produces PTSD and sequelae leading on to complications (e.g. alcoholism), which then cause the abnormality.

It is also possible that a combination of one or more of these factors may
be present. There seems to be no clear linear relationship between the
severity of a traumatic event and the eventual psychological consequences for
those involved, which implies that social and individual factors may influence
the psychological outcome. Some of the potential influencing factors were
identified in this research and it seems that, once anxiety or depression have
become established, there may be a negative feedback loop in which PTSD
becomes more likely to occur (Bracken 2002: 78-79), but further research is
necessary to clarify whether there are any causal connections.

Whilst DSM IV TR does not overtly state that PTSD is a normal response
to an abnormal (traumatic) situation, this view is implicit in some modern
approaches to PTSD. Shalev suggests that, if PTSD is seen as a normal
response to an abnormal situation, then that response may have continued
beyond its functional usefulness (the psychodynamic view); alternatively, the
behavioural view suggests that it may be a learned response which is not yet
extinguished. The research of van der Kolk and others on the psychobiological effects of traumatic stress appears to support the proposal that PTSD may
be defined as the result of a dysfunctional physiological reaction to a traumatic
stressor, which is distinguishable from the normal physiological response to
stress.

DSM IV TR suggests definitive statistical risks of PTSD following traumatic events, particularly in those people considered vulnerable, reflecting a
general perception exemplified in an extract from a training manual from the
Government of Australia:

Experience has shown that when very serious and traumatic events occur, the staff involved are at high risk for developing post-traumatic stress disorder (PTSD). Although debriefing and associated interventions may prevent the development of symptoms in less intense cases, it does not seem to do so in severe cases. As such, staff usually need additional assistance such as rapid access to treatment from trained trauma counsellors or mental health clinicians. (Human Resources Branch 1997: 3).

Yehuda and McFarlane (1995) conducted a review of relevant research findings in the decade since PTSD was first categorised. They comment that clinical researchers continue to make observations such as the relative infrequency of the disorder following exposure to trauma; the existence of risk factors other than trauma that may predict PTSD; the atypical rather than normative nature of the biological response in PTSD; and the prevalence of other pre-and posttraumatic comorbid psychiatric conditions. They suggest that there is a conflict between those who wish to normalise the status of those who have experienced trauma and those who prefer to characterise PTSD as a psychiatric illness. They suggest that the future of the traumatic stress field depends upon an acknowledgment of the competing agendas and paradigms, clarification of theoretical inconsistencies and a reformulation of conceptual issues. Recent research continues to challenge the assumption that PTSD is likely to occur after the experience of trauma. McFarlane, in a meta-analysis of epidemiological studies of PTSD following trauma, concludes:

PTSD is a predictable consequence of traumatic events, however, specific prevalence rates are determined by a range of issues, such as the intensity of exposure, the prevalence of risk factors in the population and the recruitment rates of different studies. (McFarlane and de Girolamo 1996: 144).

Perhaps it is not surprising that, given the extensive traumatic experiences of war in Croatia, psychological responses to these stressors are reported in the case study to be similarly widespread and there is a current lack of any national epidemiological study of PTSD, Acute Stress Disorder, or any other psychological and psychosomatic effects of the war in Croatia.

There is a difficulty in establishing a diagnosis of an illness where the aetiology is built into its diagnostic criteria. In addition, research has failed to establish any temporal linear causality between a traumatic stressor and the onset of PTSD. However, it is widely accepted in western approaches to psychiatry that experiencing or witnessing traumatic events is potentially harmful. Child protection law in the United Kingdom was recently amended, perhaps because the DSM IV TR criteria include the recognition that PTSD may be caused just as much by witnessing traumatic events as by directly experiencing them. The threshold criteria for significant harm in the Children Act 1989 have been amended by section 120 of the Adoption and Children Act 2002 to include in the definition of 'significant harm' the 'impairment suffered from seeing or hearing the ill-treatment of another'. Children witnessing domestic violence or other abuse at home may now fall within the new section 31(9)(b) of the Children Act 1989.

A further issue is that awareness of the psychological effects of trauma might be thought by some to risk inculcating an expectation of suffering the illness, or even producing symptomology. I encountered this difficulty in my research and elsewhere in post-war psychological, humanitarian aid and peace work. Familiarity with the DSM IV TR criteria through work or education from humanitarian aid agencies about posttraumatic stress makes it difficult to know whether consciously or subconsciously, feelings and experiences are expressed with those diagnostic criteria in mind and if so, to what extent those criteria then influence perceptions of the prevalence of psychiatric illness or symptomology.

The concept of psychiatric illness generally and the normative 'western' definitions of posttraumatic stress and PTSD have been questioned by Bracken and others, but although some focus group members several times distinguished Croatia from 'the west' in varying ways, the focus group discussions in this case study appear to show a consensual and apparently uncritical acceptance of the western approach to psychiatric illness generally and the syndrome of posttraumatic stress in particular. Croatian mental health research adopts western methods of measurement (e.g. the Hamilton Depression Scale, the Mississippi PTSD Questionnaire and Watson's PTSD Questionnaire) and descriptions of illnesses linked with DSM IV (Kadenic 1998; Klain 1998; Ljubotina and Arcel 1998; Mandic and Javornik 1998; Marusic, Kozaric-Kovacic et al. 1998) and mental health practitioners are trained in approaches reflecting western concepts of psychiatry and psychology, including the conceptual basis of depression, anxiety and PTSD. Any criticisms levelled at western psychiatry, therefore, may also be relevant to some Croatian psychiatric and mental health practice.

However, although there is a strong perception in the focus groups of wide-spread psychological suffering, there is very little suggestion from the participants of widespread or generalised formal psychiatric illness. The participants described a wide range of feelings and experiences which have some features in common with those of depression, anxiety and posttraumatic stress, but they may be describing a much wider concept which I have called here the 'post-war syndrome' which would benefit from further research and a better understanding of which could enhance the peacemaking process following violent conflict.

Complex psychological and physiological reactions to the trauma of war

All the focus groups described psychological symptoms which they had experienced and witnessed and which they attributed to the trauma of war. Some people referred specifically to 'PTSP' (Posttraumatski stresni poremecaj, the Croatian translation for PTSD), but most participants described symptoms in much more general terms.

For ethical reasons, it was not appropriate to elicit any personal accounts of individuals' traumatic experiences for research purposes. However, in the course of my work over the last ten years in Croatia and Kosovo, staff and volunteers in non-governmental organisations have given personal accounts in confidence of exposure to traumatic events, followed by persistent re-experiencing of the events through flashbacks, images, thoughts, intrusive memories and distressing dreams. Some of these people have sought formal medical, psychiatric or psychological advice and help, but others have not. Some turn to alcohol (or other substances) for symptom relief. The stress of this type of work is great and even for those involved in providing psychological assistance, sometimes the perceived social stigma of mental illness and the culture of suffering in silence remain very influential.

Depression and the emotional numbing of posttraumatic stress

In the case study, symptoms of depression were reported as common in the community, linking apathy with depression, with confusion, a lack of vision of a future and emotional numbing. The term 'depression' was used by participants to indicate a mood, rather than a formal diagnosis, but the symptoms described by the groups as 'apathy', 'emotional numbing' and 'no vision of the future' bear a remarkable similarity to the DSM IV criteria for PTSD (see Chapter 3).

Herman (1992a: 91) suggests that prolonged depression almost always accompanies trauma. Following the war in the Former Yugoslavia, many of those who sought and received help from humanitarian aid programmes had suffered catastrophic life events that were reported as capable of generating posttraumatic stress or reactive depression (Arcel, Folnegovic-Smalc et al. 1998; Weisaeth 1998), but the symptoms of depression and anxiety overlap with those of PTSD, making any differential diagnosis difficult. Psychological symptoms indicating anxiety and/or depressive states were the most frequently reported in refugee studies conducted in Croatia (Arcel, Folnegovic-Smalc et al. 1998; Ljubotina and Arcel 1998).

In addition, other psychological conditions may co-exist, increasing the distress and dysfunction of PTSD and 'leading to a high correlation between the severity of emotional numbing and the presence of melancholic features in PTSD patients' (Henigsberg, Folnegovic-Smalc et al. 2001: 544) and psychotic symptoms may also follow traumatic experiences (Bleich and Moskowitz 2000). As seen in Chapter 3, the DSM IV TR diagnosis of any psychiatric illness requires a specified number of the diagnostic criteria to be present, having subsisted for specific durations and frequencies.

The symptoms reported in the case study bear considerable similarity to the 'low energy or fatigue', 'low self esteem', 'poor concentration or difficulty making decisions' and 'feelings of hopelessness' in the DSM IV TR diagnostic criteria for Dysthymic Disorder (American Psychiatric Association 2000: 376-381). Other commonly encountered symptoms of Dysthymic Disorder may be 'feelings of inadequacy; generalised loss of interest or pleasure; social withdrawal; feelings of guilt or brooding about the past; subjective feelings of irritability or excessive anger; and decreased activity, effectiveness or productivity.'

Major Depressive Disorder is characterised by one or more Major Depressive Episodes (American Psychiatric Association 2000: 369-376), and the symptoms include 'depressed mood', markedly diminished interest or pleasure in all or almost all activities', fatigue or loss of energy', feelings of worthlessness or excessive or inappropriate guilt' and 'diminished ability to think or concentrate or indecisiveness.' The criteria also include 'recurrent thoughts of death (not just fear of dying)' and 'suicidal ideation without a specific plan or a suicide attempt or a specific plan for committing suicide'.

DSM IV-TR reports that Major Depressive Disorder is associated with increased pain and physical illness, deceased physical social and role functioning and a high risk of mortality by suicide, with increased risk in individuals aged over 55 (American Psychiatric Association 2000: 371). This is relevant to the case study because the risk of suicide was reported as a major concern, along with family violence. Suicides were reported as having increased since the war and were noted among war veterans, youth and the elderly. Causal factors attributed to suicidal ideation by the focus group participants included insufficient money on which to live, family problems, property problems and a lack of effective psychological help. Suicide was perceived by some as an extreme form of emotional withdrawal, resulting from an inability to communicate or deal with high levels of distress, or the results of an extreme level of suppression; 'people actually hide their problems'. This view is supported by other therapists in Croatia, for example Pavlovic and Marusic (2001). One could understand how the interrelationship and possible co-existence of social, economic and physical hardship, depression and posttraumatic stress could create or exacerbate the 'severity of emotional numbing and the presence of melancholic features' reported by Henigsberg, Folnegovic-Smalc et al. (2001: 544) and lead to the situations described by the focus groups.

The PTSD criterion C (1) refers to efforts to avoid thoughts, feelings or conversations associated with the trauma and C (2) refers to efforts to avoid activities, places or people that arouse recollections of the trauma. There were many descriptions amongst the participants of people hiding their problems and of undercurrents of tension. There were references in the groups to holding back feelings and memories, becoming numb and not opening 'Pandora's box'. Reminders of the past were seen as both positive and negative. They could trigger negative emotions but some people felt the need to remember the past as an incentive to create a different future. Remembrance is addressed later in the context of peacebuilding. Silence about the past, or not expressing feelings, was described as 'suppressed mourning'. This suppression was not generally perceived as helpful because it generates psychological tension; '…people try to put their hurts under the carpet but it make a very big press on them'. Others in the groups perceived silence to be a result of peer pressure or a cultural expectation of repression of emotions. This was not generally seen as a good thing and some described the visible relief they had felt themselves in talking, or seen in individuals in group-work when people gave free expression to their feelings, a view confirmed by the reports of Croatian psychiatrists (Simunkovic and Arcel 1998). In the focus groups, silence was also construed as a defence mechanism, necessary in time of war to cope, but with the implication that perhaps this is now no longer necessary in the present safety of peacetime; 'this was to keep the collective sanity during the war, to keep everybody on the sort of level you need to keep functioning'.

Bracken (2002: 211) suggests that 'therapy can have the effect of increasing the isolation of suffering individuals by encouraging a narrow focus on their memories, thoughts and beliefs.' If Bracken means an egocentric focus on the content of memories, this would be a valid criticism if the need for re-socialisation remains unmet. As seen in Chapter 2, Curle identified the problem of 'desocialisation' for thousands of returning prisoners of war and he describes the vital process of reintegration into work, family and community through the work of the CRUs in 1945-6. The community approach to post-war trauma relief such as that provided by the five projects in Croatia extends way beyond simply addressing individual emotions in isolation from others. Their work provides an opportunity for people to open up their awareness to hear and empathise with the experience of others and to establish and consolidate psychological and social reconnection, important components of healing (Simunkovic and Arcel 1998). The work of the projects therefore meets both aspects of Bracken's criticism. The focus group participants described sharing the experience of suffering as offering emotional relief, despite a perceived local culture of silence. Even in the context of a group of people who are unfamiliar with each other, sharing feelings was seen as helpful, although initially difficult. Suicide was seen as attributable in part to the lack of opportunity or desire to talk to someone about problems 'openly' and 'honestly'. The group members were highly critical of those who try to repress the feelings of others and in all the groups there was a consensus that talking and communication of problems is psychologically beneficial, a view confirmed by other Croatian mental health practitioners (Simunkovic and Arcel 1998).

Psychological arousal of posttraumatic stress: intrusive memories

Participants reported generalised fear, anxiety, insomnia, fear of open spaces, fear of darkness and psychosis. Anger was widely reported and particularly noted amongst children, in and out of school. Two participants related events where anger in public places had flared up into violence with lethal weapons. Others noted the increase in domestic violence, also suggesting that children copy anger they have experienced in their home. This increased arousal, evidenced by anger and irritability, is reflected in the PTSD criterion D (2) and it is characteristic of posttraumatic stress.

Van der Kolk offers an explanation for the hyperarousal and re-experiencing of posttraumatic stress, suggesting that excessive stimulation of the central nervous system at the time of the traumatic event might result in a chronic psychobiological dysregulation (van der Kolk 1997: 255). He suggests that neuronal changes occur with a negative impact on learning, habituation and stimulus discrimination. The findings of Le Doux (1987, 1992) and Davis, Walker et al (1997) identified the critical role of the amygdala in cue conditioning and stimulus discrimination. The hyperarousal which occurs on reminders of the trauma and also in response to intense but neutral stimuli (e.g. the acoustic startle reflex) may provoke undifferentiated 'flight or fight' responses (Yehuda, Southwick et al. 1990 in van der Kolk 1997: 18). It is thought likely that serotonin has a role in regulating that hormonal balance and that decreased serotonin levels correlate with increased impulsivity and aggression (van der Kolk 1994: 257).

Van der Kolk suggests that physiological arousal can trigger trauma-related memories and that, conversely, the memories precipitate physiological arousal. The memory trace is therefore reinforced and those affected are literally 'unable to put the trauma behind them' (Van der Kolk 1994: 253, 260).

DSM IV-TR records no repetitive pattern of physiological arousal with associated intrusive memories in Major Depression but it is interesting to note that although individuals suffering Major Depressive Episodes or Dysthymic Disorder usually describe their mood as sad or 'down in the dumps', their mood may be irritable rather than sad. Some people tend to emphasise their bodily aches and pains rather than their feelings. Others may be emotionally volatile:

> Many individuals report or exhibit increased irritability (e.g. persistent anger, a tendency to response to events with angry outbursts or blaming others, or an exaggerated sense of frustration over minor matters). In children and   adolescents, an irritable or cranky mood may develop rather than a sad or dejected mood. (American Psychiatric Association 2000: 349)

Similarly:

'Children and adolescents with Dysthymic Disorder are usually irritable and cranky as well as depressed. They have low self-esteem and poor social skills and are pessimistic.' (American Psychiatric Association 2000: 377- 378)

In social and economic circumstances where there are prevailing conditions of difficulty, for example the financial hardship, violence, and loss described in the case study, anger and frustration may be exacerbated and coping mechanisms may be depleted or inadequate. It is easy to understand how the domestic violence and aggression described in the case study might arise when domestic pressures feel intolerable. Children living with volatile family members and subjected to aggression may respond similarly themselves. The case study revealed instances of direct interpersonal violence between neighbours, mistrust and verbal abuse and aggressive acts such as vandalism and stealing or poisoning land. If one accepts Korn's description of the process of enculturation as the encoding of sensory information as percepts, it is possible that in an environment where acts of violence are the norm, a resignation to or acceptance of aggression may be generated within a family system, or in a locality, contributing to cultural violence (Galtung 1990; Miall, Ramsbotham et al 1999: 15). The participating projects describe this syndrome in talking about the research issues of peacefulness and unpeacefulness in their community, discussed later in this chapter.

Participants noted the prevalence of substance abuse, mainly alcohol, drugs and smoking in adults. They expressed particular concern about an increase in young people drinking and smoking, taking the view that for young teenagers 'this is very serious'. The amount of illegal drug use was seen to be increasing and there is reported over-use of prescription drugs. Van der Kolk (1996: 188) points out that in the aftermath of trauma, those affected may make efforts to regain control over affect regulation by methods such as self-mutilation, bingeing and purging, or the use of alcohol and drugs. Interestingly, self-mutilation was not mentioned at all in the focus groups.

Alcohol is reported to be 'the oldest medication for the treatment of post-traumatic stress and may well be an effective short term medication for sleep disturbances, nightmares and other intrusive PTSD symptoms' (van der Kolk 1996: 191). Cessation of drinking may cause a rebound effect, in which the intrusions return. He comments that 'self help groups such as Alcoholics Anonymous seem to have grasped this issue intuitively and with extraordinary insight, seem to have incorporated effective posttraumatic treatment in their twelve steps'. In 2002, a local businessman was setting up a meeting of Alcoholics Anonymous in Osijek with the assistance of Dr Tauber. By 2005, that Alcoholics Anonymous meeting had grown sufficiently to hold a conference.

A high proportion of people in this area smoke tobacco and frequent smoking breaks are expected in workshops and group meetings. There were no statistics available about the recreational use of non-prescribed drugs, but their use also impacts on the psychological effects of trauma. 'Heroin has powerful effects on muting feelings of rage and aggression, whereas cocaine has significant antidepressant action' (van der Kolk 1996: 191). DSM IV-TR, however, warns that substance dependence (particularly cocaine or alcohol) may contribute to the onset or exacerbation of Major Depressive Disorder (American Psychiatric Association 2000: 373).

One might question whether the present lack of trust widely reported by the focus groups is linked in any way with the hypervigilance associated with experience of trauma described in the DSM IV-TR criterion D (4) for PTSD. However, given the description by the participants of violent outbursts on the streets, inter ethnic conflict amongst former friends, neighbours and relatives, continuing feelings of insecurity would be entirely understandable.

Physiological effects of posttraumatic stress

'After trauma, body and mind suffer simultaneously' (Ljubotina and Arcel 1998: 231). Medical staff and other project members described an increased number of physical ailments and psychosomatic conditions following the war, including circulatory system problems; also gastrointestinal problems, asthma and endocrine and immune system problems. Reporting on their work with returning female refugees, psychiatrists commented, 'Many of the somatic symptoms indicate a high level of physiological arousal indicative of PTSD reactions and anxiety states.' (Ljubotina and Arcel 1998: 235).

DSM IV-TR records in discussion of Major Depressive Episode that, 'Some individuals emphasise somatic complaints (e.g. bodily aches and pains) rather than reporting feelings of sadness' (American-Psychiatric-Association 2000: 349). Culturally, perhaps physical symptoms are more socially acceptable. An emphasis on somatic symptoms rather than recognition of psychological needs was noted in Croatian war survivors (Simunkovic and

Arcel 1998: 145; Popovic 1998: 169). 'Clients find organic, somatic disorders far more acceptable than psychological disorders' (Kraljevic, Bamburac et al. 1998: 173).

There are suggestions of organic effects of stress. In a paper addressing work with torture victims, Kraljevic, Bamburac et al (1998: 173), referring to a client with rheumatoid arthritis, explain that in psychodynamic theory, some psychosomatic diseases are explained by an inability to express anger: 'Hence aggression is suppressed and is then directed to one of the organic systems.' They then suggest that the appearance of rheumatoid arthritis '… is greatly influenced by stress' and 'the combination of the medical and psychological approach contributed complementarily to the improvement of both the mental and clinical status of our client'. This combined approach is proposed as a treatment model (Kraljevic, Bamburac et al. 1998: 178).

Post-war restoration and rehabilitation in Eastern Slavonia

The physical and economic pressures in Eastern Slavonia leave people little time to deal with psychological issues. Financial resources are limited for medical and social care. For those who have severe psychological problems, hospitalisation (with drug interventions) was understood by the participants to be the only residential resource in the region. Domestic violence was noted by the focus groups as prevalent, but they commented that there are no SOS help lines and there is only one refuge in Osijek, with three or four beds for residents, and this has to serve the whole region. There were few other social resources for the treatment of alcoholism, so far as the groups were aware, save for hospitalisation, but in Osijek there is now the new Alcoholics Anonymous meeting.

One person, referring to the level of mental health provision, said that 'There is a reasonably good, not quite a western standard, but a fairly high standard of psychology and psychiatry in Croatia'. I felt that this remark was probably intended as limited praise, but sadly, it was rather typical of comments I have heard in other areas from foreign professionals in non-governmental organisations who arrive to provide post-war humanitarian aid. The problem is that local professionals feel either patronised or de-skilled by such an assumption of the superiority of undefined and intangible 'western' approaches with a concomitant devaluing of local training and experience. The speaker went on to explain that there is a problem of getting good mental health practitioners from the major cities and universities to outlying areas such as Eastern

Slavonia. A participant from Zupanja said that some small villages, despite many traumatic events, had great difficulty in obtaining psychological help. The general perception in the groups was of limited mental health provision with present resources insufficient to meet local needs.

I wanted to find out more about some of the local mental health treatment facilities in the region and also spoke informally with mental health practitioners working in Osijek, Zupanja and Vukovar about local facilities and methods of treatment for trauma. Information about the national approach to the regulation of mental health provision and the treatment of posttraumatic stress was elicited from consultation with the University of Zagreb Department of Psychiatry, a non-governmental organisation and research material including the Croatian Medical Journal.

The focus groups, whilst discussing local mental health resources, did not mention some of the resources that had been described by mental health practitioners as available. The reason for this was unclear. If there is a lack of information, this could perhaps be improved by establishing regular communication between government mental health service providers, local mental health practitioners and service users to clarify local needs and the availability and location of resources. The non-governmental organisations and local residents would benefit from a public list of local resources for the purpose of making appropriate referrals.

There was also generalised concern in the focus groups about the perceived overload in the mental health system, causing a time pressure for mental health practitioners. Stemming from this high workload, they identified specific problems. The groups felt that there is a reticence in the general population to seek help from psychiatrists, who are perceived as mostly prescribing medication and being very busy, working within the constraints of a lack of time and funding. They are perceived to have insufficient time for adequate personal therapeutic contact with individuals, giving anecdotal evidence of time pressure leading to lack of empathy and inattention to the detail of a patient's concerns. More than one focus group member described the experiences of patients of brief consultations, followed by provision of a prescription and then being quickly dismissed. It is unclear whether the effect of these pressures may have contributed to the use of drugs as the preferred method of treatment by psychiatrists and general practitioners. Possible explanations of this phenomenon may be that medication may be perceived to be more effective than talking; that psychiatrists and general practitioners do not have the emotional resources or time to provide longer consultations for each patient; or that the provision of medication may indirectly relieve the organisational pressure on health professionals by limiting the consultation time with each patient. Most interventions by psychiatrists and general practitioners for psychiatric illness were described by the focus groups as based on medication.

The similarity of PTSD symptoms to those of other psychiatric disorders may cloud diagnosis and present problems in treatment. However, the psychobiological symptoms of PTSD are distinctive (Yehuda and McFarlane 1995). Van der Kolk et al. suggest that traumatic stress needs to be treated differently at various phases of people's lives after the trauma and that the pharmacological treatments that may be effective at one stage may not be so effective at another. They recommend initial management with drugs that decrease autonomic arousal, decreasing the nightmares and flashbacks, promoting sleep and preventing the limbic kindling that underlies PTSD symptomology. At a later stage, if PTSD is established, serotonin re-uptake blockers may be 'helpful in allowing people to attend to current tasks and to decrease their dwelling upon past fears, interpretations and fixations' (van der Kolk, McFarlane et al. 1996: 424-425). Other reports of research into medication for PTSD (Davidson, Swartz et al. 1985; van der Kolk, Dreyfuss et al. 1994) suggest that the appropriate psychopharmacological treatment for posttraumatic stress should vary according to the time lapse after the traumatic event and should be guided by the person's presenting symptoms. They suggest that, if medication is necessary, the optimum treatment approach may be a combination of drugs, along with psychological and social support.

A doctor working in Croatia explained that various combinations of drugs may be used to treat posttraumatic stress and that some of these cause side effects and additional difficulties for patients. An additional problem, which may occur in post-war humanitarian aid work, is that donors provide supplies of psychotropic drugs, but these may be out of date or medications less frequently used elsewhere in Europe because of their known side effects and/or because of their expense. I was told that the reason that expense is relevant is that some unscrupulous donors may provide supplies of expensive drugs free of charge initially, hoping that, once the free supply from the donor ceases, the prescribing body or the patient will then buy that drug. Alternatively, in some situations, insurance companies refuse to pay for the more expensive drugs, so some companies may seek good publicity by giving these drugs to 'needy' countries.

Clients in one counselling group of war veterans were reported to be taking combinations of as many as six to twelve medications simultaneously with the risk that they develop addictions to these drugs or that they may combine them with alcohol. Posttraumatic stress is notoriously difficult to treat with medication and treatment often has to be experimental to find the right combination for the patient at that moment in time. Acknowledging the uncertain effects of drug combinations and the existence of potential side effects in newer drugs, there is a need for further clinical research into medication for treating posttraumatic stress.

In Eastern Slavonia, apart from medication, psychoanalytical and psychodynamic approaches predominate in psychiatry. Clinical psychologists in Croatia mostly tend to use cognitive and behavioural approaches for the psychological treatment of posttraumatic stress, treatment modalities which are also recommended in the UK by the National Institute of Clinical Excellence (NICE) Guideline No 26 of March 2005.

In Croatia, clinical psychologists, psychotherapists and counsellors mainly use the humanistic therapies, including transactional analysis and gestalt therapy. Music therapy, play therapy and group therapy are used with children. Some specialist treatments, including EMDR, are also used for the treatment of trauma. Following the war, other treatment approaches are being explored and a local resident in Osijek told me that alternative therapies such as reiki are gaining in popularity.

In Eastern Slavonia, a number of factors might mitigate against seeking help for psychological distress. One of the main symptoms of posttraumatic stress and of depression, as discussed earlier, is apathy. The concomitant lack of self-confidence, motivation and assertiveness in itself mitigates against seeking appropriate help. The focus group research indicated that social and economic problems were regarded as paramount and only when these were satisfactorily addressed could people feel safe enough to tackle mental health issues, reflecting Maslow's hierarchy of needs and Curle's conditions of peace.

Psychiatric diagnosis can disempower and stigmatise individuals by labelling their experience as pathology. In the 1996 and 1997 workshops in Zupanja, the participants clearly indicated that they did not regard themselves as clinically ill, but many did feel that they and their communities were suffering psychologically. It is in my view inappropriate (and some would say insulting) to broadly categorise the psychological pain of the survivors of war or ethnic cleansing as widespread clinical mental illness. Nevertheless, survivors may well be in need of material and social support and could be helped by community-based projects offering problem-focused and emotion-focused coping strategies (Arcel, Folnegovic-Smalc et al. 1998: 46). This attitude is recognised in training for major disasters (De Wolfe 2000). Curle records that this approach of being normal, but suffering, was prevalent amongst the returning prisoners of war in the 'transitional communities' of the CRUs. The soldiers were treated with understanding and empathy and with recognition of their loyalty to comrades and their understandable guilty feelings for having survived when their comrades had perished. This sense of solidarity and mutual social support proved important in their reintegration into family and social life (Curle 2001b).

A diagnosis of mental illness may attract social stigma in the community. It could also prove reductionist, serving 'to silence other possibilities' (Bracken 2002: 4). Conversely, psychosocial problems may be ignored in the presence of obvious medical needs (Hecimovic 1998: 128-129).

> Highly placed administrative officials in the health sector have a predominantly biological medial orientation and are not trained to observe psycho-social problems, so they think that they do not exist. They cannot even guess the real magnitude of the needs for psycho-social help and consequently cannot plan adequate answers/solutions. Sometimes it seems that it is enough to have a good will, common sense, or love and sympathy for the victims, as well as strong will to reinstate order, to solve the problem. (Hecimovic 1998: 123)

When NGOs are designing programmes for humanitarian aid, we could do more to ensure that social and psychological help is offered in ways acceptable to the local community.

Van der Kolk, McFarlane et al. (1996: 425) emphasise that only a limited proportion of people who are traumatized later develop PTSD. They suggest that, immediately people are exposed to traumatic situations and suffer post-traumatic stress, the most appropriate treatment is to place emphasis on self-regulation and re-building, to establish security and predictability. This requires 'active involvement in adaptive action, such as the re-building of damaged property, engagement with other victims and active engagement in the physical care of oneself and other survivors'.

> The initial response to trauma needs to consist of reconnecting individuals with their ordinary supportive networks and having them

engage in activities that re-establish a sense of mastery. It is obvious that the role of mental health professionals in these initial recuperative efforts is quite limited. (Van der Kolk, McFarlane et al. 1996: 425)

This psychosocial approach to trauma healing is remarkably similar to the holistic approach adopted by Adam Curle, Eric Trist and 'Tommy' Wilson in the CRUs some fifty years earlier (Curle 1946a, 1946b; Curle 2001).

The work of the five projects exemplifies just this type of activity. Their community-based approach to trauma healing and peacemaking is explored later in this chapter.

Coping with memories from the past

Van der Kolk's theory would suggest that in the context of the aftermath of war, those who suffer from posttraumatic stress may have difficulty in coping with or overcoming the cycle of intrusions of traumatic memories. Van der Kolk describes the possibility of people becoming fixated on the past, in some cases being obsessed with the trauma (van der Kolk 1994: 253). Reporting work with the victims of torture '...the most noticeable aspect is the extreme attachment of the victim to the torture situation. Every thought, reaction, attempt to forget and inclusion in reality is bound up with the traumatic situation in which torture occurred'(Simunkovic and Arcel 1998: 147). This might explain why some people continue to regularly revisit painful and diffi-cult memories, even years after the events. An example might be the deep grief and loss experienced by the women presenting the travelling exhibition of photographs of the exhumation of mass graves, which included their family members, mentioned in the case study. This phenomenon of traumatic re-experiencing might also render people vulnerable to exploitation by the media or others. In these circumstances, it is all too easy to generate an emotional response to reminders of the past. Following a war, this could complicate the task of peacemaking, for example when political activists repeatedly re-arouse feelings of grief and anger in local people who have missing relatives or inter-fere with the natural process of mourning and reintegration of family life. The past must be addressed in a way that is helpful to the mourning process (Worden 1995) and enhances hope for the future.

Academics have explored the role of memory in ethnic conflict and painful memories clearly impact upon the peacemaking process (Cairns and Roe 2002). Following the 1991-95 war, the community in Eastern Slavonia is left with many painful memories. Loss and bereavement was a theme throughout the focus groups. The communities had suffered widespread loss of family, homes, jobs, relationships and security. All the groups stressed the significance of the widespread loss of social identity, which one participant said was a constant theme in the therapeutic groups with which he was working. The pain of loss was described as 'deep' and 'devastating' for many. There was a perceived need to remember the past, honouring acts of bravery and social care and remembering loved ones who had perished. In contrast, there was also a need to learn from the past and move on from it into a new future. The cycle of traumatic stress may impede this movement forward: 'War and victims are something that the community wants to forget' but the 'victims wish to forget but cannot' (Herman 1992b: 7-8). For some people, professional medical or psychological help may prove necessary if memories of the past create an unbearable burden in their present lives. Research with loss, grief and traumatic stress demonstrates that the successful integration of painful memories requires the liminality of psychological change in which the past merges with the present into a positive context of hope for the future. There was consensus in the focus groups that for those people who are not psychiatrically ill, this psychological change does not necessarily have to be carried out with professional mental health practitioners and they felt that they could help effectively with this work.

The unrecognised needs of children in the community

In wartime, children are subjected to the most severe forms of maltreatment … children are deprived of their home, toys, pets, food and clothes. They are exposed to cold, physical abuse. They receive no medical care and they are forced to watch family members being abused, or even killed. Since war changes relationships between adults (parents, teachers, neighbours, friends) and simultaneously alters the moral and ethical norms of society, the result is lack of support and structures that are indispensable to the normal development and mental health of children. (Kocijan-Hercigonja, Skrinjaric et al. 1998b: 340-341)

An issue of concern is the unrecognised needs of children and their families. The groups reported aggression and anti-social behaviour amongst children and the use of alcohol, drugs and cigarettes discussed earlier. Families have had to face loss, transitions and bereavement. The incidence of family break up and divorce is high. The disruption of attachments and separation from carers and other significant family members caused by bereavement or family break up is a significant factor in the development of younger children (Bowlby 1969; Winnicott 1957). Some group members felt strongly that the psychological needs of children are not sufficiently recognised or met, saying that, outside their families, children are not asked about their feelings and schools do not have adequate psychological help. Younger children may be affected by the traumatic stress of their older siblings or family members. Mir i dobro reported that successful workshops had been carried out with bereaved children, but that the interest in bereavement counselling has now decreased. CWWPP regularly provides seminars and discussion groups for gymnasium (secondary school) teachers, to assist them to recognise and address traumatic stress as it arises in the school environment. Some of the members of Mir i dobro are teachers and they have created in their classes the space for expression and discussion of feelings. The Centar za mir encourages work with schools, particularly the opportunity for children to express their views freely.

Children who were wounded have special additional medical and psychological needs (Kocijan-Hercigonja, Skrinjaric et al. 1998b: 341). A particular concern expressed by several researchers is that parents are not always aware of the emotional problems of their children (Kocijan-Hercigonja, Skrinjaric et al. 1998b: 342; Matacic 1998: 347; Pantic 1998: 352). The child who presents no behavioural disturbances or anti-social behaviour may be ignored, on the basis that they do not have an overt psychological problem, particularly when parents are pre-occupied with their own troubles and struggling to survive (Pantic 1998: 352). Fear, guilt or shame may prevent a child from expressing his or her needs (Hecimovic 1998: 124).

Family therapy provides an opportunity to enable the family as a whole to come to terms with the changing roles engendered by bereavement or disability in a family member (Kocijan-Hercigonja, Skrinjaric et al. 1998b). 'Family therapy and other forms of psychological support to traumatised families must constitute an obligatory element of the programme of psychosocial help for traumatised children' (Kocijan-Hercigonja, Skrinjaric et al. 1998a).

'Post-war syndrome': collective suffering and community healing

Post-war syndrome is a term for the collective social and psychological effects of war. It includes psychological suffering but it is not suggested that post-war syndrome is a psychiatric condition (although parts of the suffering described have features in common with the criteria of various psychiatric illnesses). The post-war syndrome is one aspect of the 'Black Cloud' of which Curle writes in the preface to this book. Whatever the label, the people of Eastern Slavonia are still suffering as a consequence of the war more than ten years after it ended. 'They are suffering from the misery of lost happiness, peace of mind, beloved persons, of haunting memories' (Curle 2001: 1).

The important point here is that a successful approach to alleviate the suffering of the post-war syndrome may require treatment for the clinically 'labelled' things such as posttraumatic stress, anxiety, grief and depression. It must also address the social issues and damaged interpersonal relationships that cause suffering in the community. The post-war syndrome includes, for example, homelessness, unemployment or poverty and the sense of alienation arising from ethnic or racial discrimination and inter-ethnic tensions. The work of the projects to alleviate post-war syndrome is inextricably interlinked with the process of peacemaking.

Summerfield, who has carried out extensive trauma relief work in non-western areas (Summerfield 1996, 1999; Summerfield and Hume 1993), suggests that suffering in non-western cultures must be understood as a collective phenomenon and the western individualist biomedical approach is inappropriate to understand the collective sense of suffering in some cultures. Bracken (2002: 70-71) agrees and posits that 'cultural factors are not only important in determining the degree of dislocation facing individuals in times of war, but culture determines how people cope with their suffering and seek help'. In Eastern Slavonia, despite the acceptance of western medical principles, the focus group discussions suggest that within the post-war syndrome is a community experience of trauma requiring a social response from the whole community.

In his work with the CRUs, Curle describes the 'desocialisation' and 'unsettled' psychological state of the former prisoners of war. They were not 'ill' but they were unhappy and felt alienated from the society to which they returned. Their treatment in the CRUs was an innovative combination of psychological support, social reconnection, education in seminars and workshops and 'job rehearsals' to allow the opportunity to practise a working role in business, trades and crafts. Those needing psychiatric treatment also had the opportunity for private consultations (Curle 2001). The ethos of the CRUs was both psychological and social. Adam Curle, as a result of reading my account of this research, revisited his notes on the work of the CRUs and he then considered its contemporary relevance.

I believe that the experience of the CRUs provides grounds for hope and that units of this kind, adapted to suit present-day circumstances, might help those who have experienced the trauma of war and violence. (Curle 2001: 5)

Curle's work with the Centar za mir in Osijek, with the development of workshops, community projects, seminars and networks of social support, implemented the approach of the CRUs.

The silent war: perceptions of peacefulness and unpeacefulness in Eastern Slavonia, considered in the context of Curle's theory of peacemaking

Adam Curle adopts the Tibetan Buddhist philosophy which proposes that everything with life co-exists and is interconnected 'within a field of force in which all affect and are affected by each one of the others' (Curle 1987: 1). 'The boundaries between us are hallucinations' (Curle 1987: 22). He also adopts as a value the Buddhist concept of the three 'poisons' which cause suffering: first, the ignorance of our true nature; second, greed and yearning; and the third, hatred and jealousy (Curle 1995a: 16-20). 'The three poisons provide the basis of selfishness, alienation from others, acquisitive greed, competitiveness and dislike, from which most violence grows' (Curle 1995a: 20). Proliferation of the three poisons has resulted in the modern 'pursuit of power and profit' (Curle 1999: 10). Globalisation, which exercises power through worldwide market forces, emphasises material success, exploiting the poor and powerless. Curle suggests that the result of this reckless and selfish pursuit of power and profit is pollution, famine, bigotry and violence. He realises that mediation and conflict resolution are useful for specific situations at transient moments in history, but he suggests that the primary way to secure world peace is to combat the three poisons by cultivating awareness and a culture of peace, first within oneself and then by generating widespread psychological change (Curle 1999: 21).

Adam Curle's perception accords with the basic perception of self in a sociocentric-organic non-western culture, as opposed to the egocentric-contractual self in western cultures (Holdstock 1994: 241). Organic cultures see the self as contextual, 'linked to each other in an interdependent system, members of organic cultures take an active interest in one another's affairs and feel at ease in regulating and being regulated' (Schweder and Bourne 1989: 132). Perhaps the former Yugoslavia would have been seen as partly organic until the 1991-95 war, but in the analysis of Schweder and Bourne, Croatia would now appear to have become a non-organic culture as it moves towards accession to the European Union.

Curle suggests that the true development of a human group should be measured, not in terms of wealth or life expectancy, but by the conditions that contribute most to our well-being. One conceptual framework for measuring human needs is that of Maslow and as discussed in Chapter 2, similar criteria are found in the proposition that certain human satisfactions must be met in order to create the foundation for peaceful relationships (Curle 1995a: 96; Curle 1998; Curle 1999). Curle identifies these as *safety* (the freedom from violence: no war, no death squads, no corrupt police, a fair judicial system and provision for medical or financial crises); *sufficiency* (enough employment, food and basic material requirements such as shelter and healthcare to provide a strong physical and mental basis for the full development of our potential); *satisfaction* (where material progress is not gained at great psychic or cultural cost and enjoyment of food, education and communal activities); *stimulus* (the encouragement and opportunity to follow our own personal talents and inter-ests in work, art and other creative fields of study or sport); and *service* (the chance to take some role in the ordering of local, national or international affairs) (Curle 1999: 32). Curle's categories are similar to those of Galtung, who suggests that the categories of human needs might include survival (to avoid violence), well-being (to avoid misery), identity (to avoid alienation) and freedom (to avoid repression) (Galtung 1994: 72).

The psychological changes necessary for peacemaking are broader than those for healing psychological trauma. Peacemaking involves the establish-ment of a non-violent value system. If Curle's theory of the causes of violence is accepted as a value, then the tasks of peacemaking include achieving the structural conditions necessary for peace concomitantly with generating psychological change to combat alienation and separation.

The existence of at least some of the structural and cultural conditions necessary for peace may be taken as indicators of the level of peacefulness attained in a community. Adopting Curle's criteria and definitions, we can consider the focus groups' perceptions of their communities in Eastern Slavonia from the perspective of his categories.

Safety

The groups reported a continuing sense of danger, both physical and psychological. There are unexploded land mines remaining in outlying land, presenting constant real and immediate threat to life. There are incidents of violence on the streets and a reported increase in criminal activity. Participants reported that the community still feels 'endangered' by acts of aggression and damage to property. The participants described the continuation of ethnic tension and verbal ethnic aggression. There is a perceived increase of domestic violence and therefore for many adults and children, their home is not a safe place, with possible aggression from siblings, or parents and other carers. The groups felt that all this creates a cumulative adverse psychological effect, particularly on children, causing concern both for mental health and peacemaking.

Sufficiency

The community is suffering generalised economic hardship, which causes tension and there is thought to be a greater division between poverty and riches than before the war. The former communist government was seen by some to have been oppressive 'spiritually', reducing the confidence of the people, but others thought that it provided a sense of safety and security for some people, but because the government was also perceived to have taken responsibility for community decision-making, some focus group members felt that the general population is currently unprepared for accepting the full financial responsibility for themselves and their families and that, if they were to take more responsibility, they might be less destructive. The groups saw this present lack of confidence and self-reliance as a block to developing businesses and organisations in the community. Another perceived difficulty is the development of mechanisation and information at too great a speed for the community to assimilate. The result of this lack of sufficiency is that 'unemployed people, youths, cannot see a future'. The lack of economic sufficiency was seen as a potential cause of street violence.

Satisfaction

Curle describes satisfaction as material progress at minimal psychic cost. Material satisfactions rely on resources and are subject to the limitations of supply and demand. Maslow's hierarchy of human needs (Huitt 2002; Maslow 1943, 1954; Maslow and Lowery 1998) suggests that the basic elements of safety and security and physiological requirements should be met as a precursor to psychological growth towards self-actualisation. Curle's concept of satisfaction implies material growth within a value system, transcending the boundaries between Maslow's categories. In 2002, the focus group participants felt that Croatia was developing, although hampered by economic hardships, but that standards of behaviour and morals had deteriorated and that human rights issues require attention.

Stimulus

Stimulus and satisfaction are linked, because a value system that respects individual rights and freedoms and a sense of collective responsibility was seen as important in the process of peacemaking. Adam Curle defines stimulus as a combination of the aesthetic enjoyment of life and individual freedom to pursue talents and interests. One comment in the groups was that in the communist times, the Serbian and Croatian nationalities held similar systems of value and neither of them was xenophobic or fascistic. There is a need to rebuild a shared value system, to combat delinquency, addictions and violence. The consensual perception amongst the focus groups is that there is a need for innovative thinking and implementation of new ideas. Over the years since the war, the projects themselves have created many new community activities.

Service

There have been some positive psychological outcomes from the war, including the 'posttraumatic growth' and 'creative casualties'. Positive developments mentioned by participants related to service to the community, for example, the mobilisation of social cohesion and resistance and the development of compassion, altruism and social awareness. Some participants reported spiritual growth. Health researchers reported that many refugees who had been exposed to severe trauma responded with extraordinary resourcefulness and courage in their fight for survival. However because of financial pressures, many of the unpaid project workers have difficulty in continuing their present level of service to the community.

'Burn-out' and 'compassion fatigue' are well known risks for local and international staff and helpers. Helpers may suffer vicarious trauma in which, although they may not have directly experienced traumatic events, they become traumatised by the accounts of such events from others and by witnessing the suffering of others. The focus groups mentioned this as a problem that they had noticed in themselves and also in mental health workers and clergy, on physical, emotional and spiritual levels. Mental health practitioners recorded 'burn-out' after the war (Franciskovic, Pernar et al. 1998; Ljubotina and Arcel 1998) and it has been noted in other humanitarian aid programmes (Milivojevic 1999;

Urlic 1999). The participants felt that ongoing support for helpers is essential, with practical measures to prevent and address burn out.

Burn-out may be attributable to a number of factors including personality, the nature of the work and the environment (Adjukovic and Adjukovic 1998; Hecimovic 1998). In the demanding task of post-war recovery, organisations and managers need a thorough understanding of the pressures of specific locations and tasks and knowledge of the needs and attributes of their personnel. Personnel should be selected for their ability and stamina in carrying out their tasks and provided with appropriate managerial or professional supervision. There is a considerable body of literature on the role of supervision in counselling and psychotherapy (BACP 1996; Feltham C. 1999; Hackney 1984; Hawkins 1996; Jacobs 1996; Proctor 1987; Villas-Boas Bowen 1986). Regular appraisals with re-evaluation of allocated work where necessary and peer assessment or evaluations of work carried out by the staff involved in humanitarian aid could assist in avoiding or at least mitigating burn-out. A number of positive ways in which the staff of a humanitarian aid project in Croatia supported each other during their work is described by Halilovic (1998: 285).

Adam Curle's view of active peacemaking: effecting structural and cultural change for peace

Curle (1999: 52), envisaging this world as one of systems and subsystems, suggests that our global social systems and structures are more prone to evolutionary than revolutionary change. He advocates active steps to effect change at all levels in society, transforming the direct, cultural and structural violence, attitudes and behaviours associated with the global pursuit of power and profit. He recognises that this global structural and psychological change:

> ...will require a vast educational effort, by millions of people. In order to build up the power, they will necessarily need to be aware of what they are doing, what is being done to them and what they need to transform themselves and society. The actual tools, the object lessons they will then use, will vary enormously – politics, economic changes, psychology, industrial and agricultural reform, etc... But it is the mind, the spirit, in which they are used that will give them the spread and the strength. (Curle 1999: 58)

Curle has written several accounts of the work of the Centar za mir and Bench We Share (Curle 1999: 63-69; Curle 1995a, 1995b; Curle 1996) and Mir i dobro (Curle 1995, 1998). Below is the projects' own view of their work,

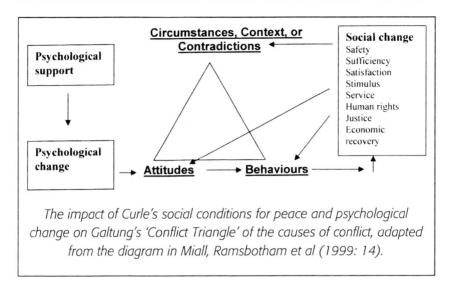

The impact of Curle's social conditions for peace and psychological change on Galtung's 'Conflict Triangle' of the causes of conflict, adapted from the diagram in Miall, Ramsbotham et al (1999: 14).

along with their suggestions for the creation of the necessary psychological changes for peace.

The restoration of human rights

One of Curle's conditions for peace is safety and security, which includes access to justice (Curle 1999: 32). The focus groups saw the restoration of equality of economic opportunity at all levels as a prerequisite for peace. The recognition and restoration of human rights through honesty in politics and the implementation of human rights laws is therefore a priority in their work. The Centar za mir has an active human rights office funded by European grants and staffed by experienced lawyers who provide the community with legal advice and representation on human rights issues. They provide information to the public, raising awareness of human rights issues and remedies for breaches of law and conventions.

Public justice for war crimes and responsibility for past actions

Derek Summerfield, a psychiatrist working with the Medical Foundation for the Victims of Torture, with many years' experience of work abroad with the victims of war, wrote: 'I think that it may apply universally that victims suffer more over time when they are denied societal acknowledgment, let alone reparation, for what has been done to them' (Summerfield 1996: 32). He suggests a role for humanitarian aid workers in protecting the indigenous

Justice and Peace

Peace and justice are inseparable;
Like a man and woman they create
Through love.

Justice is love spread widely
So that all may live in safety;
Peace is harmony protecting justice.

Peace without justice is oppression,
Justice, without peace, cruelty;
Together, they abolish violence.

organisations in countries where there are human rights violations and in providing material for the purposes of justice. Summerfield adds: 'Relief workers are in a position to collate, translate, publish and distribute such testimonies and, where possible, to present them to war crimes tribunals, truth commissions and governments. Indigenous organisations addressing rights and justice need to be supported; here too, their links with overseas agencies or human rights groups may lessen the risk that they will be eliminated' (Summerfield 1996: 32). During the war, Katarina Kruhonja and Kruno Sukic of the Centar za mir staff were threatened with death if they continued their human rights activities (a threat which they courageously ignored) and it is possible that their international connections protected them to some degree. It is not yet known whether the actions taken during the war against Katarina, Kruno and others will in the future become the subject of restorative justice. The Centar za mir now has the support of the present government and is housed in premises in Osijek provided by the local authority. It still has some of its original staff, including its able administrator Branka Kaselj, who has developed facilities and resources for the rapidly growing organisation. It has become a feature of the local community, continuing to develop new projects, the latest of which is a new community mediation centre in Osijek opening in January 2006 under the directorship of Sonja Stanic. There is more about this new project later in this chapter.

The focus groups suggested that bringing responsibility for past actions to public awareness and the public implementation of justice for criminal acts during the war would contribute significantly to the reduction of tension and the establishment of a sense of trust. Rigby considers the respective merits of justice in peacemaking and the purpose of forgiving and forgetting the past, trials and purges, compensations and reparation (Rigby 2001: 1-12). Lederach (1995: 20) makes it clear that reconciliation following war involves relinquishing both the victim role and the search for vengeance. He writes that truth and justice, tempered with mercy, contribute significantly to reconciliation and a durable peace. Curle summarises the need for peace combined with justice in a poem (see opposite).

Working towards economic recovery

Curle suggests that sufficiency including resources to meet basic human needs is necessary for peace. He suggests that the present global pursuit of power and profit causes and promotes cultural and structural violence. Economic hardship and inequality arose in Eastern Slavonia following the wartime destruction of factories, shops and offices. After the war, foreign economic assistance was seen as essential to the recovery of the Croatian economy. The government encourages the development of small businesses and financial self-reliance is seen as important. The Centar za mir has projects planned for training local people in a variety of business skills and CWWPP is willing (subject to funding) to provide workshops in democratisation, including an understanding of local government policy and the development of the skills of letter writing, communication and negotiation with local authorities.

Education for peace

Curle (1971: 174-176) holds that education and development is a vital part of creating the conditions of peace, by providing people with the psychological stability they need in order to lead good, constructive lives and to build positive co-operative human relationships (Woodhouse 1991: 33). Writing on psychological change, Curle refers to the development of 'inner awareness' which he sees as a source of strength to balance the destructiveness of the three poisons and also self-blame, guilt and recrimination and their counterparts, conceit and self-satisfaction based on illusion (Curle 1999: 86-87). He also advocates the development of compassion and awareness of the common humanity between self and the other (Curle 1999: 176). In terms of global peacemaking, he suggests that in order to combat the global pursuit of power and profit, it is necessary 'to bring about changes in perception, *changes of heart*, on a scale massive enough to influence *systems*' (Curle 1999: 53).

Four of the focus groups felt that education is vitally important in the peacebuilding process, as a means of generating attitude change in this and future generations. They expressed the need for peace education for both adults and children. The purpose of peace education was defined as 'learning non-violence, increasing self-esteem and self-confidence' and it was thought that peace should be affirmed in education as a human value. Some teachers said that they were already including peace education in their lessons, incorporating debates about tolerance and understanding.

It was also said in the groups with some sadness that, in some schools, peace education initiatives had proved ineffectual, using borrowed programmes that were never implemented. In order to avoid this outcome, it was suggested that pupils and parents should take the initiative. Teachers in the projects suggested that suitable ways of working with children are workshops in small groups of about ten children. They also recommended forming a committee with pupils and parents to design and implement programmes of non-violent education and teaching pupils peer mediation skills. One Centar za mir staff member is already running non-violent communication projects in local schools.

Peace education and skills training for adults is seen as important, combined with opportunities for formal professional training and evaluation. There are hopes for a specialist academic peace study centre, perhaps associated with a university, similar to the Department of Peace Studies at Bradford University. Proposals have also been put forward for donor funding by CWWPP to set up an institute for peace studies and/or a centre for social transformation in Vukovar.

Post-war syndrome

The literature and the case study revealed widespread social and psychological effects of the war in Eastern Slavonia, termed in this thesis the post-war syndrome. One major component of the post-war syndrome identified in this research is mental suffering, which may arise from, or result in, posttraumatic stress, depression, anxiety, substance abuse or any other psychological consequence of the traumatic experience of war. There has been no epidemiological survey of the physical and mental health of the community and CWWPP has recommended that epidemiological research should be carried out to assist in

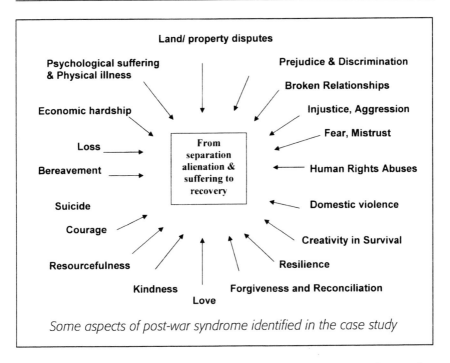

Some aspects of post-war syndrome identified in the case study

the planning and provision of health and social services appropriate to the needs of the community.

The post-war syndrome includes physical and psychological suffering, economic hardship, loss, bereavement, disputes over land and property, injustices and human rights abuses, prejudice and discrimination, fear, mistrust and other societal consequences of the trauma of war which generates the psychological alienation and separation identified by Adam Curle. Modern peace theorists note the 'invisible effects' of war and the need for psychosocial healing, citing the recommendation that, for victims of war in 'outside help is needed at five psycho/social levels: emotional/survival interventions, task-oriented interventions, psychologically oriented group interventions, counselling and intensive psychotherapy' (Agger and Mimica 1996: 27 in Miall, Ramsbotham et al. 1999: 209-210). This research suggests that we could go further and that the task of alleviating the effects of the post-war syndrome include psychological and social approaches for mental suffering which can be implemented and combined with the task of peacemaking, and, with specialist psychological and psychiatric help available for referral where necessary, ordinary people can do much to help each other.

Following war, it is necessary to look at posttraumatic stress, not from the narrow diagnosis of PTSD, but from the much wider perspective of general psychological reactions to the post-war syndrome. The social and psychological suffering following war is varied and extensive. PTSD may constitute a part of the suffering for some people, but it is inadequate and inappropriate as a global description for such wide-ranging suffering. Not only should other possible comorbid conditions be taken into account, for example, anxiety and depression, but in addition, the psychological consequences of inter-ethnic conflict where work, homes, relationships and lost lives disrupt trust and security. Agger (2001: 245) describes survivors in a state of demoralisation, helplessness and hopelessness, feeling 'lonely, frightened, sad, bitter, lost and restless.' The case study data reflect these feelings of isolation and alienation, (concepts described by Adam Curle in his writing over many years as a significant part of the cause of unpeacefulness) which the projects endeavour to address with psychological support and peacemaking activities. Further research could explore the nature of collective or cultural suffering within communities, because collective suffering may respond better to a community approach to healing. The group work of the projects may not only answer some of the criticisms of Western individualism in therapy, but might also provide the most appropriate response to collective or cultural trauma.

Transformation in the post-war syndrome: generating psychological change for peace

Inner peace to outer action

We have already seen how the activities of the projects in Croatia are carrying forward Curle's approach to healing the psychological trauma of war as one aspect of the process of peacemaking. Curle's work began in the CRUs, which changed the lives of returning prisoners of war, facilitating psychological recovery from posttraumatic stress, restoring confidence and hope, reinstating lost social skills and enabling the former prisoners to return to work. The activities of the projects go further than this. They are endeavouring to influence not only the internal world of those affected by the war, but also to challenge and change the unpeaceful aspects of the external world around them.

There is a striking similarity between Curle's view that peace is an inward state, evidenced by outer actions (Curle 1990) and the words of a member of the Centar za mir that we need '...to gain peace from within or from inside

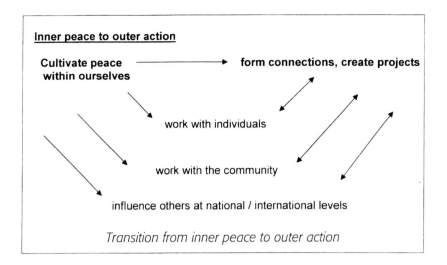

Transition from inner peace to outer action

ourselves. So, it is necessary to change ourselves first, working actually from the inside towards the outside'. The project members recognise that exploration of the internal world may yield helpful insights that can then be transferred outwards to improve relationships and life in the community.

Transition from inner peace to outer action

In workshops and groups the Centar za mir has been able to influence politicians, and uses the media whenever possible. Communication with the present Zupan of Osijek resulted in his membership of the Centar za mir. The legal service of the Centar za mir has an advocacy role in the community and in the courts, endeavouring to address injustice and to draw attention to areas for reform. The Centar za mir holds a biannual week of peace culture in Osijek and for the project's tenth anniversary in 2002 it organised public events including a concert with a nationally famous singer from Vojvodina.

Mediation: direct service to the community

More recently, the Centar has developed a new mediation service 'Medijacija Centar za mir' under the able leadership of Sonja Stanic, and I was appointed supervisor to the project. Funded for three years by the British embassy, the mediation service has now trained volunteer mediators drawn from the regions of Osijek, Beli Manastir and Vukovar. Mediators receive a free training. In return they undertake to provide a voluntary service to their community for two years. Mediations will be free to the recipients of the service. The training in Osijek and Beli Manastir is now completed and a service in Vukovar will follow later. The new Osijek Centar Medijacija opened in January 2006, providing community mediation in disputes between neighbours and in other community, family, ethnic and workplace matters.

In 2005, the Croatian government adopted a strategy for the reform of the judicial system, and passed the Law of Conciliation, which permits the courts to allow mediations within the court process in all civil matters, subject to specific conditions. The implementation of the Law of Conciliation is subject to the production of procedural guidance by the Ministry of Justice. In Croatia, the Ministry of Justice is planning to bring in pilot projects in commercial mediation experimentally during 2006, and then to widen the use of mediation alongside the court process. The Centar za mir has already trained judges, lawyers and local professionals as mediators and they are preparing to participate in the local implementation of the Law of Conciliation.

Mediations are not likely to take place within the court buildings and in the direct context of the court process in the near future. Senior judges are waiting to see the results of commercial mediation pilot projects during 2006 and for the Ministry of Justice to provide the necessary regulations and guidance before they will implement mediation generally within the court system. However, it is legally possible now for mediation to run alongside the court process if the courts are willing to permit this by, for example, adjourning the case upon the request of all the parties for an attempt to resolve the matter. The Centar za mir will have to wait and see whether the local judiciary will be willing to do so.

Counteracting alienation and separation

Curle, referring to interconnectedness, wrote of the Centar za mir members:

> 'They have a more than average sensitivity to shared consciousness or to what I have termed the extended mind. I don't mean by this anything that might be termed magical or mystical, merely a faculty which we all possess, some of us to a considerable degree' (Curle 1999: 65).

Both Adam Curle and Carl Rogers emphasised the interconnectedness of all living matter. Empathy is a core condition for creating the therapeutic conditions of psychological change in Rogers' person-centred approach to therapy (Mearns and Thorne 1998: 39-58). I believe that empathy lies on a continuum of interconnectedness within the extended mind. At one end of the continuum is a basic level of empathy, of active listening and giving undivided attention. At the other is a deep psychic connection, such as that Curle describes with the Dalai Lama (Curle 1999: 58). In creating a culture of peace, the cultivation of empathy and psychological connection counteracts the sense of alienation and separation and may be a significant step in moving from inner peace to generating collective outer peacefulness.

Roshchin (1986: 22) refers to a study of adolescents in Yugoslavia in 1974, in which the researchers found a highly developed sense of nationalism, but also the absence of the feeling of alienation and social aloofness toward other nationalities, which he attributes to their education and the social influences of their environment. This confirms the data from the case study about the situation before the 1991-95 war, but also contrasts with the perceptions of the focus groups of the present situation. What caused this change? Curle suggests that alienation and separation are both the cause and result of violence and impede peacemaking, creating psychological disconnection in the post-war syndrome. All the projects endeavour to re-establish psychological and social connection between the people in their community.

Dispersing the Black Cloud: recognising and healing the psychological suffering of the post-war syndrome

The case study data suggest that the somatic symptoms noted and described by the focus groups resemble those noted in posttraumatic stress, for example heart problems and endocrine abnormalities. Whilst noting the difficulties inherent in western approaches to diagnosis, measurement and treatment, it is clear that medical and mental health professionals and volunteers in Croatia consider that it is important for people providing trauma relief to recognise the somatic symptoms of posttraumatic stress. It is possible that emphasis on biomedicine influences the reporting of symptoms, masking the reporting of psychological needs. Practitioners point out that, in the aftermath of war, survivors and refugees are more likely to seek medical help for somatic problems than to ask for psychological help (Kraljevic, Bamburac et al. 1998: 173). Western terminology may be adapted to local language. In one study, refugees from Croatia and Bosnia were reported to be more likely to avoid the stigma of psychological symptoms by saying they suffered from 'nerves', by which they meant insomnia, passivity or restlessness, crying and quick temper. The term 'nerves' also implies the need for a medical doctor to give tranquillising medicine, rather than a psychiatrist or psychologist (Arcel,

Folnegovic-Smalc et al. 1998: 56). In this situation, awareness of the somatic symptoms of traumatic stress is essential in that colloquial descriptions of symptoms may suggest the need for therapeutic help or psychological support in addition to any necessary medication. Sensitivity to the needs of the sufferer may then also lead to the provision of appropriate social or psychological support in a way that avoids attracting the perceived social stigma of mental illness.

The research participants identified areas of inadequacy in present psychiatric and general medical practice. For example, a beneficial change would involve a shift away from the perceived emphasis on medication to an increase in individual consultation time and listening to patients. The focus groups were asked specifically about the therapies currently in use in their community for the treatment of the psychological effects of war. They mentioned a number of specific approaches including medication (pharmacotherapy), which they identified as the predominant medical and psychiatric approach. A psychologist said that she relies on the psychodynamic approach and behavioural tasks. The groups also specifically mentioned the use of bodywork (particularly with mine victims), eye movement desensitisation and reorganisation, the work of Victor Frankel and the Rogerian approach. One participant mentioned the use of bibliotherapy and psychodrama with victims of rape.

The central aim of many current western approaches to trauma treatment is the emotional processing of traumatic memories. By processing is meant the struggle for restoration of homeostasis in the individual psyche so that other experiences and behaviour can proceed without disruption (Rose 2002: 61). The cognitive, psychodynamic and behavioural approaches mentioned in the focus groups as helpful include a common valuing of the therapeutic benefit of remembering and talking about traumatic experiences, and reframing unhelpful thought patterns to increase confidence, mastery and self esteem: for example a psychologist explained, 'Give them one little thing to do per day, in order to make them feel that they have mastered something, that they feel more empowered and more in control of their life again'.

The psycho-social work of the projects demonstrates a clear consensus of opinion that sharing joys and sorrows is helpful. The projects initiate group work and shared practical activities. The participants mentioned with approval art therapy, dance therapy, drama therapy and body therapies, all of which pay attention to both somatic and psychological symptoms, facilitating the vocalisation, expression, or enactment of memories, thoughts and feelings in various ways within a supportive and empathic therapeutic environment.

Some group members said that they were training in reiki and others are exploring the possibilities of various alternative therapies, including relaxation methods. Some of these new techniques do not require disclosure or discussion of past traumatic events and these approaches therefore might be useful where there is a reluctance to share feelings. They may be more socially acceptable than formal mental health treatment. Reiki and other non-western approaches appear to be growing in popularity. Reiki is an energy-based therapeutic treatment involving elements of relaxation and therefore treatment may have a calming effect. Self-treatment may be learnt, furthering a sense of empowerment and control. A new reiki group was forming in Osijek. Other of focus group members offer the laying on of hands and spiritual healing within the religious framework of their respective faiths. Dodir nade offers spiritual healing as part of its activities.

Other therapies, each in their own way, combine the principles of western psychiatry, psychophysiology and eastern traditional energetic approaches, for example, eye movement rapid desensitization (EMDR) see (Shapiro 1988; 1995; 1996; 1999) and thought field therapy (TFT) see (Callaghan 2000; 2001a; 2001b). These approaches may be specifically used for the treatment of traumatic stress. There have been a number of clinical evaluations of EMDR in relation to efficacy in the treatment of posttraumatic stress. There have so far been few clinical trials of TFT and further research in controlled conditions is required. Therapeutic approaches that potentially defuse anger or calm labile emotions are of particular interest in the context of peacemaking. The use of TFT and its derivatives (for example emotional freedom therapy) may be helpful in situations where people are unwilling or unable to discuss traumatic events.

Bracken and others attribute western individualism and cultural limitations to some therapeutic approaches for the treatment of psychological trauma. There should be further exploration of the use of non-western and traditional approaches to healing within the context of different ethnicities and cultures, and in addition to the commonly used western psychological treatment modalities, the use of 'energy' and 'power' based trauma treatments should be explored in research.

Psycho-social work in building peace

Whilst acknowledging the role of mental health treatment where necessary, the participants felt that members of the local community could help each other '...even us who are not psychologists, but who have a goodwill and who have some kind of sly notions about what trauma is and how to deal with trauma, that is an enormous help to people very often'. This view is supported by John Lampen: 'I believe that we can all do this work, in God's strength, not our own' (Lampen 1987: 33). Along with Lampen and Curle, many of the focus group members expressed strong religious or spiritual beliefs underpinning their work. They do not wish to convert others to their religion, but they derive personal strength from their beliefs and their religious communities.

The focus groups felt that psychotherapy or other therapeutic approaches for the relief of posttraumatic stress may be sometimes necessary, but they also envisaged a wider range of activities in peacemaking, creating a safe psychological space in which time and attention are provided for listening to feelings and sharing discussion.

The staff and volunteer helpers in the projects live in the community in which they work. They have the advantage of the ability to identify local needs, designing their programmes appropriately and they can adapt quickly to changes in prevailing circumstances. They often express a feeling of responsibility for helping the local community and therefore endeavour to meet too many 'out of hours' demands on their time and energy. This may eventually lead to compassion fatigue or 'burn-out' and in the focus group discussions several participants expressed perceptions of personal and generalised tiredness. The groups recognise burn out as a phenomenon that they would wish to avoid and this became a regular topic in staff meetings over the years. There should be a staff support programme in all humanitarian aid projects, particularly those working in post-conflict areas, areas where daily life is stressful and particularly where staff are subjected to traumatic events.

Does talking about traumatic experiences help?

The projects' activities are underpinned by the assumption that remembering and verbalisation of traumatic experiences alleviates psychological suffering. Despite the criticisms made by Bracken, Summerfield and others of western approaches to the diagnosis and treatment of psychiatric illness, this belief remains supported by Croatian and international research findings (Pantic 1998; van der Kolk 1996: 194).

One of the mysteries of the mind is that as long as the trauma is experienced in the form of speechless terror, the body continues to react to conditioned stimuli as a return of the trauma, without the capacity to define alternative courses of action. However, when the triggers are identified and the individual gains the capacity to attach words to somatic experiences, these experiences appear to lose some of their terror. (Harber and Pennebaker 1992) in (van der Kolk 1996)

Many people, like Rigby, are 'not convinced of the appropriateness of opening up the past and talking about it as a means of dealing with the hurt.' He adds: 'At a commonsense level it would seem obvious that most people want to forget about the pains of the past and get on with their lives. Why should anyone want to relive past traumas by talking about them?' (Rigby 2001: 1).

In some areas or groups of people this may be the culturally normative response to trauma. However, the research on the psychology and psychobiology of posttraumatic stress indicates that, for some people, memories and feelings from the past may surface to awareness unbidden in waking hours or during sleep in disturbing dreams. Although these people may struggle to avoid the psychological effects of the past, they may not be able to simply tell themselves to forget about it or to put it behind them (van der Kolk 1994: 233).

There was consensus amongst the focus groups in the case study that the provision of a supportive atmosphere in which people can explore their experience and share their feelings is helpful to recovery from trauma. Their approach involves listening to others in an atmosphere of love and respect, reflecting the core conditions of empathy, acceptance (non-judgementalism) and unconditional positive regard which are the basis of Carl Rogers' person centred approach to therapy (Rogers 1957). Sharing laughter is considered as important as sharing sorrow. One participant emphasised that the element of healing lies in the relationship between people and that the therapeutic modality chosen is of lesser importance. Modalities can be chosen to suit specific needs.

In my own experience as a psychotherapist, I have found that some people find it helpful to talk about their past, whilst others (for all sorts of diverse reasons) may not be ready or willing to revisit past traumas. This may change from time to time in a person's life, or it may not. Fresh traumatic events or unexpected triggers may act like a fishing line to hook up and unexpectedly raise past events to the surface of memory, demanding attention. People may come to feel safer and more able to trust others enough to risk facing suppressed emotional pain. People, events and situations vary widely and if we as therapists respect diversity we cannot adopt a 'one size fits all' approach in therapy.

Reducing anxiety and mistrust in the community

Two fundamental aims of psychotherapy for PTSD have been described as the 'deconditioning of anxiety' and 'altering the way victims view themselves and their world by re-establishing a sense of personal integrity and control' (van der Kolk, McFarlane et al. 1996: 420). For those who were helpless victims in the past, reclaiming a sense of personal power and control and relinquishing the role of victim may also be a prerequisite for reconciliation. Rigby contends that 'At the core of any reconciliation process is the preparedness of people to anticipate a shared future. For this to occur, they are required not to forget, but to forgive the past and thus be in a position to move forward together' (Rigby 2001: 12). As Curle found in the CRUs, helping people to move out of the hopelessness and powerlessness of their victim role may require considerable psychological and social support. Perhaps when their basic human needs are met, people find it easier to re-establish psychological connection on a basis of equality, letting the past rest because they feel safe in the present and hopeful for the future. At this point they may be more able to forgive.

Provision of formal and informal psychological help

Only one of the participating projects, CWWPP, offers formal psychotherapy in the form of individual and group work. The remaining four projects describe their work as the provision of 'psychological support', although they sometimes colloquially refer to their work as 'therapy' or 'therapeutic'.

A member of Mir i dobro is a clinical psychologist providing psychotherapy with children and families in the local community. Her expertise has been of value to the work of Mir I dobro in the provision of knowledge and training.

The Centar za mir also has several excellent local psychologists involved with its community work over the years and it uses visiting mental health professionals occasionally to provide training in specialist areas.

The Bench We Share, Dodir nade and Centar za mir staff and volunteers use the term 'therapy' loosely in describing the community work of their projects, but said that they would make a referral, with consent, to a mental health practitioner if any person with whom they were working needed professional help. Some staff feel that they have insufficient experience to handle deep or powerful emotions and are therefore happy to leave in-depth emotional work to the professionals. In discussing their work with children, staff were clear that they wish to respect professional boundaries and are aware of legal responsibilities, therefore they describe their work in schools specifically as 'psychological support' rather than 'therapy'.

The activities of the projects may be carried out in a supportive social climate created with individuals, dyads or in groups, but as one participant pragmatically put it, 'Groups are more economic'. The projects facilitate various forms of group work in their local communities, providing opportunities to share feelings and experiences which they have found to be effective in counteracting a sense of alienation or isolation through hearing the problems of others and knowing at the same time that someone cares. Group work may prove challenging for both participants and facilitators in that '...the interpersonal aspects of the trauma, such as mistrust, betrayal, dependency, love and hate, tend to be replayed...' (van der Kolk, McFarlane et al. 1996: 420). The project staff realise that some people are not psychologically ready for the challenge of work in big groups and they use individual discussion as a preparatory step towards working in dyads and then in larger groups.

The work of the projects begins with the healing of the psychological effects of the war, extending to generating a culture of non-violence. The five groups' approach to the development of peaceful attitudes appears to be similar. They generate social change by modelling and encouraging attitudes of acceptance, non-violence and tolerance.

Managing diversity and facilitating ethnic integration

Ethnic tension is seen as a major block to peace in the community in Osijek and Vukovar. In one focus group, debate arose about the issue of working with multi-ethnic groups and consensus was that in places like Vukovar, which has experienced severe violence and has high levels of ethnic tension, separate work may be necessary initially, to prepare for integration when individuals are psychologically ready. Integration is not only problematic on the basis of ethnicity. Former soldiers who fought in the 1991-95 war are treated by some of the community as heroes, but some war veterans expect or claim preferential treatment, or have an income which is denied to others, causing resentment. Inequalities of income were described as exacerbating other existing tensions. Returning refugees may face criticism from family and

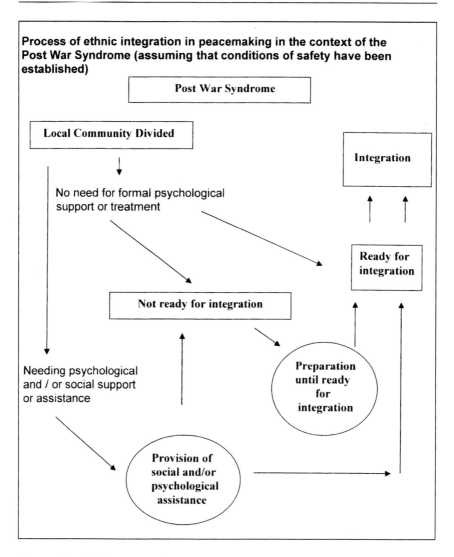

former friends for having fled from their villages and for not staying to fight.

The focus groups felt that the return of refugees should be managed carefully and reintegration carried out with sensitivity to the needs of both the returning refugees and the local population who had remained during the war. They mentioned the legal problems that arise in the community after the return of refugees over land boundaries and property rights and the economic problems arising from the loss of work.

The Centar za mir continues to be active in the community in providing moral and psychological support to refugees and to other marginalized groups in the local community. It regularly runs workshops for a wide variety of groups, including women, refugees, parents or carers of the mentally ill, divorced or separated people and carers of the elderly and has initiated a number of local schemes for young people.

The Bench We Share carried out a number of projects to aid reintegration of the community in Baranja and in other areas of Eastern Slavonia, providing community mediation for local disputes over land, property and other issues between returning refugees and local residents, or between neighbours. Dusanka Ilic, Director of the Bench We Share and others use the greeting 'Palisood'. It did not sound Croatian to me, and I asked what it meant. Dusanka explained, laughing, that she invented it and it is an acronym for 'Peace and love in spite of our differences'. The Bench We Share also carried out workshops in schools and in the community on topics of local interest, including health issues, an example of which was the 'Dr Tooth' dental advice for children and cookery classes. A successful longer-term multi-ethnic community project of the Bench We Share was the restoration of a castle and park as a monument and recreation area for public use in Darda. All these activities were offered with the intention to encourage peaceful attitudes and reintegration of the community. Currently, the Bench We Share is suffering from a lack of funds and sadly its activities have been reduced.

Staff and volunteers from the Centar za mir are involved in a wide variety of peace education programmes, community activities and community mediation projects in neighbouring towns and villages, working to facilitate integration. Eko selo, a farm in Latinovac, is a successful project run by a gifted clinical psychologist Branka Drabek, who facilitates multi-ethnic residential workshops and training. The farm has, I think, been featured on Croatian national television. Those who live and work there provide an inspiring model of successful multi-ethnic integration and a peaceful way of life.

Dodir nade runs multi-ethnic workshops in a number of areas in Eastern Slavonia, designed to assist the reintegration of the community. There is an emphasis on healing in the work of Dodir nade. The project runs a modular programme. The theme of the first module of workshops is on mental and physical health and then the theme broadens in subsequent modules to consider the health of the community, which includes addressing psychological change for peace.

Despite the conflict in Eastern Slavonia between the Serbs and Croats during the war, the staff of CWWPP said that these two ethnicities have many similarities and shared values. Interestingly, the focus groups said little about cross-cultural issues in debating the peacefulness or unpeacefulness of the community, save for the general views already reported. In Eastern Slavonia, the Moslem population is very small and their needs were not mentioned at all in the focus groups, nor were those of the Roma, although it was noted that the Roma are a marginalized minority. A main topic for the groups was that of the individual's perception of their identity, which is an issue for many people after the war. Ethnically mixed marriages were common before the war and the focus groups commented that many families had broken up as a result of the war. Identity is an issue for parents, their children and the wider family, embodying concepts of ethnicity, culture and religion. Given children's need for secure attachments with their primary carers and significant family members for their psychological well being (Bowlby 1969), these patterns of family disruption should be considered and appropriate psychological support offered, where necessary, to those children and families affected.

A participant in the case study suggested that 'defusing' is necessary before 'merging' or integration can begin. Once tension is 'defused', the projects can help individuals in the community towards integration. The issue of bringing of Serbs and Croats together in workshops was the subject of debate in the CWWPP focus group in Vukovar, an area where ethnic tensions are great. The participants considered whether workshops should be integrated from the start of a programme, or whether people should be offered separate workshops and then be brought together when they are ready. The consensus was that careful preparatory work is necessary before integration, either by discussion or by joint activities. The group considered the benefits of shared tasks with a common goal, for example the project for the restoration of a public park in Darda mentioned earlier in this chapter, which had been successfully facilitated by the Bench We Share.

A reason for failure to seek psychological help is that physical safety is not established and the person is preoccupied with the problems of survival. Psychological work should follow on from the primary task of establishing at least a basic level of physical and psychological safety.

How much power and control should funders have?

Funding (and lack of funds) can be problematic for the projects. Donors who hold the purse strings may try to control project activities. There is a risk that projects may also adapt programmes to suit the expectations of western funders (Summerfield 1996: 223-24). The focus groups reported pressure exerted on projects from time to time to conform to the expectations or requirements of donors, which they resisted with attempts at negotiation. They felt that foreign donors did not always understand or take into account local needs and conditions. One specific area of disagreement with donors was integration. One project, in a team discussion, expressed a consensus of frustration that a foreign donor had expected ethnic integration to be implemented by bringing Serbs and Croats in Vukovar together immediately, without separate preparation, into multi-ethnic workshops. The project concerned felt that this was an unrealistic expectation, arising from the donors' lack of understanding of the particular needs of that community. In Vukovar, tensions were generally considered to be too high to bring Serbs and Croats together in workshops without very careful preparation and so the projects recommended preparatory work in separate groups. The issue was finally resolved with the donors by negotiation.

Donors should make efforts to hear and respect the views of those who live and work within their recipient communities. Donors did not require implementation of specific psychological treatment approaches, but time limitations were often imposed. One project was obliged to provide short therapeutic programmes each of three months, but staff felt strongly that these short programmes would be inadequate to meet identified local needs. Perceived or actual pressure to comply with donor requirements creates undue stress for non-governmental organisations. Representatives of donors coming to carry out evaluations and visiting professionals may assume or be accorded inappropriate authority, undermining the confidence of local project staff. Foreign donors operating from their own well-equipped and well-staffed offices may not understand the practical problems of working in post-war zones (which may well include coping with adverse conditions, intermittent electricity, water and communication and a general lack of resources and facilities) so they may unwittingly make unrealistic requirements of projects, for example, expecting documents, prompt return of telephone calls, emails or faxes, fast creation of budgets, accounts and evaluations and creating unreasonable demands upon the skills and time of the projects, adding to their workload and to their stress.

Can non-professionals provide effective psychological assistance?

There was a consensus in the groups that people in the local community can help each other, supported by information and training where necessary. This non-professional psychological peer support offered by the projects is important in a culture where there is a social stigma in seeking psychological help. Participants also thought that some might fail to seek help because they feared others would not want to listen to their painful experiences and that people might need to repeat their story over and over again, something with which others might have difficulty if they are preoccupied with their own needs and problems.

Generally the focus group participants felt able to cope with listening to the troubles of others, provided they could refer individuals to a professional for psychiatric help or psychotherapy where necessary. Distinctions were made between psychological therapy and psychosocial activities and this was relevant particularly in work with children, respecting professional boundaries.

Self-awareness was seen as an important skill in helpers. They need to be aware of their own strengths, weaknesses and needs, which if left unmet could impair their helping skills or result in burn out.

Potential contribution of an understanding of posttraumatic stress to the process of peacebuilding

An understanding of the role of posttraumatic stress in the process of peacebuilding following war contributes to the creation of the social context for recovery and reintegration. The level and nature of psychosocial help is culturally determined and the knowledge and wisdom of indigenous populations may be underused in the planning and provision of humanitarian aid programmes following war.

'Cultural factors are not only important in determining the degree of disruption and dislocation facing people in times of war, but culture also determines how people cope with their suffering and seek help' (Bracken 2002: 71).

> Psychological trauma is not like physical trauma: people do not passively register the impact of external forces (unlike, say a leg hit by a bullet) but engage with them in an active and problem-solving way. Suffering arises from and is resolved in, a social context. (Summerfield 1996: 25 in Bracken 2002: 71)

In Eastern Slavonia, the focus groups noted psychological states which include avoidance, psychic numbing, increased arousal and hypervigilance. The emotional climate they described included widespread mistrust, problems of identity, social withdrawal, aggression, anger and fear. It would be difficult to separate out the effects attributable to posttraumatic stress and other psychological effects of war, including depression. My research was not designed to establish diagnostic or causal connections and therefore the observations that follow are limited in this respect. The psychological effects of war, including posttraumatic stress, may at the least hinder societal movement towards integration and peace, or it may at worst generate unpeacefulness. The physiological effects of posttraumatic stress create a combination of emotional numbing coupled with increased arousal and the likelihood of undifferentiated responses to stressors. This combination could lead to inappropriate or unrestrained response to present stressors, particularly in the post-war syndrome, which includes financial hardship and housing problems.

The focus groups described an increase in domestic violence and incidents of street violence. The 'de-socialisation' noted by Curle in the CRUs and the emotional numbing and dissociation linked with posttraumatic stress may hinder the ability of those affected to engage fully on cognitive and emotional levels in general social interaction, blocking empathy and congruence and adversely affecting their participation in the emotionally demanding tasks of peacemaking. Curle initially suggested that education and development are vital to counteract the effects of alienation and separation (Curle 1971: 174-176); but, recognising the prevalence of psychological suffering in Eastern Slavonia and referring to the work with Mir i dobro, he later suggested that counselling (including by this term professional therapeutic activities and community psychological support) may also be helpful in the peacemaking process (Curle 1997; Curle 1998; Curle 2001; Curle 2001).

Modern peace theorists do not appear to take the effects of posttraumatic stress sufficiently into account in their proposals for peacebuilding and reconciliation. In *Building Peace* (Lederach 1997) and in *Preparing for Peace* (Lederach 1996), there is no mention of the effects of posttraumatic stress in the authors' peacebuilding models, which is surprising since Lederach acknowledges that 'individuals are affected by conflict both negatively and positively – for example, in terms of their physical well-being, self-esteem, emotional stability, capacity to perceive accurately and spiritual integrity' (Lederach 1997: 82). Galtung (1994: 21) refers to alienation, but not in the context of posttraumatic stress. Rigby (2001: 67-68) writes empathically of those who are bereaved and grieving, but he is not convinced of the appropriateness of opening up the past and talking about it as a means of dealing with psychological pain. Miall, Ramsbotham and Woodhouse do, however, note the 'invisible effects' of war and the need for psychosocial healing. Citing from an evaluation of psychosocial assistance to victims of war in Bosnia-Herzegovina and Croatia by Agger and Mimica (1996: 27), they suggest that 'outside help is needed at five psycho/social levels: emotional/survival interventions, task-oriented interventions, psychologically oriented group interventions, counselling and intensive psychotherapy' (Miall, Ramsbotham and Woodhouse 1999: 209-210). This apparent lack of recognition by modern peace theorists of the depth of the impact of posttraumatic stress and its role in the process of post-war peacemaking contrasts sharply with the views of the projects constituting the case study.

The focus groups stressed the importance of addressing the psychological aspects of war, including posttraumatic stress (CWWPP refers to psychotrauma) in the peacemaking process. The projects each expressed awareness of the impact of posttraumatic stress on the community and they endeavour to address it in their work. Therapy was seen in all the groups as part of the preparation for peace, a prelude to integration. However, 'therapy' was defined to include psychosocial interventions, which could be carried out by ordinary people and distinguished from 'psychotherapy', which was seen as a professional activity. I reflected upon whether my presence (as I am known to be a psychotherapist) might have unduly influenced the responses in the focus groups, biasing them towards these references to therapy. This is possible, but even if this were the case, the amount of work carried out by the projects to heal the hurts of war over the past ten years constitutes cogent evidence of their belief that psychological healing is an integral part of the peacemaking process.

Adam Curle's approach to peacemaking may have profoundly influenced the projects' thinking on this issue. He was present at the first workshop of the Centar za mir on peacemaking in 1992 and has many friendships with the Centar za mir staff. They know that he has written widely since 1971 of alienation and separation as causal factors of conflict, drawing on his background in psychology and anthropology in understanding and explaining the damage which traumatic experiences may inflict on the human psyche. He has consistently associated alienation and separation with the trauma of war. In his papers published after the workshops with Mir i dobro, Curle considers counselling as a potential agent for psychological change in the process of peace building (Curle 1997; Curle 1998; Curle 2001).

It is likely that others who have shared information about traumatic stress and PTSD also influenced the Eastern Slavonian projects. An example is John Lampen, a Quaker with twenty years' experience of working with emotionally disturbed adolescent boys. He stresses the need for healing the psychological effects of conflict and violence in the process of peacemaking in *Mending Hurts* (Lampen 1987). He has visited the Centar za mir and he is known to some of the staff in the projects through his work in Eastern Slavonia and Western Sirmium. He explains the risk of 'holding powerful and distressing feelings inside' (1987: 23). He feels that ordinary people can help each other in this situation and that in the shared space between people in an atmosphere of loving attention the painful feelings can emerge and be met with empathy and support: 'to find our courage, to meet the other person in his or her anger, depression, disorientation or frozen state, to listen' (Lampen 1987:33).

The mandate of the CWWPP (2000, 2003) confirms the need to address psychological trauma and conflict concomitantly. Psychological support should be offered as part of the peacemaking process. It is here that the understanding of posttraumatic stress is helpful, both in recognising when and where the need for psychological support arises and also in provision of appropriate professional therapeutic interventions and/or community activities. Psychological support can be given appropriately in the community by one person to another, but in some cases formal medical or psychiatric treatment may be necessary. Referrals may be made in situations where the project members feel that they have insufficient knowledge, skills or emotional resources to cope with others' overwhelming emotions. Professional help may be required because of specific psychological or medical problems with which the sufferer feels unable to cope on a day-to-day basis without specialist medical or psychiatric care.

Therapeutic and peacemaking activities may be combined, either sequentially, as we did in the workshops with Mir i dobro in 1996 and 1997, or concurrently. Conceptual insights from these disciplines may contribute to separate programmes. In creating a culture of peace, or in offering any therapeutic intervention or training, it is important that the values of the therapists and peacemakers are not imported or imposed in cultures where such concepts and values are of little social or cultural importance or relevance.

The trauma healing and peacemaking workshops with Mir i dobro, in 1996 and 1997 which we facilitated under Adam Curle's supervision, developed ideas, techniques and skills to alleviate the effects of posttraumatic stress in the local community, focussing on the needs of children and their families. The workshops implicitly accepted the normative 'western' concepts and diagnoses of mental illness including PTSD, whilst also acknowledging individual and cultural differences in life experiences and reaction to traumatic stressors. The first workshop in 1996 included a wide variety of ideas and techniques from various counselling and psychotherapy modalities, designed to provide opportunities to express past and present thoughts and feelings and to reframe and integrate perceptions of distressing events through the use of talking, active listening, narratives, drama, art, music, poetry and role play. Following this workshop, we put together a resource pack, *Loss, Bereavement and Trauma*, containing information and activities for use by counsellors and volunteer helpers working in the UK and abroad (Brown and Mitchels 1997).

At the request of Mir i dobro, the members of the workshop met again the following year and after discussion of their experiences in the intervening period, went on to develop a variety of peacemaking exercises and activities which could be used with children in their community. Adam Curle's subsequent reference to this work in *Counselling for Peace*, (Curle 1998), confirmed the academic link between trauma healing and peacemaking which has been explored in this book.

Positive aspects of the post-war syndrome

The positive aspects of the post-war syndrome reported in the case study include accounts of courage and resourcefulness, love, kindness, forgiveness, resilience and creativity in survival, including the development of a variety of new skills. In the work of the Civil Resettlement Units (CRUs), Curle and others noted that many of the former prisoners showed remarkable personal development following their traumatic experiences. They 'coped with pain, confusion and separation from their lived ones without losing hope or the ability to help and encourage their companions in captivity.' He considered that they had 'gained an exceptional new awareness and power' (Curle 2001: 5), perceiving a similar strength in others with whom he worked, including the staff and volunteers of the projects in Croatia. Some men in the CRUs may have possessed these qualities before their traumatic experiences, but many of the men gained from their experience in the CRUs. If it is accepted that the CRUs modelled the creation of the necessary psychological conditions to promote psychological healing, then if society can reproduce those conditions in various ways, internal energies and perceptions might be redirected to effect a transition from unhealed traumatic stress towards internal peacefulness.

Combating the social stigma of mental illness

The teaching of the symptoms of PTSD to national mental health professionals after war may be welcomed by doctors in providing a medical diagnosis for evident suffering, but may be unwelcome to survivors who do not want to be regarded as 'ill' or 'crazy' (Agger 2001: 246). The case study shows that the social stigma of mental illness is strong in Eastern Slavonia and in these circumstances, psychological support from peers and the community, such as that provided by the projects, would be regarded as a welcome alternative to medication and formal mental health treatment. Mental health treatment should be made available on confidential referral where necessary, for example where the sufferer feels unable to cope with daily life without medical or psychiatric help, or where the project staff or volunteers feel unable or unqualified to offer appropriate or effective help. Consideration might be given to the provision of more day-care and residential mental health treatment in less formal, non-hospital environments, avoiding the social stigma of hospital admission and reducing the pressure on limited hospital resources.

Addressing the impact of PTSD on children and families

Although the research has revealed limitations in the definition and diagnosis of PTSD, nevertheless, raising awareness of the general psychological and physical symptoms of posttraumatic stress, including the impact of numbing of affect, hypervigilance and intrusions on children's behaviour is helpful in recognising and responding to their emotional and physical needs. The research data revealed, for example, that parents are neither sufficiently aware of their own needs, nor do they always recognise the extent of the suffering of their children and they may ignore or misinterpret their children's behaviour. Parents who have to cope with all the problems of the post-war syndrome may minimise or even deny their children's experiences or accounts of suffering. Failure to recognise the signs and symptoms of posttraumatic stress deprive a child of immediate and appropriate help, leaving the child vulnerable to subsequent traumatic events or to the later onset of illness. Although causal factors and long-term consequences of posttraumatic stress remain unclear, a concern is that failure to recognise the needs of severely traumatised children may lead to serious or long-term consequences in their adult life, potentially affecting their ability to make and sustain relationships and possibly affecting their ability to parent effectively.

Ed Cairns from the University of Ulster (1987, 1996) has made a significant contribution to the understanding of the impact of conflict on children, but nevertheless it seems that very little has been done to explore the syndrome of posttraumatic stress in children from a psychobiological perspective and particularly in the context of non-western cultures. There is also little known about 'the interplay between trauma processing and the different developmental tasks of childhood' (Dyregrov 1995: 46). In the post-war syndrome in Croatia, many children were separated from parents and carers, and the long-term effects of loss, bereavement and trauma on children in this region may only become apparent as time progresses following the war. The long term familial effects of the wartime disruption of early attachments may emerge perhaps as they themselves become parents.

There is little clinical consensus regarding the relative effectiveness of the many approaches used to treat traumatized children who have the symptoms of PTSD. In addition to pharmacotherapy, therapeutic work with children includes the use of systemic family therapy and group activities, which might include drama, music and play. In treating posttraumatic stress, the focus of most psychotherapeutic activities with children is 'exposure based' in that it aims to create a physically and emotionally safe environment for the free expression of feelings and memories in relation to the traumatic events, which can then be addressed within the therapeutic relationship or therapeutic group setting. Practitioners have noted that further empirical research is particularly needed to evaluate the efficacy of pharmacotherapy for children. Empirical research would also assist practitioners to assess the potential efficacy of different treatment modalities in treating posttraumatic stress in a variety of situations and cultures, for example, the less exposure based approaches, which include thought field therapy (TFT) and its derivatives. These modalities are insufficiently researched and are unlikely to be widely used in the UK until the National Institute of Clinical Excellence (NICE) is satisfied by evidence of successful treatment in clinical trials. Traditional healing and energy healing approaches might also usefully be explored further for use in both western and non-western cultures.

Further research in the pharmacological treatment of posttraumatic stress

There have been significant developments in recent years in pharmacological treatments for posttraumatic stress, but perhaps because of the complexity of diagnosis and the shifting pattern of posttraumatic stress and its associated psychological conditions, further research is required in establishing effective medication for the treatment of PTSD. In the complex syndrome of posttraumatic stress, health practitioners may take a pragmatic, perhaps experimental approach to the use of pharmacotherapy. Research participants criticised prescriptions for some people suffering from PTSD of 'weird' mixtures of several drugs, some of which have side effects causing additional difficulties for those taking them. In the view of some mental health specialists, posttraumatic stress needs to be treated differently at various phases of people's lives after the trauma. Pharmacological treatments that may be effective at one stage may not be so effective at another. Drug treatments should be tailored to meet the needs of individual symptomology and combination drug therapy is therefore sometimes appropriate. New treatments are under consideration, but further research is necessary to identify the most effective treatments and drug combinations. Pharmacological agents for PTSD treatment in childhood have also received little empirical investigation.

Into the future: effecting psychological change for peace

All the five projects in the case study are working to effect social and psychological change, altering the internal world of those affected by war and influencing political, economic and social circumstances through their public activities, thereby addressing the attitudes, behaviours and contradictions of Galtung's triangle of the causes of conflict. The work of the projects addresses the 'invisible legacy' of war 'grounded in individual and collective trauma' with the concomitant 'destruction of relationships and the loss of trust, confidence, dignity and faith' (Stiefel 2001: 265). This invisible legacy forms part of what I have termed the post-war syndrome. It can be addressed with a range of techniques and activities, but the work of Adam Curle and the projects would suggest that the most important psychological elements of peacemaking in the post-war syndrome are the restoration of interconnectedness, relationship and empowerment through loving attention and psychological support.

Some theorists see humanitarian aid as an immediate response to need and not as part of a longer term programme of rehabilitation and recovery 'It helps people get through the most difficult phases after the war, but is probably not crucial in terms of the longer-term rebuilding process.' (Stiefel 2001: 267). This view has implications for the development of programmes for the relief of trauma and for peacemaking. The research confirmed a prevailing view amongst all the groups that psychosocial work and psychological support needs to be available to the community in the long-term. Activities may vary as circumstances change, adapting to social and economic changes in the community.

At the early stages of recovery from posttraumatic stress, when intrusions predominate, exposure based approaches that allow expression of feelings and memories associated with the traumatic events might be most helpful, but later when avoidance symptoms (for example, suspicion and anger) lead people into interpersonal problems 'primary attention needs to be paid to the stabilization of the social realm' (van der Kolk, McFarlane et al. 1996: 425). The focus groups were convinced that talking and sharing experience in a safe, supportive and empathic emotional climate helps to heal trauma and they try to provide this in their community-based work. Summerfield rightly points out that 'Suffering arises from and is resolved in, a social context,' and therefore a community-based approach might be the most effective, provided it is long-term and includes preventive work.

Any treatment approaches which address psychological suffering, particularly that of posttraumatic stress, PTSD, depression, anxiety, phobias, and/or debilitating feelings of guilt, fear, anger and shame, or which provide relaxation and psychological calming and which can be taught and used as self-help by individuals, may prove useful in creating inner peace which might then be reflected in outer acts in the process of peacemaking. Some therapies for the relief of posttraumatic stress require re-exposure to the traumatic experiences within the therapeutic alliance. Other treatment modalities, which might potentially be used to alleviate the symptoms of posttraumatic stress, for example, acupuncture and energy healing, may not require any outward disclosure or discussion of inner memories of the traumatic events. In circumstances where the nature of the traumatic events or personal or cultural circumstances prohibit or inhibit discussion of the trauma, treatment approaches which do not require re-exposure to traumatic memories may be more socially acceptable.

The type of therapy appears to be less important than the quality of relationship and psychological connection created between those participating. Although psychiatric assistance or medication may be necessary in some cases, generally people are not perceived to be formally psychiatrically 'ill', but they *are* suffering. Members of a community can share with each other the task of healing the psychological suffering of the post-war syndrome. This avoids social stigma and empowers people to create and sustain social relationships, gradually increasing their risk-taking in sharing emotion and experience.

Humanitarian aid programmes provided following war would benefit from an understanding of the needs of peacemaking combined with an awareness of the nature and effects of posttraumatic stress and information about a variety of treatment approaches, including traditional and non-western approaches to trauma healing.

The Centar za mir, Bench We Share, Dodir nade and Mir i dobro all create opportunities for members of the local community to come together in a wide variety of activities and workshops. The project staff expressed very clearly the problem of creating peace in the post-war syndrome and their proposed solution: 'war starts at first in our head' and 'first we need peace with ourselves'. The Coalition for Work with Psychotrauma and Peace (CWWPP) offers direct therapeutic work and counselling training. The projects use the individual gifts and skills of their members creatively, adapting to the changing needs of the community, for example, current projects relate to issues of reconciliation; music and entertainment; caring for mentally or terminally ill relatives at home; coping with a family as a single parent; democratisation, human rights abuses and restorative justice. The Centar za mir and CWWPP have the advantage of premises and offices in which workshops and training can be provided. The sense of stability, continuity and availability of psychological support provided by the Centar za mir for the community of Osijek and by the other projects for their communities has the potential to provide an important contribution to healing the post-war syndrome.

Whatever the definitions and criticisms of the diagnostic criteria for PTSD or any other formal psychiatric illnesses associated with the experience of war, the reality is that, after traumatic events, people do suffer psychologically. Whether suffering is categorised as PTSD, depression, anxiety or something else, or remains undiagnosed, as Adam Curle points out in *The Wounds of War* (Curle 2002), it is still suffering, however it is conceptualised and labelled. Our concern as practitioners must be to find a way to help people through that suffering with psychological and social approaches that work holistically in the context of the local community, adapting to different situations and cultures.

The boundaries between therapy and peacemaking are fluid and permeable. Insights can flow between them and each has something to offer the other. During this research there have been some amazing events and coincidences. But then, perhaps that is not so very surprising! One unexpected outcome was the opportunity to bring Adam Curle back into contact with Jean Clark, a highly respected counsellor and psychotherapist in Norwich, who in 1951 was a student taught by Adam Curle at Oxford. Jean was my professional counselling supervisor at the time when I started working with Adam in Croatia. Now retired, she has become a close friend. Adam and Jean have corresponded and found that they both share a love of poetry. They both are so creative that they have already generated new ideas and now are planning their next publications ...

Jean, who is as much a pioneer in counselling as Adam is in peace making, describes liminality, the edges of awareness where boundaries dissolve and where there is an opportunity for change. Carl Rogers' peace work with groups in Northern Ireland and in Africa, and in a smaller way our work in Croatia, shows that liminality achieved within a community can be an immensely powerful agent for change:

> ...liminality can be a space of time where we can be what we are, where we can relate to each other as persons in our brokenness in communitas, where status is irrelevant and through this experience we can grow. Perhaps this is one of the profound learnings from our often painful and fearful times of transition, if we choose to be aware. Liminality is a space where we can gain some view of who we are and where we might be in the cosmos, to reflect where we have come from and what we might be in the pattern of social relations and who we are person to person in open relationships, in communitas. (Clark 1988: 11)

The transition from the sense of separation and alienation to inner peace and outer peacefulness requires courage, awareness and acceptance of self, of others and of uncertainty. With increasing awareness, the definitions and boundaries of self and other may disintegrate and merge into a collective 'we', as the Centar za mir found in its very first workshop with Adam Curle. A safe, therapeutic space created by professionals, friends or a community can provide the environment in which we can experience the liminality within which lies the opportunity for the psychological change from unpeacefulness to peace.

Adam Curle wrote the first words in this book. I also want to end it with his words, looking forward to the future through his eyes, with positivity, hope and understanding.

So, above all, love, let's love and do it generously and with a full heart; and be deeply sorry for those who find loving hard; and if you do, be courageous to face the difficulties on the way. And spare an affectionate thought for the Black Cloud; its displeasing ways are the products of its pains. (Curle 2006: 9)

Bibliography

Note: For the assistance of peace studies students, this bibliography includes all the publications of Adam Curle traced during this research. A collection of Curle's publications and some of his earlier unpublished work is stored in the Curle Library at the University of Bradford.

Aarts, P. G. and Op den Velde, W. (1996). Prior traumatization and the process of aging: theory and clinical implications. *Traumatic stress: the effects of overwhelming experience on mind, body and society*. van der Kolk, B. A., Mcfarlane, A. C. and Weisaeth, L., Eds. London, New York, The Guilford Press: 359-377

Abueg, F. R. and Chun, K. M. (1996). Traumatization stress among Asians and Asian Americans. *Ethnocultural aspects of Posttraumatic Stress Disorder: issues, research and clinical applications*. Marsella, A. J., Friedman, M. J., Gerrity, E. T. and Scurfield, R. M., Eds. Washington D.C., American Psychological Association: 285-300

Adjukovic, M. and Adjukovic, D. (1998). Mental health care for helpers: experiences from a training programme. *War, violence, trauma and the coping process*. Arcel, L. T., Ed. Zagreb, International Rehabilitation Council for Torture Victims (IRCT): 314-318

Adler, A. (1974). *Understanding human nature*. London, George Allen & Unwin Ltd

Agger, I. Reducing trauma during ethno-political conflict: a personal account of psycho-social work under war conditions in Bosnia. *Peace, conflict and violence*. Christie, D. J., Wagner, R. and Winter, D., Eds. Upper Saddle River, N.J., Prentice Hall

Agger, I. (1996). *Trauma and healing under state terrorism*. London, Zed Books

Agger, I. (2001). Reducing trauma during ethno-political conflict. *Peace, conflict and violence*. Christie, D. J., Wagner, R. and Du Nann Winter, D., Eds. Upper Saddle River, N.J., Prentice Hall: 240-261

Agger, I. and Mimica, J. (1996). *Psychosocial assistance to victims of war in Bosnia-Herzgovina and Croatia: an evaluation*. Brussels, European Community Humanitarian OSCE (ECHO)

Agger, I., Vuk, S. and Mimica, J. (1995). *Theory and practice of psychosocial projects under war conditions in Bosnia-Herzgovina and Croatia*. Zagreb, European Community Humanitarian OSCE (ECHO) / ECTF

Albucher, R. C. and Liberzon, I. (2002). "Psychopharmacological treatment in PTSD: a critical review." *Journal of Psychiatric Research* **36**(6): 355-367

Aldridge, D. (1996). *Music therapy research and practice in medicine: from out of the silence*. London, Jessica Kingsley

Aldwin, C. M., C.M, S. and Lachman, M. (1996). "The development of coping resources in adulthood." *Journal of Personality* **64**: 91-113

Aldwin, C. M. and Sutton, K. J. (1998). A developmental perspective on post-traumatic growth. *Post-traumatic growth: positive changes in the aftermath of crisis*. Tedeschi, R. G., Park, C. L. and Calhoun, L. G., Eds. Mahwah, N.J, Lawrence Erlbaum: 43-63

Allen, I. M. (1996). PTSD among African Americans. *Ethnocultural aspects of Posttraumatic Stress Disorder: issues, research and clinical applications*. Marsella, A. J., Friedman, M. J., Gerrity, E. T. and Scurfield, R. M., Eds. Washington D.C., American Psychological Association: 209-238

Allwood, M. A., Bell-Dolan, D. and Husain, S. A. (2002). "Children's trauma and adjustment reactions to violent and nonviolent war experiences." *Journal of the*

American Academy of Child and Adolescent Psychiatry **41**(4): 450-457

Alternatives to Violence Project , A. *Training manual, levels 1 and 2, and facilitator training.* London, AVP Britain

Altrichter, H. (1990). *Quality features in an action research strategy.* 'Il methodo della ricerca – azione applicato all educazione frascati ', University of Klagenfurt Italy

American Academy of Medical Acupuncture (2003). *Conditions for which medical acupuncture may be indicated in a hospital setting,* American Academy of Medical Acupuncture. **2003**

American Dance Therapy Association (2003). *What is dance/movement therapy?* American Dance Therapy Association. **2003**

American-Psychiatric-Association (1952). *Diagnostic and statistical manual of mental disorders I.* Washington DC, American Psychiatric Association

American-Psychiatric-Association (1968). *Diagnostic and statistical manual of mental disorders II.* Washington DC, American Psychiatric Association

American-Psychiatric-Association (1980). *Diagnostic and statistical manual of mental disorders III.* Washington DC, American Psychiatric Association

American-Psychiatric-Association (1987). *Diagnostic and statistical manual of mental disorders III (R).* Washington DC, American Psychiatric Association

American-Psychiatric-Association (1994). *Diagnostic and statistical manual of mental disorders IV.* Washington D.C., American Psychiatric Association

American-Psychiatric-Association (2000). *Diagnostic and statistical manual of mental disorders IV.TR* Washington D.C., American Psychiatric Association

Andreasen, N. J. (1984). *The broken brain.* New York, Harper and Row

Andreasen, N. J. (1997). "Linking minds and brain in the study of mental illness: a project for scientific pathology." *Science* **275**: 1586-1593

Andreasen, N. J. and Norris, A. S. (1972). "Long-term adjustment and adaptation mechanisms in severely burned adults." *Journal of Nervous and Mental Disorders* (154): 352-362

Andreasen, N. J., Noyes, R. J., Hartford, C. E., Brodland, G. and Proctor, S. (1972). "Management of emotional reactions in seriously burned adults." *New England Journal of Medicine* (286): 65-69

Arcel, L. T. (1998). Sexual torture of women as a weapon of war- the case of Bosnia-Herzgovina. *War, violence, trauma and the coping process.* Arcel, L. T., Ed. Zagreb, International Rehabilitation Council for Torture Victims (IRCT): 183-211

Arcel, L. T., Folnegovic-Smalc, V., Kozaric-Kovacic, D. and Marusic, A. (1995). *Psychosocial help to war victims: women refugees and their families.* Copenhagen, International Rehabilitation Council for Torture Victims (IRCT)

Arcel, L. T., Folnegovic-Smalc, V., Tocilj-Simunkovic, G., Kozaric-Kovacic, D. and Ljubotina, D. (1998). Ethnic cleansing and post-traumatic coping. War violence, PTSD, depression, anxiety, and coping in Bosnian and Croatian refugees. A transactional approach. *War, violence, trauma and the coping process.* Arcel, L. T., Ed. Zagreb, International Rehabilitation Council for Torture Victims (IRCT): 45-78

Arcel, L. T. and Tocilj-Simunkovic, G., Eds. (1998). *War, violence, trauma and the coping process.* Zagreb, International Rehabilitation Council for Torture Victims

Ayalon, O. (1992). *Rescue!* Haifa, Chevron Publishing

Azar, E. (1990). Protracted international conflicts. *Conflict: readings in management and resolution.* Burton, J. W. and Dukes, F., Eds. London, Macmillan

BACP (2002). *Ethical framework for good practice in counselling and psychotherapy.* Rugby, British Association of Counselling and Psychotherapy

Baker, F. (2001). "Rationale for the effects of familiar music on agitation and orientation levels of people in posttraumatic amnesia." *Nordic Journal of Music Therapy* **10**(1): 32-41

Bakran, Z., Bobinac-Georgievski, A., Dzidic, I., Jelic, M. and Eldar, R. (2001). "Medical rehabilitation in Croatia- Impact of the 1991-1995 War: past problems, present state, future concerns." *Croatian Medical Journal* **42**(5): 556-564

Bandler, R. (1997). *Neuro-Linguistic Programming: the presuppositions of NLP*, www.purenlp.com. **2003**

Bandler, R. and Grinder, J. (1979). *Frogs into princes: Neuro-Linguistic Programming*. Moab, Utah, Real People Press

Barkham, J. (1999). The Facilitator Development Institute (Britain) workshops. *Experiences in relatedness: groupwork and the Person Centred Approach*. Lago, C. and MacMillan, M., Eds. Ross on Wye, PCCS Books: 123-136

Beck, A. (1970). "Role of fantasies in psychotherapy and psychopathology." *Journal of Nervous and Mental Diseases* **150**: 3-17

Beck, A. (1972). *The diagnosis and management of depression*. Philadelphia, University of Pennsylvania Press

Berberovic, M. (1998). Nurse in a psychosocial programme. *War, violence, trauma and the coping process*. Arcel, L. T., Ed. Zagreb, International Rehabilitation Council for Torture Victims (IRCT): 265-269

Bercovitch, J., Anagnoson, J. T. and Wille, D. (1991). "Some conceptual issues and empirical trends in the study of successful mediation in international relations." *Journal of Peace Research*. **28**(1): 7-17

Berne, E. (1991). *Transactional Analysis in psychotherapy*. London, Souvenir Press

Bisbey, S., Bisbey, L.B. (1999). *Brief therapy for posttraumatic stress disorder*. Chichester, Wiley

Blank, A. S. (1993). The longitudinal course of posttraumatic stress disorder. *Posttraumatic Stress Disorder: DSM-IV and beyond*. Davidson, J. R. T. and Foa, E. B., Eds. New York, American Psychiatric Press: 3-22

Bleich, A. and Moskowitz, L. (2000). "Posttraumatic Stress Disorder with psychotic features." *Croatian Medical Journal* **41**(4): 442-445

Boeree, G. (1997). *Karen Horney*, www.ship.edu. **2003**

Bolton, D. and Hill, J. (1996). *Mind, meaning and mental disorder. The nature of causal explanation in psychology and psychiatry*. Oxford, Oxford University Press

Bonne, O., Brandes, D., Gilboa, A., Gomori, J. M., Shenton, M. E., Pitman, R. K. and Shalev, A. Y. (2001). "Longitudinal MRI study of hippocampal volume in trauma survivors with PTSD." *The American Journal of Psychiatry* **158**(8): 1248-1251

Borba, M., Borba, C (1978). *Self-esteem, a classroom affair*. San Francisco, USA, Harper Collins

Borris, E., Diehl, P.F (1988). Forgiveness, reconciliation, and the contribution of international peacekeeping. *Psychology of Peacekeeping*. Langholtz, H., Ed. Westport, CT. & London, Praeger: 207-222

Boulding, E. and Forsberg, R. (1998). *Abolishing war*. Boston, Boston Research Center for the 21st Century

Boulding, K. (1962). *Conflict and defense: a general theory*. New York, Harper and Row

Boutros-Ghali, B. (1992). *An agenda for peace*. New York, United Nations

Boutros-Ghali, B. (1994). *An agenda for development, report of the Secretary-General A/48/935*. New York, United Nations Department of Public Information

Bowlby, J. (1969). *Attachment and loss*. New York, Basic Books

Bracken, P. (1987a). "Mania following head injury." *Br J Psychiatry* **150**: 690-2

Bracken, P. (1987b). "Science and psychoanalysis." *Aust N Z J Psychiatry* **21**(2): 137-9

Bracken, P. (1993). "Post-empiricism and psychiatry: meaning and methodology in cross-cultural research." *Social Science and Medicine* **36**: 265

Bracken, P. (1998). Hidden agendas: deconstructing posttraumatic stress disorder.

Rethinking the trauma of war. Bracken, P. and Petty, C., Eds. London, Free
Association Books

Bracken, P. (2001). "Post-modernity and Post-Traumatic Stress Disorder." *Soc Sci Med*
53(6): 733-43

Bracken, P. (2002). *Trauma, culture, meaning and philosophy.* London, Whurr

Bracken, P. and Coll, P. (1985). "Homocystinuria and schizophrenia. Literature review and
case report." *J Nerv Ment Dis* **173**(1): 51-5

Bracken, P., Giller, J. E. and Summerfield, D. (1995). "Psychological responses to war and
atrocity: the limitations of current concepts." *Social Science and Medicine* **40**: 1073-
1082

Bracken, P., Giller, J. and Summerfield, D. (1993). "Psychological responses to war and
atrocity: the limitations of current concepts." *Social Science and Medicine* **40**: 1073-
1082

Bracken, P., Thomas, P (1999). "Cognitive therapy, cartesianism and the moral order."
European Journal of Psychotherapy, Counselling and Health 2(3): 325-344

Bracken, P. J., Giller, J. E. and Kabaganda, S. (1992). "Helping victims of violence in
Uganda." *Med War* **8**(3): 155-63

Bracken, P. J., Giller, J. E. and Sekiwanuka, J. K. (1996). "The rehabilitation of child
soldiers: defining needs and appropriate responses." *Med Confl Surviv* **12**(2): 114-25

Bracken, P. J., Giller, J. E. and Summerfield, D. (1995). "Psychological responses to war
and atrocity: the limitations of current concepts." *Soc Sci Med* **40**(8): 1073-82

Bremner, J. D., Southwick, S. M., Johnson, D. R., Yehuda, R. and Charney, D. S. (1993).
"Childhood physical abuse and combat-related posttraumatic stress disorder in
Vietnam veterans." *American Journal of Psychiatry* **150**(2): 253-259

Brett, E. A. (1996a). The classification of posttraumatic stress disorder. *Traumatic Stress:
the effects of overwhelming experience on mind, body and society.* van der Kolk, B. A.,
McFarlane, A. C. and Weisaeth, L., Eds. New York, Guilford Press

Brett, E. A. (1996b). The classification of posttraumatic stress disorder. *Traumatic Stress:
the effects of overwhelming experience on mind, body and society.* van der Kolk, B. A.,
Mcfarlane, A. C. and Weisaeth, L., Eds. London, New York, The Guilford Press: 117-
128

Breuer, J. and Freud, S. (1955). *Studies on hysteria: project for a scientific psychology.*
London, Hogarth Press

Brewin, C. R. (2001). "A cognitive neuroscience account of posttraumatic stress disorder
and its treatment." *Behaviour Research and Therapy* **39**: 373-393

Brewin, C. R., Dalgliesh, T. and Joseph, S. (1996). "A dual representation theory of
posttraumatic stress disorder." *Psychological Review* **103**: 670-686

Brewin, C. R., Rose, S. and Andrews, B. (2002). Screening to identify individuals at risk
after exposure to trauma. *Reconstructing early intervention after trauma.* Orner, R. and
Schnyder, U., Eds. Oxford, Oxford University Press

Briere, J. N. (1992). *Child abuse trauma: theory and treatment of the lasting effects.*
London, Sage

British Association of Art Therapists (2002). *What is Art Therapy?* British Association of Art
Therapists. **2003**

Brom, B., Kleber, R. J. and Defares, P. B. (1989). "Brief psychotherapy for posttraumatic
stress disorder." *Journal of Consulting and Clinical Psychology* **57**: 607-612

Brom, B., Kleber, R. J. and Hofman, M. (1993). "Victims of traffic accidents: incidence and
prevention of posttraumatic stress disorder." *Journal of Clinical Psychology* **49**(2): 131-
140

Brown, D. P. and Fromm, E. (1986). *Hypnotherapy and Hypnoanalysis.* Hillsdale, N.J.,
Erlbaum

Brown, T. and Mitchels, B. (1997). *Loss, bereavement and trauma*. Norwich, Watershed Publications, Norfolk

Bryant, A. (1949). *Samuel Pepys: the man in the making*. London, The Reprint Society

Bryant, R. A. (2001a). "Posttraumatic stress disorder and mild brain injury: controversies, causes and consequences." *Journal of Clinical and Experimental Neuropsychology: Official Journal of the International Neuropsychological Society* 23(6): 718-728

Bryant, R. A. (2001b). "Posttraumatic stress disorder and traumatic brain injury: can they co-exist?" *Clinical Psychology Review* 21(6): 931-948

Bucalic, V., Pavlekovic, N. and Ponjaric, N. (1998). Dental treatment and psychological well-being. *War, violence, trauma and the coping process*. Arcel, L. T., Ed. Zagreb, International Rehabilitation Council for Torture Victims (IRCT): 278-280

Burgess, A. W. and Holmstrom, L. (1974). "Rape trauma syndrome." *American Journal of Psychiatry* 131: 981-986

Burgess, J. (1996). "Focusing on fear." *Area* 28(2): 130-136

Burns, J. L., Labbe, E., Arke, B., Capeless, K., Cooksey, B., Steadman, A. and Gonzales, C. (2002). "The effects of different types of music on perceived and physiological measures of stress." *Journal of Music Therapy* 39(2): 101-116

Burton, J. W. (1965). *International relations: a general theory*. Cambridge, Cambridge University Press

Burton, J. W. (1968). *Systems, states, diplomacy and rules*. Cambridge, Cambridge University Press

Burton, J. W. (1969). *Conflict and communication: the use of controlled communication in international relations*. London, Macmillan

Burton, J. W. (1972). *World society*. Cambridge, Cambridge University Press

Burton, J. W. (1979). *Deviance, terrorism and war*. Oxford, Martin Robinson

Burton, J. W., Ed. (1990). *Conflict: human needs theory*. The Conflict Series. London, Macmillan Press

Burton, J. W. and Dukes, F., Eds. (1990a). *Conflict: practices in management, settlement and resolution*. London, Macmillan

Burton, J. W. and Dukes, F., Eds. (1990b). *Conflict: readings in management and resolution*. The Conflict Series. London, Macmillan Press

Burton, J. W., Dukes, F. and Mason, G., Eds. (1990). *Conflict: resolution and provention*. The Conflict Series. London, Macmillan Press

Cahill, S. P., Carrigan, M. H. and Frueh, B. C. (1999). "Does EMDR work? And if so, why? A critical review of controlled outcome and dismantling research." *Journal of Anxiety Disorders* 13(1-2): 5-33

Cairns, E. (1996) *Children and Political Violence*. Oxford, Blackwell Publishers.

Cairns, E. (1987) *Caught in Crossfire*. New York, Syracruse Press.

Cairns, E. and Roe M. D., (Eds). (2002). *The Role of Memory in Ethnic Conflict*. Basingstoke, Palgrave.

Callaghan, R. (2000). *Stop the nightmares of trauma*. Chapel Hill, N.C, Professional Press

Callaghan, R. (2001a). "The impact of Thought Field Therapy on heart rate variability." *Journal of Clinical Psychology* 57(10): 1153-1170

Callaghan, R. (2001b). "Thought Field Therapy: response to our critics and a scrutiny of some old ideas of social science." *Journal of Clinical Psychology* 57(10): 1251-1260

Callaghan, R. J. and Trubo, R. (2001). *Tapping the healer within*. New York, Contemporary Books

Carbonell, J. and Figley, C. (1999). "Promising PTSD treatment approaches." *Traumatology* 5(1): 4

Centar Za Mir (2000). *Centre for Peace, on-Violence and Human Rights, Osijek*. Osijek, Centre for peace, Non-Violence and Human Rights, Osijek

Chemtob, C. M., Bauer, G. B., Neller, G., Hamada, R., Glisson, C. and Stevens, V. (1990). "Post-traumatic stress disorder among special forces Vietnam veterans." *Military Medicine* **155**: 16-20

Clark, J. (1988). *Change is boundaries dissolved.* Norwich, The Norwich Centre for Personal and Professional Development

Clark, J. (2002). The loneliness and freedoms of change. *Freelance counselling and psychotherapy: competition and collaboration.* Clark, J., Ed. London, Brunner-Routledge, Taylor and Francis Group

Clarkson, P. (1990). *Gestalt counselling in action.* London, Sage

Clarkson, P. (1995). *The therapeutic relationship.* London, Whurr Press

Coalition for Work with Psychotrauma and Peace (2000). *The CWWPP: philosophy and mandate, activities since 1995.* Vukovar, Coalition for Work with Psychotrauma and Peace

Coalition for Work with Psychotrauma and Peace (2003). *The CWWPP: philosophy and mandate, activities since 1995, and plans for the future.* Vukovar, Coalition for Work with Psychotrauma and Peace

Cohen, B. D. and Schermer, V. L. (2002). "On scapegoating in therapy groups: a social constructivist and intersubjective outlook." *International Journal Of Group Psychotherapy* **52**(1): 89-109

Cohen, R. (1996). *Negotiating Across Cultures,* U.S. Institute of Peace

Cohena, J. A., Mannarino, A. P. and Rogal, S. (2001). "Treatment practices for childhood posttraumatic stress disorder." *Child Abuse & Neglect* **25**(1): 123-135

Cole, P. M., Putnam, F.W., (1991). "Effect of incest on self and social functioning: a developmental psychopathology perspective." *Journal of Consultant Clinical Psychology* **60**(174-184)

Collins, R. L., Taylor, S. E. and Skokan, L. A. (1990). "A better world or a shattered vision? Changes in life perspectives following victimisation." *Social Cognition* **8**: 263-285

Comte, A. (1830 – 1842). *Cours de philosophie positive*

Cooke, B. (2001). The social psychological limits of participation. *Participation, the new tyranny.* Cooke, B., and Kothari, U., Ed. London, Zed Books: 102-122

Cooke, B. and Kothari, U. (2001). *Participation: the new tyranny?* London, Zed Books

Cottrell, D., Boston, P. and Sahapiro, D. (2003). *Systemic Family Therapy manual,* www.psyc.leeds.ac.uk/research/ lftrc/manuals/SFT/manual. **2003**

Coulson, A. (1999). Experiences of separateness and unity in person centred groups. *Experiences in relatedness: groupwork and the Person Centred Approach.* Lago, C. and MacMillan, M., Eds. Ross on Wye, PCCS Books: 167-180

Croatia National Bank Council (1999). *Gradska Banka Osijek, Komercijalna Banka Zagreb and Zupanska Banka Zupanja.* **2003**

Curle, A. American Friends Service Committee. Involvement in Southern Africa

Curle, A. *"Heretical firefighting."*

Curle, A. *"Peacemaking in the 21st century."*

Curle, A. *"Steps towards peacemaking."*

Curle, A. *"Towards transforming a global culture of violence."*

Curle, A. *The Transforming Force: Aspects of Non-Violence*

Curle, A. *"The worthlessness of war."*

Curle, A. *Your mind and how it works,* Foundry Press: 271-286

Curle, A. (1926). *Love and Blackmail (unpublished)*

Curle, A. (1938). *A Desert Journey*

Curle, A. "Nationalism and higher education in Ghana." *Universities Quarterly:* 229-242

Curle, A. (1946a). *A follow-up survey of resettlement among returned prisoners of war.* War Office 1946. London: 15

Curle, A. (1946b). *Some methods of facilitating the resettlement of returned prisoners of war.* War Office. London: 12

Curle, A. (1946c). "The teacher face to face with himself in relation to the community." *The New Era in Home and School* **36**(1): 1-6

Curle, A. (1948a). *Human satisfactions in rural life.* Proceedings of the Sixth Agricultural Conference of Agricultural Economists

Curle, A. (1948b). "A theory of psycho-social interaction." *Proceedings of the Seventh International Conference of Anthropology and Ethnology* **1948**

Curle, A. (1949a). "Incentives to work: an anthropological appraisal." *Human Relations* **1**: 41-47

Curle, A. (1949b). "Participant action research with special reference to rural communities." *Bulletin of the British Psychological Society*

Curle, A. (1949c). "The sociological background to incentives." *Occupational Psychology* **23**(1): 21-29

Curle, A. (1949d). "A theoretical approach to action research." *Human Relations* **3**: 269-280

Curle, A. (1949e). "Toilet training in early childhood." *Proceedings of the Royal Society of Medicine* **52**(11): 905-909

Curle, A. (1951a). "A conference on the methodology of social surveys." *International Social Science Bulletin* **3**(3): 629-634

Curle, A. (1951b). "Human affairs." *Biology* **17**(2)

Curle, A. (1951c). *Uses of psychosocial research methods.* UNESCO

Curle, A. (1952a). *Education for freedom.* The Times Educational Supplement

Curle, A. (1952b). "The function of educational psychology." *Bulletin of Education* **29**: 12-15

Curle, A. (1952c). "Impressions of modern German psychology." *Bulletin of the British Psychological Society* **1952**

Curle, A. (1952). "Kinship structure in an English village." *Man* **100**: 68-69

Curle, A. (1952d). "Our 'crisis' seen in terms of human relationships." *The New Era in Home and School* **35**(5): 122-124

Curle, A. (1952e). "War crisis seen in terms of human relationships." *The New Era in Home and School* **33**(1): 122-123

Curle, A. (1952f). "What happened to three villages?" *The Listener* **Vol 58 (XLVIII)**(No 1242): 1027-1028

Curle, A. (1953). "Education and conformity." *The New Era. Bulletin of the Institute of Education of the University College of the South West of England (University of Exeter)* **1**: 8-10

Curle, A. (1953a). "Children and their social relationships 1." *Bulletin of the Institute of Education of the University College of the South West of England (University of Exeter)* (3): 6-7

Curle, A. (1953b). "Children and their social relationships 2." *Bulletin of the Institute of Education of the University College of the South West of England (University of Exeter)* (2): 3-4

Curle, A. (1953c). "Kinship and conformity." *The New Era in Home and School* **5**: 8-10

Curle, A. (1953d). *Studies of behaviour and concepts of freedom.* An Inaugural Address, University College of the South West of England (University of Exeter), University College of the South West of England (University of Exeter)

Curle, A. (1954). "Some psychological factors in rural society." *Tribus* **4-5**: 250-255

Curle, A. (1955). *Psychoanalysis and the study of society.* Bristol Meeting of the British Association, Bristol, British Association

Curle, A. (1955a). "The contribution of psycho-analysis to the understanding of human behaviour (a symposium with J. Nuttin and C. de Loncheaux)." *The Advancement of*

Science XII (49): 548-563

Curle, A. (1955b) Education in rural areas. *Looking forward in education*. Judges, A. V.,
    Ed.: 156-173

Curle, A. (1955c) "From student to teacher status." *The New Era in Home and School*
    36(2): 21-23

Curle, A. (1955d) "Huxley's 'brave new world." *The New Statesman and Nation* XLIX
    (1257): 508-509

Curle, A. (1955e) "A matter of communication." *The Listener* III (1331): 566-567

Curle, A. (1955f) The psychological theory of group work. *Social Group Work in Great
    Britain*. Kuenstler, Ed.: 135-155

Curle, A. (1955g) "The teacher face to face with himself in relation to the community." *The
    New Era in Home and School* 36(1): 1-6

Curle, A. (1955h) "The year book of education 1954." *British Journal of Educational
    Studies* 1955(5)

Curle, A. (1956a). *Community organisation and family welfare in European problem areas*.
    Ministry of Social Work, the Hague. The Hague: 22

Curle, A. (1956b). *Problems of social change*. The Government of Pakistan Planning
    Board.

Curle, A. (1957a). *The child and the community*. Proceedings of the First All-Pakistan
    Child Welfare Conference 1957, Pakistan, Proceedings of the First All-Pakistan Child
    Welfare Conference

Curle, A. (1957b). *The first five year plan*, Government of Pakistan Planning Board

Curle, A. (1957c). *Nomadism in Kalat Division*. Mimeographed Government of Pakistan
    Planning Board.: 12

Curle, A. (1957d). *Problems of resettlement in the Chittagong Hill tracts*. Mimeographed
    Government of Pakistan Planning Board. 14

Curle, A. (1957e). *The school curriculum and social and cultural tradition*. UNESCO: 57

Curle, A. (1957f). *The special areas and other tribal territories*. The First Five-Year Plan
    Government of Pakistan Planning Board: 639-652

Curle, A. (1958a). *The desert areas of Thar Parkar district*. Mimeographed. Government of
    Pakistan Planning Board. 22

Curle, A. (1958b). *Development in the far North of Pakistan*. Mimeographed. Government
    of Pakistan Planning Board. 33

Curle, A. (1958c). *The present labour policy*. Mimeographed. Government of Pakistan
    Planning Commission. 11

Curle, A. (1958d). *Principles of regional development*. Mimeographed. Government of
    Pakistan Planning Board. 15

Curle, A. (1960a). "Social service: part III human resources and welfare." *The Second Five
    Year Plan. Government of Pakistan Planning Commission* , : 311-391; 329-396; &
    397-414

Curle, A. (1960b). "Tradition, development and planning." *The Sociological Review* 8

Curle, A. (1960c). "Social Service; Part IV Regional Development." *The Second Five- Year
    Plan. Government of Pakistan Planning Commission*: 311-391; 329-396; & 397-414

Curle, A. (1961). "The role of education in under-developed societies." *School Inspection
    and In-Service Training* 42: 87-98

Curle, A. (1961a). "Dangers in Ghana." *Amnesty* 4: 2

Curle, A. (1961b). Foreword. *Social survey of Tefle: child development monographs*. D.K.
    Fiawoo, Ed., No 2 Institute of Education. Legon. 2

Curle, A. (1961c). "Fra elev-til laererstatus." *Unge Paedagoger*. 22 argana (Nr 4): 9-14

Curle, A. (1961d). "Further thoughts on teacher training." *The New Era in Home and
    School* 42(1): 1-4

Curle, A. (1961e). *The role of education in developing societies.* Inaugural Lecture. University College of Ghana

Curle, A. (1961f). "Sir George Robertson: an early fieldworker." *Man* **LXI**: 1-25 & 15-19

Curle, A. (1961g). "Undervisningsvalsenets funktion i de underudviklede lande." *Unge Paedagoger.* **22 argana** (Nr 5,6,7): 10

Curle, A. (1962a). "African nationalism and higher education in Ghana." *Universities Quarterly* **16**(3): 229-243

Curle, A. (1962b). "Letter from Jamaica." *Universities Quarterly* **16**(3)

Curle, A. (1962c). Social and economic problems of increasing human resources in underdeveloped countries. *The year book of education.* Bereday and Lauwerys, Eds.: 528-53

Curle, A. (1962d). "Some aspects of educational planning in underdeveloped areas." *Havard Educational Review* **32**(3)

Curle, A. (1963a). *Economic and social development: educational investment in the Pacific community,* American Association of Colleges for Teacher Education

Curle, A. (1963b). *Education, administration and development.* Occasional papers. Comparative Administration Group, American Society for Public Administration

Curle, A. (1963c). *Educational strategy for developing societies: a study of educational and sociological factors in relation to economic growth.* London, Tavistock

Curle, A. (1964a). "Education, politics, and development." *Comparative Education Review* **7**(3)

Curle, A. (1964b). *World campaign for universal literacy: comment and proposal.* Occasional Papers in Education and Development, No 1 1964. Havard. USA

Curle, A. (1965). Critical implications of the education explosion. *The year book of education 1965.* Bereday and Lauwerys, Eds.

Curle, A. (1966). *Planning for education in Pakistan: a personal case study.* London, Tavistock Publications

Curle, A. (1967). MSS. *Education and technological change* (Unpublished)

Curle, A. (1968a). *Educational planning: the adviser's role,* UNESCO International Institute for Educational Planning

Curle, A. (1968b). The new university. *The new university.* Lawlor, J., Ed. London, Routledge and Kegan Paul Ltd

Curle, A. (1968c). *Problems of professional identity: an examination of training for human resource development and educational planning.* New York, Education and World Affairs Report No 6 1968

Curle, A. (1968d). Universities in a changing world: innovation and stagnation. *The New University.* Lawlor, J., Ed. London, Routledge

Curle, A. (1969a). The Devil's advocate view. *Agents of change: professionals in developing countries.* Benveniste, G. and Illchman, W., Eds. New York, Praeger

Curle, A. (1969b). Education, politics and development. *Scientific investigations into comparative education.* Eckstein, M. and Noah, H. J., Eds. Toronto,Ontario, Macmillan.

Curle, A. (1969c). *Educational problems of developing societies with case studies of Ghana and Pakistan.* New York, Praeger.

Curle, A. (1970a). Aid and its implications. *Problems of economic development.* Prasi, D., Ed. London, WRI

Curle, A. (1970b). *Educational strategies for developing societies.* London, Tavistock

Curle, A. (1970c). *Friendschaffen: in der offentlichkett und im privaten.* Luxembourg, FWWCC

Curle, A. (1970d). *L'identite professionelle de l'education,* UNESCO Institut international de planification de l'education

Curle, A. (1970e). *The professional identity of the education planner*, UNESCO International Institute for Educational Planning

Curle, A. (1970f). *A psychological background for universalism*

Curle, A. (1971a). "Education cast in a broader development role." *Modern Government* (March 1971)

Curle, A. (1971b). Education, politics and development. *Education in comparative and international perspectives.* Gezi, K., Ed. Chicago, SF, Atlanta, Dallas, Montreal, Toronto, London, Sydney, Holt, Rinehard & Winston Inc: 302

Curle, A. (1971c). *Making peace.* London, Tavistock

Curle, A. (1971d). *Gelisen cemiyetlerde egitimin roli.* Kamisonu Yayinlari: 3, Cahit Okurer Sosyal Lhimler

Curle, A. (1972). *Mysticos y militantes.* Buenos Aires/ London, Tavistock

Curle, A. (1972a). *Mystics and militants- a study of awareness, identity and social action.* London, Tavistock

Curle, A. (1972). "Seminar Notes Peace Studies and the U235."

Curle, A. (1973a). "Adam Curle appointed to the Chair of Peace Studies, Bradford." *The Friend* **131**(10)

Curle, A. (1973b). *Education for liberation.* London, Tavistock

Curle, A. (1973c). The education of teachers. *Education at home and abroad.* Lauwerys, J., Tayar, G., Ed. London, Routledge and Kegan Paul Ltd

Curle, A. (1973d). *Educational problems of developing societies: with case studies of Ghana, Pakistan, and Nigeria.* New York: London, Praeger

Curle, A. (1973e). *Educational psychology a contemporary view.* Del Mar, California, Communications research Machines Inc

Curle, A. (1973f). "Professor of peace studies." *The Friend* **131**(10): 2-3

Curle, A. (1973g). "Teaching peace." *World Issues* **27**: 6

Curle, A. (1974a). *Contribution of education to freedom and justice.* Education for Peace Proceedings for the First World Conference of the World Council for Curriculum and Instruction, University of Keele, ISP Science and Technology Press

Curle, A. (1974b). "Education for peace: the international dimension." *London Educational Review*: 33-38

Curle, A. (1974c). *Education in developing societies (Hindi edition).* Bombay, Oxford University Press

Curle, A. (1974d). *Peace and co-operation.* 1974 Ernest Bader Common Ownership Lecture, Scott Bader Commonwealth Centre, Scott Bader Commonwealth Centre

Curle, A. (1975a). "Conspiracy case in context." *The Friend* **133**(6): 139

Curle, A. (1975b). *Reconciliation, violence and anger.* New Malden, Fellowship of Reconciliation, 9 Coombe Road, New Malden, Surrey, KT3 4QA

Curle, A. (1975c). *The scope and dilemmas of peace studies, an inaugural lecture.* Bradford, University of Bradford

Curle, A. (1975d). "A word for this time." *Friends Journal* (15 October 1975): 515-518

Curle, A. (1976a). Education for a technical explosion. *Hidden factors in technological change.* Coggin, E. and Semper, E., Eds. Oxford, Toronto, NY, Sydney, Paris, Frankfurt, Pergamon Press

Curle, A. (1976b). Peace studies. *The year book of world affairs.* Keeton, G. W., Schwartenberger, Ed. London, The London Institute of World Affairs, Stevens and Sons Ltd. **30**

Curle, A. (1976c). "Violence or non-violence? A Christian dilemma." *The Clergy Review* **LXI**(2): 44-49

Curle, A. (1977d). *Educacion Liberadora problems de pedagogia.* Barcelona, Editorial Herder

Curle, A. (1977e). *Estrategia educativa.* Barcelona, Editorial Herder

Curle, A. (1977c). *Peace and love the violin and the oboe.* London, Lindsey press

Curle, A. (1977d). "Reflections on working in a university." *Studies in Higher Education* **2**(1)

Curle, A. (1977e). "That of God." *Quaker Monthly* **56**(5): 81-85

Curle, A. (1978a). "Peace studies at Bradford – the first five years." *The Friend* **136**(39): 1213

Curle, A. (1978b). *Peacemaking, public and private.* Occasional Papers; 5; Office of the Dean of Women, Queens University, Kingston, Ontario. Kingston, Ontario

Curle, A. (1978c). *Peacemaking, public and private.* Philadelphia, Wider Quaker Fellowship: A program of the Friends World Committee for Consultation, 1506, Race Street, Philadelphia PA 19102

Curle, A. (1978d). "Seven enemies." *The Friend*: 1121-1122

Curle, A. (1978e). "Towards a different society." *Quaker Monthly* **57-8**: 150

Curle, A. (1978). *Vredestichten als Openbara en Prive Aktiviteit.* Canada, Queens University Publishing

Curle, A. (1979). "Looking abroad: vigour and veritas." *The Friend* **137**(38): 1167

Curle, A. (1979a). "Looking abroad: the material and the sacramental." *The Friend* **137**(12): 329

Curle, A. (1980a). Action research as part of peacemaking. *Social science – for what? Festschrift for Johan Galtung.* Holm, H. H. and Rudeng, E., Eds. Oslo, Bergen, Tromso, Universitesforlaget

Curle, A. (1980b). *The basis of Quaker work for peace and service.* London, Friends House

Curle, A. (1980c). "Bears and lions." *The Friend* **138**(8): 217

Curle, A. (1980d). "Life-styles- human and machine." *The Friends Quarterly* **22**(1): 213

Curle, A. (1980e). "Peace studies in universities." *World Studies Journal* **1**(4): 5-12

Curle, A. (1980f). "Wars of liberation: a fact of international life." *The Friend* **138**(31): 1 August 1980

Curle, A. (1981a). "Do our nuclear weapons protect us more than they imperil us?" *Science and Public Policy* **8**(5): 350-360

Curle, A. (1981b). "Looking abroad: digging into Pendle Hill." *The Friend* **139**(11): 307

Curle, A. (1981c). "Looking abroad: Tibetans outside Tibet." *The Friend* **141**(33): 1039

Curle, A. (1981d). *Preparation for peace.* Canada, Canadian Yearly Meeting.

Curle, A. (1981e). *Security through disarmament.* QUND Seminar, Geneva

Curle, A. (1981f). "South Africa in bondage: time for compassion and action." *South African Working Party of the American Friends Service Committee*

Curle, A. (1981g). *True justice: Quaker peacemakers and peacemaking.* London, Swarthmore Press

Curle, A. (1982a). "Can We Speak truth in Love?" *Quaker Monthly* **61**(10): 193-196

Curle, A. (1982b). A letter to Sigrid Helliesen Lund. *Quakerism, a way of life: in homage to Sigrid Helliesen Lund* Norway, Kvekerforlaget

Curle, A. (1982c). "Sources of peace and violence." *Churches Register* **3**: 20-21

Curle, A. (1982d). "Universities in the third world." *Pacific Perspective* **12**(1): 4-7

Curle, A. (1982e). "What do Friends really mean?" *The Friend* **140**(38): 1165

Curle, A. (1983a). "Abnormality in the context of different cultural settings." *The Friend* **141**(19): 581

Curle, A. (1983b). "The compassionate will." *Quaker Monthly* **62**(12): 253

Curle, A. (1983c). "Conflict resolution simplified." *The Friend* **141**(29): 911

Curle, A. (1983d). Do our nuclear weapons protect us more than they imperil us? Defence and energy issues. *Science and Society* London, Heinemann

Curle, A. (1983e). *Europe and non-violent defence*. European Security: Nuclear or Conventional Defence? Geneva, Pergamon Press

Curle, A. (1983f). *The fire in the peat*. London, Quaker Peace and Service Friends House, Euston Road London NW1 2BJ

Curle, A. (1983g). "Looking abroad: the fire in the peat." *The Friend* **141**(7): 189

Curle, A. (1983h). *Nuclear and /or conventional forces in European security*. Groupe de Bellerive International Colloquium, Geneva

Curle, A. (1983i). "Making peace." *The Internationalist* **121**: 27

Curle, A. (1983j). *Nuclear forces in European security*. Groupe de Bellerive, Geneva

Curle, A. (1983k). "Tentative notes for the shambhala recruits." *The Friend* **141**(31): 975

Curle, A. (1983l). "Das feuer im moor (The fire in the peat)." *Der Quaker* **6**: 104-106

Curle, A. (1983m). "Three stages in the process of peacemaking." *The Internationalist* **121**: 27

Curle, A. (1984a). "Education for peace." *Educare – Journal of Life Education* **1**(1): 7-8

Curle, A. (1984b). *Jesus, the Heretic*

Curle, A. (1984c). "Looking abroad: our common membership." *The Friend* **142**(8): 239-240

Curle, A. (1984d). "Looking abroad: visions of the future." *The Friend* **142**(42): 1331-1333

Curle, A. (1984e). The nature of peace. *Issues in peace education*. Reid, C., Ed. South Glamorgan. The United World College of the Atlantic: 8-12

Curle, A. (1984g). "Visions of a new world." *The Friend* **142**(42): 1331-1332

Curle, A. (1985). "Looking abroad: insular pressures in education." *The Friend* **143**(29)

Curle, A. (1986a). *In the middle: non-official mediation in violent situations*. Oxford, Berg

Curle, A. (1986b). "Leading out or shoving in?" *Educare – Journal of Life Education* **2**(3): 44-46

Curle, A. (1986c). "Looking abroad: a bureau of trained mediators." *The Friend* **144**(12)

Curle, A. (1986d). "Mediation: steps on the long road to negotiated settlement of conflicts." *Transnational Perspectives* **12**(1): 5-7

Curle, A. (1986e). *Non-violent political struggle*. Conference on Non-Violent Political Struggle, London, Quaker Peace and Service

Curle, A. (1987b). *Recognition of reality: reflections and prose poems*. Stroud, Hawthorn Press

Curle, A. (1988a). "Labels." *Quaker Monthly* (October 1988)

Curle, A. (1988b). "The terminology of peacemaking." *Conflict Resolution Notes* **5**(3): 26-27

Curle, A. (1989a). *Document arising from the consultation of Quaker experience of political mediation*. Old Jordans, Buckinghamshire, UK

Curle, A. (1989b). "A key to awareness." *The Friend* (October): 1375-1376

Curle, A. (1990a). "Letter from the Peace Brigade." *Quaker Monthly* **69**(9): 186-187

Curle, A. (1990b). Peace studies. *Peace is the way*. Wright, C. and Augarde, T., Eds. Cambridge, The Lutterworth Press: 121-124

Curle, A. (1990c). "Peacemaking:' inner' state and 'outer' act." *The Friends Quarterly*

Curle, A. (1990d). "Third party peacemaking." *Interdisciplinary Peace Research*: 62-73

Curle, A. (1990e). *Tools for transformation-a personal study*. Stroud, Hawthorn Press

Curle, A. (1991a). *A dialogue for universalists*. London, Quaker Universalist Group.

Curle, A. (1991b). "Transformation." *Engaging Buddhism*: 29-31

Curle, A. (1992a). Peacemaking: the middle way. *Reconciliation in the post cold war era: challenges to Quaker international affairs work* Philadelphia, Pennsylvania, American Friends Service Committee: 5-9

Curle, A. (1992b). *Peacemaking – the middle way*. Philadelphia, Pennsylvania, Bridges. Quaker International Affairs. International Division of the American Friends Service Committee

Curle, A. (1992c). "Small circles: work for peace in the former Yugoslavia." *The Friend* **150**(40): 1265-1268

Curle, A. (1992d). A spirit of optimism. *Waging peace.* Krieger, D. a. K., F, Ed. Chicago, Illinois, The Noble Press

Curle, A. (1992e). *The transforming force: aspects of non-violence*, London, Carlssons

Curle, A. (1992f). "Unclenching the fist around the heart." *The Friend* **150**(35): 1103-1105

Curle, A. (1992g). "What prospects for peace in the former Yugoslavia?" *The Friend* **150**(39): 1229-1230

Curle, A. (1993a). "In a climate of moral anarchy." *The Friend* **151**(34): 1071-1072

Curle, A. (1993b). "Peace and development." *CHEC Journal* **11**: 29-30

Curle, A. (1993c). "Small circles for peace." *Horizons: Community Aid Abroad* **1**(4): 14-15

Curle, A. (1993d). *Some notes on Quakerism and Buddhism.* Birmingham, Woodbrooke Interfaith Centre

Curle, A. (1993e). Steering the world away from violence. *Voices on the threshold of tomorrow.* Fuerestein, G. and Fuerestein, T., Eds. Madras, London, Quest Books

Curle, A. (1993). "Unclench the fist around the heart." *World Goodwill Newsletter* **1**(1): 6-7

Curle, A. (1994a). "Forgiveness?" *Fellowship* **60**(7/8): 9

Curle, A. (1994b). "New challenges for citizen peacemaking." *Medicine and War* **10**(2): 96-105

Curle, A. (1994c). "Reflections on forgiveness." *Fellowship* **July/August**: 4

Curle, A. (1994d). "Some notes on Quakerism and Buddhism." *Quaker Monthly* **73**(10): 212-213

Curle, A. (1994e). *Towards a global awareness of peace services.* Towards a Global Awareness of Peace Services, Stensnas, Sweden, Christian Council of Sweden, Life and Peace Institute, Uppsala

Curle, A. (1995). *Another way.* Oxford, Jon Carpenter

Curle, A. (1995a). "A forgotten Balkan town." *Coordinating Committee for Conflict Transformation Newsletter* **2**: 1-2

Curle, A. (1995b). "Reconstituting the council." *Fellowship* **61**(7/8): 21

Curle, A. (1995c). *Ways out of war.* London, Quaker Peace and Service

Curle, A. (1996). "Following the light." *The Friend* **154**(51): 5-6

Curle, A. (1996a). *After the Cold War.* The Friend. **154**: 7-8

Curle, A. (1996b). "After the Cold War 2: violence and alienation." *The Friend* **154**(25): 11-12

Curle, A. (1996c). "After the Cold War 3: compassionate prophecy." *The Friend* **154**(27): 7-8

Curle, A. (1996d). Problemas de pacificacion contemporanea. *Construir a Paz: Cultura Para las Paz.* Jares, X. R., Ed.

Curle, A. (1996e). "Small circles for peace." *Community Aid Abroad*: 14-15

Curle, A. (1996f). *Training for situations of alienation and violence*, Unpublished

Curle, A. (1997a). *Counselling for peace*

Curle, A. (1997b). "Public health II : the psychological dimension." *Medicine, Conflict and Survival* **13**: 23-26

Curle, A. (1997c). "Public health III : hatred and reconciliation." *Medicine, Conflict and Survival* **13**: 37-47

Curle, A. (1997d). "Public health IV : reversing the cycle of violence." *Medicine, Conflict and Survival* **13**

Curle, A. (1998). "Counselling in Croatia: a peaceful future?" *The Friend*: 4-6

Curle, A. (1998a). "Happiness as a right." *The International Journal of Human Rights*: 77-83

Curle, A. (1999). *To tame the Hydra.* Charlbury Oxford, Jon Carpenter

Curle, A. (1999a). *Ghandi: the great soul of the century*. Ontario, Canada, Centre for Peace Studies, McMaster University

Curle, A. (2001). *The wounds of war*. London (draft)

Curle, A. (2001a). From the Somme to the Hydra. *Living in godless times*. Leonard, A., Ed. Edinburgh, Floris Books: 95-119

Curle, A. (2001b). "Social healing of the wounds of war." *Committee for Conflict Transformation Support Newsletter* **14**(Autumn 2001): 3-6

Curle, A. (2003). *Letter*. Mitchels, B.

Curle, A. (2006) *Fragile Voice of Love* Charlbury Oxford, Jon Carpenter

Curle, A., Boulding, E (2000). *Reflections on peace: the state of the world*. Building a Culture of Peace, Burlington, New Jersey, Pendle Hill's Religion and Social Issues Forum and Bryn Mawr College Graduate School of Social Work and Social Research

Curle, A., Dugan, M. (1971). "Peacemaking: stages and sequences."

Curle, A. and Trist, E. L. (1948). "Transitional communities and social reconnection." *Human Relations* **1**(1 & 3.): 74

Curle, A., Wilson, A. E. and Trist, E. L. (1952). Transitional communities and social reconnection: a study of the civil resettlement of British prisoners of war. *Readings in Social Psychology*. Swanson, Newcomb and Hartley, Eds.: 561-580

Curle, A., Yudelman, M. (1965). The goals of education in underdeveloped countries. *Challenge and change in American education*. Harris, S., Deitch, K., and Lavenshon, Ed. Berkely. CA, McCutchan Publishing: 103-112

D.H.S.S. (1970). *The battered baby*. London, Department of Health and Social Security and the Welsh Office

Daly, R. (1983). "Samuel Pepys and post-traumatic stress disorder". *British Journal of Psychiatry* **143**: 64-68.

Danieli, Y. (1992). *Child survivors as orphans, offspring and parents*, United Nations Publications

Davidson, J., Swartz, M., Krishnan, R. and Hammett, E. (1985). "A diagnostic and family study of posttraumatic stress disorder." *American Journal of Psychiatry* (142): 90-93

Davidson, J. R. T. and van der Kolk, B. A. (1996). The psychopharmacological treatment of posttraumatic stress disorder. *Traumatic stress: the effects of overwhelming experience on mind, body and society*. van der Kolk, B. A., Mcfarlane, A. C. and Weisaeth, L., Eds. London, New York, The Guilford Press: 510-524

Davidson, P. R. and Parker, K. C. H. (2001). "Eye Movement Desensitization and Reprocessing (EMDR): a meta-analysis." *Journal of Consulting and Clinical Psychology* **69**(2): 305-316

Davis, M., Walker, D. L. and Lee, Y. (1997). "Amygdala and bed nucleus of the stria terminalis: differential roles in fear and anxiety measured with the acoustic startle reflex." *Philosophical Transactions of the Royal Society* **352**: 1675-1687

de Bloch, J. (1898). *The war of the future*

de Girolamo, G. and McFarlane, A. C. (1996). The epidemiology of PTSD: a comprehensive review of the international literature. *Ethnocultural aspects of Posttraumatic Stress Disorder: issues, research and clinical applications*. Marsella, A. J., Friedman, M. J., Gerrity, E. T. and Scurfield, R. M., Eds. Washington D.C., American Psychological Association: 33-86

de Jong, J. T., Komproe, I. H., Ivan, H., van Ommeren, M., El Masri, M., Araya, M., Khaled, N., van de Put, W. and Somasundarem, D. (2001). "Lifetime events and posttraumatic stress disorder in four post-conflict settings." *Journal of the American Medical Association* **286**(5): 555-562

De Jongh, A., Ten Broeke, E. and Renssen, M. R. (1999). "Treatment of specific phobias with Eye Movement Desensitization and Reprocessing (EMDR): protocol, empirical status, and conceptual issues." *Journal of Anxiety Disorders* **13**(1-2): 69-85

de Vries, M. W. (1996). Trauma in a cultural perspective. *Traumatic stress: the effects of overwhelming experience on mind, body and society.* van der Kolk, B. A., Mcfarlane, A. C. and Weisaeth, L., Eds. London, New York, The Guilford Press: 398-416

De Wolfe, D. (2000). *Field manual for mental health and human service workers in major disasters.* Washington, D.C., National Mental Health Services Knowledge Exchange Network

Denton, D. (1981). "Understanding the life world of the counsellor." *Journal of Personnel and Guidance* **59**: 596-599

Denzin, N. K. and Lincoln, Y. S., Eds. (2000). *Handbook of qualitative research.* London, Sage

Desaprecidos (2003). *Wall of memory*, Desaprecidos.org

Descartes, R. (1968). *Discourse on method and the meditations.* London, Penguin Books

Desjarlais, R., Eisenberg, L., Good, B. and Kelinman, A. (1995). *World mental health: problems and proprieties in low- income countries.* New York, Oxford University Press

Deutsch, K. W. (1967). *Arms control and the Atlantic alliance.* New York, Wiley

Deutsch, K. W. (1968). *The analysis of international relations.* Englewood Cliffs, NJ, Prentice Hall

Deutsch, M. (1995). "William James: the first peace psychologist." *Peace and Conflict: Journal of Peace Psychology* **1**(1): 27-35

Devilly, G. J. and Spence, S. H. (1999). "The relative efficacy and treatment distress of EMDR and a cognitive-behavior trauma treatment protocol in the amelioration of Posttraumatic Stress Disorder." *Journal of Anxiety Disorders* **13**(1-2): 131-157

Dilic, S. (1998). Primary health care: what we lack in our work. *War, violence, trauma and the coping process.* Arcel, L. T., Ed. Zagreb, International Rehabilitation Council for Torture Victims (IRCT): 258-264

DiNicola, V. F. (1996). Ethnocultural aspects of PTSD and related disorders among children and adolescents. *Ethnocultural aspects of Posttraumatic Stress Disorder: issues, research and clinical applications.* Marsella, A. J., Friedman, M. J., Gerrity, E. T. and Scurfield, R. M., Eds. Washington D.C., American Psychological Association: 389-414

Donnelly, C. L. and Amaya-Jackson, L. (2002). "Post-traumatic stress disorder in children and adolescents: epidemiology, diagnosis and treatment options." *Paediatric Drugs* **4**(3): 159-170

Douglass, B. G. and Moustakas, C. (1985). "Heuristic inquiry: the internal search to know." *Journal of Humanistic Psychology* **25**(3): 39-55

Draguns, J. D. (1996). Ethnocultural considerations in the treatment of PTSD. *Ethnocultural aspects of Posttraumatic Stress Disorder: issues, research and clinical applications.* Marsella, A. J., Friedman, M. J., Gerrity, E. T. and Scurfield, R. M., Eds. Washington D.C., American Psychological Association: 459-504

Duffey, T. (1998). *Culture, conflict and peacekeeping.* Peace Studies. Bradford, University of Bradford

Dukes, F. (1990). Action research. *Conflict: readings in management and resolution.* Burton, J., and Dukes, F.,, Ed. London, Macmillan: 288-298

Dunant, H. (1862). *A memory of Solferino*

Duncan, R. D., Benjamin, E. S., Kilpatrick, D. G., Hanson, R. F. and Resnick, H. S. (1996). "Childhood physical assault as a risk factor for PTSD, depression and substance abuse: Findings from a national survey." *American Journal of Orthopsychiatry* **66**(3): 437-448

Dunn, D. (1995). "Articulating the alternative: the contribution of John Burton." *Review of International Studies* **21**: 197-208

Dybdahl, R. "Children and mothers in war: an outcome study of a psychosocial intervention program." *Child Development* **72**(4): 1214-1230

Dyregrov, A. (1989). "Caring for helpers in disaster situations: psychological debriefing." *Disaster Management* **2**: 25-29

Dyregrov, A. (1995). *Grief in children: a handbook for adults*. London, Jessica Kingsley Publishers, Ltd

Economic and Social Research Council (2003). *General terms and conditions of ESRC studentships*, ESRC. **2003**

Egendorf, A. (1981). *Legacies of Vietnam*. Washington, D.C., U.S. Government Printing Office

Ehlers, A. and Clark, D. (2000). "A cognitive model of posttraumatic stress disorder." *Behaviour Research and Therapy* **38**: 319-345

Ehlers, A., Mayou, R. A. and Bryant, B. "Cognitive predictors of posttraumatic stress disorder in children: results of a prospective longitudinal study." *Behaviour Research and Therapy* **In Press, Uncorrected Proof**

Einstein, A. and Freud, S. (1933). *Why war?* Paris, Institute of Intellectual Co-operation, League of Nations

Elliott, R., Davis, K. L. and Slatic, E. (1998). Process-experiential therapy for posttraumatic stress difficulties. *Handbook of experiential psychotherapy*. Greenberg, L. S., Watson, J. C. and Lietaer, Eds. New York, Guilford Press

Ellis, A. (1962). *Reason and emotion in psychotherapy*. Secaucus, New Jersey, Stuart

Ellis, A. (1994). *How to cope with a fatal illness: the rational management of death and dying*. New York, Barricade Books

Ellis, A. (1996). *Stress counselling: a rational emotive behaviour approach*. London, Cassell

Emery, V. O., Emery, P. E., Shama, D., K, Quiana, N. A. and Jassani, A. K. (1991). "Predisposing variables in PTSD patients." *Journal of Traumatic Stress* (4): 325-343

Englund, H. (1998). "Death, trauma and ritual: Mozambican refugees in Malawi." *Social Science and Medicine* **46**: 1165-1174

Enright, R. D., Human Development Study Group (1994). "Piaget on the moral development of forgiveness: identity or reciprocity?" *Human Development* **37**(63-80)

Enright, R. D., Santos, M., Al-Mabuk, R (1989). "The adolescent as forgiver." *Journal of Adolescence* **21**: 95-110

Epstein, S. (1991). The self-concept, traumatic neurosis, and the structure of personality. *Perspectives in personality: self and emotion*. Ozer, D., Healey, J. M., Jr and Stewart, A. J., Eds. London, Jessica Kingsley. **3**: 63-98

Erickson, M. H. and Rossi, E. L. (1979). *Hypnotherapy: an exploratory casebook*. New York, Irvington

Erickson, M. H., Rossi, E. L. and Rossi, S. (1976). *Hypnotic realities: the induction of clinical hypnosis and forms of indirect suggestion*. New York, Irvington

Erikson, E. (1950). *Childhood and society*. New York, W.W. Norton & Company, inc.

Erikson, E. (1968). *Identity, youth and crisis*. London, Faber

Erikson, E. (1970). *Ghandi's truth: on the origins of militant nonviolence*. London, Faber

Eriksson, C. B., Vande Kemp, H., Gorsuch, R., Hoke, S. and Foy, D. W. (2001). "Trauma exposure and PTSD symptoms in international relief and development personnel." *Journal of Traumatic Stress* **14**(1): 205-219

Etzioni, A. (1967). Sociological perspectives in strategy. *Transactions of the sixth world congress of sociology*. **2**

Fairhurst, I. and Merry, T. (1999). Groupwork in counsellor training. *Experiences in relatedness: groupwork and the Person Centred Approach*. Lago, C. and MacMillan, M., Eds. Ross on Wye, PCCS Books: 49-62

Federn, P. (1952). *Ego, psychology and the psychoses.* New York, Basic Books

Feltham C., D. W. (1999). *Developing counsellor supervision.* London, Sage

Fetherston, A. B. (2000). *From conflict resolution to transformative peacebuilding: reflections from Croatia.* Bradford, Department of Peace Studies, University of Bradford, BD7 1DP

Fetherstonhaugh, D., Slovic, P., Johnson, S. and Friedrich, J. (1998). Insensitivity to the value of human life: a study of psychosocial numbing. *The psychology of peacekeeping.* Langholtz, H., Ed. Westport, Conn. and London, Praeger: 75-88

Figge, P. (1999). Client centred psychotherapy in groups: understanding the influence of the client-therapist relationship on therapy outcome. *Experiences in relatedness: groupwork and the Person Centred Approach.* Lago, C. and MacMillan, M., Eds. Ross on Wye, PCCS Books: 93-95

Finkelhor, D. (1986). *A Sourcebook on Child Sexual Abuse.* Finkelhor, D., Ed. Beverley Hills, Sage Publications

Finkelhor, D. and Browne, A. (1986). Initial and long-term effects: a conceptual framework. *A sourcebook on child sexual abuse.* Finkelhor, D., Ed. Beverley Hills, Sage Publications

Fisher, R. J. (1990a). Needs theory, social identity and conflict. *Conflict: human needs theory.* Burton, J., Ed. London, Macmillan: 89-112

Fisher, R. J. (1990b). *The social psychology of intergroup and international conflict.* New York, Springer Verlag

Fisher, R. J. and Keashly, L. (1991). "The potential complementarity of mediation and consultation within a contingency model of third party intervention." *Journal of Peace Research.* 28(1): 29-42

Flores, J. G. and Alonso, C. G. (1995). "Using focus groups in educational research." *Evaluation Review* 91: 84-101

Foa, E. B., Johnson, K. M., Feeny, N. C. and Treadwell, K. R. (2001). "The Child PTSD Symptom Scale: a preliminary examination of its psychometric properties." *Journal of Clinical Child Psychology* 30(3): 376-384

Foa, E. B. and Kozak, M. J. (1986). "Emotional processing of fear: exposure to corrective information." *Psychological Bulletin* 99: 20-35

Foa, E. B. and Meadows, E. A. (1997). "Psychological treatments for posttraumatic stress disorder: a critical review." *American Review of Psychology* 48: 449-480

Foa, E. B. and Riggs, D. S. (1993). *Posttraumatic stress disorder in rape victims.* American psychiatric press review of psychiatry. Oldman, J., Riba, M. B. and Tasman, A., American Psychiatric Association. 12

Foa, E. B., Steketee, G. and Rothbaum, B. O. (1989). "Behavioural/cognitive conceptualisation of posttraumatic stress disorder." *Behaviour Therapy* 20: 155-176

Folkes, C. E. (2002). "Thought field therapy and trauma recovery." *International Journal Of Emergency Mental Health* 4(2): 99-103 *Follett.* New York, Harper

Folnegovic-Smalc, V., Kozaric-Kovacic, D., Marusic, A. and Skrinjaric, L. (1998). Time course of psychological adaptation and development of psychological disturbances in refugees and displaced persons. *War, violence, trauma and the coping process.* Arcel, L. T., Ed. Zagreb, International Rehabilitation Council for Torture Victims (IRCT): 79-85

Forbes, D., Creamer, M. and Biddle, D. (2001). "The validity of the PTSD checklist as a measure of symptomatic change in combat-related PTSD." *Behaviour Research and Therapy* 39(8): 977-986

Foucault, M. (1971). *Madness and civilisation: a history of insanity in the age of reason.* London, Tavistock

Fowle, C. R. (1999). *Stepping-stones to reconciliation in the Former Yugoslavia: case* study – the Bench We Share Project, Slavonia and Baranja, Croatia. Department of Peace Studies. Bradford, University of Bradford

Fowle, C. R. (2002). "Autumn in Croatia." Footprint (8)

Fowler, H. W. and Fowler, F. G., Eds. (1964). The concise oxford dictionary. London, Oxford University Press

Foxen, P. (2000). "Cacophony of voices: a K'iche' Myan narrative of remembrance and forgetting." Transcultural psychiatry 37: 355-381

Franciskovic, T., Pernar, M., Moro, L. and Roncevic-Grzeta, I. (1998). Aggravating and mitigating factors in the 'burn out' syndrome. War, violence, trauma and the coping process. Arcel, L. T., Ed. Zagreb, International Rehabilitation Council for Torture Victims (IRCT): 319-325

Frank, J. D. (1974a). "Psychotherapy: the restoration of morale." American Journal of Psychiatry (131): 271-274

Frank, J. D. (1974b). "Theraputic components of psychotherapy. A 25 year progress report of research." Journal of Nervous and Mental Disorders (159): 325-342

Frank, J. D. (1982). Theraputic components shared by all psychotherapies. Psychotherapy Research and Behaviour Change. Harvey, J. H. and Parks, M. M., Eds. Washington D.C., American Psychological Association. 1: 9-37

Frank, J. D. (1993). Persuasion and healing: a comparative study of psychotherapy. Baltimore, John Hopkins University Press

Frankfort-Nachmias, C. and Nachmias, D. (1996). Research methods in the social sciences. London. New York. Sydney. Auckland, Arnold

Freud, A. (1927). Four lectures on child analysis. The writings of Anna Freud: introduction to psychoanalysis (1922-1935) London, Hogarth. 1

Freud, S. (1922). Introductory lectures on psychoanalysis: a course of twenty-eight lectures delivered at the University of Vienna. London, Allen & Unwin

Freud, S. (1954). Introduction to psychoanalysis and the war neuroses. London, Hogarth Press

Freud, S. (1959). Group psychology and the analysis of the ego. London, Hogarth Press

Freud, S. (1961). Beyond the pleasure principle. London, Hogarth Press

Freud, S. (1962). The aetiology of hysteria. London, Hogarth Press

Freud, S. (1973). New introductory lectures on psychoanalysis. Harmondsworth, Penguin

Freud, S. (1975). The psychopathology of everyday life. Harmondsworth, Penguin

Freud, S. (1976). The interpretation of dreams. Harmondsworth, Penguin

Freud, S. (1983). Some general remarks on hysterical attacks. On psychopathology: inhibitions, symptoms and anxiety and other works. Sigmund Freud. Richards, A., Ed. London, Penguin. 10

Freud, S. (1984). Two short accounts of psychoanalysis. Five lectures on psychoanalysis. Strachey, J., Ed. Singapore, Penguin

Freud, S., Ed. (1991a). Beyond the pleasure principle. The Penguin Freud library. On psychology: the theory of psychoanalysis. Harmondsworth, Penguin

Freud, S. (1991b). Jokes and their relation to the unconscious. Harmondsworth, Penguin

Freud, S. and Breuer, J. (1893). On the psychical mechanism of hysterical phenomena preliminary communication

Friedman, M. J. (2002). "Future pharmacotherapy for post-traumatic stress disorder: Prevention and treatment." Psychiatric Clinics of North America 25(2): 427-441

Friends., R. S. o. (1995). Quaker faith and practice. Londo, Friends House, Euston Road, London

Freire, P. (1970). Pedagogy of the oppressed. New York, Herder and Herder

Fulford, K. W. M. (2002). Foreword. Trauma, culture, meaning and philosophy. Bracken, P., Ed. London, Whurr

Fuller, R. C. (1982). "Carl Rogers, religion, and the role of psychology in American culture." *Journal of Humanistic Psychology* **22**(4): 21-32

Gaines, A. (1992). Ethnopsychiatry. The cultural construction of the psychiatries. *Ethnopsychiatry: the cultural construction of the professional and folk psychiatries.* Gaines, A., Ed. Albany, NY, State University of New York Press

Galtung, J. (1969). Conflict as a way of life. *Progress in mental health.* Freeman, H., Ed. London, Churchill

Galtung, J. (1976). "Three realistic approaches to peace: peacekeeping, peacemaking, peacebuilding." *Impact of Science on Society* **26**: 103-115

Galtung, J. (1994). *Human rights in another key.* Cambridge, Polity Press

Galtung, J. (1996). *Peace by peaceful means: peace and conflict, development and civilisation.* London, Sage

Garfield, D. A., Fichtner, C. G., Leveroni, C. and Mahableshwarkar, A. (2001). "Open trial of nefazodone for combat veterans with posttraumatic stress disorder." *Journal of Traumatic Stress* **14**(3): 453-460

Geddes, L. A. (1991). "History of magnetic stimulation of the nervous system." *Journal of Clinical Neurophysiology* **8**(1): 3-9

Gerbode, F. (1990). "Repeating viewing instructions without variation." *Journal of Metapsychology* **3**: 3-4

Gerbode, F. (2002). *Critical issues in trauma resolution,* TIR.org. **2002**

Gerrity, E. T. and Solomon, S. D. (1996). The treatment of PTSD and related stress disorders: current research and clinical knowledge. *Ethnocultural aspects of Posttraumatic Stress Disorder: issues, research and clinical applications.* Marsella, A. J., Friedman, M. J., Gerrity, E. T. and Scurfield, R. M., Eds. Washington D.C., American Psychological Association: 87-104

Gibbs, A. (2002). "Focus groups." *Social Research Update* (19)

Gilboa-Schechtman, E. and Foa, E. B. (2001). "Patterns of recovery from trauma: the use of intraindividual analysis." *Journal of Abnormal Psychology* **110**(3): 392-400

Glaser, B. and Strauss, A. (1967). *The discovery of grounded theory.* Chicago, Aldine

Glasser, W. (1965). *Reality therapy.* New York, Harper Collins

Glasser, W. (1998). *Choice theory.* New York, Harper Collins

Glasser, W. (2000a). *Reality therapy in action.* New York, Harper Collins

Glasser, W. (2000b). *Reality therapy in the year 2000.* The Evolution of Psychotherapy Conference, Anaheim Convention Center, Anheim, C.A., The William Glasser Institute

Glasser, W. and Glasser, C. (1999). *The language of choice theory.* New York, Harper Collins

Glasser, W. and Glasser, C. (2000). *Getting together and staying together: solving the mystery of marriage.* New York, Harper Collins

Glenny, M. (2000). *The Balkans 1804-1999: nationalism, war, and the great powers.* London, Granta Books

Goldman, E. (2003). *The five rhythms,* Oak-Wood. Co.Uk. **2003**

Goleman, D. (1985). *Vital lies, simple truths: the psychology of self-deception.* New York, Simon and Schuster

Goss, J. D. and Leinbach, T. R. (1996). "Focus groups as alternative research practice." *Area* **28**(2): 115-123

Gottleib, S. (1993). *Nation against state.* New York, Council on Foreign Relations Press

Grant, M. (2000). "EMDR: a new treatment for trauma and chronic pain." *Complementary Therapies in Nursing and Midwifery* **6**(2): 91-94

Green, B. L. (1990). "Defining trauma: terminology and generic stressor dimensions." *Journal of Applied Social Psychology* **20**(1632-1642)

Green, B. L. (1994). "Psychosocial research in traumatic care: an update." *Journal of

Traumatic Stress **7**: 341-362

Green, B. L. (1996). Cross-national and ethnocultural issues in disaster research. *Ethnocultural aspects of Posttraumatic Stress Disorder: issues, research and clinical applications.* Marsella, A. J., Friedman, M. J., Gerrity, E. T. and Scurfield, R. M., Eds. Washington D.C., American Psychological Association: 341-362

Green, B. L., Wilson, J. P. and Lindy, L. D. (1985). Conceptualizing post-traumatic stress disorder: a psychosocial framework. *Trauma and its wake.* Figley, C., Ed. New York, Brunner Mazel. **1**

Greenbaum, T. L. (2000). *Moderating focus groups.* London, New Delhi, Sage

Greenberg, L. S., Rice, L. N. and Elliott, R. (1993). *Facilitating emotional change: the moment by moment process.* Guilford Press

Greenwald, R. (1996). "The information gap in the EMDR controversy." *Professional Psychology: Research and Practice* **27**(1): 67-72

Greenwald, R. (1999). "The power of suggestion: comment on EMDR and mesmerism: a comparative historical analysis." *Journal of Anxiety Disorders* **13**(6): 611-615

Gregg, G. (2003). *A sketch of Albert Ellis,* The Albert Ellis Institute, New York. **2003**

Griffin, J. and Tyrrell, I. (2001). *The shackled brain: how to release locked in patterns of trauma.* Chalvington, European Studies Institute

Griffin, J. and Tyrrell, I. (2003). *Human givens.* Chalvington, Human Givens Publishing

Griffith, J. L. (2002). "Living with threat and uncertainty: what the Kosavars tell us." *Family Process* **41**(1): 24-27

Grossman, D. (2001). "On killing. II: the psychological cost of learning to kill." *International Journal of Emergency Mental Health* **3**(3): 137-144

Grujic-Koracin, J. (1998). Problems with pelvic inflammatory disease in refugee women-survivors of sexual torture. *War, violence, trauma and the coping process.* Arcel, L. T., Ed. Zagreb, International Rehabilitation Council for Torture Victims (IRCT): 274-277

Guay, S., Mainguy, N. and Marchand, A. (2002). "Disorders related to traumatic events. Screening and treatment." *Canadian Family Physician Medecin de Famille Canadien* **48**: 512-517

Gusman, F. D., Stewart, J., Hiley Young, B., Riney, S. J., Abueg, F. R. and Blake, D. D. (1996). A multicultural developmental approach for treating trauma. *Ethnocultural aspects of Posttraumatic Stress Disorder: issues, research and clinical applications.* Marsella, A. J., Friedman, M. J., Gerrity, E. T. and Scurfield, R. M., Eds. Washington D.C., American Psychological Association: 439-458

Hackney, H., Goodyear, R (1984). Carl Rogers' client-centred approach to supervision. *Client centred therapy and the Person Centred Approach.* Levant, R., Shlien, J., Ed. New York, Praeger

Hageman, I., Anderson, J. S. and Jorgenson, M. B. (2001). "Posttraumatic stress disorder: a review of psychobiology and pharmacotherapy." *Acta Psychiatrica Scandinavica* **104**(6): 411-422

Halilovic, S. (1998). Psychosocial help as a coping skill for non-professionals who are themselves refugees. *War, violence, trauma and the coping process.* Arcel, L. T., Ed. Zagreb, International Rehabilitation Council for Torture Victims (IRCT): 283-288

Harber, K. D. and Pennebaker, J. W. (1992). Overcoming traumatic memories. *The handbook of emotion and memory: research and theory.* Christianson, S. A., Ed. Hillsdale, N.J., Erlbaum

Harre, R., Gillett, G (1994). *The discursive mind.* Thousand Oaks, Sage Publications

Harris Hendricks, J., Black, D. and Kaplan, T. (1993). *When father kills mother: Guiding children through trauma and grief.* London, Routledge

Harris, W. S., Gowda, M., Kolb, J. W., Strychaz, C., Vacek, J. L., Jones, P. G., Forker, A., O'Keefe, J. H. and McCallister, B. D. (1999). "A randomized, controlled trial of the effects of remote, intercessory prayer on outcomes of patients admitted to the coronary care unit." *Archive of Internal Medicine* **159**: 2273-2278

Hautamaeki, A. and Coleman, P. G. (2001). "Explanation for low prevalence of PTSD among older Finnish war veterans: social solidarity and continued significance given to wartime sufferings." *Ageing and Mental Health* **5**(2): 165-174

Hawkins, P. and Shoet, R. (1996). *Supervision in the helping professions.* Milton Keynes., Philadelphia, Open University Press

Hecimovic, V. (1998). Unrecognised needs for psychosocial help in the modern war. *War, violence, trauma and the coping process.* Arcel, L. T., Ed. Zagreb, International Rehabilitation Council for Torture Victims (IRCT): 123-130

Hendrick, D. (1994). *Community relations, conflict resolution and prevention: an exploration with special reference to the Muslim community in Bradford.* Peace Studies. Bradford, University of Bradford

Henigsberg, N., Folnegovic-Smalc, V. and Moro, L. (2001). "Stressor characteristics and post-traumatic stress disorder symptom dimensions in war victims." *Croatian Medical Journal* **42**(5): 543-550

Herman, J. L. (1981). *Father daughter incest.* Cambridge Mass, Havard University Press

Herman, J. L. (1992a). "Complex PTSD: a syndrome in survivors of prolonged and repeated trauma." *Journal of Traumatic Stress* **5**: 377-391

Herman, J. L. (1992b). *Trauma and recovery.* London, Harper Collins

Herman, J. L. (1993). Sequelae of prolonged and repeated trauma: evidence for a complex post-traumatic syndrome (DESNOS). *Posttraumatic Stress Disorder: DSM IV and beyond.* Davidson, R. T. and Foa, E. B., Eds. Washington D.C, American Psychiatric Association

Herman, J. L., Perry, J. C. and van der Kolk, B. A. (1989). "Childhood trauma in Borderline Personality Disorder." *American Journal of Psychiatry* **146**(490-495)

Heron, J. (1971). *Experience and method.* Surrey, Human Potential Research Project; University of Surrey

Heron, J. (1992). *Feeling and personhood.* London, Sage

Hobson, R. F. (1985). *Forms of feeling: the heart of psychotherapy.* London, Tavistock

Hodgkinson, P., Stewart, M (1991). *Coping with catastrophe. A handbook of disaster management.* London, Routledge

Hoffman, J. (1999). A person centred approach to the facilitation of citizens' juries: a recent development in public consultation. *Experiences in relatedness: groupwork and the Person Centred Approach.* Lago, C. and MacMillan, M., Eds. Ross on Wye, PCCS Books: 107-109

Holbrook, T. L., Hoyt, D. B., Stein, M. B. and Sieber, W. J. (2001). "Perceived threat to life predicts Posttraumatic Stress Disorder after major trauma: risk factors and functional outcome." *The Journal of Trauma* **51**(2): 287-292; discussion 292-293

Holdstock, L. (1994). Can we afford not to revison the person centred concept of self? *Beyond Carl Rogers.* Brazier, D., Ed. London, Constable: 229-253

Holman, R. (1991). *Ethics in social research.* Harlow, Longman

Homans, P. (1980). *Jung in context.* Chicago, University of Chicago Press

Hoppe, M. J., E.A, W., D.M, M., M.R, G. and A, W. (1995). "'Using focus groups to discuss sensitive topics with children'." *Evaluation Review* **91**(1): 102-114

Horney, K. (1937). *The neurotic personality of our time.* London/New York, W.W.Norton

Horney, K. (1939). *New ways in psychoanalysis.* London, Kegan Paul

Horney, K. (1950). *Neurosis and human growth.* London/New York, W.W. Norton

Horney, K. (1992). *Our inner conflicts.* London/New York, W.W. Norton

Horney, K. (1993). *Feminine psychology.* London/New York, W.W. Norton

Horney, K. (1994). *Self analysis.* London/New York, W.W. Norton

Horowitz, M. (1976). *Stress response syndromes*. North Vale NJ, Jason Aronson

Horowitz, M. (1979). Psychological responses to serious life events. *Human stress and cognition*. Hamilton, V. and Warburton, D. M., Eds. New York, Wiley

Horsbrugh, H. J. N. (1974). "Forgiveness." *The Canadian Journal of Philosophy* **4**: 240-244

Hoshmand, L. L. S. T. (1989). "Alternative research paradigms: a review and teaching proposal." *The Counselling Psychologist* **17**(1): 3-79

Hough, R. L., Canino, G. J., Abueg, F. R. and Gusman, F. D. (1996). PTSD and related disorders among Hispanics. *Ethnocultural aspects of Posttraumatic Stress Disorder: issues, research and clinical applications*. Marsella, A. J., Friedman, M. J., Gerrity, E. T. and Scurfield, R. M., Eds. Washington D.C., American Psychological Association: 301-340

Houston, G. (1998). *The red book of groups*. London, The Rochester Foundation

Huitt, W. (2002). *Maslow's hierarchy of needs*, Educational Psychology Interactive. **2003**

Human Resources Branch, D. o. H. S. (1997). *Resource guide for Critical Incident Stress Debriefing in human service agencies*. Melbourne, Human Resources Corporate Resources Division, Department of Human Services

Hytten, K. (1989). "Helicopter crash in water: Effects of simulator escape training." *Acta Psychiatrica Scandinavica* **80**: 73-78

International Federation of Red Cross and Red Crescent Societies (1993). *World disaster report*. Dortrecht, The Netherlands, Martinus Nijhoff

Ivanisevic, M., Vince, A., Milkovic-Vukelic, D. and Arcel, L. T. (1998). Papanicolaou findings in refugee patients. *War, violence, trauma and the coping process*. Arcel, L. T., Ed. Zagreb, International Rehabilitation Council for Torture Victims (IRCT): 270-273

Jacobs, M., Ed. (1996). *In search of supervision*. Buckingham Philadelphia, Open University Press

James, W. (1995). "The moral equivalent of war." *Peace and Conflict: Journal of Peace Psychology* **1**: 17-26

Janet, P. (1889). *L' automatisme psychologique*. Paris, Alcan

Janis, I. L. (1991). Groupthink. *The organisational behaviour reader*. Kolb, D., Rubin, I. R. and Osland, J. S., Eds. New Jersey, Prentice Hall

Janoff-Bulman, R. (1992). *Shattered assumptions. Towards a new psychology of trauma*. New York, The Free Press

Jaspers, K. (1963). *General psychopathology*. Manchester, Manchester University Press

Jegen, M. E., Sr (1996). *Sign of hope*. Uppsala, Life and Peace Institute

Jenkins, J. H. (1996). Culture, emotion and PTSD. *Ethnocultural aspects of Posttraumatic Stress Disorder: issues, research and clinical applications*. Marsella, A. J., Friedman, M. J., Gerrity, E. T. and Scurfield, R. M., Eds. Washington D.C., American Psychological Association: 165-182

Jenkins, P. (1997). *Counselling, psychotherapy and the law*. London, Sage

Johnson, C., Shala, M., Sejdijaj, X., Odell, R. and Dabishevci, K. (2001). "Thought Field Therapy: soothing the bad moments of Kosovo." *Journal of Clinical Psychology* **57**(10): 1237-1240

Jones, E. (1964). *The life and work of Sigmund Freud*. Middlesex, UK, Pelican

Joseph, S. (1998). "Traumatic amnesia, repression and hippocampus injury due to emotional stress, corticosteroids and encephalins." *Child Psychiatry and Human Development* **29**(2): 169-185

Joseph, S. and Linley, A. (2002). "EMDR: what's the evidence?" *Counselling and Psychotherapy Journal* **13**(3): 18-19

Joseph, S., Williams, R. and Yule, W. (1993). "Changes in outlook following disaster: The preliminary development of a measure to assess positive and negative responses."

Journal of Traumatic Stress **6**: 271-279

Joseph, S., Williams, R. and Yule, W. (1997). *Understanding posttraumatic stress: a psychosocial perspective on PTSD and treatment.* West Sussex, Wiley

Journal of the American Medical Association (editorial) (1995). "Posttraumatic stress disorder: psychology, biology, and the Manchunian war between false dichotemies." *Journal of the American Medical Association* **152**: 963-965

Kadenic, M. (1998). Primary health care: somatic diseases and treatment. *War, violence, trauma and the coping process.* Arcel, L. T., Ed. Zagreb, International Rehabilitation Council for Torture Victims (IRCT): 246-253

Kardiner, A. (1941). *The traumatic neuroses of war.* New York, Hoeber

Keane, T. M., Kaloupek, D. G. and Weathers, F. W. (1996). Ethnocultural considerations in the assessment of PTSD. *Ethnocultural aspects of Posttraumatic Stress Disorder: issues, research and clinical applications.* Marsella, A. J., Friedman, M. J., Gerrity, E. T. and Scurfield, R. M., Eds. Washington D.C., American Psychological Association: 183-208

Kebo, A., Sehovic, J. and Masic, S. (1998). Refugee line: information and advice for urgent social, psychological, medical and legal problems. *War, violence, trauma and the coping process.* Arcel, L. T., Ed. Zagreb, International Rehabilitation Council for Torture Victims (IRCT): 135-140

Keh-Ming-Lin, Poland, R. E., Anderson, D. and Lesser, I. M. (1996). Ethnopsychopharmacology and the treatment of PTSD. *Ethnocultural aspects of Posttraumatic Stress Disorder: issues, research and clinical applications.* Marsella, A. J., Friedman, M. J., Gerrity, E. T. and Scurfield, R. M., Eds. Washington D.C., American Psychological Association: 505-528

Kelman, H. C. (1965). *International behaviour: a social-psychological analysis.* New York, Holt, Rinehart & Winston

Kelman, H. C. (1973). "Violence without moral restraint." *Journal of Social Issues* **29**(4): 25-62

Kelman, H. C. (1990). Interactive problem-solving: a social psychological approach to conflict resolution. *Conflict: readings in management and resolution.* Burton, J., Ed. London, Macmillan. **1**: 199-215

Kelman, H. C. (1996). The interactive problem-solving approach. *Managing global chaos: sources of and responses to international conflict.* Crocker, C. A., Hampson, F. O. and Aall, P., Eds. Washington, D.C., United States Institute of Peace Press: 501-520

Kerman, C. E. (1974). *Creative tension: the life and thought of Kenneth Boulding.* Ann Arbor, University of Michigan Press

Kimmel, P. R. (1998). Cultural and ethnic issues of conflict and peacekeeping. *The psychology of peacekeeping.* Langholtz, H., Ed. Westport, Conn. and London, Praeger: 57-71

Kingston Friends, W. G. (1988). *Ways and means: an approach to problem solving.* London, Kingston Friends

Kirmayer, L. J. (1988). Mind and body as metaphors: hidden values in biomedicine. *Biomedicine examined.* Lock, M., Gordon, D. Ed. Dordrecht, Kluwer Academic Publishers

Kirmayer, L. J. (1989). "Cultural variations in the response to psychiatric disorders and mental distress." *Social Science and Medicine* **29**: 327-329

Kirmayer, L. J. (1996). Confusion of the senses: implications of ethnocultural variations in somatoform and dissociative disorders for PTSD. *Ethnocultural aspects of Posttraumatic Stress Disorder: issues, research and clinical applications.* Marsella, A. J., Friedman, M. J., Gerrity, E. T. and Scurfield, R. M., Eds. Washington D.C., American Psychological Association: 131-164

Kitzinger, J. (1994). "The methodology of focus groups: the importance of interaction between research participants." *Sociology of Health* **16**(1): 103-121

Kitzinger, J. (1995). "Introducing focus groups." *British Medical Journal* **311**: 299-302

Klain, E. (1998). Transference and countertransference in psychoanalytic psychotherapeutic approach to war victims. *War, violence, trauma and the coping process.* Arcel, L. T., Ed. Zagreb, International Rehabilitation Council for Torture Victims (IRCT): 155-167

Klain, E. and Pavic, L. (1999). "Countertransference and empathic problems in therapists/helpers working with psychotraumatized persons." *Croatian Medical Journal* **40**(4): 466-472

Klain, E., Pavicacute, L. (2002). "Psychotrauma and reconciliation." *Croatian Medical Journal* **43**(2): 126-137

Klain, E. and Pavicacute, L. (2001). "Psychotrauma and reconciliation." *Croatian Medical Journal* **43**(2): 126-137

Klein, M. (1932). *The psychoanalysis of children.* London, Hogarth

Kleinman, A. (1977). "Depression, somatisation and the new "cross-cultural psychiatry"." *Social Science and Medicine* **11**: 3-10

Kleinman, A. (1982). "Neuraesthenia and depression: a study of somatitization and culture in China." *Culture, Medicine and Psychiatry* **6**: 117-190

Kleinman, A. (1987). "Anthropology and psychiatry. The role of culture in cross-cultural research on illness." *British Journal of Psychiatry* **151**: 447-454

Kleinman, A. (1988). *Re-thinking psychiatry. From cultural category to personal experience.* New York, The Free Press

Kleinman, A. (2001). "Cross-cultural psychiatry: a psychiatric perspective on global change." *Havard Review of Psychiatry* **9**: 46-47

Klejin, W. C., Hovens, J. E. and Rodenberg, J. J. (2001). "Posttraumatic stress symptoms in refugees: assessments with the Havard Trauma Questionnaire and the Hopkins Symptom Checklist-25 in different languages." *Psychological Reports* **88**(2): 527-532

Kocijan-Hercigonja, D., Skrinjaric, L. and Maroevic, S. (1998a). Psychological problems of children in war. *War, violence, trauma and the coping process.* Arcel, L. T., Ed. Zagreb, International Rehabilitation Council for Torture Victims (IRCT): 335-339

Kocijan-Hercigonja, D., Skrinjaric, L. and Maroevic, S. (1998b). Wounded and traumatised children in war. *War, violence, trauma and the coping process.* Arcel, L. T., Ed. Zagreb, International Rehabilitation Council for Torture Victims (IRCT): 340-344

Kolb, L. C. (1987). "Neurophysiological hypothesis explaining posttraumatic stress disorder." *American Journal of Psychiatry* **144**: 989-995

Kolb, L. C. (1989). "Letter to the editor." *American Journal of Psychiatry* **146**: 811-812

Kolb, L. C. (1993). "The psychobiology of PTSD: perspectives and reflections on the past, present and future." *Journal of Traumatic Stress* **6**: 293-304

Kolnai, A. (1973-1974). "Forgiveness." *Proceedings of the Aristotelian Society* **74**: 91-106

Koppel, H. (2002). "High speed therapy?" *Counselling and Psychotherapy Journal* **13**(1): 20-21

Korn, M. L. (2002). *Cultural aspects of the psychotherapeutic process.* 53rd Institute on Psychiatric Services: treatment guidelines, culture and outcomes, Orlando, Florida, American Psychiatric Association

Kostovic, I., Judas, M. and Henigsberg, N. (1993). "Medical documentation of human rights violations and war crimes on the territory of Croatia during the 1991-1993 war." *Croatian Medical Journal* **34**(285-293)

Kozaricacute-Kovacicacute, D. and Kocijan-Hercigonja, D. (2001). "Assessment of post-traumatic stress disorder and comorbidity." *Military Medicine* **166**(8): 677-680

Kozaricacute-Kovacicacute, D., Kocijan-Hercigonja, D. and Jambrosicacute, A. (2002).

"Psychiatric help to psychotraumatized persons during and after war in Croatia."
Croatian Medical Journal **43**(2): 221-228

Kozaric-Kovacic, D., Folnegovic-Smalc, V. and Marusic, A. (1998). Refugees with
psychological disturbances and psychiatric hospitalisation: When and why? *War,
violence, trauma and the coping Process.* Arcel, L. T., Ed. Zagreb, International
Rehabilitation Council for Torture Victims (IRCT): 101-106

Kozaric-Kovacic, D., Folnegovic-Smalc, V. and Marusic, A. (1995). "International
Rehabilitation Council for Torture Victims (IRCT): experiences after two years of
providing psychological support to women-victims of war and their families from
Bosnia and Herzgovina and Croatia." *Croatian Medical Journal* **36**(69-77)

Kraljevic, R., Bamburac, L., Markeljevic, J. and Kadenic, M. (1998). A multidisciplinary
approach to working with family members of torture victims- a case of rheumatoid
arthritis. *War, violence, trauma and the coping process.* Arcel, L. T., Ed. Zagreb,
International Rehabilitation Council for Torture Victims (IRCT): 172-180

Krueger, R. A. (1988). *Focus groups: a practical guide for applied research.* Newbury
Park, CA, Sage Publication

Kruhonja, K., Ed. (2000). *I choose life: building a democratic society based on the culture
of non-violence-post-war peace building in Eastern Croatia.* Osijek, Croatia, Centre for
Peace, Osijek

Kubler-Ross, E. (1991). *On death and dying.* London, Routledge

Kuhn (1970). *The structure of scientific revolutions.* Chicago, University of Chicago Press

Kumar, R. (1999). *Research methodology.* London. Thousand Oaks. New Delhi, Sage

Kutchins, H. and Kirk, S. (1999). *Making us crazy. DSM, the psychiatric Bible and the
creation of mental disorders.* London, Constable

Ladame, F. (1999). "Transference and countertransference: two concepts specific to
psychoanalytic theory and practice." *Croatian Medical Journal* **40**(4): 455-457

Lago, C. and MacMillan, M. (1999). PCA groups: past, present... and future? *Experiences
in relatedness: groupwork and the Person Centred Approach.* Lago, C. and MacMillan,
M., Eds. Ross on Wye, PCCS Books: 29-46

Lamont, G., Burns, S (1993). *Values and visions.* Manchester, Manchester Development
Education Project

Lampen, J. (1987). *Mending hurts.* London, Quaker Home Service

Lang, P. (1977). "Imagery and therapy." *Behaviour Therapy* **8**: 862-886

Langholtz, H. (1998a). The evolving psychology of peacekeeping. *The psychology of
peacekeeping.* Langholtz, H., Ed. Westport, Conn. and London, Praeger: 5-30

Langholtz, H., Ed. (1998b). *Psychology of peacekeeping.* Westport, CT. & London,
Praeger

Lantz, M. S., Buchalter, E. N. and American Association for Geristric, P. (2001).
"Posttraumatic stress. Helping older adults cope with tragedy." *Geriatrics* **56**(12): 35-36

Latham, R., Ed. (1978). *The illustrated Pepys: extracts from the diary.* London, Book Club
Associates

Lauterbach, D. and Vrana, S. (2001). "The relationship among personality variables,
exposure to traumatic events, and severity of posttraumatic stress symptoms." *Journal
of Traumatic Stress* **41**(1): 29-45

Le Doux, J. E. (1986). "Sensory systems and emotion: a model of affective processing."
Integrative Psychiatry **4**: 237-243

Le Doux, J. E. (1987). Emotion. *Handbook of physiology.* Plum, F., Ed. Bethseda,
American Psychological Society: 416-459

Le Doux, J. E. (1992a). Emotion and the amygdala. *The amygdala: Neuroboliogical
aspects of emotion, memory and mental dysfunction.* Aggleton, J. P., Ed. New York,
Wiley-Liss: 339-352

Le Doux, J. E. (1992b). Emotion as memory: Anatomical systems underlying indelible neural traces. *Handbook of emotion and memory*. Christianson, S. A., Ed. Hillsdale, N.J, Erlbaum

Le Doux, J. E. (1994). "Emotion, memory and the brain." *Scientific American* **5**(50-57)

Le Doux, J. E., Romanski, L. and Xagoraris, A. (1991). "Indelibility of subcortical emotional memories." *Journal of Cognitive Neuroscience* **1**: 238-243

Leder, D. (1997). *Modern social theory*. London, UCL Press

Leder, D. (1998). *Sociological practice: linking theory and social research*. London, Sage

Lederach, J. P. (1996). *Preparing for peace: conflict transformation across cultures*. New York, Synacruse University Press

Lederach, J. P. (1997). *Building peace: sustainable reconciliation in divided societies*. Washington D.C., United States Institute of Peace

Leff, J. (1988). *Psychiatry around the globe*. London, The Royal College of Psychiatrists

Leibovici, L. (2001). "Effects of remote, retroactive intercessory prayer on outcomes in patients with bloodstream infection: randomised controlled trial." *British Medical Journal* **323**: 1450-1451

Levin, P., Lazrove, S. and van der Kolk, B. A. (1999). "What psychological testing and neuroimaging tell us about the treatment of Posttraumatic Stress Disorder by Eye Movement Desensitization and Reprocessing." *Journal of Anxiety Disorders* **13**(1-2): 159-172

Lewis, W. A. (1959). *The Principles of Economic Planning*. London, Allen & Unwin

Lifton, R. J. (1967). *Death in life: survivors of Hiroshema*. New York, Random House

Lindberg, K. A. (1998). *What is Music Therapy?* Music Therapy Info Link. **2003**

Lindy, J. D. (1996). Psychoanalytic psychotherapy of posttraumatic stress disorder: The nature of the therapeutic relationship. *Traumatic stress: the effects of overwhelming experience on mind, body and society*. van der Kolk, B. A., Mcfarlane, A. C. and Weisaeth, L., Eds. London, New York, The Guilford Press: 525-536

Linley, A. (2000). "Transforming psychology... the example of trauma." *The Psychologist* **13**(7): 353-359

Ljubotina, D. and Arcel, L. T. (1998). Suffering of the body and mind: predictors for psychosomatic problems in female refugees. *War, violence, trauma and the coping process*. Arcel, L. T., Ed. Zagreb, International Rehabilitation Council for Torture Victims (IRCT): 231-245

Loncar, M. (1998). Sexual torture of men in the war. *War, violence, trauma and the coping process*. Arcel, L. T., Ed. Zagreb, International Rehabilitation Council for Torture Victims (IRCT): 212-217

London School of Biodynamic Psychotherapy (2003). *Biodynamic Psychotherapy: A precis of theory and practice*, London School of Biodynamic Psychotherapy. **2003**

Loughrey, G. (1997). Civil violence. *Psychological trauma: a developmental approach*. Black, D., Newman, M., Harris-Hendriks, J. and Mezey, G., Eds. London, Gaskell: 156-160

Lugris, V. (2001). *Vicarious traumatisation in therapists: contributing factors, PTSD symptomology, and cognitive distortions*

Lund, M. (1996). *Preventing violent conflicts: a strategy for diplomacy*. Washington, DC, United States Institute of Peace Press

Lytle, R. A., Hazlett-Stevens, H. and Borkovec, T. D. (2002). "Efficacy of Eye Movement Desensitization in the treatment of cognitive intrusions related to a past stressful event." *Journal of Anxiety Disorders* **16**(3): 273-288

MacCulloch, M. J. and Fieldman, P. (1996). "Eye Movement Desensitisation treatment utilises the positive visceral element of the investigatory reflex to inhibit the memories of post-traumatic stress disorder: a theoretical analysis." *British Journal of Psychiatry*

169: 571-579

MacIntosh, J. (1981). "Focus groups in distance nursing education." *Journal of Advanced Nursing* **18**: 1981-1985

MacKay, H. and Cross, M. (2001). "Putting the scientist practitioner metaphor to the test: A trainee therapist's leap of good faith in the treatment of PTSD." *Counselling Psychology Review* **16**(2): 12-23

Mackay, H. C., West, W., Moorey, J., Guthrie, E. and Margison, F. (2001). "Counsellors' experiences of changing their practice: learning the psychodynamic-interpersonal model of therapy." *Counselling and Psychotherapy Journal* **1**(1): 29-40

Maguire, P. and Parkes, C. M. (1998). "Surgery and loss of body parts." *Bmj* **316**(7137): 1086-8

Mandela, N. (1995). *Long Walk to Freedom*. London, Abacus

Mandic, N. and Javornik, N. (1998). "Posttraumatski stresni poremecaj i radna sposobnost." *Social Psychiatry* **26**: 75-81

Manson, S., Beals, J., O'Nell, T., Piasecki, J., Bechtold, D., Keane, E. and Jones, M. (1996). Wounded spirits, ailing hearts: PTSD and related disorders among American Indians. *Ethnocultural aspects of Posttraumatic Stress Disorder: issues, research and clinical applications*. Marsella, A. J., Friedman, M. J., Gerrity, E. T. and Scurfield, R. M., Eds. Washington D.C., American Psychological Association: 255-284

March, J. S. (1993). What constitutes a stressor? The criterion 'A' issue. *Post-traumatic Stress Disorder: DSM IV and beyond*. Davidson, J. R. T. and Foa, E. B., Eds. Washington D.C., American Psychiatric Association

Marczak, M., Sewell, M (2002). *Using focus groups for evaluation*, University of Arizona. **2002**

Marmar, C. R., Neylan, T. C. and Schoenfeld, F. B. (2002). "New directions in the pharmacotherapy of posttraumatic stress disorder." *Psychiatric Quarterly* **73**(4): 259-270

Marsella, A. J. (1982). Culture and mental health: an overview. *Cultural conceptions of mental health and therapy*. Marsella, A. J. and White, G. M., Eds. Dordrecht, Reidal Publishing Company

Marsella, A. J. and Friedman, M. J. (1996). Posttraumatic Stress Disorder: an overview of the concept. *Ethnocultural aspects of Posttraumatic Stress Disorder: issues, research and clinical applications*. Marsella, A. J., Friedman, M. J., Gerrity, E. T. and Scurfield, R. M., Eds. Washington D.C., American Psychological Association: 11-32

Marsella, A. J., Friedman, M. J., Gerrity, E. T. and Scurfield, R. M., Eds. (1996a). *Ethnocultural aspects of Posttraumatic Stress Disorder: issues, research and clinical applications*. Washington. D.C., American Psychological Association

Marsella, A. J., Friedman, M. J., Gerrity, E. T. and Scurfield, R. M. (1996b). Ethnocultural aspects of PTSD: some closing thoughts. *Ethnocultural aspects of Posttraumatic Stress Disorder: issues, research and clinical applications*. Marsella, A. J., Friedman, M. J., Gerrity, E. T. and Scurfield, R. M., Eds. Washington D.C., American Psychological Association: 529-539

Marsella, A. J., Friedman, M. J., Gerrity, E. T. and Scurfield, R. M. (1996). Preface. *Ethnocultural aspects of Posttraumatic Stress Disorder: issues, research and clinical applications*. Marsella, A. J., Friedman, M. J., Gerrity, E. T. and Scurfield, R. M., Eds. Washington D.C., American Psychological Association: Preface

Marsella, A. J., Friedman, M. J. and Huland Spain, E. (1996). Ethnocultural aspects of PTSD: an overview of issues and research directions. *Ethnocultural aspects of Posttraumatic Stress Disorder: issues, research and clinical applications*. Marsella, A. J., Friedman, M. J., Gerrity, E. T. and Scurfield, R. M., Eds. Washington D.C., American Psychological Association: 105-130

Martenyi, F., Brown, E. B., Zhang, H., Koke, S. C. and Prakash, A. (2002). "Fluoxetine v. placebo in prevention of relapse in post-traumatic stress disorder." *British Journal of Psychiatry* **181**(4): 315-320

Martenyi, F., Brown, E. B., Zhang, H., Prakash, A. and Koke, S. C. (2002). "Fluoxetine versus placebo in posttraumatic stress disorder." *The Journal of Clinical Psychiatry* **63**(3): 199-206

Martz, E. and Cook, D. W. (2001). "Physical impairments as risk factors for the development of posttraumatic stress disorder." *Rehabilitation Counselling Bulletin* **44**(4): 217-221

Marusic, A., Kozaric-Kovacic, D., Arcel, L. T. and Folnegovic-Smalc, V. (1998). Validity of three PTSD scales in a sample of refugees and displaced persons. *War, violence, trauma and the coping process*. Arcel, L. T., Ed. Zagreb, International Rehabilitation Council for Torture Victims (IRCT): 93-100

Masheder, M. (1986). *Lets co-operate*. London, Peace Education Project

Maslow, A. (1943). "A theory of human motivation." *Psychological Review* **50**: 370-396

Maslow, A. (1954). *Motivation and personality*. New York, Harper & Row

Maslow, A. (1968). *Towards a psychology of being*. Princeton, N.J., Van Nostrand

Maslow, A. (1971). *The farther reaches of human nature*. New York, The Viking Press

Maslow, A. and Lowery, R., Eds. (1998). *Toward a psychology of being*. New York, Wiley and Sons

Mason, J. (2000). *Qualitative researching*. London, Sage

Mason, J. W., Giller, E. L., Kosten, T. R., Ostroff, R. B. and Podd, L. (1986). "Urinary free-cortisol levels in Posttraumatic Stress Disorder patients." *Journal of Nervous and Mental Diseases* **34**(145-159)

Masunaga, S. and Ohashi, W. (1977). *Zen Shiatsu*. Tokyo and New York, Japan Publications

Matacic, S. (1998). Psychopathology in war-traumatised children. *War, violence, trauma and the coping process*. Arcel, L. T., Ed. Zagreb, International Rehabilitation Council for Torture Victims (IRCT): 345-350

Mc Ivor, R. (1997). Theoretical models of PTSD- physiological and biological mechanisms. *Psychological trauma- a developmental approach*. Black, D., Newman, M., Harris Hendricks, J. and Mezey, G., Eds. London, Gaskell

McCann, L. I., Pearlman, L.A (1990). *Psychological trauma and the adult survivor: theory, therapy, and transformation*. New York, Bruner/Mazel

Mcfarlane, A. C. (1985). "The effects of stressful life events and disasters: research and theoretical issues." *Aust NZ J Psychiatry* (19): 409-421

McFarlane, A. C. (1989). "The aetiology of post-traumatic morbidity: predisposing, precipitating and perpetuating factors." *British Journal of Psychiatry* (154): 221-228

McFarlane, A. C. and de Girolamo, G. (1996). The nature of traumatic stressors and the epidemiology of posttraumatic reactions. *Traumatic stress: the effects of overwhelming experience on mind, body and society*. van der Kolk, B. A., Mcfarlane, A. C. and Weisaeth, L., Eds. London, New York, The Guilford Press: 129-154

Mcfarlane, A. C. and van der Kolk, B. A. (1996). Trauma and its challenge to society. *Traumatic stress: the effects of overwhelming experience on mind, body and society*. van der Kolk, B. A., Mcfarlane, A. C. and Weisaeth, L., Eds. London, New York, The Guilford Press: 24-46

McFarlane, A. C. and Yehuda, R. (1996). Resilience, vulnerability and the course of posttraumatic reactions. *Traumatic stress: the effects of overwhelming experience on mind, body and society*. van der Kolk, B. A., Mcfarlane, A. C. and Weisaeth, L., Eds. London, New York, The Guilford Press: 155-181

McMillen, C., Zuravin, S. and Rideout, G. (1995). "Perceived benefits from childhood sexual abuse." *Journal of Consulting and Clinical Psychology* **63**(1037-1043)

McNally, R. J. (1999). "On eye movements and animal magnetism: a reply to Greenwald's defense of EMDR." *Journal of Anxiety Disorders* **13**(6): 617-620

McNally, R. J. (2001). "Tertullian's motto and Callaghan's method." *Journal of Clinical Psychology* **57**(10): 1171-1174

Mead, C., Ed. (1996). *Journeys of discovery: creative learning from disaster.* London, National Institute for Social Work

Mearns, D. and Dryden, W., Eds. (1990). *Experiences of counselling in action.* London, Sage

Mearns, D. and Thorne, B. (1988). *Person-Centred Counselling in action.* London, Sage

Mearns, D. and B. Thorne (2000). *Person-Centred Therapy Today: new frontiers in theory and practice.* London, Sage.

Medcins Sans Frontieres (1997). *Refugee health: an approach to emergency situations.* London, Macmillan

Merton, R. K. and Kendall, P. L. (1946). "The focused interview." *American Journal of Sociology* **51**: 541-557

Miall, H., Ramsbotham, O. and Woodhouse, T. (1999). *Contemporary conflict resolution: the prevention, management and transformation of deadly conflicts.* Cambridge, Polity Press

Michenbaum, D. (1994). *Treating Post-Traumatic Stress Disorder. A handbook and practice manual for therapy.* Ontario, Wiley

Midwest College (2003). *Layman's guide to Acupuncture,* Midwest College. **2003**

Mikus-Kos, A. (1998). Psychosocial and mental health training- a critical approach to an important aspect of helping refugees. *War, violence, trauma and the coping process.* Arcel, L. T., Ed. Zagreb, International Rehabilitation Council for Torture Victims (IRCT): 305-313

Milgram, S. (1963). "Behavioural study of obedience." *Journal of Abnormal and Social Psychology* **67**: 371-378

Milgram, S. (1974). *Obedience to authority.* New York, Harper and Row

Milivojevic, L. (1999). "Complexity of therapist's feelings in the work with war traumatized patients." *Croatian Medical Journal* **40**(4): 503-507

Milkovic-Vukelic, D., Bek, R. and Ostojic, D. (1998). The outreach approach in health care for a refugee population. *War, violence, trauma and the coping process.* Arcel, L. T., Ed. Zagreb, International Rehabilitation Council for Torture Victims (IRCT): 254-257

Mill, J. S. (1953). A System of logic. *Readings in philosophy of science.* P.P, W., Ed. New York, Scribner's

Mitchell, C. R. (1981). *The structure of international conflict.* London, Macmillan

Mitchell, C. R. (1991). Recognising conflict. *Peacemaking in a troubled world.* Woodhouse, T., Ed. Oxford, Berg: 209-225

Mitchell, C. R. (1993). Problem-solving exercises and theories of conflict resolution. *Conflict resolution theory and practice.* Sandole, J. D. and van der Merwe, H., Eds. Manchester, Manchester University Press: 78-84

Mitchell, C. R. and Webb, K. (1988a). Mediation in international relations. *New approaches to international mediation.* Mitchell, C. and Webb, K., Eds. London, New York, Connecticut, Greenwood Press: 1-15

Mitchell, C. R. and Webb, K., Eds. (1988b). *New approaches in international mediation.* Contributions in political science. New York. London, Greenwood

Mitchell, J. T. (1983). "When disaster strikes: the critical incident stress debriefing process." *Journal of Emergency Medical Services* (8): 36-39

Mitchell, J. T. and Dyregrov, A. (1993). Traumatic stress in disaster workers and emergency personnel: prevention and intervention. *International handbook of traumatic stress syndromes.* Wilson, J. P. and Raphael, B., Eds. New York, Plenum Press: 905-914

Mitchell, J. T. and Everly, G. S. (2000). Critical incident stress management and critical incident stress debriefings: evolutions, effects and outcomes. *Psychological debriefing.* Raphael, B. and Wilson, J. P., Eds. Cambridge, Cambridge University Press: 71-90

Mitchels, B. (2002a). "Ten years of peacemaking in Croatia." *The Friend* (July): 6-7

Mitchels, B. (2002b). "With a little help from our friends." *Holding the pattern* (Summer): 6-7

Mitchels, B. (2002c) Leading Humanity into Peace: Revolution or Evolution? Peace and Conflict, Journal of Peace Psychology. 2002 8 (1) 89-93

Mitchels, B. (2003). Healing the wounds of war and more: an integrative approach to peacemaking. The work of Adam Curle and others in Osijek, Zupanja and Vukovar, Croatia. *British Journal of Guidance & Counselling*, Nov 2003 Vol. 31 (4) 403-416

Mollica, R. F., Sarajlic, N., Chernoff, M., Lavelle, J., Vukovic, I. S. and Massagli, M. P. (2001). "Longitudinal study of psychiatric symptoms, disability, mortality, and emigration among Bosnian refugees." *JAMA: the Journal of the American Medical Association* **286**(5): 546-554

Moore, R. H. (1993). Traumatic incident reduction: a cognitive-emotive treatment of post-traumatic stress disorder. *Innovations in Rational-Emotive Therapy.* Dryden, W. and Hill, L., Eds. Newbury Park, C.A., Sage

Moore, R. H. (2002). *Psychological Foundations of Traumatic Incident Reduction (TIR),* TIR. org. **2002**

Moreno, Z. (1979). "Escape me never." *Group Psychotherapy, Psychodrama and Sociometry* **32**: 5-12

Morgan, D. L. (1988). *Focus groups as qualitative research.* Newbury Park, CA, Sage Publications

Morgan, D. L. and Kreuger, R. A. (1993). When to use focus groups and why. *Successful focus groups.* Morgan, D. L., Ed. London, Sage Publications

Morgan, D. L. and Spanish, M. T. (1984). "Focus groups: a new tool for qualitative research." *Qualitative Sociology* **7**: 253-270

Morgenthau, H. J., Thompson, K.W. (1993). *Politics among nations. The struggle for power and peace.* New York, McGraw-Hill

Moro, L., Franciskovic, T., Varenina-Novakovic, G. and Urlic, I. (1998). War trauma: influence on individuals and community. *War, violence, trauma and the coping process.* Arcel, L. T., Ed. Zagreb, International Rehabilitation Council for Torture Victims (IRCT): 86-92

Morris, L. P. (2000). Is consensus about debriefing possible? *Psychological debriefing.* Raphael, B. and Wilson, J. P., Eds. Cambridge, Cambridge University Press: 321-326

Moustakas, C. (1990a). "Heuristic research, design and methodology." *Person Centred Review* **5**(2): 170-190

Moustakas, C. (1990b). *Heuristic research, design, methodology and applications.* London, Sage

Moustakas, C. (1994). *Phenomenological research methods.* London, Sage

Mowrer, O. H. (1960). *Learning theory and behaviour.* New York, Wiley

Muris, P., Merckelbach, H., Holdrinet, I. and Sijsenaar, M. (1998). "Treating phobic children: effects of EMDR versus exposure." *Journal of Consulting and Clinical Psychology* **66**(1): 193-198

Murphy, J. G., Hampton, J (1988). *Forgiveness and mercy.* Cambridge, Cambridge University Press

Murray, H. (1938). *Explorations in personality.* New York, Oxford University Press

Myers, C. S. (1940). *Shell shock in France.* Cambridge, Cambridge University Press

Natiello, P. (1999). Sexism, gender dynamics and the Person Centred Approach.

Experiences in relatedness: groupwork and the Person Centred Approach. Lago, C. and MacMillan, M., Eds. Ross on Wye, PCCS Books: 63-76

National Association for Drama Therapy (2003a). *Drama therapy*, National Association for Drama Therapy.

National Association for Drama Therapy (2003b). *National Association for Drama Therapy*, National Association for Drama Therapy.

National Federation of Spiritual Healers (2003). *What is healing?* National Federation of Spiritual Healers.

Nelson-Jones, R. (1991). *The theory and practice of counselling and psychology.* London, Cassell

Newman, E., Kaloupek, D. G. and Keane, T. M. (1996). Assessment of posttraumatic stress disorder in clinical and research settings. *Traumatic Stress: the effects of overwhelming experience on mind, body and society.* van der Kolk, B. A., Mcfarlane, A. C. and Weisaeth, L., Eds. London, New York, The Guilford Press: 242-278

Nicolaidis, S. (2002). "A hormone-based characterization and taxonomy of stress: possible usefulness in management." *Metabolism: Clinical and Experimental* 51(1): 31-36

Nieves-Grafals, S. (2001). "Brief therapy of civil war-related trauma: a case study." *Cultural Diversity & Ethnic Minority Psychology* 7(4): 387-398

Norris, F., Perilla, J., Ibanez, G. E. and Murphy, A. D. (2001). "Sex differences in symptoms of posttraumatic stress: does culture play a role?" *Journal of Traumatic Stress* 14(1): 7-28

Norris, F. H. (1992). "Epidemiology of trauma: frequency and impact of different potentially traumatic events on different demographic groups." *Journal of Consulting and Clinical Psychology* 60(3): 409-418

North, C. S., Spitznagel, E. L. and Smith, E. M. (2001). "A prospective study of coping after exposure to a mass murder episode." *Annals of Clinical Psychiatry: Official Journal of the American Academy of Clinical Psychiatrists* 13(2): 81-87

North, J. (1987). "Wrongdoing and forgiveness." *Philosophy* 62: 499-508

Nunnerley, M. and Mitchels, B. (2002). *Cross cultural research: international and local perspectives*

Nys, Y., Parkes, C. O. and Thomasset, M. (1986). "Effects of suppression and resumption of shell formation and parathyroid hormone on uterine calcium-binding protein, carbonic anhydrase activity, and intestinal calcium absorption in hens." *Gen Comp Endocrinal* 64(2): 293-9

O'Connell, J. and Curle, A. (1985). *Peace with work to do.* Leamington Spa, Berg

Ohashi, W. (1979). *Do it yourself Shiatsu.* London, Unwin

Oppenheimer, R., Howells, K., Palmer, L. and Chandler, D. (1985). "Adverse sexual experiences in childhood and clinical eating disorders: a preliminary description." *Journal of Psychosomatic Research* 19: 157-161

Oquendo, M. A., Echavarria, G., Galfalvy, H. C., Grunebaum, M. F., Burke, A., Barrera, A., Cooper, T. B., Malone, K. M. and John Mann, J. (2003). "Lower cortisol levels in depressed patients with comorbid post-traumatic stress disorder." *Neuropsychopharmacology: Official Publication Of The American College Of Neuropsychopharmacology* 28(3): 591-598

OSCE (2002). *Report on community trauma in Eastern Croatia.* Vukovar, OSCE

O'Shea, B. (2001). "Posttraumatic Stress Disorder: a review for the general psychiatrist." *International Journal of Psychiatry in Clinical Practice* 5(1): 11-18

Page, S., Wosket, V. (1998). *Supervising the counsellor.* London, Routledge

Pantic, Z. (1998). Integrative group therapy with refugee children. *War, violence, trauma and the coping process.* Arcel, L. T., Ed. Zagreb, International Rehabilitation Council for Torture Victims (IRCT): 351-360

Parkes, C. M. (1980). "Bereavement counselling: Does it work?" *British Medical Journal* **281**: 3-6

Parkes, C. M. (1986a). "Bereavement counselling." *Lancet* **1**(8492): 1277-8

Parkes, C. M. (1986b). "Care of the dying. The role of the psychiatrist." *British Journal of Hospital Medicine* **36**(4): 250, 252, 254-5

Parkes, C. M. (1988). "Not always!" *Journal of Palliative Care* **4**(1-2): 50-2

Parkes, C. M. (1991). "Planning for the aftermath." *Journal of the Royal Society of Medicine* **84**(1): 22-5

Parkes, C. M. (1993). "Psychiatric problems following bereavement by murder or manslaughter." *British Journal of Psychiatry* **162**: 49-54

Parkes, C. M. (1995). "Guidelines for conducting ethical bereavement research." *Death Studies* **19**(2): 171-81

Parkes, C. M. (1998a). "Bereavement in adult life." *British Medical Journal* **316**(7134): 856-9

Parkes, C. M. (1998b). "The dying adult." *British Medical Journal* **316**(7140): 1313-5

Parkes, C. M. (1998c). "Facing loss." *British Medical Journal* **316**(7143): 1521-4

Parkes, C. M. (2000). "Commentary: prognoses should be based on proved indices not intuition." *British Medical Journal* **320**(7233): 473

Parkes, C. M. (2001). "Bereavement dissected—a re-examination of the basic components influencing the reaction to loss." *Israeli Journal of Psychiatry Related Sciences* **38**(3-4): 150-6

Parkes, C. M. (2003). *Untitled.* Mitchels, B. Halifax

Patton, M. Q. (1990). *Qualitative Evaluation and Research Methods.* Newbury Park, C.A., Sage

Pavelic, D. (1998a). Non-professionals and professionals: encounter between the necessary and the inevitable. *War, violence, trauma and the coping process.* Arcel, L. T., Ed. Zagreb, International Rehabilitation Council for Torture Victims (IRCT): 299-302

Pavelic, D. (1998b). A refugee and his professional self. *War, violence, trauma and the coping process.* Arcel, L. T., Ed. Zagreb, International Rehabilitation Council for Torture Victims (IRCT): 295-298

Pavlov, I. P. (1926). *Conditioned reflexes: an investigation of the physiological activity of the cerebral cortex.* New York, Dover Publications

Pavlov, I. P. (1927). *Conditioned reflexes.* New York, Oxford University Press

Pavlovic, E. and Marusic, A. (2001). "Suicide in Croatia and in Croatian immigrant groups in Australia and Slovenia." *Croatian Medical Journal* **42**(6): 669-672

Pearsall, J., Ed. (1999). *The concise oxford dictionary.* Oxford, Oxford University Press

Perls, F., Hefferline, R. F. and Goodman, P. (1990). *Gestalt therapy.* London, Souvenir Press

Perry, B. D., Polland, R. A., Blakley, T. L., Baker, W. L. and Vigilants, B. (1995). "Childhood trauma, the neurobiology of adaptation, and 'use-dependent' development of the brain: how 'states' become 'traits'." *Infant Mental Health Journal* **16**(4): 271-291

Pitman, R., Orr, S. (1990). "The black hole of trauma." *Biological Psychiatry* **26**: 221-223

Pitman, R. K., Shin, L. M. and Rauch, S. L. (2001). "Investigating the pathogenesis of Posttraumatic Stress Disorder with neuroimaging." *Journal of Clinical Psychiatry* **62**(17): 47-55

Pitman, R. K., Sparr, L. F., Saunders, L. S. and McFarlane, A. C. (1996). Legal issues in Posttraumatic Stress Disorder. *Traumatic stress: the effects of overwhelming experience on mind, body and society.* van der Kolk, B. A., Mcfarlane, A. C. and Weisaeth, L., Eds. London, New York, The Guilford Press: 378-397

Polak, P. R., Egan, D., Vandebergh, R. and Williams, W. V. (1975). "Prevention in mental health: a controlled study." *American Journal of Psychiatry* **132**: 146-149

Polkinghorne, D. (1984). *Methodology for the human sciences.* Albany, State University of New York Press

Popovic, S. (1998a). Grief and psychosoma- a case report on a wounded soldier. *War, violence, trauma and the coping process.* Arcel, L. T., Ed. Zagreb, International Rehabilitation Council for Torture Victims (IRCT): 168-171

Popovic, S. (1998b). Understanding grief and bereavement: Psychosomatic symptoms of sexually tortured women. *War, violence, trauma and the coping process.* Arcel, L. T., Ed. Zagreb, International Rehabilitation Council for Torture Victims (IRCT): 218-221

Popovic, S. and Dizdarevic, U. (1998). Refugee line: psychological and medical problems of callers and methods of treatment. *War, violence, trauma and the coping process.* Arcel, L. T., Ed. Zagreb, International Rehabilitation Council for Torture Victims (IRCT): 118-120

Popper, K. (1959). *The logic of scientific discovery.* London, Hutchinson/Routledge

Popper, K. (1963). *Conjectures and refutations: the growth of scientific knowledge.* London, Routledge

Popper, K. (1972). *Objective knowledge.* Oxford, Clarendon Press

Powell, R. A., Single, H. M. and Lloyd, K. R. (1996). "Focus groups in mental health research: enhancing the validity of user and provider questionnaires." *International Journal of Social Psychology* **42**(3): 193-206

Proctor, B. (1987). Supervision, a co-operative exercise in accountability. *Enabling and ensuring supervision in practice.* Marken, M. and Payne, M., Eds. Leicester, National Youth Bureau

Putnam, F. W. (1989). *Diagnosis and treatment of Multiple Personality Disorder.* New York, Guilford Press

Putnam, F. W., Guroff, J. J. and Silberman, E. K. (1986). "The clinical phenomenology of multiple personality disorder: review of 100 recent cases." *Journal of Clinical Psychiatry* **47**: 285-293

Pynoos, R. S., Steinberg, A. M. and Goenjian, A. (1996). Traumatic stress in childhood and adolescence: recent developments and current controversies. *Traumatic Stress: the Effects of Overwhelming Experience on Mind, Body and Society.* van der Kolk, B. A., Mcfarlane, A. C. and Weisaeth, L., Eds. London, New York, The Guilford Press: 331-359

Race, K. E., Hotch, D. F. and Parker, T. (1994). "Rehabilitation program evaluation: use of focus groups to empower clients." *Evaluation Review* **18**(6): 730-740

Rachman, S. (1980). "Emotional processing." *Behaviour, Research and Therapy* **18**: 51-60

Rahimi, Z. (2001). *Milan Systemic Family Therapy: uses and cautions in working with refugees,* www.torturecare.org.uk. **2003**

Rapaport, M. H., Endicott, J. and Clary, C. M. (2002). "Posttraumatic Stress Disorder and quality of life: results across 64 weeks of sertraline treatment." *The Journal of Clinical Psychiatry* **63**(1): 59-65

Raphael, B. (1977). "Preventive intervention with the recently bereaved." *Archives of General Psychiatry* **34**(12): 1450-1454

Raphael, B., Meldrum, L. and McFarlane, A. C. (1995). "Does de-briefing after psychological trauma work?" *British Medical Journal* **310**: 1479-1480

Raphael, B., Wilson, J., Meldrum, L. and McFarlane, A. C. (1996). Acute preventive interventions. *Traumatic Stress: the effects of overwhelming experience on mind, body and society.* van der Kolk, B. A., Mcfarlane, A. C. and Weisaeth, L., Eds. London, New York, The Guilford Press: 463-479

Raphael, B. and Wilson, J. P., Eds. (2000). *Psychological debriefing.* Cambridge, Cambridge University Press

Rapoport, A. (1966). Models of conflict: cataclysmic and strategic. *Conflict in society*. de Reuck, A., Ed. London, Churchill

Raven Recording (2003). *About Gabrielle Roth*, Raven Recording. **2003**

Reason, P. (1988). *Human inquiry in action*. London, Sage

Reason, P. (1994). *Participation in human inquiry*. London, Sage

Reason, P. and Heron, J. (1986). "Research with people: the paradigm of co-operative experiential enquiry." *Person Centred Review* 1(4): 456-476

Reason, P. and Rowan, J., Eds. (1981). *Human inquiry: a sourcebook of new paradigm research*. Chichester, Wiley

Reder, P., Duncan, S. and Gray, M. (1994). *Beyond blame: child abuse tragedies revisited*. London and New York, Routledge

Reynolds, M. and Brewin, C. R. (1998). "Intrusive cognitions, coping strategies and emotional responses in depression, post-traumatic stress disorder, and a non-clinical population." *Behaviour Research and Therapy* **36**: 135-147

Reynolds, R. (1995). *Bridging the gap of peace in Bosnia*, CNN. **2003**

Rigby, A. (2001). *Justice and reconciliation*. London, Lynne Reiner Publishers, Inc

Ring, K. (1984). *Heading towards Omega: in search of the meaning of the near-death experience*. New York, Dodd, Mead and Co

Ritsher, J. B., Struening, E. L., Hellman, F. and Guardino, M. (2002). "Internal validity of an anxiety disorder screening instrument across five ethnic groups." *Psychiatry Research* **111**(2-3): 199-213

Rittenhouse, J. A. (2000). "Using Eye Movement Desensitization and Reprocessing to treat Complex PTSD in a biracial client." *Cultural Diversity and Ethnic Minority Psychology* **6**(4): 399-408

Robin, R. W., Chester, B. and Goldman, D. (1996). Cumulative trauma and PTSD in American Indian communities. *Ethnocultural aspects of Posttraumatic Stress Disorder: issues, research and clinical applications*. Marsella, A. J., Friedman, M. J., Gerrity, E. T. and Scurfield, R. M., Eds. Washington D.C., American Psychological Association: 239-254

Roet, B. (1986). *Hypnosis: a gateway to better health*. London, Weidenfield and Nicholson

Rogers, C. (1944) "Wartime issues in family counselling." *Journal of Home Economics*. 36 (7) 390-393

Rogers, C. (1945) Counseling with the returned serviceman and his wife *Marriage and Family Living* 7,4 (1945) 82–84

Rogers, C. (1942). *Counselling and Psychotherapy: newer concepts in practice*. Boston, Houghton Mifflin

Rogers, C. (1957). "The necessary and sufficient conditions of therapeutic personality change." *Journal of Consulting Psychology* 21(2): 95-103

Rogers, C. (1961)). *On becoming a person*. Boston, Houghton Mifflin (latest edition 1995)

Rogers, C. (1980). *A way of being*. Boston, Houghton Mifflin (latest edition 1995)

Rogers, C. (1982a). "A psychologist looks at nuclear war: its threat, its possible prevention." *Journal of Humanistic Psychology* 22(4): 9-19

Rogers, C. (1982b). "Reply to Rollo May's letter to Carl Rogers." *Journal of Humanistic Psychology* 22(4): 85-89

Rogers, C. (1985). "Toward a more human science of the person." *Journal of Humanistic Psychology* 25(4): 7-24

Rogers, C. (1986). "The Rust workshop: A personal overview." *Journal of Humanistic Psychology* 26(3): 23-45

Rogers, C. (1987a). "Inside the world of the Soviet professional." *Counselling and Values* 32(1): 46-67 and in *Journal of Humanistic Psychology* 27, 3 (1987) 277–304

Rogers, C. (1987b). "Journal of South African trip (January 14-March 1, 1986)."

Counselling and Values **32**(1): 21-38

Rogers, C. (1987c). "Steps towards world peace, 1948-1986: tension reduction in theory and practice." *Counselling and Values* **32**(1): 12-17

Rogers, C. (1987d). "The underlying theory: drawn from experience with individuals and groups." *Counselling and Values* **32**(1): 38-46

Rogers, C. (1989). "The necessary and sufficient conditions of personality change." *Journal of Consulting and Clinical Psychology* **21**(2): 95-103

Rogers, C. (1992). "The necessary and sufficient conditions of therapeutic personality change." *Journal of Consulting and Clinical Psychology* **60**(6): 827-832

Rogers, C. (1995). *Client Centred Therapy*. London, Constable and Company Ltd (original 1965)

Rogers, C. and Malcolm, D. (1987). "The potential contribution of the behavioural scientist to world peace." *Counselling and Values* **32**(1): 10-12

Rogers, C. and Ryback, D. (1984). "One alternative to nuclear planetary suicide." *The Counselling Psychologist* **12**(2): 3-12

Rogers, C. and Sanford, R. (1987). "Reflections on our South African experience (January-February 1986)." *Counselling and Values* **32**(1): 17-21

Rogers, C. and Stevens, B. (1967). *Person to person. The problem of being human: a new trend in psychology*. Walnut Creek, CA. Real People Press

Rogers, C. and Whiteley, J. M. (2003a). *Facilitating peace: insights from three experiences*, Quest for Peace Video Series. **2003**

Rogers, C. and Whiteley, J. M. (2003b). *Mutual understanding and communication in creating a facilitative climate for peace: interview with Carl Rogers*, Quest for Peace Video Series. **2003**

Root, M., P (1996). Women of color and traumatic stress in 'domestic captivity': Gender and race as disempowering statuses. *Ethnocultural aspects of Posttraumatic Stress Disorder: issues, research and clinical applications*. Marsella, A. J., Friedman, M. J., Gerrity, E. T. and Scurfield, R. M., Eds. Washington D.C., American Psychological Association: 363-388

Rose, S. (2002). "Theoretical approaches to psychological trauma: implications for research and practice." *Counselling and Psychotherapy Research* **2**(1): 61-72

Rosen, G. M. and Powel, J. E. "Use of a symptom validity test in the forensic assessment of Posttraumatic Stress Disorder." *Journal of Anxiety Disorders* **In Press, Uncorrected Proof**

Rosen, S., Ed. (1982). *My voice will go with you: the teaching tales of Milton H. Erickson*. New York, W.W. Norton & Company

Rosenberg, S. D., Mueser, K. T., Friedman, M. J., Gorman, P. G., Drake, R. E., Vidaver, R. M., Torrey, W. C. and Jankowski, M. K. (2001). "Developing effective treatments for posttraumatic disorders among people with severe mental illness." *Psychiatric Services (Washington, D.C.)* **52**(11): 1453-1461

Rosenheck, R. and Fontana, A. (1996). Ethnocultural variations in service use among veterans suffering from PTSD. *Ethnocultural aspects of Posttraumatic Stress Disorder: issues, research and clinical applications*. Marsella, A. J., Friedman, M. J., Gerrity, E. T. and Scurfield, R. M., Eds. Washington D.C., American Psychological Association: 483-504

Roshchin, S. (1986). "Psychological problems of the political development of personality." *Journal of Humanistic Psychology* **26**(4): 7-47

Rosner, R. (2001). "Between search and research: how to find your way around? Review of the article "Thought Field Therapy- soothing the bad moments of Kosovo"." *Journal Of Clinical Psychology* **57**(10): 1241-1244

Rot, N. (1974). "Forms of national attachment." *Studia Psychologica* **16**: 233-239

Rothbaum, B. O. and Foa, E. B. (1996). Cognitive-Behavioural Therapy for Posttraumatic Stress Disorder. *Traumatic stress: the effects of overwhelming experience on mind, body and society.* van der Kolk, B. A., Mcfarlane, A. C. and Weisaeth, L., Eds. London, New York, The Guilford Press: 491-509

Rothbaum, B. O., Meadows, E. A., Resick, P. and Foy, D. W. (2000). Cognitive Behavioural Therapy. *Effective treatments for Post-Traumatic Stress Disorder.* Foa, E. B., Keane, T. M. and Friedman, M. J., Eds. New York, Guilford Press

Russell, D. E. H. (1984). *Sexual exploitation: rape, child sexual abuse, and sexual harassment.* Beverley Hills, C.A., Sage

Russell, D. E. H. (1986). *The secret trauma.* New York, Basic Books

Ruzek, J. I., Riney, S. J., Leskin, G., Drescher, K. D., Foy, D. W. and Gusman, F. D. (2001). "Do post-traumatic stress disorder symptoms worsen during trauma focus group treatment?" *Military Medicine* **166**(10): 898-902

Salem, P. e. (1997). Conflict resolution in the Arab world: selected essays New York, American University of Beirut

Salmon, K. and Bryant, R. A. (2002). "Posttraumatic stress disorder in children: the influence of developmental factors." *Clinical Psychology Review* **22**(2): 163-188

Samson, C. (1995). "The fracturing of medical dominance in British psychiatry?" *Sociology of Health and Illness* **17**(245-268)

Sanford, R. (1999). Experiencing diversity. *Experiences in relatedness: groupwork and the Person Centred Approach.* Lago, C. and MacMillan, M., Eds. Ross on Wye, PCCS Books: 77-92

Sapolsky, R., Hideo, E., Rebert, C. S. and Finch, C. E. (1990). "Hippocampal damage associated with prolonged glucocorticoid exposure in primates." *Journal of Neuropsychiatry* **10**: 2897-2902

Saraceno, B., Saxena, S. and Maulik, P. K. (2002). Mental health problems in refugees. *Psychiatry in society.* Gaebel, W., Ed. New York, John Wiley & Sons Ltd: 193-220

Sartorius, N. (2001). "Is pain a somatic symptom?" *Croatian Medical Journal* **42**(2): 127-129

Sayer, A. (1999). *Method in social science.* London, Routledge

Scheck, M. M., Schaeffer, J. A. and Gilette, C. (1998). "Brief psychological intervention with traumatized young women: the efficacy of Eye Movement Desensitization and Reprocessing." *Journal of Traumatic Stress* **11**(1): 25-44

Scheibe, S., Bagby, R. M., Miller, L. S. and Dorian, B. J. (2001). "Assessing Posttraumatic Stress Disorder with the MMPI-2 in a sample of workplace accident victims." *Psychological Assessment* **13**(3): 369-374

Schelling, T. (1960). *The strategy of conflict.* London, Oxford University Press

Schelling, T. (1966). *Arms and influence.* New Haven, Conn, Yale University Press

Schelling, T. C. (1980). *The Strategy of conflict.* Cambridge, MA, Havard University Press

Schlenger, W. and Fairbank, J. (1996). Ethnocultural considerations in understanding PTSD and related disorders among military veterans. *Ethnocultural aspects of Posttraumatic Stress Disorder: issues, research and clinical applications.* Marsella, A. J., Friedman, M. J., Gerrity, E. T. and Scurfield, R. M., Eds. Washington D.C., American Psychological Association: 415-438

Schnurr, P. P., Friedman, M. J. and Bernardy, N. C. (2002). "Research on Posttraumatic Stress Disorder: epidemiology, pathophysiology, and assessment." *Journal of Clinical Psychology* **58**(8): 877-889

Schweder, R. A. and Bourne, E. J. (1989). Does the concept of the person vary cross-culturally? *Cultural conceptions of mental health and therapy.* Marsella, A. J., White, G.M., Ed. London, D. Reidal Publishing Company: 97-137

Scragg, P., Grey, N., Lee, D., Young, K. and Turner, S. (2001). "A brief report on the Penn

Inventory for Posttraumatic Stress Disorder." *Journal of Traumatic Stress* **14**(3): 605-611

Selimbasicacute, Z., Pavlovicacute, S., Sinanovicacute, O., Vesnicacute, S., Petrovicacute, M., Ferkovicacute, V. and Cipurkovicacute-Mustacevicacute, A. (2001). "Posttraumatic Stress Disorder: effects of psychosocial treatment in children." *Medicinski Arhiv* **55**(1): 25-29

Sells, M. A. (1998). *The bridge betrayed*. Berkeley and Los Angeles C.A., University of California Press

Selye, H. (1956). *The stress of life*. New York, McGraw-HIll

Shalev, A. Y. (1996). Stress versus traumatic stress: from acute homeostatic reactions to chronic psychopathology. *Traumatic stress: the effects of overwhelming experience on mind, body and society*. van der Kolk, B. A., Mcfarlane, A. C. and Weisaeth, L., Eds. London, New York, The Guilford Press: 77-101

Shapiro, F. (1988). "Efficacy of the eye movement desensitization procedure in the treatment of traumatic memories." *Journal of Traumatic Stress* **1**: 199-223

Shapiro, F. (1995). *Eye Movement Rapid Desensitization*. New York, Guilford Press

Shapiro, F. (1996). "Eye Movement Desensitization and Reprocessing (EMDR): evaluation of controlled PTSD research." *Journal of Behavior Therapy and Experimental Psychiatry* **27**(3): 209-218

Shapiro, F. (1999). "Eye Movement Desensitization and Reprocessing (EMDR) and the Anxiety Disorders: clinical and research implications of an integrated psychotherapy treatment." *Journal of Anxiety Disorders* **13**(1-2): 35-67

Shepherd, B. (2000). *A war of nerves; soldiers and psychiatrists 1914-1994*. London, Jonathan Cape / Routledge

Showalter, E. (1985). *The female malady: women, madness and English culture 1830-1980*. New York, Pantheon

Silber, L. and Little, A. (1996). *The death of Yugoslavia*. London, Penguin

Silverman, M. (2003). "The influence of music on the symptoms of psychosis: a meta-analysis." *Journal of Music Therapy* **40**(1): 27-40

Simunkovic, G. T. and Arcel, L. T. (1998). Group psychotherapy with victims of torture. *War, violence, trauma and the coping process*. Arcel, L. T., Ed. Zagreb, International Rehabilitation Council for Torture Victims (IRCT): 143-154

Skinner, B. F. (1953). *Science and human behaviour*. New York, Macmillan Free Press

Skinner, B. F. (1991). *The behaviour of organisms: an experimental analysis*, B.F. Skinner Foundation

Skinner, B. F. (2002a). *Beyond freedom and dignity*, Hackett Publishing Co

Skinner, B. F. (2002b). *Verbal behaviour*. Action, MA, Copley

Smajkic, A., Weine, S., Djuric-Bijedic, Z., Boskailo, E., Lewis, J. and Pavkovic, I. (2001). "Sertraline, Paroxetine, and Venlafaxine in refugee Posttraumatic Stress Disorder with depression symptoms." *Journal of Traumatic Stress* **14**(3): 445-452

Smith, J. A., Scammon, D. L. and Beck, S. L. (1995). "Using patient focus groups for new patient services." *Joint Commission Journal on Quality Improvement* **21**(1): 22-31

Smith, M. (1998). *Social science in question*. London, Sage

Solomon, Z., Laror, N. and McFarlane, A. C. (1996). Acute posttraumatic stress reactions in soldiers and civilians. *Traumatic stress: the effects of overwhelming experience on mind, body and society*. van der Kolk, B. A., Mcfarlane, A. C. and Weisaeth, L., Eds. London, New York, The Guilford Press: 102-116

Soper, B., Milford, G. and Rosenthal, G. (1995). "Belief when evidence does not support theory." *Psychology and Marketing* **12**(5): 415-422

Southwick, S. M., Morgan, A., L.M, N., Bremner, D., Nicholaou, A. L., Johnson, D. R., Rosenheck, R. and Charney, D. S. (1993). "Trauma-related symptoms in veterans of

Operation Desert Storm: a preliminary report." *American Journal of Psychiatry* (150): 1524-1538

Spock, B. M. (1946). *Common sense book of baby and child-care.* New York, Sloan and Pearce

Stalekar, V., Gregurek, R. and Jelic, M. (1998). War trauma and its consequences: working with wounded war veterans. *War, violence, trauma and the coping process.* Arcel, L. T., Ed. Zagreb, International Rehabilitation Council for Torture Victims (IRCT): 107-117

Staub, E. (1989). *The roots of evil: the origins of genocide and other group violence.* New York, Cambridge University Press

Staub, E. (1996a). "Breaking the cycle of violence: helping victims of genocidal violence heal." *Journal of Personal and Interpersonal Loss* 1: 191-197

Staub, E. (1996b). "Preventing genocide: activating bystanders, helping victims and the creation of caring." *Peace and Conflict: Journal of Peace Psychology* 2(189-201)

Staub, E. (1998). Early intervention: prediction and action. *The psychology of peacekeeping.* Langholtz, H., Ed. London, Praeger: 31-39

Staub, E., and Pearlman, L (1996). *Trauma and the fulfilment of the human potential.* Institute of Traumatic Stress Studies, San Francisco, CA, ISTSS

Stein, D. (1999). *Essential Reiki.* Freedom, C.A., Crossing Press

Stevens, A. and Price, J. (2000). *Evolutionary psychiatry: a new beginning.* London, Routledge

Stevenson, D. (2003). *Freud's division of the mind,* Brown University. **2003**

Stewart, D. W. and Shamdasani, P. N. (1990). *Focus groups: theory and practice.* Newbury Park, CA, Sage Publications

Stewart, D. W. and Shamdasani, P. N. (1992). *Focus groups: theory and practice.* London, Sage

Stiefel, M. (2001). Participatory Action Research as a tool for peacebuilding. *Peacebuilding, a field guide.* Reychler, L. a. P., Ed. London, Lynne Reinner: 265-276

Strachey, J. (1983). Sigmund Freud, a sketch of his life and ideas. *On psychopathology.* Strachey, J., Ed. Harmondsworth, Penguin Books. 10: 19-20

Strauss, A. and Corbin, J. (1990). *Basics of qualitative research: Grounded Theory procedures and techniques.* Newbury Park.C.A., Sage

Stubbs, P. and Soroya, B. (1996). "War trauma, psycho-social projects and social development in Croatia." *Medicine, Conflict and Survival* 12: 303-314

Summerfield, D. (1995). "Raising the dead: war, reparation and the politics of memory." *British Medical Journal* 311: 495-497

Summerfield, D. (1996). *The impact of war and atrocity on civilian populations: basic principles for NGO intervention and a critique of psychosocial trauma projects.* Relief and Rehabilitation Network Paper No. 14. London, Overseas Development Institute

Summerfield, D. (1999). "A critique of seven assumptions behind psychological trauma programmes in war-affected areas." *Social Science and Medicine* **48**: 1449-1462

Summerfield, D. (2001). "The invention of Posttraumatic Stress Disorder and the social usefulness of a psychiatric category." *British Medical Journal* **322**(7278): 95-98

Summerfield, D. and Hume, F. (1993). "War and Posttraumatic Stress Disorder: the question of social context." *Journal of Nervous and Mental Diseases* **181**: 522

Tauber, C. (2001). *Mandate for work with psychotrauma and peace.* Vukovar, Croatia, CWWPP Gunduliceva 18, 3200 Vukovar, Croatia

Taylor, C. (1997). *Philosophical arguments.* Cambridge MA, Havard University Press

Taylor, S., Thordarson, D. S., Maxfield, L., Fedoroff, I. C., Lovell, K. and Ogrodniczuk, J. (2003). "Comparative efficacy, speed, and adverse effects of three PTSD treatments: Exposure Therapy, EMDR, and Relaxation Training." *Journal of Consulting and*

Clinical Psychology **71**(2): 330-338

Taylor, S. E. (1983). "Adjustment to threatening events: a theory of cognitive adaptation." *American Psychologist* **38**: 1161-1173

Tedeschi, R. G. (1999). "Violence transformed: Post-traumatic Growth in survivors and their societies." *Aggression and Violent Behaviour* **4**(319-341)

Tedeschi, R. G. and Calhoun, L. G. (1995). *Trauma and transformation: growing in the aftermath of suffering.* Thousand Oaks, C.A., Sage

Tedeschi, R. G. and Calhoun, L. G. (1996). "The Post-traumatic Growth Inventory: measuring the positive legacy of trauma." *Journal of Traumatic Stress* **9**(455-471)

Tedeschi, R. G., Park, C. L. and Calhoun, L. G. (1998). Post-traumatic Growth: conceptual issues. *Post-traumatic Growth: positive changes in the aftermath of crisis.* Tedeschi, R. G., Park, C. L. and Calhoun, L. G., Eds. Mahwah, N.J, Lawrence Erlbaum: 1-22

Terzimehic, A., Biscevic, E., Halilovic, S., Pekez, A., Sahovic, N. and Mujadzic, H. (1998). Experiences and feelings of non-professionals working with refugees. *War, violence, trauma and the coping process.* Arcel, L. T., Ed. Zagreb, International Rehabilitation Council for Torture Victims (IRCT): 289-294

Thayer Gaston, E. and Sears, W. (2003). *Music Therapy principles,* Warchild.org. 2003

Thorne, B. (1998). *Person-Centred Counselling: therapeutic and spiritual dimensions.* London, Whurr.

Thorne, B. (2003). *Carl Rogers.* London, Sage.

Tocilj-Simunkovic, G. (1998). When can psychotherapy for survivors of sexual torture begin? *War, violence, trauma and the coping process.* Arcel, L. T., Ed. Zagreb, International Rehabilitation Council for Torture Victims (IRCT): 222-228

Turnbull, G. and McFarlane, A. C. (1996). Acute treatments. *Traumatic stress: the effects of overwhelming experience on mind, body and society.* van der Kolk, B. A., Mcfarlane, A. C. and Weisaeth, L., Eds. London, New York, The Guilford Press: 480-490

Turner.S.W, McFarlane, A. C. and van der Kolk, B. A. (1996). The therapeutic environment and new explorations in the treatment of posttraumatic stress disorder. *Traumatic stress: the effects of overwhelming experience on mind, body and society.* van der Kolk, B. A., Mcfarlane, A. C. and Weisaeth, L., Eds. London, New York, The Guilford Press: 537-558

U.K. Reiki Federation (2003). *Defining Reiki.*

UNICEF (1996a). *State of the World's children.* Oxford, Oxford University Press

UNICEF (1996b). *UNICEF survey documents horrors experienced by Rwandan children during 1994 genocide.* New York, UNICEF

Urlic, I. (1999). "Aftermath of war experience: impact of anxiety and aggressive feelings on the group and the therapist." *Croatian Medical Journal* **40**(4): 486-492

Ursano, R. J., Grieger, T. A. and McCarroll, J. E. (1996). Prevention of posttraumatic stress: consultation, training and early treatment. *Traumatic stress: the effects of overwhelming experience on mind, body and society.* van der Kolk, B. A., Mcfarlane, A. C. and Weisaeth, L., Eds. London, New York, The Guilford Press: 441-462

Ury, W. (2000). *The third side.* London, Penguin

van den Dungen, P. (1977). "Varieties of peace science: an historical note." *Journal of Peace Science* **2**(2 Spring 1977): 239-257

van den Dungen, P. (1983). "Jean de Bloch: a 19th century peace researcher." *Peace Research* **15**(3): 21-27

van den Dungen, P. (1996). Initiatives for the pursuit and institutionalisation of peace research. *Issues in peace research.* Broadhead, L., Ed. Bradford, Department of Peace Studies, University of Bradford: 5-32

van der Kolk, B. A. (1988). "The trauma spectrum: the interaction of biological and social events in the genesis of the trauma response." *Journal of Traumatic Stress* **1**: 273-290

van der Kolk, B. A. (1994a). *The body keeps the score: memory and the evolving psychobiology of posttraumatic stress.* Boston, Massacheusetts, Massacheussets General Hospital Trauma Clinic, Havard Medical School: 253-265

van der Kolk, B. A. (1994b). "The body keeps the score: memory and the evolving psychobiology of posttraumatic stress." *Havard Review of Psychiatry* **1**(5): 253-265

van der Kolk, B. A. (1996a). The body keeps the score- approaches to the psychobiology of Posttraumatic Stress Disorder. *Traumatic stress: the effects of overwhelming experience on mind, body and society.* van der Kolk, B. A., Mcfarlane, A. C. and Weisaeth, L., Eds. New York, The Guilford Press

van der Kolk, B. A. (1996b). The body keeps the score: approaches to the psychobiology of Posttraumatic Stress Disorder. *Traumatic stress: the effects of overwhelming experience on mind, body and society.* van der Kolk, B. A., Mcfarlane, A. C. and Weisaeth, L., Eds. London, New York, The Guilford Press: 214-241

van der Kolk, B. A. (1996c). The complexity of adaptation to trauma: self-regulation, stimulus discrimination and characterological development. *Traumatic stress: the effects of overwhelming experience on mind, body and society.* van der Kolk, B. A., Mcfarlane, A. C. and Weisaeth, L., Eds. London, New York, The Guilford Press: 182-213

van der Kolk, B. A. (1996d). Trauma and memory. *Traumatic stress: the effects of overwhelming experience on mind, body and society.* van der Kolk, B. A., Mcfarlane, A. C. and Weisaeth, L., Eds. London, New York, The Guilford Press: 279-302

van der Kolk, B. A. (1997). "The psychobiology of Posttraumatic Stress Disorder." *Journal of Clinical Psychiatry* **58**(9): 16-24

van der Kolk, B. A., Dreyfuss, D., Michaels, M., Shera, D., Berkowitz, B., Fisler, R. and Saxe, G. (1994). "Fluoxetine in Posttraumatic Stress Disorder." *Journal of Clinical Psychiatry* **55**(12): 517-522

van der Kolk, B. A., Greenberg, M., Boyd, H. and Krystal, J. (1985). "Inescapable shock, neurotransmitters, and addiction to trauma: toward a psychobiology of post traumatic stress." *Journal of Biological Psychiatry* **20**: 314-325

van der Kolk, B. A. and Mcfarlane, A. C. (1996). The black hole of trauma. *Traumatic stress: the effects of overwhelming experience on mind, body and society.* van der Kolk, B. A., Mcfarlane, A. C. and Weisaeth, L., Eds. London, New York, The Guilford Press: 3-24

van der Kolk, B. A., McFarlane, A. C. and van der Hart, O. (1996). A general approach to the treatment of Posttraumatic Stress Disorder. *Traumatic stress: the effects of overwhelming experience on mind, body and society.* van der Kolk, B. A., Mcfarlane, A. C. and Weisaeth, L., Eds. London, New York, The Guilford Press: 417-440

van der Kolk, B. A., Mcfarlane, A. C. and Weisaeth, L., Eds. (1996). *Traumatic stress: the effects of overwhelming experience on mind, body and society.* London, New York, The Guilford Press

van der Kolk, B. A., Roth, S. and Pelcovitz, D. (1992). *Field trials for DSM IV, Posttraumatic Stress Disorder II; disorders of extreme stress.* Washington D.C, The American Psychiatric Association

van der Kolk, B. A., van der Hart, O. and Marmar, C. R. (1996). Dissociation and information processing in Posttraumatic Stress Disorder. *Traumatic stress: the effects of overwhelming experience on mind, body and society.* van der Kolk, B. A., Mcfarlane, A. C. and Weisaeth, L., Eds. London, New York, The Guilford Press: 303-332

van der Kolk, B. A., Weisaeth, L. and van der Hart, O. (1996). History of trauma in psychiatry. *Traumatic stress: the effects of overwhelming experience on mind, body and society*. van der Kolk, B. A., Mcfarlane, A. C. and Weisaeth, L., Eds. London, New York, The Guilford Press: 47-76

van Humbeeck, G., Van Audenhove, C., De Hert, M., Pieters, G. and Storms, G. (2002). "Expressed emotion; a review of assessment instruments." *Clinical Psychology Review* **22**(3): 321-341

van Lommel, P., van Wees, R., Meyers, V. and Elfferich, I. (2001). "Near-death experience in survivors of cardiac arrest: a prospective study in the Netherlands." *The Lancet* **358**: 2039-2042

van Minnen, A., Arntz, A. and Keijsers, G. P. J. (2002). "Prolonged exposure in patients with chronic PTSD: predictors of treatment outcome and dropout." *Behaviour Research and Therapy* **40**(4): 439-457

Veenema, T. G. and Schroeder-Bruce, K. "The aftermath of violence: children, disaster, and Posttraumatic Stress Disorder." *Journal Of Pediatric Health Care: Official Publication Of National Association Of Pediatric Nurse Associates & Practitioners* **16**(5): 235-244

Vellacott, J. (1981). *Introduction to preparation for peace*. Canadian Quaker pamphlet, Argenta Friends School Press. No 11 Argenta, Canada

Vidovic, V. (1991). *The children's responses to war and exile in Croatia*. Zagreb, University of Zagreb, Croatia

Villas-Boas Bowen, M. (1986). "Personality differences and Person Centred Supervision." *Person Centred Review* **1**(3): 291-309

Volkan, V. (1999). "Individual and large-group identity: parallels in development and characteristics in stability and crisis." *Croatian Medical Journal* **40**(3): 458-465

von Neumann, J. and Morganstern, O. (1944). *The theory of games and economic behaviour*. Princeton, Princeton University Press

Wahba, A. and Bridgewell, L. (1976). "Maslow reconsidered: a review of research on the need hierarchy theory." *Organisational Behaviour and Human Performance* **15**: 212-240

Warren, R. and Zgourides, G. D. (1991). *Anxiety Disorders: a rational emotive perspective*. Elmsford, New York, Pergamon Press

Webb, K. (1988). The morality of mediation. *New Approaches to International Mediation*. Mitchell, C. and Webb, K., Eds. London, New York, Connecticut, Greenwood Press: 16-28

Weber, E. H. (1834). De pulsu, resorptione, auditu et tactu. *Annotationes Anatomical et Physiological* Leipzig, Koehler

Weine, S. M., Kuc, G., Dzudza, E., Razzno, L. and Pavkovic, I. (2001). "PTSD among Bosnian refugees: a survey of providers' knowledge, attitudes and service patterns." *Community Mental Health Journal* **37**(3): 261-271

Weisaeth, L. (1998). Psychiatric problems in war. *War, violence, trauma and the coping process*. Arcel, L. T., Ed. Zagreb, International Rehabilitation Council for Torture Victims (IRCT): 25-33

Weisaeth, L. (2001). "Acute posttraumatic stress: non-acceptance of early intervention." *Journal of Clinical Psychiatry* **62**(117): 35-40

Weiss, E. (1950). *Principles of psychodynamics*. New York, Grune and Stratton

Wenzel, T., Pritz, E., Farkas-Erlacher, B. and Wurbel, G. (1998). Experiences from a neighbouring country- the importance of comprehensive solutions to refugee care. *War, violence, trauma and the coping process*. Arcel, L. T., Ed. Zagreb, International Rehabilitation Council for Torture Victims (IRCT): 131-134

Wertz, F. J. (1985). Methods and findings in the study of a complex life event: being criminally victimised. *Phenomenology and psychological research*. Giorgi, A., Ed. Pittsburgh, Duquesne University Press

Wessells, M. (1996). "Assisting Angolan children impacted by war: blending Western and traditional approaches to healing." *Coordinators Notebook: An International Resource for Early Childhood Development* **19**: 33-37

Wessells, M. (1997). "Child soldiers." *Bulletin of the Atomic Scientists* **53**(6): 32-39

Wessells, M., Kostelny, M (1996). *The Graca Machel/UN study on the impact of armed conflict on children: implications for early childhood development.* New York, UNICEF Working Paper

West, W. (1996). "Using human inquiry groups in counselling research." *British Journal of Guidance and Counselling* **24**(3): 347-356

West, W. (1997). *Integrating psychotherapy and healing: an enquiry into the experiences of counsellors and psychotherapists whose work includes healing.* Psychology. Keele, University of Keele. U.K.

West, W. (1998a). "Critical subjectivity: use of self in counselling research." *Counselling* **9**(3): 228-230

West, W. (1998b). "Developing practice in a context of religious faith: a study of psychotherapists who are Quakers." *British Journal of Guidance and Counselling* **26**(3): 365-375

West, W. (1998c). "Passionate research: heuristics and the use of self in counselling research." *Changes* **16**(1): 60-6

West, W. (1998d). "Spirituality and work." *Friends Quarterly* **31**(3): 138-142

West, W. (2000). *Psychotherapy and spirituality.* London, Sage

West, W. (2001). "Beyond grounded theory: the use of a heuristic approach to qualitative research." *Counselling and Psychotherapy Research* **1**(2): 126-131

West, W. and Mansor, A. T. (2002). "Hearing what research participants are really saying: the influence of researcher cultural identity." *Counselling and Psychotherapy Research* **2**(4): 253-258

Whitby, S. (1993). *A history of peace studies at the University of Bradford.* Peace Studies. Bradford, Bradford

White, G. E. and A.N, T. (1995). "Anonymized focus groups as a research tool for health professionals." *Qualitative Health Research* **5**(2): 256-261

White, G. M. M., A.J., (1982). Cultural concepts of mental health and therapy Dorderecht, Reidal Publishing Company

Williams, K. (2003). *Near-death experiences and the afterlife*, Near-Death Experiences and the Afterlife. **2003**

Williams, M. B. (1994). *Handbook of post trauma therapy.* Westport, Greenwood Press

Williams, R. and Joseph, S. (1999). Conclusions: an integrative psychosocial model of PTSD. *Posttraumatic Stress Disorder: concepts and therapy.* Yule, W., Ed. Chichester, Wiley

Williams, S. W., Sue. (1992). "Being in the middle by being on the edge." *Quaker Peace and Service*

Wilson, A. T. W., Trist, E. L. and Curle, A. (1990). Transitional communities and social reconnection: the civil resettlement of British prisoners of war. *The Social engagement of social science: the socio-psychological perspective.* Trist, E. L. and Murray, H., Eds. Philadelphia, The University of Pennsylvania Press. **1**: 88-112

Wilson, J. P. (1988). Culture and trauma. *Human adaptation to extreme stress: from holocaust to Vietnam.* Wilson, J. P., Harel, Z. and Kahana, B., Eds. New York, Plenum: 38-71

Wilson, J. P. (1989). *Trauma, transformation and healing.* New York, Brunner/Mazel

Wilson, J. P. and Walker, A. J. (1989). The psychobiology of trauma. *Trauma, transformation and healing.* Wilson, J. P., Ed. New York, Brunner/Mazel: 21-37

Wilson, S. A., Becker, L. A. and Tinker (1995). "Eye Movement Desensitization and

Reprocessing (EMDR) treatment for psychosocially traumatised individuals." *Journal for Consulting and Clinical Psychology* **63**: 928-937

Wilson, S. A., Becker, L. A. and Tinker, R. H. (1997). "Fifteen-Month follow-up of Eye Movement Desensitization and Reprocessing (EMDR): treatment for Posttraumatic Stress Disorder and psychological trauma." *Journal of Consulting and Clinical Psychology* **65**(6): 1047-1056

Winnicott, D. W. (1957). *The child and the family*. London, Tavistock

Wood, J. K. (1999). Toward an understanding of large group dialogue and its implications. *Experiences in relatedness: groupwork and the Person Centred Approach*. Lago, C. and MacMillan, M., Eds. Ross on Wye, PCCS Books: 137-166

Woodhouse, T. (1991). Making peace: the work of Adam Curle. *Peacemaking in a troubled world*. Woodhouse, T., Ed. New York, Oxford, Berg

Woodhouse, T. (1998). The psychology of conflict resolution. *The psychology of peacekeeping*. Langholtz, H., Ed. Westport, Conn. and London, Praeger: 153-166

Worden, J. W. (1995). *Grief counselling and grief therapy: a handbook for mental health practitioners*. London, Tavistock/Routledge

Wuthnow, R. (1991). *Acts of compassion: caring for others and helping ourselves*. Princeton, N.J, Princeton University Press

Yalom, I. D. (1985). *The theory and practice of group psychotherapy*. New York, Basic Books

Yarrow, M. (1978). *Quaker experiences in international conciliation*. Yale, University of Yale

Yehuda, R., Giller, E. L., Levengood, R. A., Southwick, S. M. and Siever, L. J. (1995). Hypothalamic-pituitary-adrenal functioning in post-traumatic stress disorder: expanding the concept of the stress response spectrum. *Neurobiological and clinical consequences of stress: from normal adaptation to PTSD*. Friedman, M. J., Charney, D. S. and Deutsch, K. W., Eds. Philadelphia, Lippincott-Raven

Yehuda, R., Kahana, B., Schmeidler, Southwick, S. M., Wilson, S. and Giller, E. L. (1995). "Impact of cumulative lifetime trauma and recent stress on current posttraumatic stress disorder symptoms in Holocaust survivors." *American Journal of Psychiatry* (152): 1815-1818

Yehuda, R. and McFarlane, A. C. (1995). "Conflict between current knowledge about Posttraumatic Stress Disorder and its original conceptual basis." *American Journal of Psychiatry* **152**: 1705-1713

Yehuda, R., Southwick, S. M., Krystal, J., Bremner, D., Charney, D. S. and Mason, J. W. (1993). "Enhanced suppression of cortisol following dexamethason administration in Posttraumatic Stress Disorder." *American Journal of Psychiatry* **150**: 83-86

Yehuda, R., Southwick, S. M. and Mason, J. W. (1990). Interactions of the hypothalamic-pituitary adrenal axis and the catecholaminergic system of the stress disorder. *Biological assessment and treatment of PTSD*. Giller, E. L., Ed. Washington D.C., American Psychiatric Press

Yehuda, R., Southwick, S. M., Nussbaum, G., Wahby, V., Mason, J. W. and Giller, E. L. (1990). "Low urinary cortisol excretion in patients with PTSD." *Journal of Nervous and Mental Diseases* **174**: 145-159

Yeomans, T. (1994). *Soul wound and psychotherapy*. The Concord Institute Pamphlet Series. Mass USA

Yerkes, R. M. and Dodson, J. D. (1908). "The relation of strength of stimulus to rapidity of habit-formation." *Journal of Comparative and Neurological Psychology* **18**: 459-482

Young, A. (1995). *The harmony of illusions. Inventing Posttraumatic Stress Disorder*. Princeton, N.J., Princeton University Press

Zaidi, L. Y. and Foy, D. W. (1994). "Childhood abuse and combat-related PTSD." *Journal of Traumatic Stress* (7): 33-42

Zarowsky, C. and Pederson, D. (2000). "Rethinking trauma in a transnational world." *Transcultural Psychiatry* **37**: 291-293

Zimbardo, P. G. (1972). "Pathology of imprisonment." *Society* **10**(6): 4-8

Zoellner, L. A., Sacks, M. B. and Foa, E. B. (2001). "Stability of emotions for traumatic memories in acute and chronic PTSD." *Behaviour Research and Therapy* **39**(6): 697-711